EVERY GOOD PATH

T&T Clark Enquiries in Theological Ethics

Series editors
Brian Brock
Susan F. Parsons

EVERY GOOD PATH

Wisdom and Practical Reason in Christian Ethics and the Book of Proverbs

Andrew Errington

LONDON • NEW YORK • OXFORD • NEW DELHI • SYDNEY

T&T CLARK
Bloomsbury Publishing Plc
50 Bedford Square, London, WC1B 3DP, UK
1385 Broadway, New York, NY 10018, USA

BLOOMSBURY, T&T CLARK and the T&T Clark logo are
trademarks of Bloomsbury Publishing Plc

First published in Great Britain in 2020
Paperback edition first published 2021

Copyright © Andrew Errington, 2020

Andrew Errington has asserted his right under the Copyright,
Designs and Patents Act, 1988, to be identified as Author of this work.

For legal purposes the Acknowledgements on p. ix constitute
an extension of this copyright page.

All rights reserved. No part of this publication may be reproduced or
transmitted in any form or by any means, electronic or mechanical,
including photocopying, recording, or any information storage or retrieval
system, without prior permission in writing from the publishers.

Bloomsbury Publishing Plc does not have any control over, or responsibility for,
any third-party websites referred to or in this book. All internet addresses given
in this book were correct at the time of going to press. The author and publisher
regret any inconvenience caused if addresses have changed or sites have
ceased to exist, but can accept no responsibility for any such changes.

A catalogue record for this book is available from the British Library.

Library of Congress Cataloging-in-Publication Data
Names: Errington, Andrew (Lecturer), author.
Title: Every good path: wisdom and practical reason in Christian ethics
and the Book of Proverbs / Andrew Errington.
Description: 1 [edition]. | New York: T&T Clark, 2019. |
Includes bibliographical references and index.
Identifiers: LCCN 2019016120 | ISBN 9780567687692 (hardback) |
ISBN 9780567687722 (epub)
Subjects: LCSH: Christian ethics. | Wisdom. | Practical reason. |
Bible. Proverbs.–Criticism, interpretation, etc. | O'Donovan, Oliver.
Classification: LCC BJ1275.E77 2019 | DDC 241–dc23
LC record available at https://lccn.loc.gov/2019016120

ISBN: HB: 978-0-5676-8769-2
PB: 978-0-5676-9894-0
ePDF: 978-0-5676-8770-8
eBook: 978-0-5676-8772-2

Typeset by Integra Software Services Pvt. Ltd.

To find out more about our authors and books visit
www.bloomsbury.com and sign up for our newsletters.

For Lauren
אֵשֶׁת חַיִל

CONTENTS

Acknowledgments	ix
List of Abbreviations	xi
INTRODUCTION	1

Chapter 1
THE COMPLEXITIES OF PRACTICAL REASON IN
THE *NICOMACHEAN ETHICS* OF ARISTOTLE

	19
Introduction	19
1 Happiness and Reason	20
2 Wisdom and Prudence	26
3 Deliberation	29
4 The Practical Syllogism	32
Conclusion	38

Chapter 2
THE NATURE AND FOUNDATION OF MORAL REASONING IN
THOMAS AQUINAS

	39
Introduction	39
1 Reason and Wisdom	41
2 Kinds of Action	48
3 Eternal Law and Divine Providence	59
a. Law, Divine Reason, and Nature	59
b. The Concept of Eternal Law	65
c. Eternal Law and Proverbs Chapter Eight	69
4 Prudence	71
5 Deliberation and the Practical Syllogism	78
Conclusion	86

Chapter 3
PRACTICAL REASON AND THE WAYS OF WISDOM

	89
Introduction	89
1 The Puzzle of Proverbs Chapter Eight	90
2 The Nature of Wisdom in the Book of Proverbs	100
a. The Alterity of Wisdom	103
b. "Getting" Wisdom: Wisdom and Practical Knowledge	116
c. Proverbs 8 Reconsidered	123

3 Reflections on Aquinas's Understanding of Practical Reason — 126
    a. Wisdom, Creation, and Eternal Law — 126
    b. Deliberation, Prudence, and Words of Instruction — 134
Conclusion — 140

Chapter 4
WORLD ORDER AND DELIBERATION IN THE WORK OF OLIVER O'DONOVAN — 141
  Introduction — 141
  1 The Generic Character of Moral Reasoning
    in *Resurrection and Moral Order* — 142
    a. Paul Ramsey's "The Case of the Curious Exception" — 143
    b. Resurrection and Moral Order — 144
  2 The Elevation of Moral Reason in *Ethics as Theology* — 153
    a. The Shape of Practical Reason — 157
    b. Faith, Love, and Wisdom — 164
    c. Hope and Prudent Deliberation — 169
    d. The Perfecting of Agency — 175
  3 The Reconciliation of Nature and History — 181

Chapter 5
WISDOM, CREATION, AND CHRISTIAN ETHICS — 193
  Introduction — 193
  1 Wisdom and Creation — 194
  2 Nature, History, and Created Order — 199
    a. Moral Order and Resurrection — 199
    b. David VanDrunen and David Kelsey on Created Order in Proverbs — 203
  3 Moral Discernment and the Naming of Actions — 210
    a. Hercules at the Crossroads — 211
    b. Scripture and the Construal of Actions — 217
  4 Theory, Practice, and Christian Ethics — 221

Bibliography — 227
General Index — 235
Index of Scripture References — 242

ACKNOWLEDGMENTS

"Those who attend to a word find good" (Prov. 16:20). It has been a joy and privilege to have been given time to attend to the word that is the book of Proverbs. This gift of God has come through many people. This book first took shape through doctoral study at the University of Aberdeen, which was made possible by friends, family, and church communities in Australia and Scotland. The prayers, encouragement, generosity, and blessing of Andrew and Louisa Greenwell, Greg and Beth Hammond, Ted and Jenny Kerr, Jill Flinders, Fiona Volke, Jill and Ian McGilvray, Roger Bray, Roger Fitzhardinge, Sally Coombes, David and Amelia Höhne, Stephen and Anne Judd, Polly Seidler, Luke and Valerie Charlton, Martin and Jasmine Kemp, Frank and Tracey Szanto, Rod and Ronelle Pratt, Michael and Jenna Jones, Roger Abrahams, Greg Anderson, David and Clare Ryan, Tom Swanton, Rob and Julie Kerr, Ben and Leal Beazley, James and Celia Toose, Matthew Tyson and Meg Hallahan, Laura Yeates, Ben and Jen Williams, Jay and Karen Spence, Ellaina and Lachlan Welsman, James and Honoria Brennan, and others made this a work of partnership in ministry. I would not have embarked on this journey were it not for the encouragement of Andrew Cameron, Peter Jensen, and my uncle Neil Chambers; and I also acknowledge them with gratitude. Trinity Church Aberdeen became a home and family to us in Aberdeen, and allowed me to keep clear in mind the things that matter most.

I gratefully acknowledge the financial assistance of the University of Aberdeen, the Latimer Trust, the Menzies Centre for Australian Studies at King's College London, the Australian Research Theology Foundation, and Moore Theological College. The last phase of this work has been completed at St Mark's National Theological Centre, in Canberra, and as a research fellow of the Public and Contextual Theology Research Centre, Charles Sturt University. I am grateful to all these institutions for their interest in and support of this project.

This work has been enriched by the insights and challenges of many others. The generous and insightful divinity faculty and my fellow students in theological ethics made the University of Aberdeen a wonderful place to research. I am especially grateful for the friendship of Michael Mawson, Kevin Hargaden, Ben Paulus, and Daniel Patterson. More recently, the careful attention and responses of my doctoral examiners, Paul Nimmo and Christopher Insole, have been an honor to receive and a help to clearer thinking. The value of this study may in the end lie in its capacity to open up lines of critical response such as the ones they raised. I am also grateful to Raymond Van Leeuwen, for his comments on the central chapter on Proverbs, which both stimulated my thinking afresh and saved me from blunders.

It was a surprise and delight to get to know, and be advised, by Stanley Hauerwas. He saw what I ought to be thinking about well before I did. Brian Brock gave me freedom to move, renounced defensiveness, and cared deeply not only about the quality of the work, but even more its truthfulness. The other editor of this series, Susan Parsons, has been generous and encouraging to me far beyond what I deserved, since I first submitted an article to *Studies in Christian Ethics* some years ago.

The genesis of this study lies over a decade ago, when I prepared a series of Bible studies on the book of Proverbs and read *Resurrection and Moral Order*. I have not stopped thinking about either. I wrote to Professor O'Donovan upon finishing the book to express my gratitude. That acquaintance has now become a friendship that has been a joyful gift. O'Donovan has written that "the teacher who first opens a disciple's eyes gestures towards a wide horizon."[1] Although the present work moves clumsily in a slightly different direction, my indebtedness to O'Donovan's work is great.

My wife and I have been supported by our families well beyond what we could have expected. Especial thanks to Chris and Marianne, for your faithful, wonderful visits; and to my mother, Megan Chambers. "The crown of the aged is their grandchildren; the beauty of children, their parents" (Prov. 17:6). I want also to acknowledge my beloved grandparents on my mother's side, Ross and Audrey Chambers, both of whom died during this research. They had the wisdom to inscribe Prov. 3:5-6 into the Greek New Testament they gave me when I began training for the ministry many years ago, and they embodied the kind of wisdom this study is all about.

Next to last, I want to acknowledge two sets of dear friends. David and Angela Gibson, with their children, made Aberdeen, for us, "a place of springs" (Ps. 84:6). And Joel Morrison and Meredith Lake were the friends who, like the proverb says, "stick closer than a brother" (Prov. 18:24).

Finally, those who have traveled most closely with me: thank you Frances, Owen, and Angus, for being part of the journey, and bearing it so well. And most of all, the beloved companion of my youth, Lauren, to whom this study is dedicated. Indeed, a strong and noble wife. It is a privilege to walk the path with you. "'Well and truly blessed!' her children say; her husband stands too, and sings her praise" (Prov. 31:28).

---

1. *SWT*, 56.

ABBREVIATIONS

Complete citations may be found in the Bibliography.

ACCS	J. Robert Wright, ed. *Ancient Christian Commentary on Scripture*, Vol. 9
CD	Karl Barth, *The Church Dogmatics*
DT	Augustine, *On the Trinity* (*De Trinitate*)
EIR	Oliver O'Donovan, *Entering into Rest*
EN	Aristotle, *Nicomachean Ethics*
F&S	Oliver O'Donovan, *Finding and Seeking*
NPNF	Schaff and Wace, eds. *A Select Library of the Nicene and Post-Nicene Fathers of the Christian Church*
RMO	Oliver O'Donovan, *Resurrection and Moral Order*
SLE	Thomas Aquinas, *Sententia Libri Ethicorum*
ST	Thomas Aquinas, *Summa Theologiae*
SWT	Oliver O'Donovan, *Self, World, and Time*

INTRODUCTION

Then you will understand righteousness, judgment, and rectitude—every good path.
—Prov. 2:9[1]

It is a very bad idea to join a violent criminal gang. In essence, this is the advice with which, after an initial prologue, the book of Proverbs begins (1:8-19). It is a piece of instruction that has seemed innocuous to some readers. Of course, troubles of our own day, such as the recruitment of young people by terrorist groups, have made us realize that it is not advice that can be taken for granted. Nevertheless, this teaching can seem an odd way for the book to begin.

The passage is where it is, however, because it illustrates some of the core dynamics of the book of Proverbs. Notice the following points. First, the passage pictures a contest of invitations. The fundamental question faced by the son addressed in v. 8 is, to whom will he listen. He may listen to his father's instruction and his mother's teaching, or he can listen to the voice of "sinners" trying to "hoodwink" (*yĕpatûkā*) him—"If they *say* ... do not go with them." In this, we meet one of the guiding thoughts of the book of Proverbs: that living wisely is most basically a matter of attending to the right words.

Second, notice that these contesting invitations presume that the moral agent, the son, is a desiring being, who is and will be drawn hither and thither by various attractions. The deceitful appeals of the sinners aim at the son's desires: "Let's get all precious wealth! Let's fill our houses with spoil! ... There will be one money

---

1. All translations of Proverbs are my own, from the Hebrew text prepared by J. Fichtner, in Biblica Hebraica Stuttgartensia Volume 12, *Iob et Proverbia*, ed. K. Elliger and W. Rudolph (Stuttgart: Deutsche Bibelstiftung, 1977). I have, however, referred frequently to other English translations, especially in the following works: Stuart Weeks, *Instruction and Imagery in Proverbs 1-9* (Oxford: Oxford University Press, 2007), 180-92; Michael Fox, *Proverbs 10-31* (Anchor Bible; New Haven, CT: Yale University Press, 2009), 1071-115; Roland E. Murphy, *Proverbs* (Word Biblical Commentary 22; Nashville: Thomas Nelson, 1998); the *New Revised Standard Version Bible: Anglicized Edition,* copyright © 1989, 1995 National Council of the Churches of Christ in the United States of America; and the *Holy Bible, New International Version*®, NIV®. Copyright © 1973, 1978, 1984, 2011 by Biblica, Inc.™

bag for all of us!" Yet the parental voice, in its own way, also sets forth something desirable. "Listen my son to your father's instruction, and do not forsake your mother's teaching, for they are a graceful garland for your head, and a necklace for your neck." These attractions are of a different kind to those offered by the sinners. They offer a picture of beauty and nobility, rather than mere wealth and pleasure. Still, they are attractions. They hold out to the son a vision of his good, inviting him to see *his* good in what is truly good. This appeal to desire, and to different kinds of desires, is also a central dynamic of the book of Proverbs, in which wisdom and folly will be imagined as two women, holding out the promise of goods for those who "love" and "embrace" (4:6-9) them—though goods of very different orders. The very idea of *wisdom* entails an acceptance that human beings are motivated by a desire for their own good. The book of Proverbs would not simply reject the premise from which so much of the ethical thought of the ancient world began, that all human beings desire *eudaimonia*, that is, want their lives to succeed. However, it is also true that at the very heart of Proverbs lies a distinctive claim about what this involves, namely, that wisdom *is* righteousness, and that the beginning of wisdom is the fear of the Lord.

Third, notice the way in which the difference between wisdom and folly is plain and predictable. There is an inevitability to the consequences of the actions proposed by the sinners that is not all that difficult to understand: "they ambush their own blood and lie in wait for their lives! So goes the path of all who seek unjust gain—it takes the life of its master." Verse 17 is difficult, but the point is clearly to draw an analogy with an action that is bound to fail.[2] "It is useless spreading a net in full view of all the birds." Here we glimpse another basic assumption of the book of Proverbs, which will be central to this study: wisdom, in the book of Proverbs, is correlated to creation, and the limited, determinate possibilities it presents. Wisdom is not first and foremost about subjective dispositions or intellectual states; it is about the way the created world itself is hospitable to certain forms of action, and not others.

The central metaphor for this reality in Proverbs is that of ways and paths, three words for which are used in vv. 8-19 (*derek, nĕtîbâ*, v. 15; *ʾōraḥ*, v. 19).[3] The metaphor reflects what we will call the alterity of wisdom. Wisdom and folly lie before the agent like paths; they are there to be discerned, and taken or avoided. "My son, do not walk with them in the way; draw back your foot from their path" (v. 15). It is not that a person cannot *have* wisdom or *be* wise in any sense. "Wisdom will enter your heart," Proverbs will say (2:10). Yet wisdom is not merely an ability; it is a determinate reality, realized in action. It is "righteousness, judgment, and rectitude—every good path" (2:6-9). To "get wisdom" is to be able to take up certain forms of action. There are *ways* of wisdom, and there are dead-ends of folly. This is why Proverb begins with the voice of a parent trying to get their child to "see reason," and make good choices: it is because wisdom is something

---

2. See Stuart Weeks, *Instruction and Imagery*, 195.
3. The other main term used in Proverbs is *maʿĕgāl*.

objective, a good path that lies before the child. The issue is not, fundamentally, being a wise person; it is going down a wise path.

This study explores these patterns of thinking in the book of Proverbs, and asks what difference they make to our understanding of Christian ethics. Its central thesis is that the way the book of Proverbs thinks about wisdom presents an important challenge to the way practical reason has been understood in the Western theological and philosophical tradition. Rather than being a perfection of speculative knowledge, which is how it was understood by both Augustine and Aristotle, and then by Thomas Aquinas, in the book of Proverbs, wisdom is a *practical* knowledge of how to act well, grounded in the reality of the world God has made. God's wisdom is a perfection, not of his theoretical knowledge, but of his action, which is why it ultimately relates to Jesus Christ crucified. "Greeks seek wisdom," wrote the apostle Paul; "we, though, proclaim Christ crucified" (1 Cor. 1:22). The book of Proverbs allows us to understand the deep structure of this contrast, and its significance for Christian ethics. This reframes our understanding of natural order and its place within moral thinking, and of the structure of moral deliberation and discernment. It also clarifies the purpose of Christian ethics as a discipline.

The strategy of this study is to bring the book of Proverbs into discussion with two significant theological accounts of the nature and foundation of practical reason in Christian ethics, one medieval—that of Thomas Aquinas—and one modern—that developed by Oliver O'Donovan. This strategy requires some explanation.

To begin with, *what is meant by the book of Proverbs?* The book of Proverbs, as it currently stands in a modern Bible, is a compilation of several compositions. There are good reasons to distinguish chs 1–9 from chs 10–31, and within 10–31 to distinguish 22:17–24:22 from various pieces before and after.[4] As Katharine Dell says, "the forms and content of Proverbs are actually quite diverse," and the different sections have different characters.[5] Others will speak of a "thick black line,"[6] or an "enormous gulf"[7] dividing Proverbs chs 1–9 from Proverbs chs 10–31. Yet the importance of these differences can be overstated. Gerhard von Rad, in

---

4. The main subsections may reasonably be said to be: 1–9; 10:1–22:16; 22:17–24:22; 24:23–34; 25–29; 30; 31. However, further divisions can be seen between chs 15 and 16, and chs 27 and 28. See Katharine Dell, *The Book of Proverbs in Social and Theological Context* (Cambridge: Cambridge University Press, 2006), 15, following R. N. Whybray, *The Composition of the Book of Proverbs* (JSOTS 168; Sheffield: Sheffield Academic Press, 1994); and Raymond C. Van Leeuwen, *Context and Meaning in Proverbs 25–27* (SBL Dissertation Series 96; Atlanta, GA: Scholars, 1988), 1–9.

5. Dell, *The Book of Proverbs*, 15.

6. Weeks, *Instruction and Imagery*, 173.

7. Gerhard von Rad, *Wisdom in Israel* (London: SCM, 1972), 57.

the same discussion in which he speaks of this "enormous gulf," concludes that "the whole difference between the earlier and later collections" is really one of emphasis and focus.[8] Similarly, Christopher Ansberry argues that Proverbs ought to be taken seriously as a whole, commenting, "Though these collections may have been formulated as discrete compositions, they have been incorporated into a larger literary discourse that evinces a reasonable degree of homogeneity in literary character, presuppositions, and perspective."[9] William Brown, likewise, has argued that chs 10–31 reflect an overarching editorial arrangement with a coherent pedagogical purpose that also makes sense in relation to chs 1–9.[10] Some of these arguments are probably overstated. I think Anne Stewart is right to insist that Proverbs "does not operate with a narrative scheme," but rather "holds coherence as a loose sequence."[11] Yet this is still a real coherence. This study therefore attempts to read the book of Proverbs as a whole, allowing chs 10–31 to inform our reading of chs 1–9, and vice versa, on the modest assumption that the editorial process that brought it together was intelligent.

More fundamentally, however, Proverbs will be read as a whole for theological reasons. This study is a work of Christian theology, and hence engages the book of Proverbs first and foremost as Holy Scripture. This means that, even if the parts can and should be appreciated in their distinctiveness, most basically the book is the whole book that in the providence of God has become part of the canon. The isolation of different parts of the book from one another can allow Proverbs to be taken to support ideas it otherwise might not.[12] This study proceeds on the assumption that this is not how the book should principally be read for Christian theology.

8. Rad, *Wisdom in Israel*, 70.

9. Christopher B. Ansberry, *Be Wise, My Son, and Make My Heart Glad: An Exploration of the Courtly Nature of the Book of Proverbs* (Beihefte zur Zeitschrift für die alttestamentliche Wissenschaft 422; Berlin: de Gruyter, 2011), 8.

10. William P. Brown, "The Pedagogy of Proverbs 10:1–31:9," in *Character and Scripture: Moral Formation, Community, and Biblical Interpretation*, ed. William P. Brown (Grand Rapids: Eerdmans, 2002), 150–82.

11. Anne W. Stewart, *Poetic Ethics in Proverbs: Wisdom Literature and the Shaping of the Moral Self* (New York: Cambridge University Press, 2016), 27, 211. Note Stewart's comments about Brown and Ansberry on pp. 27–8 and 209–11.

12. Consider one example of importance for our argument: In *Instruction and Imagery*, Stuart Weeks argues that the instruction in view in Proverbs 1–9 essentially refers to Torah. This argument rests on the premise that Proverbs 1–9 "offers very little instruction itself" (p. 126). This in turn involves two decisions. First, to treat chs 1–9 in isolation from chs 10–31, and second, to excise 6:1–19, which is in content similar to material in chs 10–31, as secondary (p. 100). This leaves 3:1–10 and 21–35 as the main didactic sections in chs 1–9. But these sections are "strongly religious" and "specifically Jewish" in character (p. 102), suggesting an association with the law. This procedure, it seems to me, is in danger of assuming the conclusion in the premises. Whatever good arguments there may be for the identification of chs 1–9 as a separable entity, these chapters are now presented to us as an introduction to "the proverbs of Solomon" (1:1), and therefore as an introduction to chs

This is also our justification for *restricting* our scope to the book of Proverbs, rather than looking at, say, the wisdom literature more broadly. The latter approach is taken in an important recent work by Paul Fiddes, *Seeing the World and Knowing God*.[13] Fiddes's work displays the complexity and sophistication of Israel's wisdom literature, and contains stimulating readings of Proverbs with which we will engage. In my view, however, the distinctive contribution of Proverbs is lost in the attempt to take in the breadth of the wisdom movement. To give one example: Fiddes reads Prov. 8:22-31 alongside the wisdom hymns in Ben Sira 24:1-22 and the Wisdom of Solomon chs 6–9.[14] While these are undoubtedly important parallels, the procedure means that the text in Proverbs is read without significant reference to parallels within the book itself, particularly 1:20-33.[15] This leads Fiddes to interpret Proverbs 8 as describing "a giving of God's self,"[16] which is, in my view, not sufficiently chastened by the first speech of Wisdom in Proverbs (1:20-33), which describes Wisdom's call being refused. This in turn has consequences for Fiddes's wider arguments. The differences of this study from these arguments arise partly from the assumption that theology owes special attention to the *book* of Proverbs, taken as a whole.

Which version of the book, though? In particular, why should we focus on the *Hebrew* text of Proverbs? An ancient version of this objection was made by Origen in a letter to Julius Africanus.[17] The letter comes in response to an enquiry about Origen's quoting a passage from the apocryphal expansions of Daniel. Origen begins by pointing out that he is well aware of the differences between "our copies [the Greek LXX] and those of the Jews." He argues, however, that we ought to receive the church's Bible ("the Seventy") because:

> Are we to suppose that that Providence which in the sacred Scriptures has ministered to the edification of all the Churches of Christ, had no thought for those bought with a price, for whom Christ died; whom, although His

10–31. This suggests that we are meant to understand the "teaching" referred to in chs 1–9 in verses such as 2:1, as, at least in part, the proverbs in 10–31. Weeks's argument amounts to saying that Proverbs 1–9 is not only distinct from chs 10–31, but inimical to it. Weeks's own judicious comments about redactors (e.g., on p. 47) should lead us to be suspicious of such a view. It is easier to see Proverbs 1–9 as making sense in its context, rather than as ruined by an editorial blunder.

13. Paul Fiddes, *Seeing the World and Knowing God: Hebrew Wisdom and Christian Doctrine in a Late-Modern Context* (Oxford: Oxford University Press, 2013).

14. Fiddes, *Seeing the World*, ch. 6.

15. Fiddes does consider this text (*Seeing the World*, 185, 352–4). However, the two passages are not really allowed to inform one another.

16. Fiddes, *Seeing the World*, 188.

17. "A Letter from Origen to Africanus," in *The Ante-Nicene Fathers*, Vol. 4, trans. F. Crombie, ed. A. Roberts and J. Donaldson (Grand Rapids: Eerdmans, 1989), 386–92. The argument in view is found in sections 4–5.

Son, God who is love spared not, but gave Him up for us all, that with Him
He might freely give us all things?

Origen then supports his argument by quoting Prov. 22:28—"Thou shalt not remove the ancient landmarks which thy fathers have set"—understanding "thy fathers" to mean the church fathers.

Origen's argument shows us that an argument from providence can seem to lead to very different conclusions. The problem with Origen's argument, however, is not that it appeals to providence, but that it rests on a false characterization of the relationship between the church and Israel. This study proceeds on the assumption that, in relation to the books of what Christians know as the Old Testament, "the Jews" have the priority. Providence certainly had thought for those for whom Christ died—precisely by leading them to the Jewish Scriptures. "Because salvation is from the Jews" (Jn 4:22). Hence, this study engages in the first instance with the Hebrew text of the book of Proverbs.

It treats this book, however, as part of *Christian* Holy Scripture. This means that it is read as part of a wider whole that is focused on the person of Jesus Christ and includes the writings of the New Testament. This does not mean that it is read as a Christian text in a straightforward sense. This is frequently how the church fathers read Proverbs, as when, to pick one example among many, Augustine reads "dining with a ruler" in Prov. 23:1 as a reference to the Eucharist.[18] Such a way of reading is currently enjoying a renaissance. In my view, however, this movement is too quick, collapsing together moments of salvation history that need to be kept distinct. There is, as R. W. L. Moberly puts it, "a permanent hermeneutical dialectic between Israel's scripture and Jesus."[19] The book of Proverbs is a Christian text, but it is not originally a Christian text. It must first be appreciated as a text that belongs to the history of Israel. For this reason, more space is made for biblical studies scholarship than might be made in some theological readings. Yet because, on a Christian understanding, the history of Israel leads to the coming of the Messiah, Proverbs must also be read as a text that belongs to and is most meaningful within a canon that includes the New Testament. For this reason, we will keep a constant eye on the consequences of interpretations for Christian theology, and frequently draw on patristic and other theological readings.[20]

---

18. See references in *ACCS*, 146.

19. R. W. L. Moberly, *The Bible, Theology, and Faith: A Study of Abraham and Jesus* (Cambridge: Cambridge University Press, 2000), 61.

20. For a similar account of what is involved in the practice of reading texts as Holy Scripture, see David Kelsey, *Eccentric Existence: A Theological Anthropology*, 2 vols. (Louisville, Kentucky: Westminster John Knox, 2009), 132–56. Where my account differs from Kelsey's is in thinking that the practice of reading texts as Scripture involves recognizing connections not just within texts, but within the whole canon. In Chapter 5, I will suggest that Kelsey's reading of Proverbs fails to do this adequately.

This is only the barest sketch of the way Proverbs will be read in this study, particularly in Chapter 3. There are many objections to it. However, I will not expand upon it for two reasons. First, the arguments surrounding the theological interpretation of Scripture have been made by others, and it is well beyond the scope of this study to enter into them.[21] Second, the distinctive aspects of the approach taken here rest upon the arguments of this study, in particular, its argument, which will take until Chapter 5 to develop, that there is an irreducible twofoldness to God's works of creation and reconciliation. Ultimately, I think that reading Proverbs as Christian Scripture *requires* reading it as, in a sense, pre-Christian, because it is related primarily to God's act of creation, which, though connected to his work of redemption in Christ, is also distinct. Acknowledging, therefore, the questions this explanation leaves unanswered, we will move on.

In the second place, let us clarify: *what is the nature of this "discussion"?* One of the proposed participants in this discussion, Oliver O'Donovan, has described a discussion like this:

> Beginning from an intuition, we use the dialectical interplay of perspectives on a shared question to help us "know what we think" and "make up our minds." A negotiation succeeds when it achieves a compromise; a discussion succeeds only when it reaches a measure of substantial agreement. Discussion is a shared struggle to reach truth and overcome error.[22]

To conceive of this study as a discussion is a contrivance. It is a contrivance that is possible, however, because the proposed participants really do share a question. Aquinas, O'Donovan, and the book of Proverbs are each, in their own way, genuinely concerned to clarify the nature and foundation of practical reason, and its implications for ethics.

The intuition that begins this discussion is provided, however, by Aristotle. To say that the discussion is about "practical reason" is to identify it by reference to an idea first made explicit in Aristotle's distinction between "two parts of the soul with reason," in the *Nicomachean Ethics*,[23] but which has subsequently had a long history in philosophy. Discussions of practical reason today often begin with the work of Immanuel Kant, for whom the distinction between theoretical (or speculative) reason and practical reason was of fundamental, structural importance, and who thought deeply about this distinction. Yet it is Aristotle's

---

21. For an introduction, see Kevin J. Vanhoozer, *Dictionary for Theological Interpretation of Scripture* (Grand Rapids: Baker Academic and London: SPCK, 2005); Brian Brock, *Singing the Ethos of God: On the Place of Christian Ethics in Scripture* (Grand Rapids: Eerdmans, 2007), 3–95; and Daniel J. Treier, *Virtue and the Voice of God: Toward Theology as Wisdom* (Grand Rapids, MI: Eerdmans, 2006), 103–64. My own assumptions are closest to those articulated by Moberly in *The Bible, Theology, and Faith*, 39–44, 69–70.

22. *SWT*, 45.

23. See *EN* 6.1, 1139a7–13; and below, Chapter 1, Section 1.

understanding of practical reason, and of the distinction between practical and speculative thought, that has had the greatest influence on theology, because of its significance for Aquinas. Aristotle's account also orients O'Donovan's recent discussions of practical reason.[24] Proverbs, we will argue, does not quite support Aristotle's account of the matter. Yet there is much overlap, and a great deal to be learned by beginning the discussion in this way. Aristotle's intuition allows a fruitful dialectical interplay of perspectives to unfold, which can, I believe, help us to "make up our minds."

What is this intuition? It is an intuition about action, and what acting well involves. The central insight from which this discussion begins is that something different is required by the task of acting than is required by the task of thinking to a conclusion. O'Donovan points to this difference by saying that "practical reason is not deductive, but inductive."[25] As we will see, this is a profound insight. Yet it perhaps does not go far enough. The question this study will finally reach is whether the distinctive character and requirements of action finally unsettle the very category of practical *reason*. What this study seeks is greater clarity about what is involved in acting well, and what difference this makes to Christian ethics, meaning both the living of the Christian life and the discipline that reflects upon it. There is a great deal to be appreciated in both Aquinas's and O'Donovan's thinking about this question, and this study aims to draw out and consolidate their insights, particularly in relation to the complex dynamics of moral reasoning. As the discussion proceeds, it also quickly becomes clear that clarifying the nature of action requires us to think about the context that makes it possible, whether it be the context of social practices, or the created world itself. Acting well means acting in certain *kinds* of ways; and in the end, we cannot talk about *kinds* without talking about creation. Hence our interest is in the nature *and foundation* of practical reason.

A discussion is an event; something that happens, and that is shaped by the constraints of time and the kinds of contributions each speaker makes. Such is the case in this study, too. Others who have things to say about this topic do not join the discussion, and many of those who do get a word in have more things to say than they say here. In particular, important contemporary treatments of practical reason in Christian ethics are not given an extensive hearing. These include Charles R. Pinches's *Theology and Action*,[26] which is a lucid introduction to the complex questions surrounding the nature of action. This study shares Pinches's criticisms of "principle monism," and mirrors it in drawing on Aquinas's theory of action to argue that at the heart of acting well is the naming of actions.[27] This

---

24. See O'Dononvan, *SWT*, 21–5; *Common Objects of Love: Moral Reflection and the Shaping of Community* (Grand Rapids, MI: Eerdmans, 2002), 1–16; and below, Chapter 4.

25. *SWT*, 30; and below, Chapter 4, Section 2.

26. Charles R. Pinches, *Theology and Action: After Theory in Christian Ethics* (Grand Rapids, MI: Eerdmans, 2002).

27. See Pinches, *Theology and Action*, 34–58, 111–36.

is also a key emphasis in Stanley Hauerwas's understanding of practical reason, developed in many works, but most recently in *The Work of Theology*.[28] Where this study differs from Pinches and Hauerwas is in its emphasis on creation as the ground of such naming. While Pinches and Hauerwas think that names depend upon the narratives in which they are embedded, I think that they depend more fundamentally upon the world that God has made hospitable to action.[29] Another significant recent work is Daniel Westberg's *Renewing Moral Theology*,[30] which proposes a framework for Christian ethics that hinges on a sophisticated account of practical reason. Although we will not examine this work in detail, we will engage extensively with Westberg's earlier work on Aquinas, on which the more recent account is based.

In the event, after the issues are raised by Aristotle, Aquinas and O'Donovan are allowed to speak at some length, along with Proverbs. There are several reasons for this. First, it allows us to hear the different perspectives properly. "To respond before hearing—that is folly and shame," says Proverbs (18:13). The aim here is for the participants to be heard properly, their perspectives on particular questions understood in the context of their wider thought. Insofar as there is anything new in our discussion of Aquinas, it lies in observations of how different elements of his thought connect. Second, such careful listening is especially important in this case, because the topic of discussion is complex. At the beginning of his treatise on lying, Augustine warns his readers that the question to be considered is, "very full of dark corners, and has many cavern-like windings, whereby it oft eludes the eagerness of the seeker; so that at one moment what was found seems to slip out of one's hands, and anon comes to light again, and then is once more lost to sight."[31] The same is true here—and for much the same reasons. For the complexities of Augustine's treatise arise from its attention to the notion of kinds of action, which is why, as we will notice in Chapter 2, its presence can be felt in Aquinas's understanding of action. In the third place, this form of discussion is adopted so as to bring out the significance of O'Donovan's contribution. O'Donovan's work, and especially his recent trilogy, *Ethics as Theology*, has not yet received the attention that it deserves. No doubt this will change in time. I hope, however, by providing an extended, critical presentation of his position, to further the discussion and reception of his work. Finally, hearing Aquinas and O'Donovan at length is necessary in order to make it possible for Proverbs to enter the discussion. Both

---

28. Stanley Hauerwas, *The Work of Theology* (Grand Rapids, MI: Eerdmans, 2015), especially 11–31.

29. See especially Pinches, *Theology and Action*, 15–18, 50–8, 199–232. On this point note the recent suggestion by Pinches, accompanying David M. McCarthy, that there can be connections between talk of practices and talk of natural law: "Craft as a Place of Knowing in Natural Law," *Studies in Christian Ethics* 29, no. 4 (2016): 386–408.

30. Daniel Westberg, *Renewing Moral Theology: Christian Ethics as Action, Character, and Grace* (Downer's Grove, IL: IVP, 2015).

31. Augustine, "On Lying" [*De Mendacio*], *NPNF*, Vol. 3, 457 [section 1].

Aquinas and O'Donovan make use of the book of Proverbs in significant ways. Discerning the importance of these points of contact, however, and their relevance to the discussion requires that we attend to their overall schemes of thought. This, though, presses the question of why such an effort to hear from Proverbs should be made. Is this task worth the effort it requires?

Why bring the book of Proverbs into such a discussion? Let us first note an objection to doing so, a lively statement of which confronts us at the beginning of Immanuel Kant's *Groundwork of the Metaphysics of Morals*:

> All trades, crafts, and arts have gained by the division of labor, namely when one person does not do everything but each limits himself to a certain task that differs markedly from others in the way it is to be handled, so as to be able to perform it most perfectly and with greater facility. Where work is not so differentiated and divided, where everyone is a jack-of-all trades, there trades remain in the greatest barbarism. [We ought] not to carry on at the same time two jobs which are very distinct in the way they are to be handled, for each of which a special talent is perhaps required, and the combination of which in one person produces only bunglers.[32]

In trying to bring a reading of an ancient Hebrew text into a discussion about the theory of Christian ethics, are we not risking just the kind of bungling Kant warns of here? We are. The work of Bible reading and the work of theological and ethical theorizing differ markedly from each other, and require particular skills and habits. It is therefore doubtless true that in attempting to bring them together, we will not do justice to both, or perhaps either.[33] Yet, without denying this, we must insist that there is also a danger in keeping such tasks separate: on one side, the risk of leaving implications and connections inadequately examined, and therefore exposed to the danger of trivial conclusions or the appearance of self-evidence; on the other side, the risk of allowing our theoretical frameworks to float free of biblical texts that are held to be authoritative. The reality of these risks will, I think, be clear in what follows.

Christian ethics cannot avoid the risk involved in seeking to bring different kinds of investigation alongside one another. Joan Lockwood O'Donovan describes the task of Christian ethics perceptively:

> Political and moral theology at their best are faithful intellectual undertakings involving the widest and richest possible engagement of the inquiring mind with the scriptural text and with the exegetical and theological inheritance. They have the twofold purpose of glorifying God by drawing

---

32. Immanuel Kant, *Groundwork of the Metaphysics of Morals*, trans. Mary Gregor (Cambridge: Cambridge University Press, 1998), 2 [4:388].

33. For a lucid discussion of the kinds of troubles faced here, see Moberly, *The Bible, Theology, and Faith*, 151–3.

out in an orderly fashion the implications of His actions for our common and individual human actions, and also, thereby, of serving the political and moral reflection and deliberation of all His faithful people.[34]

For both of the representatives of Christian ethics considered in this study, the book of Proverbs is Holy Scripture. In the course of the *Summa Theologiae*, Thomas Aquinas quotes from almost every chapter of Proverbs. Likewise, reflection on certain parts of Proverbs has played an increasingly central role in O'Donovan's work on practical reason and moral theology. If it turns out that Proverbs has things to say in this discussion, then Christian ethics must attempt to listen to it.

And Proverbs does have things to say. It is a truth too seldom acknowledged that the book of Proverbs is the closest thing in the Bible to a book about practical reason. As Katharine Dell observes, "Guidance in ethical decision-making is at the heart of the wisdom enterprise."[35] "Decision-making," though, is too restricted. Proverbs is a book about *wisdom* and *prudence*, about the ways life may be lived successfully. It gives attention not only to the details of wisdom, but to its basic structures. It is a book about what Aristotle thought practical reason was about.

Proverbs has not received attention commensurate with this reality. This is not to say it has played no role in the history of Christian ethics, or to ignore the attention it has recently received. Proverbs ch. 8 has been a crucial text in Christian accounts of natural law. When Richard Hooker grounds his account of law in "that law eternal which God himself hath made to himself, and thereby worketh all things whereof he is the cause and author," and quotes Prov. 8:1 in support, he is drawing unmistakably on Aquinas's account of eternal law, at the center of which stood Proverbs 8.[36] Our engagement with Proverbs and with Aquinas on this point therefore connects with an influential stream of Christian thinking that remains a live line of thought today. As part of his effort to rehabilitate reformed ethics, David VanDrunen has recently argued that Proverbs makes a significant contribution to a biblical theology of natural law.[37]

Recent biblical studies have also begun to take the ethical thought of Proverbs seriously. Michael Fox's commentary on Proverbs contains extended discussion

---

34. Joan O'Donovan, "From Justification to Justice: The Cranmerian Prayer Book Legacy," in *The Authority of the Gospel: Explorations in Moral and Pastoral Theology in Honor of Oliver O'Donovan*, ed. Robert Song and Brent Waters (Grand Rapids, MI: Eerdmans, 2015), 104.

35. Dell, *The Book of Proverbs*, 150.

36. Richard Hooker, *Of the Laws of Ecclesiastical Polity*, ed. Arthur Stephen McGrade (Cambridge: Cambridge University Press, 1989), 57 [2.5]. Hooker also draws on Prov. 8:15 (16.2), another text of great significance to Aquinas in this connection, as we will see.

37. David VanDrunen, *Divine Covenants and Moral Order: A Biblical Theology of Natural Law* (Grand Rapids, MI: Eerdmans, 2014), 369. See also "Wisdom and the Natural Moral Order: The Contribution of Proverbs to a Christian Theology of Natural Law," *Journal of the Society of Christian Ethics* 33, no. 1 (2013): 153–68.

of the ethical thought of the book, in which he compares Proverbs particularly to Socratic ethics.[38] Responding to Fox, Christopher Ansberry has suggested that Aristotle's *Nicomachean Ethics* provides a better "heuristic guide" to the ethical framework of Proverbs.[39] Differently again, Michael Baris argues that Stoic philosophy is the right point of contrast.[40] Most significantly, Anne Stewart has explored the ways in which the poetic form of Proverbs encodes an approach to ethics.[41] She suggests Proverbs presents a number of "models of *mûsār* [discipline]," which reflect "a keen awareness of the complexity of moral reasoning."[42] In particular, Stewart sees a fruitful point of comparison in modern thought that draws on cognitive science to highlight the role of metaphor and imagination in moral reasoning.[43] These studies contain valuable insights, and they will be interlocutors when we turn to the book of Proverbs in Chapter 3. The diversity of their perspectives and conclusions, however, demonstrates both the potential fruitfulness of such enquiries, and that complete clarity has not yet been reached. These studies are at places weakened by insufficient critical attention to the theological and philosophical questions with which they make contact. Ansberry's study, for example, certainly highlights points of connection between Aristotle's thought and Proverbs. Yet it is limited by treating Aristotle's ethical thought as a stable, unproblematic point of reference, rather than what it is, namely, a complex proposal with inherent ambiguities that, at least for Christian theology, present challenges. This prevents Ansberry from seeing the ways Proverbs challenges aspects of Aristotle's thinking and categories at more fundamental levels. To take another example, Stewart's discussion of the significance of imaginative prototypes relies on an oversimplified account of law and moral reasoning in "the Western philosophical tradition."[44] In fact, a core aim of Aquinas's theory was to make room for the "indeterminacy" Stewart and others stress, precisely within a theory of law. What this study seeks to do, therefore, is to allow Proverbs to enter into deeper and more critical discussion with moral theology and philosophy. This is what is

---

38. Michael Fox, *Proverbs 1–9* (Anchor Bible; New York: Doubleday, 2000); and *Proverbs 10–31* (Anchor Bible; New York: Doubleday, 2009). Each volume contains appended essays. Essay six, in the second volume (934–45), is on the ethics of Proverbs.

39. Christopher B. Ansberry, "What Does Jerusalem Have to Do with Athens? The Moral Vision of the Book of Proverbs and Aristotle's *Nicomachean Ethics*," *Hebrew Studies* 51 (2010): 147–73. See also Ansberry's monograph, *Be Wise, My Son*.

40. Michael Baris, "Iniquities Ensnare the Wicked: The Ethical Theory of Proverbs 1–9," *Hebrew Studies* 56 (2015): 129–44.

41. Stewart, *Poetic Ethics*; and Anne W. Stewart, "Wisdom's Imagination: Moral Reasoning and the Book of Proverbs," *Journal for the Study of the Old Testament* 40, no. 3 (2016): 351–72.

42. Stewart, *Poetic Ethics*, 78.

43. See Stewart, *Poetic Ethics*, ch. 7; and Stewart, "Wisdom's Imagination."

44. See the discussion in Stewart, *Poetic Ethics*, 173–7.

necessary if we are to move beyond suggestive indications about the significance Proverbs may have for Christian ethics.

Furthermore, these studies are the exception to the rule. The discipline of biblical studies has long held a prejudice against taking Proverbs seriously, neatly expressed by Crenshaw's comment that the "vast majority of proverbial sayings … tend towards the banal, hardly commending themselves as worthy of careful study by serious students."[45] This prejudice endures in many quarters. Philip Davies, for instance, states, "Proverbs offers an official theology, and has all the virtues of almost anything that is official. It is half-baked."[46]

The tendency to overlook Proverbs as a significant source for Christian thinking about ethics owes something to its character. Both the other participants in our discussion characterize the book in ways that are not conducive to serious reflection. In his first inaugural sermon, Aquinas states that Proverbs represents instruction in the "first grade" of virtue—the virtue "whereby a man moderately uses the things of this world and lives among men." It is surpassed by higher wisdom, in which a man turns his back on the world and moves toward contemplation of wisdom itself.[47] Not dissimilarly, Oliver O'Donovan writes:

> Nobody would be tempted to call the compilers of the Book of Proverbs philosophers; they are moral teachers with pedagogic aims and distinctive methods; they collect and compile proverbs, and they supplement them with poetry in praise of a wisdom which crowns and coordinates all other human goals. They are unconcerned when their proverbs do not see eye to eye with each other.[48]

O'Donovan, it must be added, is by no means dismissive of the value of moral teaching.[49] Yet what both perspectives share is a reluctance to take the bulk of Proverbs seriously *as wisdom*, and to see the book as containing, despite its being a compilation, a coherent vision of the moral life.

Recently, a number of works have appeared that, like this study, suggest that such an attitude to the book is less than ideal. We have already mentioned Paul Fiddes's book, *Seeing the World and Knowing God*, which sees in the wisdom tradition, to which Proverbs is central, the potential "to make Christian doctrine

---

45. Quoted in Brown, "Pedagogy," 151.
46. Philip R. Davies, quoted in Stewart, "Wisdom's Imagination," 354. Stewart displays the continuing dominance of the "simplicity thesis" in *Poetic Ethics*, 71–8; and "Wisdom's Imagination," 353–7.
47. Thomas Aquinas, "Commendation and Division of Sacred Scripture," in *Thomas Aquinas: Selected Writings*, ed. Ralph McInerny (London: Penguin, 1998), 11. Thomas sees a parallel between the three grades of virtue set out by Plotinus in *Enneads* I.I.2.2–7 and the three books of Solomon: Proverbs, Ecclesiastes, and Song of Songs.
48. *EIR*, 34.
49. See especially *SWT*, 60–5.

anew in the context of the preoccupations of our late-modern world."[50] Along a similar line, David Ford's *Christian Wisdom: Desiring God and Learning in Love* sees wisdom as a key to re-imagining theology, and draws on the wisdom literature to do so.[51] Still, although the book of Proverbs can be glimpsed in the wings in this work, it never really takes the stage.[52]

Two other recent works engage the book of Proverbs at greater depth. Daniel J. Treier's *Virtue and the Voice of God: Toward Theology as Wisdom*[53] draws significantly on Proverbs to argue that theology should be understood as wisdom, and that this framework can clarify the place and practice of Scripture reading. In many ways, Treier's questions surrounding the interpretation of Proverbs parallel those of this study. He is drawn to wisdom by its potential to connect theory and practice,[54] and recognizes potentially illuminating connections with the thought of Aristotle.[55] He is also committed to taking seriously the New Testament's identification of Christ and wisdom, and the ways this seems to challenge assumptions about wisdom in Proverbs.[56] These will be key points of reference for this study too. The way the dots are joined here will, however, be different to how they are in Treier, even though some of the conclusions will be similar. Treier, in my view, underestimates the practical character of wisdom in Proverbs, in the interest of establishing "the linkage of *phronēsis* to *sophia*."[57] I will argue that wisdom in Proverbs has a different focus to wisdom in the New Testament, and that this should not be smoothed over, because it reflects an irreducible distinction in God's works of creation and salvation in Christ. This point is also the core disagreement we will have with Oliver O'Donovan, in Chapter 4, and so it is instructive to observe that Treier draws on O'Donovan's account of created order to resolve just this question.[58] In fact, I think that the perspective of this study provides a more secure basis for two of Treier's key conclusions: that theology's theoretical dimension lies in prevenient divine communicative action,[59] and that Christian discipleship is sustained by two kinds of reading practice.[60]

---

50. Fiddes, *Seeing the World*, 11.

51. David Ford, *Christian Wisdom: Desiring God and Learning in Love* (Cambridge Studies in Christian Doctrine; Cambridge: Cambridge University Press, 2007).

52. It is striking, for instance, that Proverbs makes very little impact, even on the first chapter, which is entitled "wisdom cries." This is a distinctive motif of Proverbs, which we will explore below, Chapter 3, Section 2a.

53. Treier, *Virtue*.

54. See Treier, *Virtue*, 3–30, 47–57.

55. See Treier, *Virtue*, 44, 51, 235 n. 91.

56. See Treier, *Virtue*, 47–61.

57. Treier, *Virtue*, 57.

58. Treier, *Virtue*, 45–6, 199.

59. Treier, *Virtue*, 183.

60. See Treier's discussion of the differences between biblical theology and theological exegesis, in *Virtue*, 203–5.

Finally, perhaps the most significant recent treatment of Proverbs is found in David Kelsey's expansive theological anthropology *Eccentric Existence*.[61] Kelsey draws on a sophisticated reading of Proverbs to articulate an arresting account of God's creative activity. Kelsey's reading of Proverbs is close to the one pursued in this study. He also comes to conclusions that are antithetical to the natural law tradition. We will therefore return to Kelsey's work at length in Chapter 5, to clarify our conclusions about the nature and function of created order in Christian ethics.

The central difference between these works and the present study is its different perspective. Where these works are oriented primarily by dogmatic questions, in this study it is questions related to ethics that are kept in view. This is not a clear-cut distinction. Kelsey's work, for instance, is deeply interested in the existential and practical consequences of the ideas he discusses, and the same is true of the other works noted. By the same token, this study is often driven deep into dogmatic territory, such as in discussing Aquinas's understanding of God's knowledge of creation. Yet there remains a difference in focus, the logic of which we will try to articulate at the close. It is the same difference observed, though not explored, by Kelsey, when he contends that the question of the logic of Christian beliefs must be distinguished from the question of the logic of living the Christian life.[62]

This different focus doubtless makes this study vulnerable to criticism from a dogmatic standpoint: my proposal about how to understand divine wisdom, for example, probably requires further clarification and development, at the least. Yet the different focus is also what gives this study a different angle on Proverbs. In fact, it is looking at Proverbs with an interest in ethical questions that discloses the deeper reasons Proverbs has often been overlooked. There are two such reasons. First, the way Proverbs conceives of wisdom represents a fundamental challenge to the mainstream Western tradition. Aristotle said that wisdom was knowledge of "the most honourable things [*ta timiōmata*]," which is to say, things that are necessary and eternal.[63] Augustine said the same: "Wisdom consists in the contemplation of eternal things."[64] By contrast, Proverbs sees wisdom as genuinely practical. "By wisdom," says Proverbs, "a house is built" (24:3). This sentence, we will see, unsettles two distinctions that have frequently been thought basic: the distinction between the speculative and the practical, and the distinction between making and doing.

---

61. Kelsey, *Eccentric Existence*.
62. Kelsey distinguishes (1) investigation of the logic of Christian beliefs (his own project) from that of (2) the logic of coming to belief and (3) the logic of living the Christian life (*Eccentric Existence*, 27–41, 113–19). He emphasizes the dangers involved in confusing the first two investigations, but is much less attentive to the relation between the first and third, suggesting only that "pretty much the same things happen" when they are conflated (p. 82). Our criticisms of Kelsey's account in Chapter 5 could be taken to demonstrate this point.
63. *EN* 1141a18, b3.
64. *DT* 15.3.5.

An example will illustrate how this is a more fundamentally important point than it might appear. When Thomas Aquinas begins his discussion of prudence in the *Summa Theologiae*, he faces a problem posed by Proverbs for a simple separation of practical and theoretical reason.[65] Prov. 10:23, in his Bible, says that "wisdom is prudence to a man."[66] But *wisdom*, for Thomas, is the virtue of the speculative reason. We should not dismiss this objection on the basis that Thomas has been misled by the translation of Proverbs 10:23.[67] Whether or not it is posed by precisely this verse, this *is* a challenge Proverbs poses to Thomas's Aristotelian separation of wisdom and prudence. "I Wisdom [*ḥokmâ*] dwell with prudence ['*ormâ*]," declares Prov. 8:12, and the book is introduced by the promise of *both* wisdom (*ḥokmâ*) and prudence ('*ormâ*; 1:2, 4). Aquinas's conclusion that the wisdom spoken of here in Proverbs is not wisdom as such, but wisdom relative to a particular area of consideration—"the genus of human acts"—is a significant, and contestable, interpretative claim. One of the aims of this study is to clarify the nature of the challenge posed by Proverbs at this point, and to discern what difference it might make. It seems to me that this challenge is rarely taken seriously enough by the more theologically oriented studies.

The second deeper reason for the neglect of Proverbs has to do with the influence of Immanuel Kant on the notion of practical reason. It was a basic, orienting principle for Kant that practical reason was *not* about the prudential pursuit of happiness. If humanity's chief end were happiness, then reason should be side-lined, for it is, Kant thought, quite a bad instrument for attaining it. Reason is not essentially related to happiness, but involves "the idea of another and far worthier purpose of one's existence, to which therefore, and not to happiness, reason is properly destined."[68] Prudence and morality run along two quite different tracks. Practical reason's domain is morality and duty; prudence does not share in that dignity.[69]

The influence of this distinction can be seen in one of the recent attempts to take the ethical thought of Proverbs seriously. Michael Baris argues that Proverbs 1–9 presents a variation on a Stoic vision, in which "the fundamental structure of Wisdom/*logos* as moral substratum of the world is the mainstay."[70] The problem with such systems, according to Baris, is that they fall foul of Hume's is/ought argument; they cannot make the transition from description of the world to

---

65. *ST* ii-II.47.2.

66. Sapientia est viro prudentia.

67. The Hebrew is somewhat unclear. Most likely the idea is that while doing evil is "like sport" to a fool, to a man of understanding, wisdom is such, i.e. pleasurable. So Bruce Waltke, *The Book of Proverbs, Chapters 1–15*. New International Commentary on the Old Testament. (Grand Rapids: Eerdmans, 2004), 474; and Murphy, *Proverbs*, 75.

68. Kant, *Groundwork*, 9 [4:396].

69. For Kant's distinction between prudence and morality, see *Groundwork*, 26–7 [4:415–416].

70. Baris, "Iniquities Ensnare," 136.

truly moral prescription.⁷¹ How can the simplistic exhortations and warnings of Proverbs, "like the maxims of a farmer's almanac,"⁷² be thought to have truly ethical significance? "Are these the deep insights of moral wisdom the sages have to offer or merely behaviourist words to the wise?"⁷³ This alternative, however, trades on an understanding of "moral" that is foreign to Proverbs, but owes much to Kant. Baris writes: "The conceptual gap between happiness as a goal per se and what Moderns would deem a true ethic appears substantial. Ethical behaviour and intention are oriented towards others, and they do not depend on the personal satisfaction of the moral subject."⁷⁴ This is just not how Proverbs sees things. For Proverbs, the "happiness" we unavoidably seek is not merely "personal satisfaction," but a *genuinely* successful life—in Robert Spaemann's phrase, a life that "turns out well."⁷⁵ The alternative between morality and happiness rests, as it does in Kant's thought,⁷⁶ on a reduction of the concept of happiness that Proverbs, like much ancient philosophy, refuses.⁷⁷ Wisdom is about how life can turn out well. It concerns not merely the subjective experience of life, but its objective success.⁷⁸ The warnings of the "farmer's almanac," therefore, do not need to be "transform[ed] from practical maxims to unforgiving introspection," as Baris proposes, so that they are really about "the disintegration of the human self as a moral being."⁷⁹ Rather, they really are about death, failure, disaster. It is also true, we will argue, that the great and theologically significant claim of Proverbs is that wisdom is righteousness. But this is a claim that depends upon the assumption that wisdom is about how life can turn out well. It is therefore, we will further argue, a claim that is ultimately a kind of prophecy.

71. Baris, "Iniquities Ensnare," 137.
72. Baris, "Iniquities Ensnare," 132.
73. Baris, "Iniquities Ensnare," 132.
74. Baris, "Iniquities Ensnare," 137.
75. "Turn out well" is the felicitous rendering of "gelindendes Leben" in Jeremiah Alberg's translation of Robert Spaemann's *Glück und Wohlwollen: Happiness and Benevolence* (Notre Dame: University of Notre Dame, 2000).
76. Although Kant is clear that happiness is an indeterminate concept, it is still, for him, fundamentally subjective, having to do with "well-being" (see *Groundwork*, 28–9 [4:418]); or, "consciousness of the agreeableness of life"; "where each has to put his happiness comes down to the particular feeling of pleasure and displeasure in each … " (*Critique of Practical Reason*, trans. Mary Gregor [Cambridge: Cambridge University Press, 2015], 20, 23 [5:22, 25]).
77. For this argument, see Robert Spaemann, *Glück und Wohlwollen* (Stuttgart: Klett-Cotta, 1989).
78. This is why Aristotle wrestled with the problem of whether someone should only be called happy after they had died. See *Nicomachean Ethics* 1.10–11; and also Spaemann, *Glück und Wohlwollen*, 75–84.
79. Baris, "Iniquities Ensnare," 144, 140.

It remains only to preview how the discussion will unfold. It proceeds, broadly speaking, in two movements. In the first, we begin with Aristotle (Chapter 1), seeking to describe not so much his ethical thought as a whole, but the complexities surrounding the notion of practical reason that emerge in the *Nicomachean Ethics*. From this point we move to Aquinas, attempting, in Chapter 2, to grasp the overall shape of his moral theology as it pertains to the notion of practical reason. I argue that at the heart of Aquinas's thought is an understanding of the generic character of action, and that this shapes his account of prudence and moral deliberation. The theological foundation for this idea is found in the idea of eternal law, a concept that Aquinas draws from the notion that God "made the world by wisdom." For Aquinas, the biblical basis for this idea lies especially in Proverbs ch. 8. This text is therefore the point from which we begin to hear the distinctive voice of Proverbs. Struggles over the meaning of this text (Chapter 3, Section 1) lead us to ask more basic questions about how the book of Proverbs thinks about wisdom (Chapter 3, Section 2). These questions lead us to conclusions that put pressure on key features of Aquinas's thought (Chapter 3, Section 3). This brings us to the end of the first movement in the discussion. It leaves us with a number of questions, which the second movement picks up by allowing a new voice to enter. Oliver O'Donovan's work highlights many of the same issues, and particularly the importance of kinds of action, but from a different perspective. Chapter 4 allows O'Donovan to speak at length, but all the while recalling points raised in the first part of the discussion. This allows us to reflect critically on O'Donovan's work (Chapter 4, Section 3), and then to move to a concluding discussion (Chapter 5), in which we sum up the points that have been reached and suggest what they may mean. This cannot, of course, truly conclude the discussion. "A discussion," O'Donovan says, "succeeds only when it reaches a measure of substantial agreement." The contrived nature of this discussion means that there can be no true agreement. It is hoped, however, that by the end the discussion will have advanced, at least through clarifying further intuitions and shared questions from which discussion may recommence.

Chapter 1

THE COMPLEXITIES OF PRACTICAL REASON IN THE *NICOMACHEAN ETHICS* OF ARISTOTLE

Happy the person who finds wisdom

—Prov. 3:13

Introduction

This chapter has two aims. First, to prepare the way for our discussion of Thomas Aquinas in Chapter 2. "Aquinas's (unacknowledged) aim," in John Rist's words, "was coherently to appropriate Aristotle for the Augustinian tradition."[1] Although as we will see, Aquinas disagrees with and develops Aristotle's ideas in important ways, the central aspects of his understanding of practical reasoning are best viewed in the light of Aristotle's discussions. We will therefore prepare the way for our discussion of Aquinas with an orienting sketch of some of the core ideas of the *Nicomachean Ethics*.[2] Beginning from Aristotle's thinking about the relationship of happiness and reason (Section 1), we will move to his account of the virtues that correspond to theoretical and practical reason—*sophia* and *phronēsis* (Section 2).

---

1. John Rist, *Augustine Deformed: Love, Sin, and Freedom in the Western Moral Tradition* (Cambridge: Cambridge University Press, 2014), 104. On the relationship of Aquinas to Aristotle and his practical philosophy, see, among many works, Joseph Owen, "Aristotle and Aquinas," in *The Cambridge Companion to Aquinas*, ed. N. Kretzmann and E. Stump (Cambridge: Cambridge University Press, 1993), 38–59; Ulrich Kühn, *Via Caritatis: Theologie des Gesetzes bei Thomas von Aquin* (Berlin: Evangelische Verlagsanstalt, 1964), 122–8; Anthony Kenny, *Aquinas* (Oxford: Oxford University Press, 1980), 20–3; Alasdair MacIntyre, *Three Rival Versions of Moral Enquiry: Encyclopaedia, Genealogy, and Tradition* (London: Duckworth, 1990), 105–48; Ralph McInerny, *Aquinas on Human Action: A Theory of Practice* (Washington, DC: Catholic University of America Press, 1992), 161–77; and Tobias Hoffmann, ed., *Aquinas and the Nicomachean Ethics* (Cambridge: Cambridge University Press, 2013).

2. We are here concerned almost exclusively with the *Nicomachean Ethics* (*EN*). The complex questions surrounding the relationship of the *EN* to the *Eudemian Ethics* (*EE*) can safely be set aside because the *EN* was the primary text by which Aristotle's ethics was known to Thomas.

This will lead us to a more detailed discussion of Aristotle's thinking about deliberation (Section 3) and the practical syllogism (Section 4).

Providing this sketch also allows us to introduce the conceptual issues that are the focus of this study. This is the second aim of this chapter. Aristotle introduces us to the distinction between theoretical and practical reason, and the ideas of wisdom and prudence. His conception of wisdom as a perfection of speculative knowledge will have a profound influence on Thomas Aquinas, as will his notion of deliberation. Yet these ideas are also beset with ambiguities and tensions in Aristotle's thought. In particular, the distinctive character of practical thinking is partially obscured by the prominence given to a certain conception of productive skill. This will be a key point when we come to consider both Aquinas and the book of Proverbs. Therefore, just as Aristotle's thought was the chief stimulus for Aquinas's understanding of practical reasoning, it can provide a productive starting point for this discussion. It should hastily be added, though, that the sketch of Aristotle's position that follows will be roughly as satisfactory as having major monuments frantically pointed out as you pass through a city on a fast train; we must settle for a sense of the lie of the land. It is impossible to survey this material without making choices about various contentious questions, and some kind of argument. Nevertheless, many complex issues are barely touched on.

1 Happiness and Reason

The *Nicomachean Ethics* begins with an observation: that every human action "is thought to aim at some good."[3] From this starting point, Aristotle moves quickly to the idea of a highest good, which leads him to the notion of happiness (*eudaimonia*), and thence to a formal conception of practical reason as reasoning from ends to actions.[4] Before we delve further into these arguments, however, it is important to notice the form of the starting point. Aristotle begins his discussion from what "is thought" (*dokei*) to be the case, and, as John Cooper points out, throughout the discussion of happiness Aristotle "returns periodically to this dialectical home-base."[5] Thinking about ethics, Aristotle is at pains to point out,

---

3. *EN* 1.1, 1094a1. Except where otherwise stated, quotations are taken from Roger Crisp's translation of the *Nicomachean Ethics* (Cambridge: Cambridge University Press, 2000). Quotations of the Greek text are from the LOEB edition: *Aristotle: The Nicomachean Ethics*, trans. H. Rackham (Loeb Classical Library 73; Cambridge, MA: Harvard University Press, 1934).

4. There are debates about the logic of this movement, particularly as regards *EN* 1.2. See, for instance, Peter B. M. Vranas, "Aristotle on the Best Good: Is 'Nicomachean Ethics' 1094a18–22 Fallacious?" *Phronesis* 50, no. 2 (2005): 116–28. However, these questions are not important for our argument.

5. John M. Cooper, *Reason and Human Good in Aristotle* (Cambridge, MA, and London: Harvard University Press, 1975), 69. See *EN* 1095a17; 1095b23–31.

is a rough business, in which success is mostly a matter of offering "sufficient proof" for "received opinions."[6] "The truth in practical issues," as Aristotle later puts it, "is judged from the facts of our life, these being what really matter."[7] The initial premises of practical thinking are not known through formal logic, but are grasped through dialectical argument.[8]

It is important to recognize this aspect of Aristotle's practical philosophy, because it highlights the fact that Aristotle's thinking is embedded in, and draws upon, a particular social context.[9] As Richard Kraut notes, Aristotle's insistence, "that his audience have experience in ethical matters and must have been brought up in good habits suggests that he is not building his arguments on a value free foundation."[10] The *polis*, as Alasdair MacIntyre puts it, is for Aristotle "the locus of rationality," because it supplies "those systematic forms of activity within which goods are unambiguously ordered." In a real sense, there is "no practical rationality outside the *polis*."[11]

However, it is also true that Aristotle's arguments rely on categories and principles that transcend his context. Aristotle appeals at several junctures to human nature, and to reason, in ways that produce a critical standpoint upon the culture and life of the *polis*. This is particularly clear in the "function argument," in which Aristotle attempts to discern "the characteristic activity of a human being" (*to ergon tou anthrōpou*),[12] and in which he concludes that this *ergon* must have to do in some way with reason.[13] A similar kind of appeal manifests itself in the discussion of wish (*boulēsis*),[14] where Aristotle regards as deeply unsatisfying the

---

6. *EN* 1.3; 7.1, 1145b2–7.

7. *EN* 10.8, 1179a.20.

8. See Cooper, *Reason and Human Good*, 69–70.

9. I am here partially resisting the argument of Terrence Irwin, in *Aristotle's First Principles* (Oxford: Clarendon, 1988), that Aristotle developed a conception of "strong dialectic," which, by sticking to premises "that we have some good reason for accepting" (p. 476), overcomes the objection that his dialectical arguments could not yield truly "objective principles" (p. 473)—at least to the extent that this argument allows Aristotle's ideas about practical reason to wholly transcend their social context. See also Richard Kraut, "*Aristotle's First Principles*, by Terence Irwin. Book Review," *The Philosophical Review* 101, no. 2 (1992): 365–71.

10. Kraut, "*Aristotle's First Principles*," 370–1. See *EN* 1095a2–5; 1095b4–6.

11. Alasdair MacIntyre, *Whose Justice? Which Rationality?* (London: Duckworth, 1988), 141.

12. *EN* 1.7, 1097b24.

13. *EN* 1.7, 1098a2–7. For a defense of Aristotle's naturalism, see T. H. Irwin, *The Development of Ethics: A Historical and Critical Study. Volume I: From Socrates to the Reformation* (Oxford: Oxford University Press, 2007), 140–5. Note especially Irwin's point that Aristotle's idea that happiness requires the exercise of virtue over a complete life makes it very difficult to sustain a non-naturalist reading.

14. *EN* 3.2.

notion that "nothing is an object of wish by nature."[15] Aristotle's argument, as Irwin puts it, "relies indispensably on … premises about the human essence and the human good."[16] This point is also very apparent in book ten, in which Aristotle makes a case for contemplation as the greatest activity to pursue:

> And what we said above will apply here as well: what is proper to each thing is by nature best and pleasantest for it; for a human being, therefore, the life in accordance with intellect is best and pleasantest, since this, more than anything else, constitutes humanity.[17] So this life will be the happiest.[18]

This quotation raises a contentious aspect of Aristotle's practical philosophy: his views about the nature of happiness. The difficulty lies in determining how this claim in book ten, that happiness lies in contemplation, relates to what seem to be clear and careful articulations elsewhere of how happiness is found in the practical life of moral virtue. In book ten, Aristotle appears to resolve this by distinguishing between "perfect happiness" and happiness in a "secondary" sense.[19] This is not satisfying, however, because it still leaves hanging the question of how the two relate.[20] One possibility is to say that this is in fact consistent with the view Aristotle appears to develop more clearly elsewhere, namely what Irwin calls, "a comprehensive and composite view of happiness."[21] This is a conception in which a range of goods are sought not only in and for themselves, but also as parts of a whole; these goods are good as such, but better insofar as they contribute to a whole.

Although there are undoubtedly things to be said for this position,[22] it is difficult to sustain in relation to the *Nicomachean Ethics* as a whole.[23] Parts of the

---

15. *EN* 1113a.21.
16. Irwin, *Aristotle's First Principles*, 478.
17. This phrase (*eiper touto malista anthrōpos*) is contested. Irwin translates it, "if understanding, more than anything else, is the human being" (*Nicomachean Ethics*, 2nd ed. [Indianapolis: Hackett, 1999], 165). I am content with Crisp's rendering for reasons set out in what follows.
18. *EN* 10.7, 1178a5–8.
19. *EN* 1178a9.
20. For the problems here, see J. L. Ackrill, "Aristotle on Eudaimonia," in *Essays on Aristotle's Ethics*, ed. A. O. Rorty (Berkeley: University of Chicago Press, 1980), 29–33; and Joseph Dunne, *Back to the Rough Ground: "Phronesis" and "Techne" in Modern Philosophy and in Aristotle* (Notre Dame and London: University of Notre Dame Press, 1993), 239–44.
21. Irwin, *Development*, 132. This is the position Ackrill argues is set out in book one, and dominates the *EN*, though not 10.7–8 ("Aristotle on Eudaimonia," 15–33).
22. See, for example, Cooper's arguments in *Reason and Human Good*, 89–143.
23. See especially Ackrill, "Aristotle on Eudaimonia," 29–33; Anthony Kenny, *Aristotle on the Perfect Life* (Oxford: Clarendon, 1992); and Richard Kraut, *Aristotle on the Human Good* (Princeton, NJ: Princeton University Press, 1989).

text strongly suggest that happiness is most fully realized in one, "dominant"[24] activity of contemplation: "The god's activity, which is superior in blessedness, will be contemplative; and therefore the human activity most akin to this is the most conducive to happiness."[25] It is possible that this implies that the moral virtues and practical wisdom are ordered to the service of contemplation, so that Aristotle is saying both that "one will need the ethical virtues in order to live the life of a philosopher, even though exercising those virtues is not the philosopher's ultimate end,"[26] and that the *polis* requires both political activity and contemplation for its health.[27] It may be, however, that things are not so neat as that. Many interpreters feel a significant disjunction between the two conceptions of happiness. Cooper, for instance, concludes that book ten affirms the intellectualist account of happiness only with "significant reservations," and to an extent leaves the "mixed" life of moral virtue standing as a real alternative.[28] Similarly, Thomas Nagel sees a real "indecision between two accounts of *eudaimonia*" in the *Nicomachean Ethics*.[29]

How one resolves this issue will depend partly on how certain passages are read and partly on one's assumptions about the coherence of the different parts of the Aristotelian corpus.[30] One way of responding, however, is to see this tension as an inevitable consequence, given Aristotle's metaphysical commitments, of the duality we observed at the outset—between a dialectical argument that operates within the conditions of a given social context and an appeal to categories, within this argument, that transcend these conditions. The addition of "given Aristotle's metaphysical commitments" is crucial here. In and of itself, one could argue, why should the exercise of reason require anything other than the active life of social activity? There is no self-evident reason why human nature, and the human capacity for reason, cannot be fully and fittingly realized in the active life within a given, contingent social context. For Aristotle, this argument is undermined by an important metaphysical

---

24. For the language of "inclusive" and "dominant," see Ackrill, "Aristotle on Eudaimonia," 17; cf. Kraut, *Aristotle on the Human Good*, 8, n. 13; and Kenny, *Aristotle on the Perfect Life*, 6.

25. *EN* 10.8, 1178b22–23.

26. Richard Kraut, "Aristotle's Ethics," in *The Stanford Encyclopedia of Philosophy* (Summer 2014 edition), ed. Edward N. Zalta. http://plato.stanford.edu/archives/sum2014/entries/aristotle-ethics/. See also Kraut, *Aristotle on the Human Good*, especially 41–4.

27. MacIntyre, *Whose Justice?*, 142–3.

28. Cooper, *Reason and Human Good*, 177–80.

29. Thomas Nagel, "Aristotle on Eudaimonia," in *Essays on Aristotle's Ethics*, ed. A. O. Rorty (Berkeley: University of Chicago Press, 1980), 7. Ackrill, likewise, concludes that book ten is not finally reconcilable with the wider account in the *EN* ("Aristotle on Eudaimonia," 31–3).

30. Anthony Kenny argues that this question clearly distinguishes the *EN* from the *EE*, and on this basis, suggests that the *EE* is a late work. See Anthony Kenny, *The Aristotelian Ethics: A Study of the Relationship between the Eudemian and Nicomachean Ethics of Aristotle* (Oxford: Clarendon, 1978).

conviction: the existence of "eternal objects." The object of scientific knowledge (*epistēmē*), Aristotle says at one point, is "necessary" (*ex anagkēs*) and therefore "eternal" (*aidion*), because "everything that is necessary, without qualification, is eternal, and what is eternal does not come into being or cease to be."[31] Moreover, these eternal objects have an elevated status and dignity. "There are other things," Aristotle points out at a key point in book six, "far more divine in nature than human beings, such as—to take the most obvious example—the things constituting the cosmos."[32] These things Aristotle calls "the most honourable things [*ta timiōmata*]."[33]

This metaphysical commitment makes it impossible that happiness, which is realized in the exercise of reason (the function argument), could be fully realized within the practical life of the *polis*. The reason for this lies in a further principle, articulated by Aristotle at the beginning of book six: the exercise of reason is correlated to the form of the world.

> Let us assume that there are two sub-parts [of the *psychē*] with reason, one with which we contemplate those things whose first principles cannot be otherwise, and another those things whose first principles can be otherwise. For when the objects are different in kind, the part of the soul naturally related to each is different in kind, since they gain their understanding through a certain similarity and relationship between them and their objects.[34]

Here we meet for the first time a distinction that will be at the heart of this study: between theoretical and practical reason. We must note, however, the peculiar form in which Aristotle introduces this distinction. First and foremost, it is a distinction within the soul that corresponds to a distinction in the world. Because there are in fact two kinds of "object"—things whose first principles cannot be otherwise, which are necessary and eternal,[35] and things whose first principles can be otherwise, which includes "what is produced and what is done"[36]—there must be a distinction within the rational part of the soul corresponding to those two kinds of object.[37] For Aristotle, that is to say, the distinction is not simply *formal*, between "reasoning leading to action and reasoning for the truth of a

---

31. *EN* 1139b.23; cf. 3.3, 1112a22, where Aristotle says that we do not deliberate about "eternal things, such as the universe, or the fact that the diagonal is commensurable with the side."

32. *EN* 6.7, 1141a35–1141b2. Compare *Metaphysics* 6.1, 1026a26–30. See also Jonathan Barnes, *Aristotle* (Oxford: Oxford University Press, 1982), 24.

33. *EN* 1141a18, b3.

34. *EN* 6.1, 1139a7–13.

35. See *EN* 6.3, 1139b20–24.

36. *EN* 6.4, 1140a1–2.

37. On this idea, see J. A. Stewart, *Notes on the Nicomachean Ethics*, Vol. 2 (Clarendon: Oxford, 1892), 11–15; and Sarah Broadie, *Ethics with Aristotle* (New York: Oxford University Press, 1991), 262, n. 47.

conclusion," as Elizabeth Anscombe puts it.[38] That certainly *is* a valid distinction, and Aristotle goes on to distinguish practical and theoretical *thought* (*dianoia*);[39] but for Aristotle this distinction depends upon a prior distinction between kinds of object. Anscombe's observation that it is perfectly possible to reason about non-necessary things without a view to action is a genuine objection to the adequacy of Aristotle's account of the matter.[40] As we will see, it is a point that Thomas Aquinas will also make.

This is a point we will need to revisit. For now, however, we note simply that it is this distinction between fundamentally different objects of thought that produces the idea of contemplation. Contemplation (*theōria*) is the form of reasonable activity fitted to eternal and necessary objects. Contemplation is the activity of the "best element," which is either "intellect or something else we think naturally rules and guides us and has insight into matters noble and divine."[41] It is "the highest activity," both because it is the activity of "the highest element in us" and because "its objects are the highest objects of knowledge."[42]

The tension between the practical and intellectual forms of happiness is therefore inevitable. For Aristotle believes—on the basis of dialectical argument that presumes the validity of certain convictions about human nature and reason—that happiness is an activity of the soul in accordance with reason.[43] Yet his convictions about the nature of the universe—in particular, the existence of eternal objects—mean that activity in accordance with reason is not reducible to the activity of practical reason. On the contrary, activity in accordance with reason, at its purest, must be contemplation. Indeed, contemplation is, in Ackrill's words, "incommensurably more valuable" than any other activity.[44] But to affirm, this undermines precisely the social context that allowed the dialectical argument to emerge. The thought of a happiness constituted by activity that is *reasonable* is the gift of a particular social context, but the concept of reason implied therein relativizes the value of life lived in accordance with that social context. There is no practical rationality outside the *polis*, but the rationality that practical rationality implies must transcend the *polis*.

---

38. Elizabeth Anscombe, *Intention* (Oxford: Basil Blackwell, 1976), 59–60.

39. *EN* 6.2, 1139a27.

40. Anscombe, *Intention*, 59–60.

41. *EN* 10.7, 1177a15–16.

42. *EN* 10.7, 1177a20. I thus agree with Irwin's argument that Aristotle's ethical theory is deeply anchored in his metaphysics ("The Metaphysical and Psychological Basis of Aristotle's Ethics," in *Essays on Aristotle's Ethics*, ed. Rorty [Berkeley: University of California Press, 1980], 35–53). My only reservation is that this metaphysical basis is not limited to Aristotle's psychology. A similar line of thought to the one presented here is found in Nagel, "Aristotle on Eudaimonia," 11–12.

43. *EN* 1.7, 1098a3–19; 1.8, 1098b32–1099a6; 1.9, 1099b25–27; cf. 10.6, 1176a34–b8.

44. Ackrill, "Aristotle on Eudaimonia," 32.

2 Wisdom and Prudence

This is the vantage point from which we may understand another distinction of special interest to us. Aristotle says that there are two virtues corresponding to the two parts of the soul with reason. On the one hand, there is *phronēsis*, practical wisdom or prudence, which corresponds to the "calculative" (*logistikon*) part of the soul—the part oriented to things that *can* be otherwise. On the other hand, there is *sophia*, wisdom, which corresponds to the "scientific" (*epistēmikon*) part of the soul—the part oriented to those things which *cannot* be otherwise.[45] Contemplation is the activity "in accordance with wisdom," which "is agreed" to be "the most pleasant of activities in accordance with virtue."[46] Correspondingly, the core activity of practical wisdom is "deliberation" (*bouleusis*)—for "no one deliberates about what cannot be otherwise."[47]

That wisdom and practical wisdom are the "virtues" (*aretai*) of the two parts of the soul with reason means that they are the "best state" (*hē beltistē hexis*) of these two parts.[48] Aristotle's argument for why this is the case helps us understand more about the distinction between practical and theoretical reason. Aristotle begins by highlighting that for both practical and theoretical thought, "best" has to do with truth: "The characteristic activity of each of the parts related to the intellect, then, is truth; and so the virtues of each will be those states on the basis of which it will most of all arrive at the truth."[49] However, the involvement in truth of each of the two parts is somewhat different. "In the case of thought concerned with contemplation ... which is neither practical nor productive, what constitute its being good or bad are truth and falsity, because truth is the characteristic activity of everything concerned with thought."[50] Wisdom enables the soul to know truth simply. In this respect, it resembles scientific knowledge (*epistēmē*), which knows by deductive inference and intellect's (*nous*) grasp of basic principles.[51]

Practical thought is different: "In the case of what is practical and concerned with thought, its being good consists in truth in agreement with correct desire."[52] This is because practical existence, as Aristotle has previously made clear, has a fundamentally goal-oriented nature; it is about pursuit and avoidance of certain ends. "The beginning of practical reason," as Gerasimos Santas puts it, is supplied by an "object of want."[53] This does not, however, require that we impute to Aristotle

---

45. *EN* 6.1, 5, 7, 11–12. See especially 1139a10–16, 1140b20–30, 1143b15.
46. *EN* 10.7, 1177a24.
47. *EN* 6.1, 1139a15.
48. *EN* 6.1, 1139a17.
49. *EN* 6.2, 1139b12–13.
50. *EN* 6.2, 1139a27–29.
51. *EN* 6.3, 6.
52. *EN* 6.2, 1139a.29–31.
53. Gerasimos Santas, "Aristotle on Practical Inference, the Explanation of Action, and Akrasia," *Phronesis* 14, no. 2 (1969): 170.

a Humean position, in which practical reason merely serves the needs of desire. For the objects of want in question are things that are *held* to be good;[54] they are wanted, in John Finnis's words, "under a description."[55] It is simply to insist that the goal-orientated nature of practical thought means that it is irreducibly involved with desire (*orexis*), and so is fundamentally about what Aristotle calls "rational choice" (*prohairesis*). "Rational choice" means "deliberative desire" (*orexis bouleutikē*) for a particular action.[56] Movement for the sake of something (*heneka tou*), as Santas explains, is a product of "both reason (or mind) and want together."[57] Good rational choice therefore involves a coordination of truth and desire: "desire must pursue what reason asserts" (*ta auta ton [logon] men phanai tēn [orexin] de diōkein*).[58] Practical reason, that is to say, involves thinking *from* desired ends *to* desired actions.

As the virtue associated with this thinking, practical wisdom (*phronēsis*) is defined by this involvement of practical reason in both truth and desire. It involves the ability to reason "correctly"—yet not merely in an instrumental sense of correct inference.[59] Practical wisdom is not mere "cleverness," that is, the ability "to do the actions that tend towards the aim we have set ourselves."[60] Rather, practical wisdom involves the ability to deliberate *well*, in the rich sense of deliberation "that achieves something good"—"correctness regarding what is beneficial, about the right thing, in the right way, and at the right time."[61] Practical wisdom, therefore, depends on *virtue*, which "makes the aim right" (*ton skopon poiei orthon*).[62] "Manifestly, one cannot be practically wise without being good."[63] Practical wisdom is about deliberating well, "where living well as a whole is concerned."[64]

---

54. On this point, see David Wiggins, "Deliberation and Practical Reason," *Proceedings of the Aristotelian Society* 76 (1975-1976): 29-51; and John Finnis, *Fundamentals of Ethics* (Oxford: Clarendon, 1983), 26-55.

55. Finnis, *Fundamentals*, 45.

56. *EN* 6.2, 1139a24. Crisp's translation of *prohairesis* as "rational choice" is retained here despite Irwin's objection that "choice" should be avoided since Aristotle also frequently uses *hairesis* (Irwin, *Development*, 117). "Rational choice" seems equally as adequate as the alternatives, "decision" or "election."

57. Santas, "Aristotle on Practical Inference," 170.

58. *EN* 6.2, 1139a25. For this reason, Aristotle analyzes continence and incontinence in terms of disjunction between reason and desire. See *EN* 1145b9-15. On this passage, and for desire in Aristotle's theory of action more broadly, see David Charles, *Aristotle's Philosophy of Action* (London: Duckworth, 1984), 84-96.

59. *EN* 6.9, 1142b13-30.

60. *EN* 6.12, 1144a25-30.

61. *EN* 6.9, 1142b29.

62. *EN* 6.12, 1144a9.

63. *EN* 6.12, 1144a35.

64. *EN* 6.5, 1140a31.

In his insightful study *Back to the Rough Ground*, Joseph Dunne has argued that this interdependence of *phronēsis* and virtue reveals that, fundamentally, *phronēsis* is a concept related to *experience*.[65] It is a kind of knowledge that arises only in and with action itself.[66] "A person," as Aristotle says, "is practically wise not only by knowing, but also by being disposed to act [*ou tō eidenai monon phronimos alla kai tō praktikos*]."[67] *Phronēsis*, as Dunne sees it, is "an internal perfection of experience," "a habit of *attentiveness* that makes the resources of one's past experience flexibly available to one and, at the same time, allows the present situation to 'unconceal' its own particular significance."[68] By this, Dunne means to suggest that *phronēsis* is about insight into concrete situations and what, in the end, they really amount to. He gives as examples such judgments as: "I am taking out my frustrations with the boss on the children," or "I am making distractions for myself in order to avoid making this decision."[69] When Aristotle speaks of practical wisdom having to do especially with ultimate particulars,[70] Dunne suggests, what he means—or at least what by his own logic he ought to mean—is that practical reason hinges on coming to such a grasp of what concrete situations amount to. This is why, for Dunne, the practical syllogism is of minimal help for understanding *phronēsis*. Practical reasoning is not, fundamentally, deductive.[71] It is also why Aristotle could say, "We should attend to the undemonstrated words and beliefs of experienced and older people or of practically wise people, no less than to demonstrations, because their experienced eye enables them to see correctly."[72]

We will have occasion to return to Dunne's work in what follows. Many of these ideas will resonate with things we will find in the book of Proverbs, and elsewhere. Our own conclusions could be taken to lend support to Dunne's argument that *phronēsis* can provide an alternative to the enfeebling dominance of technical rationality in modern existence. For now, however, we need to attend to the fact that although these elements are present in Aristotle's thought, they are also ambiguous. As Dunne himself observes, Aristotle often allows the distinctive character of *phronēsis* to be obscured by modes of rationality that are not truly native to practice—in particular, forms of thought associated with the other kind of thing whose first principles can be otherwise, namely, "what is produced."[73] We will see this as we now turn to consider in more detail Aristotle's understanding of deliberation.

---

65. Joseph Dunne, *Back to the Rough Ground: "Phronesis" and "Techne" in Modern Philosophy and in Aristotle* (Notre Dame and London: University of Notre Dame Press, 1993), 275–95.

66. Dunne, *Back to the Rough Ground*, 290.

67. *EN* 7.10, 1152a8–9.

68. Dunne, *Back to the Rough Ground*, 305–6.

69. Dunne, *Back to the Rough Ground*, 302.

70. See *EN* 6.11, 1143b1–6.

71. Dunne, *Back to the Rough Ground*, 307–8. We will return to the practical syllogism below, Section 4.

72. *EN* 6.11, 1143b11–13.

73. Dunne, *Back to the Rough Ground*, 244–9; cf. *EN* 6.4, 1140a1–2.

3 Deliberation

Deliberation (*bouleusis*), Aristotle says, is a kind of *search* (*zētēsis*),[74] by which a person determines "how he is to act."[75] We do not deliberate about "eternal things," or things that happen of necessity or from natural causes, or by chance, nor about human affairs that do not concern us.[76] Rather, "we deliberate about what is in our power," and in relation to things that are uncertain in how they are going to come out—the kinds of things you might sometimes seek advice in.[77] More specifically, we deliberate about "means," or "things that are conducive to ends" (*tōn pros ta telē*) rather than *ends* as such.[78]

> For a doctor does not deliberate about whether to cure, nor an orator whether to persuade, nor a politician whether to produce good order; nor does anyone else deliberate about his end. Rather, they establish an end [or "taking an end as given" (*themenoi telos ti*)] and then go on to think about how and by what means it is to be achieved. If it appears that there are several means available, they consider by which it will be achieved in the easiest and most noble way; while if it can be attained by only one means, they consider how this will bring it about and by what further means this means is itself to be brought about, until they arrive at the first cause the last thing to be found.[79]

On this account, deliberation is about thinking *to* an action to be done in the light of (*from*) a given end of action, something that is desired. This end is the starting point of thinking,[80] whereas the end point of thinking (the "last thing") is the starting point of action. As Thomas Aquinas will explain it, "the order of reasoning about actions is contrary to the order of actions."[81]

It is important to be careful at this point, however, because the notion of end–means reasoning is somewhat deceptive. We therefore need to pause to observe the different ways in which this idea can be taken. The paradigm for end–means

---

74. *EN* 6.9, 1142a31; cf. 3.3, 1112b22.
75. *EN* 3.3, 1113a6.
76. *EN* 3.3, 1112a22–31.
77. *EN* 3.3, 1112a.31–1112b10.
78. *EN* 3.3, 1112b.12.
79. *EN* 3.3, 1112b.12–19.
80. In 1151a17, Aristotle says that "in actions the end for which we act is the first principle (*archē*), as assumptions are in mathematics." The concept of a first principle is being used here in a different sense to how it is used in *EN* 6.1, 1139a7–18, a potential confusion that Aristotle takes care to clarify there, saying, "The first principle of action—its moving cause, not its goal [*hou heneka*]—is rational choice" (1139a32). It is "what is done" that "can be otherwise" (*endechetai to prakton allōs echein*) (1140a33–b3).
81. *ST* I-II.14.5.

reasoning is what we might call technical deliberation.[82] One of Aristotle's basic examples is the process involved in working out the best way to draw a geometric figure.[83] However, there are real and important differences between this kind of technical deliberation and other forms of deliberation, in particular, much moral deliberation. Aristotle himself famously distinguishes the logic of "making," or production (*poiēsis*), from that of "doing," or action (*praxis*). He says that in making, to which the virtue *technē* (skill) corresponds, the end is distinct from the activity, whereas with acting, which is of course the domain of *phronēsis*, "the end is acting well [*eupraxia*] itself."[84] Two quite different ways of conceiving the relationship between ends and means are involved in this distinction. David Wiggins highlights the difference:

> It is absolutely plain what counts as my having adequate covering, or as my having succeeded in drawing a plane figure of the prescribed kind using only ruler and compass. The practical question here is only what means or measures will work or work best or most easily to those ends. But the standard problem in a non-technical deliberation is quite different. In the non-technical case I shall characteristically have an extremely vague description of something I want—a good life, a satisfying profession, an interesting holiday, an amusing evening—and the problem is not to see what will be causally efficacious in bringing this about, but to see what really *qualifies* as an adequate and practically realizable specification of what would satisfy this want. Deliberation is still *zetēsis*, a search, but it is not primarily a search for means. It is a search for the *best specification*.[85]

Elizabeth Anscombe makes a similar observation in *Intention*. "The mark of practical reasoning," she writes, reframing the means-end paradigm, "is that the thing wanted is *at a distance* from the immediate action, and the immediate action is calculated as the way of getting or doing or securing the thing wanted." She then points out that "it may be at a distance in various ways. For example, 'resting' is merely a wider description of what I am perhaps doing in lying on my bed." Finally, she notes that "acts done to fulfil moral laws will generally be related to positive precepts in this way."[86] This is a recognition of the same point made by

---

82. As Hannah Arendt acutely observes: "acting in the mode of making" has "its categorical framework of means and ends" (*The Human Condition* [Chicago: University of Chicago Press, 1958], 238).

83. Wiggins, "Deliberation," 30, highlights the significance of this point. Dunne, too, notes this point and goes on to highlight the way it actually obscures the distinctive character of *phronēsis* (*Back to the Rough Ground*, 244–74, 300–4). On this argument, see further below.

84. *EN* 6.5, 1140b6–7; cf. 1139b3–4. See Dunne, *Back to the Rough Ground*, 262–3.

85. Wiggins, "Deliberation," 38.

86. Anscombe, *Intention*, 79, emphasis original.

Wiggins, namely, that in moral questions, practical reasoning often takes the form not of calculating the way to achieve a known aim, but of discerning how actions are rightly construed, working out what a course of action would in fact "add up to." The relationship of the "means" to the "end" in action is characteristically constitutive, rather than causal.[87] Deliberation is fundamentally a matter of discerning how "the end" might appear in the present circumstances. In Wiggins's terms, "the whole interest and difficulty of the matter is in the search for adequate specifications."[88] Determining the "means" to the "end" is a matter of discerning in what, here and now, the end consists. This suggests that at the heart of moral deliberation lies an *interpretative* task: the task of rightly construing courses of action. This, we will argue, is a point of great importance.

Now, Aristotle does recognize the ambiguity of the means-end framework to some extent.[89] The fact is, however, he is not as clear about it as he might have been.[90] He is constrained by his basic decision to try, "to illuminate examples of non-technical deliberation by comparing them with a paradigm drawn from technical deliberation."[91] His "basic conceptual schema," Dunne observes, was provided by his formal account of *technē*,[92] an account which drew on what Jaako Hintikka calls "the paradigm of the craftsman,"[93] and that placed a high premium on the ability to give a communicable, theoretical account of the process of making.[94] As Aristotle puts it in the *Metaphysics*, "Things are produced from skill [*technē*] if the form of them is in the mind."[95] This is why, notwithstanding his official distinction between making and doing, Aristotle earned Hannah Arendt's ire for his "substitution of making for acting and the concomitant degradation of politics into a means to obtain an allegedly 'higher' end."[96]

Dunne further argues that this account, which took house-building (*oikodomikē*) as its paradigm example,[97] prevented Aristotle from fully appreciating the significance of other forms of *technē* that he mentions—practices such as playing music, performing gymnastics, military strategy, and navigation.[98]

---

87. See also Cooper, *Reason and Human Good*, 10–24.
88. Wiggins, "Deliberation," 38.
89. See Wiggins, "Deliberation," 30.
90. See Dunne, *Back to the Rough Ground*, 270–3, 351–6.
91. Wiggins, "Deliberation," 37.
92. Dunne, *Back to the Rough Ground*, 251.
93. Jaakko Hintikka, *Knowledge and the Known: Historical Perspectives on Epistemology* (Dordrecht: D. Reidel, 1974), 41–7.
94. Dunne, *Back to the Rough Ground*, 249–51.
95. *Metaphysics* 6.7, 1032a32.
96. Arendt, *The Human Condition*, 229. See also Hintikka, *Knowledge and the Known*, 45: "If the end or aims of any activity is the most important aspect of that activity, all activities are assimilated conceptually to the production of certain results, to making."
97. *EN* 6.4, 1140a7. See also Dunne, *Back to the Rough Ground*, 248, 442, n. 58.
98. Dunne, *Back to the Rough Ground*, 254.

These are practices, Dunne suggests, with a much greater affinity with *phronēsis*, processes "where involvement and fluidity … are ineliminable."[99] Below, we will argue, as Dunne also ultimately does, that house-building, too, is inadequately comprehended by a formal account of making where a fixed, intellectual plan is executed in a two part process, involving, in Arendt's description: "first, perceiving the image or shape (*eidos*) of the product-to-be, and then organizing the means and starting the execution."[100] When the book of Proverbs says, "By wisdom a house is built" (24:3), it does not support a conception of wisdom as an intellectual grasp of theory from which practice proceeds unproblematically. This, as we will see, has some importance for our assessment of Thomas Aquinas's understanding of wisdom. For the moment, however, we need to see that the pull of the technical conception of making, and its associated framework of means and ends, provides some explanation for the ambiguities surrounding the idea of the "practical syllogism" in Aristotle's practical thought.

4 The Practical Syllogism

In his discussion of *akrasia* in book seven, Aristotle distinguishes between two ways in which the combination of a "universal" belief and a "perception" of "particulars" produces a consequence:

> When a single belief emerges from the combination of these two, the soul must in one kind of case affirm the conclusion, while in matters of production it must immediately act. If, for example, everything sweet must be tasted, and this is sweet, in that it is one example of particular sweet things, a person who is capable and not prevented must act on this immediately.[101]

What seems to be set out here is a syllogistic account of action where a principle or rule of some kind—everything sweet must be tasted—is put into effect through the perception of a particular. The terminology seems to pick up on a number of passages in book six, in which Aristotle refers to the way in which "action is concerned with particulars."[102] Aristotle speaks of how practical wisdom is concerned not only with "universals," but also with "particulars."[103] Error in deliberation, he explains, "can concern either the universal or the particular"; and practical wisdom involves the "perception" of the "last thing," which is "what is done."[104]

---

99. Dunne, *Back to the Rough Ground*, 355.
100. Arendt, *The Human Condition*, 225.
101. *EN* 7.3, 1147a.24–31.
102. *EN* 6.7, 1141b16.
103. *EN* 6.7, 1141b15–23.
104. *EN* 1142a21–30. The relationship of deliberation to perception of particulars is mentioned already in 3.3, 1113a1.

The difficulty here is that this kind of universal–particular syllogism seems to involve a different kind of reasoning to the end–means thinking that Aristotle says characterizes deliberation. One appears to work from given principles of action; the other seems to assume only a desire for an end. "It is hardly possible," D. J. Allan influentially wrote, "to see what relation is intended between these two analyses of practical reasoning."[105]

This difficulty does not seem to have worried Aristotle nearly as much as it has modern commentators.[106] One reason for this is that, in Aristotle's thought, syllogistic reasoning seems to perform a different function in practical reasoning to end–means reasoning. The universal–particular practical syllogism often appears to serve as an explanation of how action comes about, in the sense that it accounts for the movement from a "rational choice" to an action. John Cooper, followed by Alasdair MacIntyre and others, has thus argued that the practical syllogism lies "outside the process of deliberation proper."[107] Deliberation is a discursive process that begins from an end and terminates, not in *action*, but in the choice of a "means," in *prohairesis*, which is "the decision to perform an action of some definite, specific *type*."[108] Cooper argues that the passages in book six that speak of "universals" and "particulars" (such as those noted above) should not be understood as syllogisms, but as a recognition that the selection (rational choice) of a kind of action requires the right level of specificity of knowledge.[109] Knowing that "chicken is a light meat," for instance, is not knowledge of an *individual* thing, but of a particular kind in relation to the generic category of "light meats."[110] The universal–particular practical syllogism, on the other hand, applies principally to "a very limited part of practical thinking, the final step which actually issues in the performance of an action."[111]

This argument is reasonably persuasive. However, Cooper takes a further step that is problematic. He argues that "Aristotle never says or implies that" deliberation ever takes a form that "remotely resembles" a syllogism,[112] and so suggests that the practical syllogism "ought not to be regarded as part of practical reasoning at all";[113] it, rather, "is only a way of expressing the content of the intuitive perceptual act by which the agent recognizes the presence and availability for action of the ultimate

---

105. D. J. Allan, "The Practical Syllogism," in *Autour d'Aristote: Recueil d'études de philosophie ancienne et médiévale offert à Msgr A. Mansion* (Louvain: Publications Universitaires de Louvain, 1955), 325–40, 337.

106. For a summary of the debate, see Daniel Westberg, *Right Practical Reason: Aristotle, Action, and Prudence in Aquinas* (Oxford: Clarendon, 1994), 17–25.

107. Cooper, *Reason and Human Good*, 44.

108. Cooper, *Reason and Human Good*, 23, emphasis original.

109. Cooper, *Reason and Human Good*, 27–32.

110. Cf. *EN* 6.7, 1141b15–23.

111. Cooper, *Reason and Human Good*, 24.

112. Cooper, *Reason and Human Good*, 24.

113. Cooper, *Reason and Human Good*, 51.

means previously decided upon."[114] We should make two comments about this. First, it is a bit too neat. At one point in book six, Aristotle says, "For practical syllogisms [*sullogismoi tōn praktōn*] have a first principle: 'Since such-and-such is the end or chief good,' whatever it is ... "[115] This appears straightforwardly to suggest that the process of deliberating from an end to a means can be analyzed as a syllogism. Cooper's passing over this passage, on the basis that *sullogismoi* is better translated "reasonings," is not persuasive.[116] As David Charles points out, there is considerable evidence that for Aristotle the syllogism can be a part of deliberation.[117] Most notably, Aristotle says that deliberation can fail "through false inference,"[118] and elsewhere holds that end–means reasoning can take a syllogistic form.[119] It seems clear that the distinction between deliberation and the syllogism is not so clear-cut.[120] In my opinion, this is because, as we stressed above, deliberation is often an essentially interpretative task, a matter of rightly construing a course of action. Determining the right "means" to the "end" is often a matter of discerning the meaning of a proposed action. This kind of movement is susceptible to analysis in terms of a syllogism: I want to act well; this act, because it is an act of kind X, is acting well; I should do an act of kind X.

Second, the idea that the movement mapped by the practical syllogism is of negligible significance, as an element *within* practical reasoning is highly problematic. The subsumption of the particular under the general, which as Aristotle stresses involves "perception" (*aisthēsis*),[121] should not be regarded as a mere formality that does not require "further thinking."[122] On the contrary, further thinking is often precisely what is required. In some cases, such as Cooper's example of turning on a light switch,[123] the perception involved may not seem very taxing. However, it is possible to imagine how even here the perception involved might impact the decision arrived at. What if, for example, I look for the switch and see that it is hanging from the wall, with a wire coming out? What if the switch is covered in honey? Here, of course, lies the significance of Aristotle's saying that "a person who is capable *and not prevented* must act on this immediately."[124]

---

114. Cooper, *Reason and Human Good*, 46–7.

115. *EN* 6.12, 1144a31–32.

116. Cooper, *Reason and Human Good*, 24, n. 25. It was this passage, among other things, that led Allan to his argument (see "The Practical Syllogism," 336).

117. *Aristotle's Philosophy of Action*, 136–7.

118. *EN* 6.9, 1142b22.

119. See *Posterior Analytics* 94b8–12. MacIntyre draws attention to these points in *Whose Justice?*, 135.

120. Cooper admits that Aristotle uses technical terms connected to the syllogism to describe aspects of deliberation (*Reason and Human Good*, 24).

121. *EN* 6.8, 1142a24–31.

122. Cooper, *Reason and Human Good*, 27.

123. Cooper, *Reason and Human Good*, 26–7.

124. *EN* 7.3, 1147a.30–31, and above. Emphasis added.

However, in other cases the perception involved in joining a rational desire for a kind of action to the action itself clearly is materially significant. The perception of what, in some situation, it means to tell the truth, or to honor my father, for example, may lead me to realize I do not in fact desire this kind of act in the way I thought I did. To these examples, Cooper might respond that what has happened is that deliberation has not reached a kind of action with the necessary level of specificity. To this we may reply that between a *kind* of action—*however* specific— and its actual instantiation there is always a gap to be bridged by perception, and that apart from this perception we do not yet truly know what it is that we have decided upon in deliberation. Wiggins stresses the same point: "A man may think it clear to him, in a certain situation, what is the relevant concern, yet ... may resile from the concern when he sees what it leads to, or what it costs, and start all over again."[125] The perception of the particular by which rational choice moves to action is an essential part of practical reason. Indeed, it is often the heart of the issue. "Few situations," David Wiggins reminds us, "come already inscribed with the names of all the human concerns which they touch or impinge upon," meaning that it is the minor premise that is often the crucial factor in practical reasoning.[126]

These reservations about Cooper's account should not lead us to conclude that he is entirely wrong about the function of the universal–particular practical syllogism. Within Aristotle's thought, there do seem to be two broad movements of practical thought: end–means reasoning, which begins from a desire for a good to be achieved; and the universal–particular syllogism, which begins from the proposition that something or other *should* be done. "Every man ought to walk"; "I ought to create a house"; "what I need I ought to make."[127] The first is a movement *to* the choice of an action, the second is a movement *from* a choice to an actual act.[128]

---

125. Wiggins, "Deliberation," 44.

126. Wiggins, "Deliberation," 43–4. This point is crucial both for Dunne, in *Back to the Rough Ground*, and, as we will see, for O'Donovan.

127. *De Motu Animalium* 701a14–16. Translation by A. S. L. Farquharson in *The Complete Works of Aristotle*, Vol. 1, ed. Jonathan Barnes (Princeton, NJ: Princeton University Press, 1984), 1087–96.

128. The alternatives to Cooper's account are either to say that principle-based thinking does not properly belong to Aristotle's conception of practical reasoning, or to try to harmonize the two kinds of syllogism under a common denominator. The first path is taken by Wiggins, and leaves him in a position where practical syllogisms are only ever a way of framing a situation, and never a way of bringing an objective, universal consideration to bear on the situation. The particularities of the situation become wholly authoritative. Aristotle's comments in his discussion of *akrasia* (which we quoted above) have to be dismissed as a blunder. The second route is taken by a range of scholars (see the survey in Westberg, *Right Practical Reason*, 17–25), including David Charles, who argues that universal–particular reasoning and end–means reasoning are united in expressing desire for what is seen as good (*Aristotle's Philosophy of Action*, 57–108, 262–5). To make this argument, however, Charles has to see the syllogism as having a "basic form" in which the

Yet clearly it is messier than Cooper allows. The problem is that these movements constantly bleed into each other, because of the non-technical character of much practical thinking. Deliberation, as we have said, is very often a matter of rightly construing the significance of an action. Hence, it may be thought of in terms of a process of subsumption: I want to act well (= the "end"); to do this would be to act well here and now (= the "means"). Correspondingly, the movement from a kind of action to the discernment of the instantiation of that kind in the particular situation (the movement Cooper sees under *prohairesis*) can often have deliberative significance: it can be a kind of search for how to do that kind of thing here and now. I should honor my mother. How can I do that? To respect her decisions with my children this afternoon would be honoring her! And Wiggins is right to note that sometimes—perhaps in this case when she decides to buy them enormous ice creams—this process may cause us to reconsider our initial goal, or choice. There come moments, that is to say, when the connection between what we "ought" to do and what we see as good for us becomes obscure. Sometimes time will permit "starting all over again," as Wiggins puts it; but sometimes it will not, and we will have simply to decide, in the face of an apparent clash between "the good" and "the right," whether or not to do "what has been decided by prior deliberation," as Aristotle defines *prohairesis*.[129] Ultimately, we will argue that it is for just this reason that the book of Proverbs places great stress on the need for trustworthy words of instruction in moral discernment.

One of the striking things about the *Nicomachean Ethics*, however, is the relative absence of this conflict. The two movements of practical thought—end–means thinking and universal–particular reasoning—do not encode a fundamental tension. Rather, Aristotle's thought generally seems to envisage a smooth movement from desire for one's good to determination of what one should do. This is true, moreover, despite the fact that within Aristotle's thought more broadly there are ideas that in another context might appear as "deontological." There are actions that are intrinsically bad.[130] The person who loves truth is "praiseworthy" because he avoids falsehood "in itself."[131] "Actions done in accordance with virtue are noble [*kalai*] and done for the sake of what is noble."[132] Yet these elements do not significantly disrupt the teleological framework within which they are situated.

---

major premise is indicative and "involves expressions of goodness" (p. 88). This seems to me to force Aristotle's examples of the universal–particular syllogism into a form they ill-fit. "The minimal predicate" of such syllogisms, as MacIntyre observes, "is the bare gerundive 'should be done by me'" (*Whose Justice?*, 130; cf. *De Anima* 3.11, 434a17). In my opinion, Cooper is therefore right to the extent that the practical syllogism is not a general account of practical reason, but primarily a way of thinking about how a considered desire for an action (a *prohairēsis*) gets enacted.

129. *EN* 3.2, 1112a16.
130. *EN* 2.6, 1107a.10–12.
131. *EN* 4.7, 1127b5–7. See also Cooper, *Reason and Human Good*, 78–9.
132. *EN* 4.1, 1120a23.

Aristotle can recognize that the pursuit of what is *kalon* may jeopardize one's enjoyment of pleasure. Courage, for example, may lead someone to stand their ground and be killed, even though this is a great loss.[133] Yet, the recognition of such things does not fundamentally destabilize the account of practical reasoning.[134] On the whole, there is little concern that, for example, the need to be truthful might dramatically conflict with one's ability to be happy. Indeed, the opposite is the case. There is a strong assumption that virtuous action is a generally reliable route to the life that turns out well.

This observation leads us to a final, significant point, at which we find ourselves back where we began. What undergirds this assumption about the harmony of the good and the right is the social context in relation to which Aristotle's thought is situated. Cooper recognizes this. In concluding his analysis of Aristotle's moral thought, he shows what we have just argued: that Aristotle clearly does believe in intrinsically good actions, but that this does not constitute for him "two distinct orders of value, one moral and one not," because he conceives of morally good actions as "constituent parts" of flourishing as a complex end.[135] What makes this possible, Cooper continues, is an outlook on life, that "is impressed … with the regularity and stability of human circumstances and human relationships," as opposed to one that is driven by consciousness of "wholly new and different circumstances arising which were not envisaged in the development of the traditional maxims and conceptions of the virtues."[136] A similar thought seems to me to be the central insight in MacIntyre's insistence that there is "no practical rationality outside the *polis*."[137] Aristotle's thinking, MacIntyre argues, makes sense "only from within a given *polis*, already provided with an ordering of goods, goods to be achieved by excellence within specific and systematic forms of activity, integrated into an overall rank-order by the political activity of those particular citizens."[138] It is the *polis* that provides the stability needed for virtuous action to work as a constituent part of happiness, and so allows practical reason to determine the right means by discerning a particular kind of action. There is "no practical rationality outside the

---

133. *EN* 3.9, 1117b10–17.

134. This does not mean that Aristotle was unaware of the potential problems here. Arguably, the discussion of death in book one (*EN* 1.10–11) is more destabilizing than is sometimes acknowledged. Aristotle acknowledges that death means we may only speak of someone being happy "in human terms" (1101a23), and recognizes "a puzzle about whether the dead can partake of any good or evil" (1101b1). Robert Spaemann has argued that Aristotle is deeply aware of the compromise-character of the happiness of practical life in the *polis* (Robert Spaemann, *Glück und Wohlwollen: Versuch über Ethik* (Stuttgart: Klett-Cotta, 1989), 75–84).

135. Cooper, *Reason and Human Good*, 79–82.

136. Cooper, *Reason and Human Good*, 84.

137. MacIntyre, *Whose Justice?*, 141. See also MacIntyre, *Three Rival Versions of Moral Enquiry*, 58–68.

138. MacIntyre, *Whose Justice?*, 133; cf. p. 141.

polis," because apart from the *polis* there is nothing to secure the unity of moral right and subjective good, and so no way for a particular construal of an action to be the perception deliberation requires to reach a rational choice.

Conclusion

This assumption of the unity of the good and the right was one reason Thomas Aquinas saw Aristotle's thought as open to Christian theology, which maintains, in the words of Proverbs, that "the light of the righteous shines gladly, the lamp of the wicked is put out" (13:9). Yet Aquinas could not presuppose the *polis* as that which prevents the happy life from falling apart from virtuous action.[139] For this, he looks instead to the doctrine of creation, and to God's providential movement of all things to their end.[140] While this provides Aquinas with a powerful theological grounding for Aristotle's account of practical reason, with its many strengths, it does not resolve all its problems. Moreover, the underlying ambiguities and tensions that produce these problems become less visible. The primacy of theory over practice is heightened, and the ambiguities surrounding the idea of practice and the distinction between making and doing become less pressing. The book of Proverbs will lead us to query whether all these developments were happy ones, and to reframe the way in which we appreciate Aristotle's practical philosophy. Ultimately, we will suggest that Christian theology has more to learn from Aristotle's insight that "a person is practically wise not only by knowing, but by being disposed to act," than from his claim that wisdom has to do with what cannot be otherwise.

---

139. On this point, see Robert Spaemann, "Natur," in *Philosophische Essays* (Stuttgart: Reclam, 1994), 25.

140. Having agreed with much of MacIntyre's interpretation of Aristotle, I will now disagree with his claim that "*extra ecclesiam nulla salus*" is the counterpart to "no practical rationality outside the *polis*" (*Whose Justice?*, 141). I think, rather, that Aquinas grounds practical rationality in the eternal law.

Chapter 2

THE NATURE AND FOUNDATION OF MORAL REASONING IN THOMAS AQUINAS

The Lord by wisdom established the earth.

—Prov. 3:19

Introduction

Thomas Aquinas's understanding of practical reasoning should be seen in the light of Aristotle's, but it is no mere reiteration of Aristotle's thinking. Aristotle's conception of practical reasoning, we have observed, depends on the *polis* for its coherence. Aquinas seeks to retain basic features of Aristotle's account, including the importance of seeing actions according to their kinds. Yet the *polis* no longer provides a supporting background, requiring Thomas to develop a more elaborate framework for the ends from which practical reason moves to action. His theological commitments allow him to do so. The "eternal objects" that introduced a tension into Aristotle's account of happiness become foundational. "In themselves," Aquinas explains, "divine realities are necessary and eternal, nevertheless they are the measure of the contingent things which are the subject-matter of human actions."[1] Practical reason is anchored in divine reason. "The eternal reason is the supreme rule of all human rightness."[2] His understanding of the nature of God's knowledge of creation allows Aquinas to ground an Aristotelian account of prudence and deliberation, organized by the idea that actions come in kinds, in a notion of eternal law.

This chapter gives an overview of this theological appropriation of Aristotle's description of practical reason. Such an overview runs the risks entailed by the

---

1. *ST* II-II.45.3 ad2. Ensuing references in this chapter to the *Summa Theologiae* will omit the abbreviation *ST*. The Blackfriars edition of this work (61 vols.; Cambridge: Blackfriars, 1964–1981) has primarily been consulted; however, the Benziger Brothers edition (New York: Benziger Brothers, 1911–1925) has also been used. Where not stated, English translations are from the Blackfriars edition. The Latin text is provided where terminology is important, or where my own translation is given.

2. II-II.52.2.

necessity of overlooking parts of Aquinas's thought. However, there are also dangers in limiting our focus to particular passages or issues.³ As Fergus Kerr notes, the compartmentalizing of Aquinas's thought, and especially the detaching of Aquinas's moral theory from his theology, results in misunderstanding.⁴ We therefore begin by observing Aquinas's development of Aristotle's distinction between speculative and practical reason, and what it means for the concept of wisdom (Section 1), before moving to an overview of Aquinas's thinking about kinds of action (Section 2), and eternal law (Section 3). This leads to a detailed engagement with Thomas's conception of prudence (Section 4), and the nature of deliberation (Section 5). The aim of this sequence of topics is both to display the integrity of Aquinas's moral thought and to open up key points of connection with the book of Proverbs. Aquinas's rich and complex thinking about the nature of prudence and deliberation, in which he deploys and develops Aristotle's idea of the practical syllogism, depends for its coherence on the notion that actions come in kinds. For Aquinas, this notion is anchored in a claim he finds articulated most fully in Proverbs ch. 8: that God made the world by his wisdom.

It is perhaps worth noting at the outset where the interpretation of Aquinas's moral thought that follows sits in relation to others. A good way to do this is by reference to John Bowlin's important work, *Contingency and Fortune in Aquinas's Ethics*.⁵ The core of Bowlin's argument is that Aquinas's ethics is driven by the idea that the human good is contingent and indeterminate, and therefore fundamentally a matter of prudence and the virtues.⁶ He resists the priority often assigned to natural law in Aquinas's thought, arguing instead that for Aquinas the natural law is a way of marking out the widest limits of contingency, rather than a guide to action.⁷

The treatment that follows shares much with this perspective. I, too, think that there is an important sense for Aquinas in which from the subjective perspective the human good is indeterminate, and that Aquinas sees the core challenge of

---

3. Our attention will be focused on the *Summa Theologiae*, which is Aquinas's most systematic account of the questions of interest here. Occasional reference will be made to other texts when illuminating, especially Aquinas's commentary on the *Nicomachean Ethics, Sententia libri Ethicorum* (*SLE*), Volume 47 of *Opera Omnia* (Leonine edition; Rome: 1969). This text has primarily been consulted in the English translation by C. J. Litzinger, O. P. (Notre Dame: Dumb Ox, 1964).

4. Fergus Kerr, "Doctrine of God and Theological Ethics According to Thomas Aquinas," in *The Doctrine of God and Theological Ethics*, ed. A. J. Torrance and M. Banner (London: T&T Clark, 2006), 74.

5. John Bowlin, *Contingency and Fortune in Aquinas's Ethics* (Cambridge: Cambridge University Press, 1999).

6. Bowlin, *Contingency*, especially pp. 55–92.

7. Bowlin, *Contingency*, 93–137. A similar position to Bowlin's is found in Daniel Mark Nelson, *The Priority of Prudence: Virtue and Natural Law in Thomas Aquinas and the Implications for Modern Ethics* (University Park: Pennsylvania State University Press, 1992).

moral thought as having to do with the discernment of the meaning of actions.[8] This emphasis, it will be noted, has already emerged in our discussion of Aristotle. As will become clear, I also agree that the natural law is not, for Aquinas, a sufficient guide to action.

Yet I disagree with Bowlin that this means the human good is indeterminate in the fuller sense of not having "a particular shape."[9] I maintain, on the contrary, that for Aquinas the human good certainly has a particular shape, and a highly determinate one. It is the shape marked out by both law (especially positive law) and the virtues. Bowlin argues that this would mean "grave inconsistency" in Aquinas's position,[10] but I do not think that is right. Aquinas can indeed maintain both that the human good has a determinate shape, and also that it is indeterminate for us, in the sense that in our action it is unclear in what the realization of that shape will consist. This, indeed, is the genius of Aquinas's understanding of moral reasoning, and the key to it is his generic understanding of action.

1 Reason and Wisdom

Aristotle's distinction between practical and theoretical reason is of fundamental importance for Aquinas. It is deployed throughout the *Summa Theologiae* as a basic principle.[11] Thomas makes this distinction with greater clarity than Aristotle. It has to do with a fundamental difference between thought directed to action and thought directed to knowing. "The speculative mind [*intellectus speculativus*] knows but does not relate what it knows to action, merely considering the truth; whereas we speak of the mind as practical [*practicus ... intellectus*] when it orders what it knows to action [*ordinat ad opus*]."[12] This distinction can still be described in terms of a distinction between kinds of objects. "The practical reason is concerned with things to be done, which are individual and contingent, not with the necessary things that are the concern of theoretic reason."[13] Prudence, Thomas elsewhere clarifies, is differentiated from the virtues of the speculative intellect "by a material difference of objects" (*secundum materialem diversitatem objectorum*).[14] "Wisdom, knowledge and understanding are about necessary things, whereas art and prudence are about contingent things [*contingentia*]."[15] However, strictly speaking, it is not merely the different nature of objects that differentiates the practical and theoretical intellects, but these different objects insofar as they

---

8. See Bowlin, *Contingency*, 71, 73, 80–2.
9. Bowlin, *Contingency*, 94.
10. Bowlin, *Contingency*, 94.
11. See, for example, I.14.16; 79.11; I-II.3.5; 14.3; 56.3; 91.3; II-II.47.5; 179.2.
12. I.79.11.
13. I-II.91.3 ad3.
14. II-II.47.5.
15. II-II.47.5.

require different tasks of reason.[16] Fundamentally, practical and theoretical reason is each "named from its end [*a fine denominator*]: the one speculative, the other practical."[17]

The crucial point is that the distinction to be made is not within the power of reason itself. Practical and theoretical reason are not two different things, but the one power of reason, engaged by materially different objects, and so taking on distinct "modes of apprehension,"[18] or "distinct aptitudes."[19] Aquinas thus carefully differentiates his position from one understanding of Aristotle. In his commentary on the *Nicomachean Ethics*, Aquinas calls "doubtful" Aristotle's apparent statement, in *EN* 6.1, which we discussed above,[20] that the distinction between practical and theoretical reason is between parts of the soul. He questions this division of the intellect on a range of grounds, concluding that the distinction Aristotle was actually interested in was between the intellect in itself and the intellect as working through the sensitive powers. For contingent things "are the objects of counsel and operation" only in this way. Thomas sees, that is, that the relevant distinction here is not merely between kinds of things—since contingent things can also be considered theoretically—but more fundamentally between ways in which things are engaged in thought.[21]

In fact, reason always involves a procedure from first principles,[22] from the general to the particular (*communibus ad propria*). Practical reason, like theoretical reason, has its own naturally known first principles.[23] The procedure of reason takes a different form in the theoretical reason and the practical reason only by virtue of their different objects. Because the practical reason is engaged with contingent matters (*negotiatur circa contingentia*), "in questions of action … truth and practical rectitude are not the same for everybody with respect to particulars [*propria*], but only with respect to generalities [*communia*]."[24] With Aristotle, Aquinas says that both practical and theoretical reason aim at what is true. Theoretical reason aims at the true in an absolute sense. Practical reason, however, aims at the true insofar as it is attainable in action, which means the good to be done: "as an object of desire can be truth in so far as it has the character

---

16. This clarification was required partly by Augustine's distinction between the higher and lower reason (see *DT*, book 12). In I.79.9 ad3, Thomas rejects the suggestion that this distinction correlates to Aristotle's distinction in *EN* 6.1. The higher and lower reasons are not distinct powers, nor can they be equated with the practical and theoretical intellects.

17. I.79.11. Benziger Brothers edition.

18. I.79.11. See ad1, where Thomas speaks of the *modus apprehensionis* of the practical intellect.

19. I.79.9 ad3.

20. Chapter 1, Section 1.

21. *SLE* 6.1.11-15; cf. I.14.16.

22. I.79.8.

23. I.79.12.

24. I-II.94.4, my translation. Cf. I.79.9.

of goodness, in the same way the object of the practical mind is good to be done [*bonum ordinabile ad opus*], known to be truly such [*sub ratione veri*]."[25] In practical reason, therefore, the first principle takes the form of the end, as Aristotle recognized.[26] This is also why prudence aims at "the true taken in conformity to a right appetite."[27]

Aquinas clarifies, but also complicates, this position in his discussion of divine knowledge, in question fourteen of the *Prima Pars*. This is a discussion that will have some significance in what follows, and which we must therefore linger over.[28] The crucial question, for our interest, comes in article sixteen: whether God has speculative knowledge of things.[29] The most powerful objection to such a claim is that "God's knowledge is the cause of things," as Aquinas has already argued (in article eight), but speculative knowledge is not the cause of the things it knows.[30] Yet Aristotle taught that "speculative knowledge is more excellent than practical knowledge." Therefore, it must be the case that God has speculative knowledge of things.[31] Aquinas explains how this can be by carefully distinguishing various kinds of knowledge. Knowledge, he says, "may be speculative only, or practical only, or in one aspect speculative, in another practical." The reason for this potential complexity lies in the point we have observed above, that a mere difference of objects is not sufficient to distinguish practical and theoretical reason, for it is possible to think about contingent things *without* a view to action. Thomas now develops this thought carefully. First, he points out that there *are* objects—God, at least—that can only be known speculatively, for they are not "operable" (*non sunt operabiles*). Second, he explains that it is possible to "consider operable things in a speculative mode, and not according to their being operable."[32] For example, consider a builder thinking about the properties of a house in general. This is knowledge of something that *can* be the object of action, but it is speculative knowledge of it. Third, Aquinas further considers that it is possible to know something operable without aiming at action. A builder, for example, could consider how some actual house could be built, "not with a view to building it

---

25. I.79.11 ad2.

26. For this fundamental point, see, for example, I.79.8-11; 82.1; 1-II.1.1; cf. 54.2 ad3; 65.2; 90.2.

27. 1-II.64.3.

28. This text is fundamental for Stephen J. Jensen's recent work, *Knowing the Natural Law: From Precepts and Inclinations to Deriving Oughts* (Washington, DC: Catholic University of America Press, 2015). Although I have benefited from this work, I cannot agree with Jensen that this text can constitute a kind of map for Aquinas's conception of practical reason. I will argue that this text actually contains arguments that destabilize Aquinas's overall approach.

29. I.14.16.

30. I.14.16 arg1.

31. I.14.16 s.c.

32. I.14.16, my translation: Hoc siquidem est operabilia modo speculativo considerare, et non secundum quod operabilia sunt.

but merely for the sake of knowing." Such knowledge, Thomas argues, "will be speculative, though still about what could be produced [*de re operabile*]." This kind of knowledge, Aquinas goes on to argue, is the kind of knowledge God has of those things "which he can produce but never does produce."

There is something awkward about this train of thought. It seems to end up denying the very point from which it sets out: that there is a real difference between speculative and practical knowledge. For Aquinas wants to maintain that it is possible to have knowledge that is practical "in its mode," that is, genuine knowledge of *how* to do or make some real thing, and yet not actually involved in action, and so still only practical knowledge "in theory." In a parallel discussion in *De Veritate*, he calls this "virtually practical" knowledge: "There is a type of knowledge that is capable of being ordered to an act, but this ordering is not actual. For example, an artist thinks out a form for his work, knows how it can be made, yet does not intend to make it. This is practical knowledge, not actual, but habitual or virtual."[33] He further explains that the crucial thing about such knowledge is that it does not merely think about formal properties, for example, of a house in general, but considers the actualization of a particular: "a thing is considered as something capable of execution when there are considered in its regard all the things that are simultaneously required for its existence."[34] Aquinas needs this point in order to maintain that God really does know things he could make but does not.[35] However, it appears to lead to a position in which the only thing that differentiates genuinely practical knowledge from knowledge that is still essentially theoretical—Thomas admits that "virtually practical knowledge" is still "speculative in some sense"[36]—is the addition of the will.[37] The only thing that differentiates God's knowledge of things he actually does create from his knowledge of things he could but does not create is his will to create them.

We will return to this issue below, when we discuss the eternal law.[38] We will eventually argue that a weakness in Aquinas's overall account shows itself at this point: he does not make enough space for genuinely practical knowledge, knowledge that is essentially connected to action. But the crucial issue already appears in the image of the artisan who "knows through his art even those things that have not yet been fashioned."[39] This conception, we may recall, reflects

---

33. *Questiones Disputatae De Veritate* 3.3. The translation is from *The Disputed Questions on Truth*, trans. R. W. Mulligan, S. J. (Chicago: Henry Regnery Company, 1952-1954).

34. *De Veritate* 3.3.

35. Aquinas insists on the same point for the same reason in the *Summa Contra Gentiles* I.66.3.

36. *De Veritate* 3.3 ad2.

37. This is the conclusion Stephen Jensen reaches in *Knowing the Natural Law*, 221-7.

38. Below, Section 3.

39. *Summa Contra Gentiles* I.66.3, trans. Anton C. Pegis (New York: Hanover House, 1955-1957): Artifex autem suae artis cognitione etiam ea quae nondum sunt artificiata cognoscit.

Aristotle's formal account of *technē*, where, in Hannah Arendt's description, "the light by which to judge the finished product is provided by the image or model perceived beforehand by the craftsman's eye."[40] Yet, might there in fact be a significant difference between such formal knowledge and the knowledge that accompanies the making of something in reality? Does actual making often involve a kind of knowledge that can never be present apart from action? And is that even more the case when what we are talking about is not *poiēsis*, but *praxis*?

For now, however, we need to move on to a more fundamental point about speculative and practical knowledge. For Aquinas, the distinction between practical and speculative knowledge is transcended in the simplicity of divine knowledge. At the conclusion of the article on God's speculative knowledge, discussed above, Thomas acknowledges that for God's knowledge to be perfect, he must have genuinely practical knowledge of what he makes—knowledge that is practical in its mode. But then he goes on to say that "even so his knowledge loses nothing of the excellence of speculative knowledge, because he sees all things other than himself in himself, and himself he knows with speculative knowledge. Thus in his speculative knowledge of himself he has knowledge both speculative and practical of all other things."[41]

Ultimately, for Aquinas, God knows all things simply in the act of knowing himself, the act which is his very being. In another place, Thomas gives the following, lucid explanation of his position:

> [God's] being is identical with his understanding ... As his substance is pure existence so also is it pure understanding. Here nothing is lacking that can relate to knowledge, for every hint of knowledge is held in the sheer form of knowledge ... Since his being is one, simple, firm, and enduring, it follows that by one single insight God enjoys eternal and unwavering knowledge of everything ... Indeed, in the first cause things exist more nobly even than they do in themselves, for what exists in another exists according to the mode of that one's substance, and the substance of God is his understanding. Everything that is in any way real, therefore, exists intelligibly in God at the height of his substance, and is there known completely.[42]

God knows all things perfectly, in every way in which they can be known, in the act of his own self-knowledge in which his being subsists.[43] His knowledge of what he makes—speculative and practical—is enclosed within his perfect and

---

40. Hannah Arendt, *The Human Condition* (Chicago: University of Chicago Press, 1958), 192.

41. I.14.16 ad2.

42. *De Substantiis Separatis*, 14.70-72; quoted in Thomas Gilby, *St. Thomas Aquinas: Philosophical Texts* (London: Oxford University Press, 1951), 99.

43. See also I.14.8 ad3, 14.11; I-II.93.1.

essentially speculative self-knowledge.⁴⁴ This understanding of divine knowledge shapes Aquinas's understanding of wisdom.

For Aquinas, wisdom (*sapientia*) is an intellectual perfection realized in distinct, but analogous ways: in metaphysics, in theology, and as a spiritual gift.⁴⁵ Central to all wisdom, however, is right judgment in the light of ultimate reality: "to govern and judge belongs to the wise person";⁴⁶ wisdom "judges things according to divine truth."⁴⁷ In its fullest sense, this includes judgment of practical matters. Wisdom, although primarily speculative, ultimately transcends the practical–speculative distinction. Wisdom, as given by the Spirit, "is not only theoretic but practical as well"; it involves "judgment ... of human things through divine realities by directing human actions according to divine rules."⁴⁸

Wisdom has this character because it is essentially a participation in God's own self-knowledge; it is the knowledge of the mysteries of "uncreated wisdom" (*sapientia increata*).⁴⁹ Kieran Conley explains: "Since God's knowledge is eminently both speculative and practical ... so, too, these created reflections of that divine knowledge share in their respective orders the eminent inclusion of speculative and practical values."⁵⁰ Sacred doctrine—theology—is properly speculative, but also indirectly practical, because "God in the same knowledge knows both himself and the things he has made."⁵¹ In the gift of wisdom this participation is deeply *affective*.⁵² It depends upon *caritas*, and is in some sense in all who have grace.⁵³ All wisdom is about "a certain rightness in judging according to divine norms."⁵⁴ What distinguishes the gift of wisdom is that this judgment comes not merely from the perfect use of reason, but from "a kind of instinctive affinity" (*quamdam connaturalitatem*) with divine things⁵⁵—*per modum inclinationis*, as Thomas elsewhere puts it.⁵⁶ The right judgments of wisdom are made through "a certain connaturality or union with divine things."⁵⁷

---

44. See also the first question of the *Summa*, I.1.4; and I.34.3, where Aquinas succinctly explains this point with reference to the divine Word.

45. Kieran Conley, *A Theology of Wisdom: A Study in St. Thomas* (Dubuque, IO: Priory Press, 1963), 141.

46. I.1.6.

47. II-II.45.1 ad2.

48. II-II.45.3.

49. II-II.45.6 ad2.

50. Conley, *Theology of Wisdom*, 129.

51. I.1.4, quoted in Conley, *Theology of Wisdom*, 90.

52. See Conley, *Theology of Wisdom*, 113–40.

53. II-II.45.4, 5.

54. II-II.45.2.

55. II-II.45.2.

56. I.1.6 ad3.

57. II-II.45.4. On the concept of *connaturalitas*, see Tobias Hoffmann, "Prudence and Practical Principles," in *Aquinas and the Nicomachean Ethics*, ed. Tobias Hoffmann, Jörn Müller, and Matthias Perkams (Cambridge: Cambridge University Press, 2013), 176–9.

In Aquinas's thought, the distinction between speculative and practical thinking is thus not an impermeable barrier. Ultimately, what is eternal and necessary must govern, at least in principle, what is contingent. "The things of time and eternity, are related to our thinking in such a way that the one is our way of knowing the other."[58] We discover eternal realities through temporal ones, and, "in the order of judgment we regard things of time in the light of the eternal things already known and arrange them according to eternal laws."[59] "In themselves divine realities are necessary and eternal, nevertheless they are the measure of the contingent things [*regulae contingentium*] which are the subject-matter of human actions."[60] This is why Thomas can say, clearly, that "we are directed in our actions by the knowledge of matters of faith, and of conclusions drawn therefrom."[61]

In itself, this appears to be a significant development from Aristotle's position: an explicit subordination of practical reasoning to speculative knowledge. The question, however, is whether this appearance is deceiving. What precisely does Aquinas mean by such judgment and direction? One answer is that maintained in a number of works by John Finnis.[62] Finnis acknowledges that ontologically, ethics is grounded in reality—human nature, in particular. However, he insists that this relation is not mirrored in our knowledge.[63] "Ethics is not deduced or inferred from metaphysics or anthropology."[64] Rather, theoretical and practical or "descriptive" and "evaluative" claims[65] have their own distinct kinds of reasonableness. This is not to deny any relation between the two: there is, he says, "a mutual though not quite symmetrical interdependence between the project of describing human affairs by way of theory and the project of evaluating human options with a view, at least remotely, to acting reasonably and well."[66] False theory leads to practical mistakes. "One whose knowledge of the facts of the human situation is very limited is very unlikely to judge well in discerning the practical implications of the basic values."[67]

---

58. I.79.9.

59. I.79.9.

60. II-II 45.3 ad2. Interestingly, Thomas is led to this conclusion partly by the way Colossians 4:5 speaks of *walking* in wisdom (II-II.45.3), which is a metaphor of great significance for the book of Proverbs.

61. II-II.9.3; cf. I-II.68.4; II-II.8.6; 52.2 ad2.

62. See John Finnis, *Aquinas: Moral, Political, and Legal Theory* (Oxford: Oxford University Press, 1998), 47–51, 86–90; *Natural Law and Natural Rights* (Oxford: Clarendon, 1980), 3–22; and *Fundamentals of Ethics* (Oxford: Clarendon, 1983), 1–23.

63. Finnis, *Fundamentals of Ethics*, 21; "Is and Ought in Aquinas," in *Reason in Action* (Oxford: Oxford University Press, 2011), 147.

64. Finnis, *Fundamentals of Ethics*, 22.

65. See Finnis, *Natural Law and Natural Rights*, 20.

66. Finnis, *Natural Law and Natural Rights*, 19. This passage is quoted again in both *Fundamentals of Ethics*, 22, and *Aquinas*, 51.

67. Finnis, *Natural Law and Natural Rights*, 19.

Is this a sufficient explanation of what Aquinas means by the rule and direction of wisdom and knowledge over practical matters? I think it is not. Finnis does not take sufficient account of the fact that, for Aquinas, human beings "are set towards an eternal happiness out of proportion to their natural resources."[68] When Thomas maintains that wisdom judges even practical matters, and that, to give another example, the gift of understanding, which perfects the "higher reason's" speculative knowledge of the things of faith, also "extends to certain actions,"[69] he has in mind this point, that practical reason must learn to look to a further horizon than what may be known naturally.[70] We will explore this point further below.

However, Finnis's account does warn us against overstating the rule of the speculative over the practical in Aquinas's thought. "The eternal reason is the supreme rule of all human rightness."[71] Yet practical reason does also retain its own integrity. It has its own first principles, and its own distinct ways of operating. The ambiguities in Aristotle's thought continue to exercise a pull. Hence, we cannot either agree with those who argue that Aquinas envisages a smooth process in which "oughts" are derived from "is's."[72] Aquinas does go beyond Aristotle in relating practical and speculative knowledge, but he does not abandon Aristotle's basic insight that there is a real and significant difference between thinking in order to know and thinking in order to act, between knowing what is the case and knowing how to act. Our task now is to outline Aquinas's understanding of the latter.

2 Kinds of Action

"To live well means acting well."[73] At the heart of Aquinas's moral theory is action. All creaturely life is a movement toward an end. Only God possesses happiness "by nature," "without some motion of activity towards it."[74] The peculiarly human form of this movement is action, in the sense of action that comes "from a deliberate will."[75] Human beings reach beatitude only "through many motions of

---

68. I-II.91.4; cf. ad1.

69. II-II.8.3, Benziger Brothers edition.

70. The principle appears in the very first article of the *Summa*: "Man is directed to God, as to an end that surpasses the grasp of his reason" (I.1.1).

71. II-II.52.2.

72. For example, Stephen J. Jensen (*Knowing the Natural Law*), who reads I.14.16 to imply a progressive movement from speculative knowledge to practical knowledge and thence to action. This, as one reviewer points out, renders the practical intellect redundant (W. M. Diem, "Review of Stephen J. Jensen, *Knowing the Natural Law*," *Studies in Christian Ethics* 29, no. 4 [2016]: 359).

73. I-II.57.5.

74. I-II.5.7.

75. I-II.1.1, Benziger Brothers edition. On this point, see Ralph McInerny, *Aquinas on Human Action: A Theory of Practice* (Washington, DC: Catholic University of America Press, 1992), 3–24.

activity" in the right direction, that is, by good works.⁷⁶ This, Thomas believes, was also Aristotle's view, who said that happiness is "the reward for virtuous acts."⁷⁷ Aquinas's understanding of action holds together the two most important aspects of his moral framework: virtue, on the one hand, and law, on the other. Virtues are about actions. A virtue is "a habit by which we are perfected in doing good [*ad bene agendum*]."⁷⁸ Law, too, is about action. "Law is a kind of direction or measure for human activity through which a person is led to do something or held back."⁷⁹ In Aquinas's system, law is thus essentially related to virtue, through the common term of acts: "because law is given in order to direct human acts, then how far it makes men good depends on how far these contribute to virtue."⁸⁰ Virtue concerns the *internal* principles of human action; law, the external. As Ulrich Kühn summarizes, Law treats "die Prinzipien, die die ethische Qualität der Akte von außen ... her bestimmen."⁸¹

More specifically, what connects virtue and law in Aquinas's thinking is not simply action, but action in accordance with reason. Good action means, most basically, action in accordance with reason. "When we speak of 'good' or 'evil' in human acts we take the 'reasonable' as our standard of reference."⁸² "Reason is the principle of human and moral acts."⁸³ Virtue is therefore centrally about such reasonable action. For virtues are habits, and what makes habits good or bad is their fittingness to a "determinate nature";⁸⁴ and what is distinctive in human nature is its active participation in reason. Therefore, "virtuous actions accord with human nature, because they are in agreement with reason."⁸⁵ And the virtue that is proper to humankind is "the virtue which refers to works of reason [*opera*

---

76. I-II.5.7.

77. I-II.5.7, referring to *EN* 1.9, 1099b16.

78. I-II.58.3; cf. I-II.56.3. See also Ralph McInerny, "Ethics," in *The Cambridge Companion to Aquinas*, ed. N. Kretzmann and E. Stump (Cambridge: Cambridge University Press, 1993), 202–5.

79. I-II.90.1.

80. I-II.92.1. This connection between law and virtue is not always sufficiently appreciated, for reasons that will be discussed below. It is reflected in the way a treatment of a virtue in the *Secunda Secundae* frequently concludes with a discussion of the precepts pertaining to that virtue (see II-II.16; 22; 44; 56).

81. Ulrich Kühn, *Via Caritatis: Theologie des Gesetzes bei Thomas von Aquin* (Berlin: Evangelische Verlagsanstalt, 1964), 125. Translation: "The principles that determine the ethical quality of acts from without." See also Jean-Pierre Torrell, *Saint Thomas Aquinas, Volume 2: Spiritual Master*, trans. Robert Royal (Washington, DC: Catholic University of America Press, 2003), 265, n. 33.

82. I-II.18.5.

83. I-II.19.1 ad3, Benziger Brothers edition.

84. I-II.54.3.

85. I-II.54.3.

rationis]."⁸⁶ Law, also, is most basically, "something pertaining to reason" (*aliquid pertinens ad rationem*).⁸⁷ Law, as we have seen Thomas say, "is a kind of direction or measure for human activity." But human action, as we have also seen him stress, is fundamentally about deliberate action, or action toward an end. This means, Aquinas continues, that law is about reason. For "it belongs to reason to order to the end, which is the first principle in matters of action, according to the Philosopher [Aristotle]."⁸⁸ Law, because it is a rule for *human* action, must be fundamentally about reason: it is an exposition of reason's direction to the end. Here, though, we must note again the point we broached above that the "reason" to which law and human actions correspond ultimately transcends merely natural human reason. "The rule of human actions," Aquinas maintains, "is the human reason and the eternal law. Now the eternal law surpasses human reason: so that the knowledge of human actions, as ruled by the eternal law, surpasses the natural reason, and requires the supernatural light of a gift of the Holy Ghost [the gift of understanding]." The "reason" that measures human action is not simply human reasoning, but the objective, substantive order of reason that is given by eternal law.⁸⁹

86. I-II.55.2.

87. I-II.90.1.

88. I-II.90.1, my translation: Rationis enim est ordinare ad finem, qui est primum principium in agendis secundum Philosophum.

89. II-II.8.3 ad3. This is the point at which the account given here diverges from that given by Martin Rhonheimer in "The Perspective of the Acting Person and the Nature of Practical Reason: The 'Object of the Human Act' in Thomistic Anthropology of Action," in *The Perspective of the Acting Person: Essays in the Renewal of Thomistic Moral Philosophy*, ed. Martin Rhonheimer and William F. Murphy (Washington, DC: Catholic University of America Press, 2011), 195–249. With a great deal of Rhonheimer's account I am in agreement, including his treatment of "objects" and their place in Aquinas's theory of action, and especially his emphasis on the way the concept of object has to do with the "intelligible content" of actions (pp. 209, 221). I also agree that Aquinas's account aims to put the perspective of the acting person at the center of the picture. It seems to me, however, that Rhonheimer's discussion is weakened by his consistent understanding of reason as simply the human faculty of reason—"the discursive part of the intellect" (p. 215). This means that Rhonheimer understands the idea of an object being "presented to the will by the reason" (cf. I-II.19.3) in terms of a subjective mental process. This, in turn, means that he has to understand the "non-arbitrary connection" between actions and their goodness or evil in relation to the first principles of natural law (p. 222), and leads him to what is in my view a problematic defense of the notion of intrinsically evil actions. These are to be understood as "kinds of behaviour" which "can never reasonably be chosen without contradicting some of the first practical principles which order human action to the human good" (pp. 244–5). As I will explain more fully below (Section 3), I think this implies a confidence in natural law reasoning that Thomas does not actually share. When Thomas talks about reason in relation to action, I think he primarily has in mind reason as the objective order of reality, upon which the subject has a cognitive purchase.

The idea of eternal law will occupy us shortly. For now, however, the matter at hand is the way the connection between law and virtue at the point of action thus hinges on the idea of action in accord with reason. What is it about such action that allows for this connection? The answer, for Thomas, lies in the thought that actions come in kinds. This point is made in the first question of the *Prima Secundae*, when Aquinas considers whether human acts receive their kind (*species*) from the end.[90] Yes, he answers. Just as *things* of matter and form get their kind from their form, that is, their actualization, so *actions* get their kind from their actualization, or their end—they "receive their species from the end" (*a fine speciem sortiuntur*). One objection to this position stems from the observation that the same kind of act can have different aims, which seems to suggest that the end is not a good point from which to sort acts into kinds.[91] This is an important question, and it requires Thomas to begin to give a much more complex account of kinds of action. This he does by observing that what an action is depends not merely on what it is "by nature" (*naturae*), but also on what is willed. It is the action as something willed that is morally important.[92] In the body of the article, he also introduces a new category: the object (*objectum*) of an act. The distinctive feature of human acts, he says, is that they are deliberately willed. The principle, and so the point of specification, of human acts must, therefore, be the end, because "the object of the will is the good and the end."[93]

The more complex account of kinds of action that is hinted at here is properly developed in questions 18–20 of the *Prima Secundae*. As Ralph McInerny notes, these are some of the longest questions in the *Summa*.[94] The reason is that the distinctions introduced here are crucial for the unity of Aquinas's moral theology, and in particular for the connection between virtue and law.[95] In the first instance, the focus of these questions is not on kinds of action, but on the good and evil of action. Their overall argument, however, very much concerns kinds. The central issue comes into focus in article five of question eighteen: Can *kinds* of acts (and not merely individual actions) be good or evil?[96] Aquinas's answer, in brief, is

---

90. 1-II.1.3.

91. 1-II.1.3 arg3.

92. 1-II.1.3 ad3. As Martin Rhonheimer emphasizes, this is the basis for the idea that "the perspective of the acting person" is critical ("The Perspective of the Acting Person," 195-200). (The phrase is from the papal encyclical *Veritatis Splendor*, no.78.)

93. 1-II.1.3, my translation: Objectum autem voluntatis est bonum et finis.

94. McInerny, *Aquinas on Human Action*, 79.

95. Although in other respects exemplary, especially for its clarity, Charles Pinches's reading of these questions, in *Theology and Action*, 111-36, does not, in my judgment, sufficiently reckon with this point. This allows Pinches to fit Aquinas's thought into an account of ethics in which a concept of order has a less significant place than I think it does for Thomas himself.

96. 1-II.18.5: utrum aliqua actio humana sit bona vel mala in sua specie.

"yes" because kinds of acts are either in accordance with reason, or not. "As the species of physical things are constituted from forms existing in the world of nature, so the species of moral acts are constituted from forms as conceived by reason [*prout sunt a ratione conceptae*]."[97] And reason is the standard of what is good or evil in human acts, as we have already noted.[98] This argument depends, however, upon the concept we saw introduced briefly in article three of question one: the object of an act. Aquinas's more extended logic is that *kinds* of acts are in accordance with reason, or not, because *objects* are in accordance with reason or not, and it is objects that determine kinds. As he sums it up in article eight: "every act takes its species from its object; while human action, which is called moral, takes its species from the object, in relation to the principle of human actions, which is the reason."[99] Both "the end" and "the reason" can be called the *principium* of human acts because the end is the first principle of practical reason. To speak of an object of an act, therefore, is to speak of the reasonableness of an act, because it is to speak of the end of an act viewed from the perspective of reason. As Thomas puts it a little later: "Good is presented to the will as its object by the reason: and in so far as it is in accord with reason, it enters the moral order [*pertinet ad genus moris*], and causes moral goodness in the act of the will: because the reason is the principle of human and moral acts."[100] Objects are intrinsically related to reason. Hence, because objects of acts determine their kinds, kinds of action may be either good or evil (because what is reasonable is the standard for good and evil).

This summary of Aquinas's position has still glossed over the important clarifying point that we also glimpsed above: the object in question is the object *as willed* in a particular act. Thomas points out that any actual act can be considered from two perspectives. It can be seen from without, or from within, from the perspective of the act as such, and from the perspective of the person who wills it.[101] From each perspective, the act can be said to have an "object":

> In a voluntary action, there is a twofold action, *viz.* the interior action of the will, and the external action: and each of these actions has its object. The end is properly the object of the interior act of the will: while the object of the external action, is that on which the action is brought to bear. Therefore just as the external action takes its species from the object on which it bears; so the interior act of the will takes its species from the end, as from its own proper object.[102]

---

97. I-II.18.10.
98. Cf. I-II.18.5.
99. I-II.18.8, Benziger Brothers edition.
100. I-II.19.1 ad3, Benziger Brothers edition.
101. See, again, Rhonheimer, "The Perspective of the Acting Person," 195–200.
102. I-II.18.6, Benziger Brother edition.

That is to say, actions have an "object" that is intrinsic to them in and of themselves. One of Thomas's examples is "to make use of what is one's own."[103] When seen from without, this is what determines the kind that they are. However, this is not the primary perspective from which acts may be judged good or evil. For that, they need to be seen in relation to the will, and what it purposes.[104] If one gives away one's money in order to receive praise, what is morally significant is not primarily the object of the act considered from without—to make use of what is one's own— but the object of the act considered from within, the end of the action: to get praise for oneself. Although there can be intrinsic goodness or evil in kinds of action as such—there are actions that are always, necessarily, bad, evil *secundum se*[105]—it is the end in view of the will that is the object which is most basically constitutive of what an act is.[106] For this reason, actions considered from without, that is, according to their kind apart from a purpose of the will, may in fact be morally indifferent—for example, picking up a stick, or going for a walk.[107] But when what is in view is an object that is willed and so stands in some relation to the end and to reason, then it will be a kind of action that is either good or evil, because in any particular situation a human act "is necessarily either ordered or not ordered to a due end."[108]

It is important, and illuminating, to understand Thomas's concept of the object of actions through comparison with the discussion of good and evil action in Peter Lombard's *Sentences*.[109] Briefly summarized, in distinction forty of book two of the *Sentences*, Lombard begins from the view that actions are good or evil from their end. This position, he recognizes, is complicated by the fact of actions that are intrinsically evil. This suggests that a threefold distinction is necessary: there are intrinsically good actions, intrinsically evil actions, and actions that are indifferent and determined by their ends. Yet better still, Lombard concludes, is Augustine's position in *On Lying*, where he gives a twofold distinction: there are actions whose goodness is determined by their end, and there are intrinsically evil acts. This suggests that on the whole, "the name [good or evil] is given to the deed by the

---

103. I-II.18.2.
104. I-II.18.6; cf. 20.1.
105. See I-II.20.2-3.
106. I-II.18.6 ad1; cf. 20.1: Cum autem finis sit proprium objectum voluntatis.
107. I-II.18.8. Note also Aquinas's discussion of this distinction in I-II.108.1.
108. I-II.18.9, my translation: Necesse est autem quod vel ordinetur vel non ordinetur ad debitum finem. Cf. 20.3.
109. Peter Lombard, *The Sentences. Book 2: On Creation*, trans. Giulio Silano (Toronto: Pontifical Institute of Mediaeval Studies, 2008), 198–202 [II.40.1-14]. I am here in agreement with the more detailed argument of Matthew R. McWhorter, "Intrinsic Moral Evils in the Middle Ages: Augustine as a Source of the Theological Doctrine," *Studies in Christian Ethics* 29, no. 4 (2016): 409–23. In his account of Lombard's view, however, McWhorter leaves out the final hesitation expressed in paragraphs 13–14 of distinction forty, which I will suggest is important.

disposition [i.e., the intended end]," with the *exception* of intrinsically evil acts.[110] Finally, though, Lombard also raises the point that there is something problematic about speaking, as Augustine appears to, of intrinsically evil acts being done for a good end—the will to do such evil acts means that "such things never have a good cause [i.e., intention]."[111]

Aquinas's deployment of the concept of objects of actions makes sense as an effort to uphold and consolidate the insights set out in this discussion.[112] It seems to me that Aquinas is reluctant to accept the idea that there are exceptions to the important principle that actions "receive their species from the end."[113] Yet nor is he happy to defend the priority of the end at the cost of the perspective of the acting agent. This is the possibility raised by the final part of Lombard's discussion. If we say that when an evil act (say, stealing) is done for a good intention (say, to give alms) that intention is not really good at all but in fact a kind of evil (in this case, say, fraudulently to give alms), then we have found a way of preserving the principle that the end determines the species of an action, but possibly at the cost of the agent's perspective. Aquinas rejects this in a complex discussion in question eighteen.[114] It is possible, he maintains there, genuinely to intend something of a quite different character to what is willed as the means to achieve it. The function of the concept of objects, therefore, is to uphold the objective aspect of action without either undermining the principle that action-kinds are determined by ends, or upholding this principle but sacrificing the perspective of the acting agent. Aquinas finds in the concept of objects, buttressed by further distinctions,[115] a way of correlating ends and kinds and so bringing the subjective-intentional aspect of action together with the objective aspect of action, and relating them to the order of reason.

Aquinas's aim in deploying the concept of objects is thus to prevent the subjective and objective aspects of action from sliding apart. Let us see what this entails a little more fully. On the one hand, it means that an agent's intention is not an impenetrable mystery. Internal acts have objects, and this means that they are

---

110. *Sentences* 2.40.12.

111. *Sentences* 2.40.13-14.

112. In his commentary on the Sentences, Aquinas clarifies what he thinks these insights are (*Scriptum super Sententiis*, 2.40.1): First, good and evil constitute essential differences between actions (article 1). Second, an act is not judged good or evil only on the basis of the will—the nature of the external action matters (article 2). Third, the external act *adds* something to the goodness or evil of the will (article 3). And fourth, the same action cannot be good and evil (article 4). Accessed online: http://www.corpusthomisticum.org/snp2035.html#6903.

113. I-II.1.3, and above.

114. I-II.18.7. Note the example of stealing for alms-giving, taken from Lombard's discussion, used in arg1. Thomas returns to this example in 19.7 arg3.

115. Between the external and internal act (18.6), and between intending and willing (19.7-8).

comprehensible as *kinds* of action. For objects are ends viewed from the perspective of reason, and reason has to do with the reality of the world.[116] This is why Aquinas insists that the fact that the goodness of the will depends on the object does not stand in tension with but actually entails that the goodness of the will depends on reason.[117] The will can only desire good as it is "apprehended by reason" (*a ratione apprehendatur*).[118] "The will's object is proposed to it by reason. Because the good understood is the proportionate object of the will."[119] McInerny's gloss of object, as "what one sets out to do,"[120] can be accepted providing we recognize that "what" here is not merely a formal placeholder, but has a reference to reality—the object is *what* one sets out to do, that is, one's aim as it in fact stands in the order of reason. It is, in Rhonheimer's apt description, "the intelligible content of a concrete type of action."[121] The remarkable articles on erring reason at the center of question nineteen depend upon this point.[122] An object is not an unfathomable subjective purpose, but an aim that corresponds to reality, and so makes an action susceptible to description as a kind. When Aquinas says that "the goodness of the will depends on the goodness of what is willed,"[123] "what is willed" (*voliti*) has a determinate sense: it is a kind of action comprehensible within a common world.

On the other hand, the priority given to the acting agent's perspective makes a real difference. If "the goodness of the will depends on the goodness of what is willed," that means that the intention with which an act is done shapes what it is. Indeed, it is the primary determinant of its kind, for actions, as we have already noted, "receive their species from the end." Thus, a good action done for an evil

---

116. See n. 89, above.

117. I-II.19.3.

118. I-II.19.3.

119. I-II.19.3, Benziger Brothers edition. See also I-II.19.10 and 18:10. This is the basis on which Thomas later stresses that some kinds of act are always bad, I-II.20.2.

120. McInerny, *Aquinas on Human Action*, 80.

121. Rhonheimer, "The Perspective of the Acting Person," 226. As noted above, Rhonheimer deploys this idea somewhat differently to how I am doing. He goes on to say that this "intelligible content ... is presented by reason to the will as a good." I think, rather, that reason's role has already been exhausted once we have said "intelligible." There is not some further task for reason to do beyond allowing an object to appear as intelligible.

122. I-II.19.5-6. The object of an act of will is "something proposed to it by the reason" (*objectum voluntatis est id quod proponitur a ratione*; 19.5). Hence (a) if the reason is in error, the will is still bound, for it has no independent reference point from which to judge (article 5); but also (b) neither is the will excused by erring reason, because it still wills what is in fact evil. For Aquinas, in contrast to Kant, a good will is a willing of some good, rather than a quality of willing. On this point, see especially I-II.19.2 ad2. On these questions generally, see McInerny, *Aquinas on Human Action*, 90–5. Note also Oliver O'Donovan's comments in *RMO*, 117–18.

123. I-II.19.7, my translation: bonitas voluntatis dependeat a bonitate voliti.

end becomes evil,[124] and a good intention can "redound upon," as Aquinas puts it, an act of will that is less good than the intention with which it was done.[125] Say I intend to help a friend prepare to move to a new house by cleaning up some mold, but it turns out that, although I could not have known it, the mold requires much more thorough cleaning than normal and quickly reappears, so that my friend is not, in fact, helped. Aquinas says that what has happened here is that I have willed "an object that is not proportionate" to my intended end, meaning that my will, considered abstractly, is not as good as my intention. However, "because the intention also belongs, in a way, to the act of the will, inasmuch, to wit, as it is the reason thereof," the intention still has an impact on the goodness of the will, even when what is in fact willed is less than what was intended. "It comes to pass that the quantity of goodness in the intention redounds upon the act of the will."[126]

Does that mean a good intention can make a bad action good? No. Although a good intention can ameliorate a bad action, it cannot make it wholly good. "Evil comes from each and every defect, whereas good comes from a complete and integral cause." "In order to be good [a will] must be for a good as meaning good, that is it wills what is really good and for the sake of good."[127]

A useful illustration of this point is found in Aquinas's account of the morality of lying in question 110 of the *Secunda Secundae*. The basic problem in this question is a familiar one: whether an intention to help someone (or to amuse someone) can make a lie good, rather than evil. In the terms of Aquinas's discussion, is an officious or jocular lie always a sin?[128] Among other things, the problem is posed by the story of the midwives who lied to save Hebrew babies and were rewarded by God.[129] Aquinas's answer, in the end, is that a good intention cannot change the fundamental character of a lie as "naturally evil in respect of its genus."[130] An intention may, however, mean that a lie is not a *mortal* sin—and such is the case with the midwives.[131] The basis for this position lies in Aquinas's account of action, which is recalled in article one. The fundamental nature of a lie is determined by its object. This is not "to deceive"—that may be a further intention with which a lie is uttered; "the essential notion of a lie is taken from formal falsehood, from the fact, namely, that a person intends to [habet voluntatem] say what is false."[132]

---

124. I-II.19.7 ad2.
125. I-II.19.8.
126. I-II.19.8, Benziger Brothers edition.
127. I-II.19.7 ad3.
128. See II-II.110.2, 3, 4.
129. II-II.110.3 ad2, 4 ad4; cf. Exod 1:19–21.
130. II-II.110.3, Benziger Brothers edition.
131. II-II.110.4 ad4.
132. II-II.110.1, Benziger Brothers edition. Cf. Finnis, *Aquinas*, 157: "what defines lying is not intention to deceive, but simply intention to *assert* the false."

The intention to deceive "does not belong to the species of lying, but to perfection thereof."[133] The further intention with which a lie is uttered does matter, though. An intention to deceive might make something "attain the specific nature of a lie," while an intention to help might "lessen the gravity of the sin of lying."[134] Yet the basic moral character of a lie is determined simply by the object that "a falsehood may be told."[135]

There are questions to be asked about this account, of course—not least whether this is a good interpretation of the story of the Hebrew midwives. There are also questions to be asked about the framing of the whole discussion. Much of the complexity of Aquinas's account stems from the ambiguities inherent in his foundational principle, that actions receive their species from their ends. In itself, the statement seems reasonable. What is clear, however, is that the whole difficulty lies in discerning *which* ends are determinative. This is why Aquinas is forced to make distinctions between different kinds of relation between ends and actions. He distinguishes actions that are intrinsically related to ends, like fighting well relates to winning a battle, from actions that are accidentally related to ends, like stealing relates to alms-giving.[136] He also notes that "intention can be related in two ways to an act of willing": it can precede it as its cause, and it can "run alongside, or follow it."[137] When combined with the distinction between external and internal actions, this amounts to a recognition that the principle that actions receive their species from their end is as much an invitation to think about the interplay between the objective and subjective aspects of action as it is a diagnostic tool. It is a principle by which practical reason is opened to the complexity of actions as they are performed by subjects who form purposes and construe their intentions. This, though, is not to be scoffed at. "Complexity of action," Robert Spaemann observes, "always occurs when a 'what' distinguishes itself from a 'why.'"[138] The complexity of Aquinas's account arises from its attempt to preserve the importance of a subjective perspective, the "why," without letting go of the objectivity of action, the "what" of action. Through the concept of objects, Aquinas maintains the reality of what Spaemann calls "base actions," that is, "an atomic unity that is constituted by a particular content of meaning and is identifiable by virtue of this content."[139] It is putting together how such base actions go together with subjective intention

---

133. II-II.110.1.
134. II-II.110.2.
135. II-II.110.1.
136. I-II.18.7.
137. I-II.19.7.
138. Robert Spaemann, "Individual Actions," in *A Robert Spaemann Reader: Philosophical Essays on Nature, God, and the Human Person*, ed. D. C. Schindler and Jeanne Heffernan Schindler (Oxford: Oxford University Press, 2015), 149.
139. Spaemann, "Individual Actions," 149.

that produces the complexity in Aquinas's account. Ultimately, we will argue that Aquinas is right to want to secure these different aspects of action.[140]

Finally, it should again be stressed that the link between reason and kinds of action that the concept of the will's *objectum* makes possible is crucial for Aquinas's overall understanding. It is this that opens space for the idea of law, as the movement of thought in the opening articles of question nineteen makes evident. Thomas begins by asking whether the goodness of the will depends on the object. Yes, because good and evil are specific differences, and "differences of species in acts stem from their objectives [*objecta*]."[141] Does the goodness of the will depend solely on the object? Yes, this is the crucial determinant.[142] Does, then, the goodness of the will still depend on reason? Yes, in precisely the same way as it depends on the object.[143] And then the next, striking step: does the goodness of the will depend on eternal law?[144] To which question Thomas answers, yes, because human reason is derivative upon divine reason, which is eternal law. This is only the second mention of law in the *Prima Secundae*, and the first time it is in focus.[145] That it opens the way to the treatise on law is especially clear in the response to the third argument, that eternal law cannot be a measure of goodness because it is unknowable. Aquinas replies that although eternal law is indeed unknown as such, it becomes known to us in some way, "either through natural reason ... or through some revelation given to us over and above the powers of reason."[146] These are the categories that structure the treatise on law.

The notion of objects is also an important part of Aquinas's understanding of virtues, and their relationship to law. Habits, Aquinas argues in question fifty-four, are fundamentally about action. Therefore, because actions differ in kind according to differences of object, habits must be distinguished by their objects.[147] As he recalls the point later, in the treatise on prudence: "Kinds of habits are distinguished by

---

140. Bowlin rightly highlights the subjective aspect of Aquinas's thought, how he makes space for real indeterminacy regarding the meaning of actions, and whether or not in the particular circumstances they constitute something good (see *Contingency*, 71, 73, 80–2). However, Bowlin makes less room for the other, objective side of Aquinas's account, in which we have constantly to reckon with the way actions are also good and evil in their kind. Hence, Bowlin regards Aquinas's discussion of lying as a mistake (*Contingency*, 63, n. 5), whereas I think it is consistent with his wider position.

141. I-II.19.1.

142. I-II.19.2.

143. I-II.19.3: Ergo idea bonitas voluntatis dependet a ratione eo modo quo dependet ab objecto.

144. I-II.19.4: utrum bonitas voluntatis dependeat ex lege aeterna.

145. Law is also mentioned in I-II.14.3 ad2, in relation to deliberation. On which, see Daniel Westberg, *Right Practical Reason: Aristotle, Action, and Prudence in Aquinas* (Oxford: Clarendon, 1994), 173.

146. I-II.19.4 ad3.

147. I-II.54.2.

different objects."¹⁴⁸ In response to the objection that the same kind of act can be done for different ends, corresponding to different virtuous dispositions, Thomas deploys his distinction between internal and external acts: "Purposes [*fines*], too, are themselves the objects of interior acts; which are especially connected with virtues."¹⁴⁹ That is to say, the objects by which virtues are differentiated are the objects of the internal acts, the acts of the will. This clarification is also important for the connection between virtue and law. "The precepts of law," Aquinas notes early in the treatise on law, "are concerned with human acts."¹⁵⁰ Some acts are good generically (*ex genere*). These are acts of virtue. In respect of these, "to prescribe or command is assigned as the corresponding function of law," for law, as Aristotle says, "prescribes acts of all the virtues."¹⁵¹ Later, however, Thomas clarifies the sense in which law commands acts of virtue. Law does not command all acts of virtue in the sense of all action done virtuously, but in the sense of the actions that properly belong to the virtues, for instance, the doing right that is the act of the just man, or the courageous act that belongs to the virtue of courage.¹⁵² These proper actions of virtues may be prescribed by law because they are oriented by their objects to the same good the law defends.¹⁵³ Hence, "there is no virtue of which some activity cannot be enjoined by law."¹⁵⁴

Aquinas's understanding of action thus stands at the center of his moral theology, bringing together law and virtue under the rule of reason through the concept of the objects of actions. As we will see, it is also crucial for his understanding of prudence and deliberation. For now, however, we need to follow the thought noted just above, that in Aquinas's thought the generic character of action is rooted in the notion of eternal law.

3 Eternal Law and Divine Providence

a. Law, Divine Reason, and Nature

Aquinas conceives of reasonable action as founded on an order of divine reason. "That the human reason is the rule for acts of human will so that it measures their goodness comes because it derives from the Eternal Law which is the divine reason [*ratio divina*]."¹⁵⁵ That is to say, it is *divine* reason that is the fundamental

---

148. II-II.47.11, my translation: species habituum diversificantur secundum diversitatem objecti. Cf. I-II.60.1; 62.2.
149. I-II.54.2 ad3.
150. I-II.92.2, Benziger Brothers edition.
151. I-II.92.2, referring to *EN* 5.1.
152. I-II.96.3 ad2.
153. I-II.96.3.
154. I-II.96.3.
155. I-II.19.14.

rule of human action. Eternal law is the source of all other law.[156] Natural law, for Aquinas, is not *another* law, but the rational creature's "participation" (*participatio*) in the eternal law.[157] Natural law *is* the eternal law, insofar as creatures' "tendencies [*inclinationes*] to their own proper acts and ends" are "from its impression" (*ex impressione*).[158] In rational creatures, this takes the form of responsibility: "they join in and make their own [*participatur*] the Eternal Reason through which they have their natural aptitudes [*inclinationem*] for their due activity and purpose,"[159] and they do so in an "intelligent and rational manner" (*intellectualiter et rationaliter*).[160] The natural law is simply a way of speaking about the fact that eternal law involves human beings rationally, through their awareness of a natural inclination to the end.[161] All human positive law, likewise, finds its source in eternal law, and draws its justice from that concord—"A human law has the force of law to the extent that it falls in with right reason: as such it derives from the Eternal Law."[162] Divine law, too, which is a form of positive law, gives expression to eternal law, enabling a "higher participation" in eternal law (*participatur altiori modo*).[163] Indeed, the primary function of eternal law is to provide the metaphysical underpinning for the exposition of divine law as the old and new laws, which is the overall goal of Aquinas's treatise on law.[164]

Keeping the primacy of eternal law in view guards us against two temptations. The first is to see Aquinas's understanding of practical reason as essentially a theory of natural law. Such a restricted understanding is frequently imputed to Aquinas. To take one prominent example, John Finnis argues that Aquinas's recognition, in his discussion of natural law,[165] of a set of determinate goods to be pursued entails the idea that a complete system of ethics can be constructed independently of explicitly theoretical claims.[166] A list of basic goods can be enumerated on the basis

---

156. I-II.93.3: *omnes leges a lege aeterna procedunt*. Ulrich Kühn highlights that the more explicit treatment of eternal law in the *Summa Theologiae* is a significant development from Aquinas's earlier work, particularly in the *Summa Contra Gentiles* (*Via Caritatis*, 128). Following the suggestion of Fergus Kerr, *After Aquinas: Versions of Thomism* (Malden, MA: Blackwell, 2002), 111, the discussion below is indebted to Kühn's account of Aquinas's thought.

157. I-II.91.2.

158. I-II.91.2.

159. I-II.91.2.

160. I-II.91.2 ad3.

161. See I-II.93.2. The function of *synderesis* in Aquinas's thinking is to clarify what this natural human participation in eternal law involves. *Synderesis* is the habit that preserves the practical principles imparted by nature (I.79.12).

162. I-II.93.3.

163. I-II.91.4 ad1.

164. See Kühn, *Via Caritatis*, 128–30, 144.

165. See I-II.94.2.

166. See Finnis, *Fundamentals of Ethics*, 56–79.

of practical reason, which can be reframed in terms of principles, giving a "set of genuine first practical principles identifying specific types of basic human good as to be realized, pursued, and respected."[167] From these principles can be derived further "intermediate principles," which are necessary for moral deliberation.[168] Finnis acknowledges that this is not, in fact, how Aquinas developed his own position. Aquinas "did not carry through or consolidate his own advance,"[169] by supplying the necessary intermediate principles, leaving a lacuna in his thought that needs to be filled if Aquinas is not to run into problems.[170]

Equally, a number of Finnis's critics share this restriction of practical reasoning to natural law reasoning. Stephen Jensen, for instance, states, "Aquinas does not have some broad category of practical reason, under which the natural law falls as a particular instance. Rather, to reason practically is to reason according to the natural law."[171] Similarly, Anthony Lisska argues that Aquinas's theory of natural law can be reconstructed to provide a coherent and stand-alone theory of natural law that is a sufficient basis for moral reasoning.[172]

Yet these views do not take seriously enough Aquinas's comments about the limits of human judgment and human law-making. On Aquinas's own account, the lacuna identified by Finnis cannot be filled in successfully, "because of the untrustworthiness of human judgment," necessitating "a divinely given law carrying the assurance that it cannot be mistaken."[173] The problem, as Mark Jordan sums it up, is that "the premises of the natural law are, in their generality, unable to ground sure deduction of right action."[174] Human law-making is also imperfectible: it cannot see into the human heart, nor can it do away with evil without also "taking away much that is good." Hence a law is needed that is "unspotted."[175] It was not simply, as Finnis infers, that Aquinas "felt no urgent need to carry through the philosophical explication of practical wisdom."[176] It was that he thought it impossible. Fergus Kerr observes that Aquinas's last recorded notes on natural law serve to relativize its importance: "Now although God in creating man gave him this law of nature, the devil oversowed another law in man, namely the law of

167. Finnis, *Aquinas*, 89.
168. Finnis, *Fundamentals of Ethics*, 68–70.
169. Finnis, *Fundamentals of Ethics*, 68–70.
170. See also Finnis, "Is and Ought in Aquinas," 150–5.
171. Jensen, *Knowing the Natural Law*, 37.
172. Anthony J. Lisska, *Aquinas's Theory of Natural Law: An Analytical Reconstruction* (Oxford: Clarendon, 1996).
173. I-II.91.4.
174. Mark Jordan, *Ordering Wisdom: The Hierarchy of Philosophical Discourses in Aquinas* (Notre Dame: University of Notre Dame Press, 1986), 139. As noted above (n. 89), in my view this is an important weakness in Rhonheimer's account of intrinsically evil actions in "The Perspective of the Acting Person."
175. I-II.91.4, quoting Psalm 19:7.
176. Finnis, *Fundamentals of Ethics*, 69.

concupiscence ... Since then the law of nature was destroyed by concupiscence, man needed to be brought back to works of virtue, and to be drawn away from vice: for which purpose he needed the written law."[177]

The second temptation is to think that Aquinas's account of practical reasoning actually leaves very little room for law. This position takes its cue from the modesty of Aquinas's comments about natural law. To take two examples: in *The Priority of Prudence*, Daniel Mark Nelson argues that because Aquinas does not think natural law supplies "content for our moral deliberations," prudence and the virtues simply "have priority" in practical reason.[178] They, rather than law, are what provide "moral guidance."[179] Somewhat similarly, John Bowlin concludes that if natural law does not in some way or other "specify the concrete content of morally praiseworthy action"—which it doesn't—then Aquinas should be understood to see the human good as thoroughly indeterminate, and moral deliberation pretty much exclusively the domain of prudence and the virtues.[180] There is certainly truth in these positions. When it comes to how Aquinas pictures moral deliberation in practice, prudence and the moral virtues dominate. As we will see, it is the virtues, rather than laws, that tend to supply the ends of action in concrete situations.[181] What these positions leave out, however, is consideration of other kinds of law.[182] Aquinas, indeed, does not think natural law effectively provides the principles of moral decision-making, but that does not mean we are left without any guidance from law in moral deliberations. Rather, Aquinas holds that this is why we need positive law, both divine and human, which puts us in touch with right reason— the eternal law. Bowlin rightly differentiates Aquinas's thought from Korsgaard's presentation of Kant's formal account of practical reasoning by noting how the concept of eternal law means that for Aquinas "practical reason has a moral construal."[183] What Bowlin does not sufficiently reckon with, however, is the way in which this framework allows Aquinas to give an important place to positive law. Aquinas's ethics may not be an ethics of natural law, but it is still in a real sense an ethics of law. Indeed, as we noted above, Aquinas says that "there is no virtue of which some activity cannot be enjoined by law."[184] The place of law in Aquinas's thought is in fact somewhat ambiguous. In due course, we will suggest that this is a point highlighted by the book of Proverbs.

---

177. Kerr, "Doctrine of God and Theological Ethics According to Thomas Aquinas," 80, quoting from Aquinas's *Collationes in Decem preceptis*. See also the arguments in Bowlin, *Contingency*, 93–137; and Nelson, *The Priority of Prudence*, 105–27.

178. Nelson, *The Priority of Prudence*, 97, 70.

179. Nelson, *The Priority of Prudence*, 88.

180. Bowlin, *Contingency*, 93–4.

181. See below, Section 4.

182. See especially Nelson, *The Priority of Prudence*, 87.

183. Bowlin, *Contingency*, 118.

184. I-II.96.3.

At a more fundamental level, what both of these temptations share is an unwillingness to take seriously the claim we have already noted above: that human beings are "destined to an end higher than that one matching their natural constitution."[185] "The rule of human actions," Thomas holds, "is the human reason and the eternal law. Now the eternal law surpasses human reason: so that the knowledge of human actions, as ruled by the eternal law, surpasses the natural reason, and requires the supernatural light of a gift of the Holy Ghost."[186] The gift in question here is the gift of understanding, by which the things of faith are brought to bear even upon action. Were human beings "destined only to an end not beyond their natural abilities," then "they would need no directive of reason over and above the natural law and human law built on it."[187] Yet the fact is human beings are so destined, meaning that the natural law can only ever be part of the picture of practical reasoning.[188]

The attempt, therefore, to develop Aquinas's comments about natural law into a self-contained theory of ethics runs aground on many features of Aquinas's actual presentation. As Ulrich Kühn recognizes, Aquinas thinks that law requires a *theological* explanation, and so any purely philosophical account of Aquinas's ideas about law—such as, for example, Lisska's contention that there is a "conceptual secularism" to Aquinas's theory of natural law[189]—inevitably involves a damaging "Verkürzung der Perspektive."[190]

All of this is not to say that natural reason does not correspond to a certain, relatively self-contained sphere in Aquinas's thought. The fact that it does is reflected in an ambiguity in a comment cited above. On the one hand, Aquinas can speak of the problems with human judgment and the consequent need for divine law; but on the other hand, he can say that, were human beings "destined only to an end not beyond their natural abilities," then "they would need no directive of reason over and above the natural law and human law built on it."[191] Human beings, Aquinas holds, have a natural end, and a supernatural end.[192] Natural law,

185. I-II.91.4 ad3; and see, again, I.1.1.

186. II-II.8.3 ad3.

187. I-II.91.4.

188. See especially I-II.91.4 ad3. See also Thomas's comments about the *duplex* rule of the will in I-II.71.6. Rhonheimer cites this text repeatedly ("The Perspective of the Acting Person," 205 n. 35, 208 nn. 34 and 35), using it, rightly, to emphasize the importance of the eternal law and to criticize those who overlook it. In my opinion, however, he does not adequately recognize the way the *prima regula* also surpasses the natural reason, so that natural law reasoning is never sufficient for an account of practical reasoning.

189. Lisska, *Aquinas's Theory*, 91.

190. Kühn, *Via Caritatis*, 130.

191. I-II.91.4.

192. For a helpful summary of debates around this point, see John Rist, *Augustine Deformed: Love, Sin, and Freedom in the Western Moral Tradition* (Cambridge: Cambridge University Press, 2014), 122–3, n. 22.

natural reason, and the *Old* Law relate to the former. Explaining why the law of God is twofold, Aquinas says that the common good is twofold: the Old Law is ordained to "material and earthly benefit" (*bonum sensibile et terrenum*), whereas the New Law pertains to humanity's "spiritual and heavenly good" (*bonum intelligibile et caeleste*).[193] The central reason for this differentiation has to do with salvation history. "The law bringing all to salvation could not have been given until after Christ's coming." The Old Law is not unrelated to the coming of Christ: it was, "a law which prepared [the people from whom Christ was to be born] to welcome him," and contained "the rudiments of saving justice."[194] Still, the New Law, which relates to the coming of Christ, is something genuinely and substantially new.

The same dynamics appear with the virtues. In his study of Aquinas's understanding of pagan virtue, *Ethics as a Work of Charity*, David Decosimo has drawn out some of the rich ways in which Thomas articulated this sphere of the natural.[195] Decosimo argues that Aquinas has room to welcome pagan virtue, because, among other things, he thinks that the goods of natural human virtue, and of the political good, are genuine goods.[196] For they are related to what Aquinas calls "honest goods," that is, aspects of the created order that are "intrinsically ordainable" to the final good, and thus "good *in se*."[197] Virtue that relates to these goods is thus not *"strictly* true" virtue, yet it is true virtue in an imperfect sense.[198] Decosimo clarifies that this rests on Thomas's moral ontology, in which some things are intrinsically related to the final end.[199] "There is," he says, "an intrinsic, inchoate directedness of the honest to the true and final good."[200]

Yet, there is also a real disjunction between the natural and the supernatural. This is evident especially in Aquinas's discussion of the infusion of natural moral virtues. The reality of a supernatural end means that there must indeed be infused moral virtues.[201] Yet, they also must be of a different species to the natural moral virtues.[202] The difference can, indeed, be rather pronounced: the principle of natural temperance, for instance, "is that food should not harm the health of the body, nor hinder the use of reason." With infused temperance, however, the rule is that "it behooves man to 'chastise his body, and bring it into subjection'

193. I-II.91.5.

194. I-II.91.5 ad2.

195. David Decosimo, *Ethics as a Work of Charity: Thomas Aquinas and Pagan Virtue* (Stanford, CA: Stanford University Press, 2014).

196. This argument is made particularly in chapter 8 of *Ethics as a Work of Charity* (pp. 178–98), which focuses especially on II-II.23.7.

197. Decosimo, *Ethics as a Work of Charity*, 179–80, 188. For the concept of the *bonum honestum*, see I.5.6.

198. See II-II.23.7.

199. Decosimo, *Ethics as a Work of Charity*, 182–4.

200. Decosimo, *Ethics as a Work of Charity*, 190.

201. I-II.63.3.

202. I-II.63.4.

(1 Cor. 9:27), by abstinence."²⁰³ The relation between the natural and the supernatural is not, in Aquinas's thought, altogether smooth. "The same," Aquinas insists, "applies to the other virtues."²⁰⁴

These are ideas that will occupy us again. To anticipate: ultimately, we will argue that there is something to be affirmed in Aquinas's distinction between humanity's natural and supernatural ends, and in his recognition of the potential for disjunction between them. For now, we must return to the key concept that for Aquinas relates them: the eternal law, "the eternal reason" that "is the supreme rule of all human rightness."²⁰⁵

b. The Concept of Eternal Law

What does Thomas mean by eternal law? The idea of eternal law, he says, follows from the idea that God made the world through wisdom, that "through his wisdom God is the founder of the universe of things."²⁰⁶ This entails, he argues, that eternal law is a *ratio* in God, the *summa ratio in Deo existens*, the *ratio divinae sapientiae*. By this, Thomas means something like a fundamental conception in the mind of God.²⁰⁷ *Ratio* is a term that is in this case connected with Thomas's understanding of divine ideas. In question fifteen of the *Prima Pars*, Aquinas argues that there are indeed ideas in the divine mind. With the exception of things made by chance, he explains, things can be made either by natural generation or by intellect. "Since the world is not made by chance, but is made by God acting as an intellectual agent ... there must be in the divine mind a form, to the likeness of which the world is made; and that is what we mean by an Idea."²⁰⁸ Here we meet again a now familiar picture of "making": God stands to creation, Aquinas suggests, like a builder to a house, with "the form of the house" in his mind, as "something understood by him, to the likeness of which he forms the house in matter."²⁰⁹

---

203. I-II.63.4, Benziger Brothers edition.

204. I-II.63.4, Benziger Brothers edition. I therefore cannot quite agree with Jean Porter's assessment (*The Recovery of Virtue: The Relevance of Aquinas for Christian Ethics* [Louisville, Kentucky: Westminster John Knox, 1990], 66–7) that "the specific natural ideal of humanity remains the proximate norm of morality" in Aquinas's thought. Although grace does not simply destroy nature, the "radical qualitative difference" it introduces, which Porter recognizes, makes matters complex. The natural end remains, but its importance is radically relativized.

205. II-II.52.2.

206. I-II.93.1.

207. See Kühn, *Via Caritatis*, 141–2: "'Ratio' ist hier in dem anderen, bei Thomas sehr häufigen, mehr technischen Sinne gebraucht und bedeutet soviel wie 'Wesensgrund' oder 'Sinnstruktur.'"

208. I.15.1.

209. I.15.2, Benziger Brothers edition. Note also the use of this analogy in I.14.8 and II-II.52.3.

The term *ratio* comes into play in this context. Ideas, Aquinas explains, are *rationes* "existing in the divine mind."[210] Aquinas also clarifies that the term *ratio* relates primarily to *speculative* knowledge. "As a principle of the production of things it [an idea] may be called an exemplar (*exemplar*), and belongs to practical knowledge; as a principle of knowing, it is properly called a conception (*ratio*), and can belong also to speculative knowledge."[211] Aquinas makes this same point in the discussion of practical and speculative knowledge in *De Veritate*, which we have already had occasion to discuss.[212] *Rationes* are ideas insofar as they come within speculative knowledge.[213] When, therefore, Aquinas says that the eternal law is the "*ratio* of divine wisdom," he means that the eternal law is an idea, an eternal conception of God's speculative knowledge.

This particular conception is peculiar, however, in that its substance is the whole movement of creation to its end. Eternal law is the *ratio* of God's providential ordering of all things, the *ratio divinae providentiae* and the *ratio divinae gubernationis*, as Thomas also calls it.[214] Natural contingencies and even divine election fall under the eternal law,[215] and it can be equated with God's will.[216] As Ulrich Kühn explains, behind this understanding lies Aquinas's doctrine of creation. "Das übergeordnete Prinzip der gesamten Gesetzeslehre des Thomas in einer Metapysik der Schöpfung, die die Erhaltung und Regierung einschließt, liegt."[217] God's creation of all things encompasses also his ordering of all things to their end. The logic of this teleological metaphysic is highlighted in Thomas's treatment of providence:

> God creates every goodness in things ... It is not only in the substance of created things that goodness lies, but also in their being ordained to an end, above all to their final end, which, as we have seen, is the divine goodness. This good order existing in created things is itself part of God's creation. Since he is the cause of things through his mind, and, as we have already made clear, the idea of each and every effect must pre-exist in him, the divine mind must preconceive the whole pattern [*ratio*] of things moving to their end.[218]

---

210. I.15.3: Ideae sunt rationes in mente divina existentes.

211. I.15.3.

212. *De Veritate* 3.3. See above, Section 1.

213. The Blackfriars translation of *ratio* as "exemplar" throughout the treatise on law is unfortunate, as it obscures precisely this point about the difference between *ratio* and *exemplar*.

214. I-II.93.4 arg3; 93.5 ad3; 93.4.

215. I-II.93.5-6.

216. I-II.93.4 ad1.

217. Kühn, *Via Caritatis*, 147. Translation: "The overarching principle of the whole of Thomas's teaching on law lies in a metaphysic of creation that includes its preservation and government."

218. I.22.1.

This *ratio*, Thomas concludes, "is, properly speaking, providence."[219] What God creates is not static, but things in motion, ordered to an end. Hence, the eternal knowledge of God through which he created involves not only conceptions of things as such, but also a conception of their movement. Eternal law is this conception, the *ratio* of divine wisdom and divine providence.

Indeed, it is this relation to divine providence that gives eternal law the character of *law*. For Aquinas maintains that "every law is shaped to the common good."[220] The eternal law has the character of law, therefore, because it is a conception of the movement of all things to their true and final good. This is why he also insists that the eternal law is *one ratio*: "law is directive of activities as converging to the common good. When they are so co-ordinated together then things in themselves diverse are regarded as forming a unity."[221]

Now, in articulating this idea of a conception of a direction of things to the end, Aquinas draws an analogy between the work of an artisan and the work of a governor:

> Just as in every artificer there pre-exists an idea [*ratio*] of the things that are made by his art, so too in every governor there must pre-exist the type [*ratio*] of the order of those things that are to be done by those who are subject to his government. And just as the type [*ratio*] of the things yet to be made by an art is called the art or exemplar of the products of that art, so too the type [*ratio*] in him who governs the acts of his subjects, bears the character of a law, provided the other conditions be present, which we have mentioned above.[222]

The importance of this analogy lies in the fact that it allows Aquinas to conclude that the eternal law is *summa ratio in dei existens*. Because God made all things "through his wisdom," and because he is both like an artificer in relation to what he makes and like a governor in relation to every act and motion of creation, therefore, the eternal law is the *ratio* of divine wisdom:[223]

> Wherefore as the type [*ratio*] of Divine Wisdom, inasmuch as by it all things are created, has the character of art, exemplar or idea; so the type [*ratio*] of Divine Wisdom, as moving all things to their due end, bears the character of law. Accordingly the eternal law is nothing else than the type [*ratio*] of Divine Wisdom, as directing all actions and movements.[224]

---

219. I.22.1, Benziger Brothers edition.
220. i-II.90.2. See also Kühn, *Via Caritatis*, 143.
221. i-II.93.1 ad1; cf. arg1 and I.15.2.
222. i-II.93.1, Benziger Brothers edition.
223. i-II.93.1. For the former analogy, see I.14.8: "The knowledge of God is the cause of things. For the knowledge of God is to all creatures what the knowledge of the artificer is to things made by his art" (cf. I.15.1; ii-II.52.3). For the later, see I.103.5.
224. i-II.93.1, Benziger Brothers edition.

The analogy between the artisan and the governor extends the influence of the conceptuality of "making" we have already discussed. Government is understood to involve the execution of a pre-existing mental conception in the same way that making or building is. The distinction observed above between *ratio* and *exemplar* is also being deployed here. *Ratio*, as we saw, relates primarily to speculative knowledge, whereas *exemplar* as well as *idea* in its usual sense relates to practical knowledge.[225] What Thomas is arguing by drawing an analogy between the pre-existing *ratio* of both the artisan and the governor, therefore, is that eternal law stands to the *ratio divinae sapientiae* in a parallel relationship to that of the divine ideas to the *ratio divinae sapientiae*. The pre-existing conception of the mind of God, the *ratio divinae sapientiae*, is related to creation in a twofold way: it gives the *exemplars* by which creation is formed, and it gives the *law* by which creation is perfected.

The function of the idea that the eternal law is a divine *ratio* is thus to anchor eternal law in the simplicity of divine knowledge. This also involves overcoming a tension that is fundamental in Aquinas's thought to do with the eternity of creation. For Aquinas, as we have seen, God knows all things in every way in which they may be known, in the "one single insight" that is the act of his own existence.[226] "He sees all things other than himself in himself, and himself he knows with speculative knowledge. Thus in his speculative knowledge of himself he has knowledge both speculative and practical of all other things."[227] Yet creation is not eternal; so how can God be said to know it eternally? The same problem applies to the idea of eternal law. On the one hand, if eternal law is really *of* divine wisdom, then it is in a real sense divine: "all that is attributed to the divine essence or nature does not fall under it, but in reality is itself the eternal law."[228] God the Son is not subject to the eternal law, "but rather is Himself the eternal law by a kind of appropriation."[229] On the other hand, the content and substance of eternal law are the ordering of things to their end—it is *of* divine government. It has, in Kühn's words, "den Sinn von 'Gesetz' insofern … als sie auf Außergöttliches, Nichtewiges, nämlich auf die gesamte Schöpfung Gottes bezogen ist."[230] This tension is in fact the first objection to the idea of eternal law. "Every law supposes subjects on which it is imposed," but God alone is eternal. How then can there be eternal law?[231] The same problem is raised in Aquinas's discussion of providence: "Whatever is in God, is eternal. But

---

225. See *De Veritate* 3.3.

226. See above, Section 1.

227. I.14.16 ad2.

228. I-II.93.4.

229. I-II.93.4 ad2, Benziger Brothers edition. Cf. 93.1 ad2.

230. Kühn, *Via Caritatis*, 143. Translation: *ratio* "has the sense of 'law' insofar as it is applied to non-eternal entities other than God—namely the whole of God's creation."

231. I-II.91.1 arg1.

providence is not anything eternal, for it is concerned with existing things that are not eternal."²³²

Aquinas's solution is to draw a distinction between God's eternal knowledge of creation in as much as it is *God's* knowledge, and so eternally one and simple, and this knowledge "in as much as through it all things are created," and "as moving all things to their due ends."²³³ Creatures do pre-exist eternally in God's mind,²³⁴ and yet this does not mean that those creatures are themselves eternal, for "knowledge is the cause of things in accordance with the way things are in the knowledge," and "it was no part of God's knowledge that things should exist from eternity."²³⁵ This is the distinction Aquinas has in view when he calls the eternal law the *ratio* of divine wisdom. Though about finite things, the eternal law is still prior to those things, as a form of divine knowledge. "While not as yet existing in themselves things nevertheless exist in God in so far as they are foreseen and preordained by him ... Thus the eternal concept of divine law bears the character of a law that is eternal [*aeternus divinae legis conceptus habet rationem legis aeternae*] as being God's ordination for the governance of things he foreknows."²³⁶ The problem is that eternal law is *of divine wisdom*, in one sense, and *of creation* in another. Aquinas solves the problem by distinguishing between God's knowledge in itself, and his knowledge in its relation to creatures.²³⁷ We will see that this is a theological challenge that is raised sharply by Proverbs ch. 8. This is a text that also holds a prominent place within Aquinas's thought on these matters, and it is to this place that we now turn.

c. Eternal Law and Proverbs Chapter Eight

Underpinning Aquinas's understanding of eternal law lies a significant appeal to Proverbs ch. 8. Thomas's first discussion of eternal law begins like this:

> Law is nothing but a dictate of practical reason issued by a sovereign who governs a complete community. Granted that the world is ruled by divine Providence, and this we have shown in the *Prima Pars*, it is evident that the whole community of the universe is governed by God's mind [*ratione*

---

232. I.22.1 arg2, Benziger Brothers edition.
233. I-II.93.1, see above.
234. I.19.4.
235. I.14.8 ad2.
236. I-II.91.1 ad1. Aquinas makes a parallel argument in his discussion of providence, distinguishing between "the reason of order [*ratio ordinis*], which is called providence and disposition, and the execution of order, which is termed government [*gubernatio*]." The first, he says, is eternal, and the second temporal (I.22.1 ad2, Benziger Brothers edition).
237. Kühn highlights that this problem, and Aquinas's solution, is also raised sharply by the question of the promulgation of eternal law, discussed in I-II.91.1 arg2, ad2; and 93.1 arg2, ad2. See Kühn, *Via Caritatis*, 144–6.

divina]. Therefore the ruling idea of things [*ratio gubernationis rerum*] which exists in God as the effective sovereign of them all has the nature of a law. Then since God's mind [*divina ratio*] does not conceive in time, but has an eternal concept, according to Proverbs, it follows that this law should be called eternal."[238]

The reference given is to Prov. 8:23, "I was set up from everlasting, from the beginning, or ever the earth was." The speaker is personified Wisdom, which Thomas equates with divine reason. The logic is that divine reason's *ratio* of the government of the universe must, according to the way Proverbs speaks of wisdom, be eternal.

Aquinas connects Proverbs 8 to eternal law at a number of significant points in the treatise on law. Prov. 8:15, "By me princes reign, and lawgivers decree what is just," is the text from which Thomas argues that all laws derive from eternal law.[239] The same text is used to prove that just human laws bind in conscience by virtue of their derivation from eternal law.[240] Prov. 8:29, which speaks of Wisdom's presence with God "when he gave the sea is limit," is seen to prove that natural contingencies are subject to the eternal law.[241] Later, in discussing the Old Law, Prov. 8:8, "All the words of my mouth are just," shows why the Old Testament precepts relating to foreigners cannot be wrong.[242] The implication is that the words of the Old Testament law are the words of eternal wisdom.[243] In each of these texts, the figure of Wisdom in Proverbs 8 supports the crucial link in Thomas's understanding of eternal law: between God's eternal knowledge and his providential ordering of the world.

These uses fit with Aquinas's wider understanding of this text, in which the voice of Wisdom is understood to be the voice of God himself, and in particular, the voice of the Son.[244] In Aquinas's version of the Bible, Prov. 8:22 says, "The Lord possessed me at the beginning of his way."[245] In the *Prima Pars* this is taken as the voice of "the person of begotten Wisdom," and thus evidence that the angels, because made by God, were not eternal,[246] as well as a proof that the universe did

---

238. I-II.91.1.

239. I-II.93.3.

240. I-II.96.4.

241. I-II.93.5.

242. I-II.105.3.

243. This verse is used with the same understanding in II-II.34.3.

244. As well as what follows, note the use of Prov. 8:17 in I-II.65.5 and II-II.45.5.

245. The Latin version—*Dominus possedit me initium viarum suarum antequam quicquam faceret a principio*—thus allowed Thomas to overlook the thorny problem created by the LXX translation of *qnh* as *ektisen*, which had vexed the Greek church. On this, see below, Chapter 3, Section 1.

246. I.61.2.

not always exist.[247] Prov. 8:24, which refers to Wisdom's being begotten, is used to support the point that the procession of the Word in God is called generation, because "the divine act of intelligence is the very substance itself of the one who understands."[248] This link between Wisdom and the Son lies behind the links Aquinas draws between the eternal law and the Word: although the eternal law is not a proper name for the Son, Thomas explains at one point, yet it is "appropriated to the Son, on account of the kinship between type [*ratio*] and word."[249] It is a link that continues to be important in the *Tertia Pars*, where Prov. 8:31 is taken to be spoken "by the mouth of Begotten Wisdom," and to show that there is a fitness in the union of the Son of God with human nature.[250]

For Aquinas, then, the bedrock reference point for practical reason is the eternal law, the determinate divine conception of creation's ordained movement to its end, from which all other law derives. The eternal law is rooted in the divine nature—indeed, it *is* the divine nature, divine wisdom or reason—yet it nevertheless fundamentally concerns the existence of finite creatures. It is the divine pattern for creaturely goodness. All of this, for Aquinas, is what is entailed by the belief that "through his wisdom God is the founder of the universe of things."[251] And it is Proverbs 8 that is the definitive biblical exposition of this idea. In this text, we hear the divine Son speaking as the wisdom of God that governs all things. We glimpse the divine reason that animates the cosmos, and draws it to its final goal. This text will therefore be the point from which we will begin, in the following chapter, to hear the voice of Proverbs directly. For the moment, however, we must look at the understanding of practical thinking that Aquinas builds upon this foundation.

4 Prudence

To recapitulate: the human mind is engaged by reality in two fundamentally different ways: in thought, and in action. Behind this stands the fundamental truth of God and his wisdom. He is the One whose own knowledge opens up the possibility of knowledge, and his eternal law is the ground of reasonable action. At the heart of Aquinas's account of what this grounding involves is the thought that actions come in kinds. This idea, we will now see, is also basic for Aquinas's understanding of prudence and deliberation. For it is the notion of kinds of action that allows Thomas to draw together a teleological conception of the moral life and a syllogistic conception of moral reasoning. We begin with the notion of prudence.

In explaining why the goodness of the will depends on the eternal law, Thomas quotes Ps. 4:6, "Who will show us any good? Lift up the light of thy countenance

---

247. I.46.1.
248. 1.27.2 ad.2, Benziger Brothers edition.
249. I-II.93.1 ad2, Benziger Brothers edition.
250. III.4.1.
251. I-II.93.1, and above.

upon us, O Lord," and glosses it as follows: "The light of our reason is able to show us good things and guide our will, in so far as it is the light (i.e. derived from) Thy [God's] countenance."[252] Prudence (*prudentia*), for Aquinas, is the virtue of this correspondence between divine reason and human practical reason. Following Aristotle, it is the virtue of "right reason in acting" (*recta ratio agibilium*);[253] but right reason, as we have seen, ultimately means divine reason. The "mean" or measure of prudence is not, as it is for some of the moral virtues, merely a mean relative to the moral agent, but the *real* mean, that is, reality itself: "both for the practical and in the speculative intellectual virtues the mean consists in being conformed to things [*conformitatem ad rem*]."[254] As Aquinas comments in the treatise on prudence, "The eternal reason is the supreme rule of all human rightness."[255] In Aquinas's thinking, Alasdair MacIntyre deftly observes, *prudentia* "is the counterpart in human beings to that ordering of creatures to their ultimate end which is God's providence. God creates and orders particulars and knows them precisely as what he has made and is making. We, if we act rightly, reproduce that ordering."[256] Prudence is the virtue of the human taking-of-responsibility for conformity to divine reason. For, "when a man does a good deed, not of his own counsel, but moved by that of another, his deed is not yet quite perfect, as regards his reason in directing him and his appetite in moving him."[257] The glory of prudence is that it allows an action to be chosen.[258] It is, as Jean-Pierre Torrell summarizes, "the virtue of choice and decision, of personal responsibility, of risk consciously taken. It closes the deliberative process by daring to prescribe action in a specific situation, singular each time, that will never repeat itself as such."[259]

Why, exactly, does Thomas think prudence is necessary? Here is how he answers this question:

> Prudence is a virtue of utmost necessity for human life. To live well means acting well. In order to perform an act well, it is not merely what a man does that matters, but also how he does it, namely, that he acts from a right choice [*secundum electionem rectam*] and not merely from impulse or passion. Since, however, choice is about means to an end, rightness of choice necessarily involves two factors, namely, a due end and something suitably ordained to that due end. Man is indeed directed to his due end by a virtue which perfects the soul in the appetitive part, the object of which is a

---

252. I-II.19.4.
253. II-II.47.2, 8; cf. *EN* 6.5, 1140b20.
254. I-II.64.3; cf. II-II.47.7.
255. II-II.52.2.
256. Alasdair MacIntyre, *Whose Justice? Which Rationality?* (London: Duckworth, 1988), 196.
257. I-II.57.5 ad2.
258. See I-II.57.5.
259. Torrell, *Saint Thomas Aquinas, Volume 2*, 270.

good and an end [*cuius objectum est bonum et finis*]. For a man to be rightly adapted to what fits his due end, however, he needs a habit in his reason; because counsel [*consiliari*] and choice, which are about things ordained to an end, are acts of reason. Consequently, an intellectual virtue is needed in his reason to complement it and make it well adjusted to these things. This virtue is prudence. And this, in consequence, is necessary for a good life.[260]

Acting well means acting from choice. Rightness of choice, however, involves both wanting the right thing and taking hold of it in the right way. This is a work of reason, which is why prudence is necessary. Prudence prosecutes the movement of practical reason from desired ends or goods to the particular acts by which they are attained.

What is involved in this prosecution of action? We may make a number of observations. First, the fact that prudence aims at action gives it, for Aquinas, a unique character. "The chief act of prudence will be the chief act of reason as engaged with conduct [*rationis agibilium*]." And this is to *command (praecipere)*.[261] This point follows from the different characters of practical and theoretical reason, which we observed above (Section 1): Practical reason can aim at the true only insofar as it is attainable in action, which means as a "good to be done" (*bonum ordinabile ad opus*).[262] This is why prudence aims at "the true taken in conformity to a right appetite,"[263] and why its chief act is to command. Insofar as prudence takes counsel and makes judgments, it is formally indistinguishable from theoretical reason, but prudence also issues commands, and in this way becomes categorically different.[264]

Second, prudence is essentially forward-looking. This follows from the first point. Because the chief act of prudence is that which particularly relates to action, the principal parts of prudence are those which relate to that act.[265] Effective

---

260. I-II.57.5. The references here to choice (*electio*) and counsel (*consilium*) recall Aquinas's theory of action, set out in questions 6–17 of the *Prima Secundae*. *Electio* is Aquinas's term for Aristotle's *prohairesis*. *Consilium* is the main term he uses to discuss deliberation. For an introduction, see especially Westberg, *Right Practical Reason*.

261. II-II.47.8.

262. I.79.11 ad2.

263. I-II.64.3.

264. See Westberg, *Right Practical Reason*, 194–7. The attempt by Jensen (*Knowing the Natural Law*, 144) to correlate these acts to the forms of practical knowledge discussed in I.14.16 seems to me to be a mistake. Commanding is the chief act of prudence, but the whole process is a process of "practical cognition," as Aquinas says in his treatment of the cardinal virtues (see Westberg, *Right Practical Reason*, 196).

265. Aquinas's discussion of the parts of prudence is complex and will largely be passed over. We note, however, that among the parts of prudence Aquinas lists "docility," by which he means willingness to be taught, and "shrewdness," meaning "an easy or rapid conjecture in finding the mean" (II-II.49.3-4). These are ideas that resonate with Proverbs and, notably, Aquinas appeals to Proverbs 3:5 in relation to docility.

commanding requires three things: foresight (*providentia*), circumspection (*circumspectio*), and caution (*cautio*)[266]—and the greatest of these is foresight: "Foresight is principal among the components of prudence, for all the others are necessary in order that a deed be rightly directed to the end. And so prudence takes its name from providence, that being its main feature."[267] Although some things, which fall under divine providence, are not subject to human providence, "future contingents which a man can shape to the purpose of human life are matters for prudence."[268] "The prudent man," Thomas says at the beginning of the treatise, "thinks about matters far ahead."[269]

Third, prudence depends upon a wider purchase on the order of reason. Prudence, Aquinas stresses, does not appoint the ends, but only regulates the means.[270] As he says in the passage above: "Man is indeed directed to his due end by a virtue which perfects the soul in the appetitive part, the object of which is a good and an end." In this, of course, Aquinas follows Aristotle's principle that "virtue makes the aim right, and practical wisdom the things towards it."[271] Just as Aristotle distinguishes *phronēsis* from mere cleverness,[272] for Aquinas, prudence is never merely an instrumental skill, but the habit by which we realize the *right* ends in action. Prudence cannot exist apart from the moral virtues,[273] because prudence is not merely a capacity to reason, but *right* reason about action.[274] It depends on a purchase on the order of reason. Furthermore, such a purchase cannot be had merely through thinking things through from general principles.[275] General principles, such as that we should do no evil, and the "practical science" that builds upon them are well and good. Yet, when it comes to real, particular situations, they are not enough to secure the aims prudence needs in order to act well. For, "it happens sometimes that general principles known by understanding or science are swept away in the particular case by a passion." For instance, "to one who is overcome by lust, the object of his desire seems good, although it is opposed to the universal judgment of reason."[276] Therefore, in order to be able to see, in the particular instance, what is the right kind of thing to aim at, a person "needs to be

---

266. II-II.48.1.
267. II-II.49.6 ad1.
268. II-II.49.6.
269. II-II.47.1.
270. II-II.47.6.
271. *EN* 6.12, 1144a9, and above, Chapter 1, Section 2. On Aquinas's interpretation of Aristotle here see Tobias Hoffmann, "Prudence and Practical Principles," 165–83.
272. 1144a25–30, and above, Chapter 1, Section 2.
273. I-II.58.5.
274. I-II.58.5; 65.1-2. On this point, see Nelson, *The Priority of Prudence*, 78–81.
275. What follows summarizes the core argument of I-II.58.5.
276. I-II.58.5.

perfected by certain habits, whereby it becomes, as it were, connatural to him to judge rightly about an end. This is done by moral virtue."[277]

Fourth, and for our purposes importantly, the fact that prudence depends upon a purchase on the order of reason, taking its starting points from the ends entailed by virtue, allows Aquinas to think about the work of prudence in terms of syllogistic reasoning. He states,

> Now we must observe that the reason directs human acts in accordance with a twofold knowledge, universal and particular: because in conferring about what is to be done, it employs a syllogism, the conclusion of which is an act of judgment, or of choice, or an operation. Now actions are about singulars: wherefore the conclusion of a practical syllogism is a singular proposition. But a singular proposition does not follow from a universal proposition, except through the medium of a particular proposition.[278]

This thought is fundamental to Aquinas's treatment of prudence. In practical reason, as in theoretical reason, Aquinas says, there are various, "naturally evident," general principles (*principia naturaliter nota*). These "are the ends of moral virtue." But as well as these, practical reason also reaches conclusions about the attainment of these ends, which are "arrived at in the light of those ends" (*in quae pervenimus ex ipsis finibus*).[279] These are what prudence works to, "applying universal principles to the particular conclusions of practice."[280]

In question forty-nine, Aquinas clarifies this point with explicit reference to Aristotle's idea that practical wisdom involves perception of particulars:

---

277. I-II.58.5. Aquinas's phrase for what I have glossed above as "the right thing to aim at" is a "particular principle of action" (*principia particularia agibilium*, I-II.58.5). "Particular principles of action" cannot mean individual actions as such, for that would leave no room for the work of prudence. Nor can it mean the kinds of "intermediate principles" we have seen John Finnis commend, for that is just what he is saying is insufficient. I take it, therefore, to mean right goals—reasonable ends of action—within particular situations. The general principle that adultery is evil may be known in abstract, but in the particular moment what is needed is not simply a general principle, but a particular desire to avoid adultery. This means that the particular principles that virtue supplies are still, in a way, general. They are still *kinds* of action that need to be realized in particular actions. The significance of this will be seen below.

278. I-II.76.1, Benziger Brothers edition; cf. I.86.1 ad. 2. Elsewhere, Aquinas says that "every act, whether virtuous or sinful, requires a certain deduction, syllogistic in nature." *De Malo* 3.9 arg7, quoted in Westberg, *Right Practical Reason*, 211.

279. II-II.47.6.

280. II-II.47.6, my translation: applicans universalia principia ad particulares conclusiones operabilium. See also 47.3, 16 ad3.

The reasoning of prudence terminates, as in a conclusion, in the particular matter of action [*particulare operabile*], to which, as stated above [II-II.47.3, 6], it applies the knowledge of some universal principle [*universalem cognitionem*]. Now a singular conclusion is argued from a universal and a singular proposition [*Conclusio autem singularis syllogizatur ex universali et singulari propositione*]. Wherefore the reasoning of prudence must proceed from a twofold understanding. The one is cognizant of universals, and this belongs to the understanding which is an intellectual virtue, whereby we know naturally not only speculative principles, but also practical universal principles, such as "One should do evil to no man," as shown above [II-II.47.6]. The other understanding, as stated in Ethic. [*EN* 6.11, 1143b3–5], is cognizant of an extreme, i.e. of some primary singular and contingent practical matter, *viz.* the minor premiss, which must needs be singular in the syllogism of prudence, as stated above [II-II.47.3, 6]. Now this primary singular [*principium singular*] is some singular end [*singularis finis*], as stated in the same place. Wherefore the understanding which is a part of prudence is a right estimate of some particular end.[281]

The basic idea here is clear: practical reasoning moves from a general premise to a singular conclusion via a singular premise. Hence, two moments of "understanding" (*intellectus*), that is, knowledge gained non-deductively, are required: apprehension of the general premise and perception of the singular premise. The model is one of subsumption of a particular under a universal. The difficulty comes from speaking of the singular premise as a "singular *end*." Aquinas does this because his goal is to defend the position that prudence involves a kind of understanding in both the major and the minor premise of the practical syllogism.[282] The idea of the major premise involving understanding poses no difficulty, as it is supported by the parallel to theoretical reasoning, which also begins with naturally understood principles. Practical reason has its own naturally known first principles.[283] But the idea of the minor premise involving understanding is trickier, because, as one objection puts it, understanding is about "universal and non-material things,"[284] or as Aquinas says in his commentary on the relevant passage in Aristotle, "understanding has to do with principles."[285] Aquinas overcomes this problem by recognizing that there

---

281. II-II.49.2 ad1.
282. The difference between Aristotle's and Aquinas's position at this point is illuminating. In the relevant text (1143b3–5), Aristotle says that *nous* is concerned with both first terms and last terms, but not at the same time. In practical questions, intellect is concerned "with the last term, which can be otherwise, that is, with the minor premise." Aquinas agrees with this. However, he wants also to argue that the *first* principles of practical reason are known by understanding, through *synderesis*.
283. See I.79.12 on *synderesis*, and also above, Section 1.
284. II-II.49.2 arg3.
285. *SLE* 6.9.14: intellectus est principiorum.

is a way in which the minor premise of a practical syllogism still constitutes a kind of principle (*alicuius principii*).²⁸⁶ Were this not the case, then universals could not be understood from singulars.²⁸⁷ Therefore, insofar as it is mere particularity, the minor premise of a practical syllogism represents only sense-perception.²⁸⁸ But insofar as it is a perception of the way in which a particular instantiates a kind, the minor premise constitutes a principle. It is a "singular end," that is, an end in the singular.

Now, what underpins this point and the wider understanding of prudence in terms of syllogistic reasoning is Aquinas's theory of kinds of action. This point seems to me to be often overlooked. But we are reminded of the theory of kinds when, in the passage with which our discussion began, Aquinas speaks of being directed by virtue to something "*the object* of which is a good and an end."²⁸⁹ As we saw above, at the heart of Aquinas's understanding of action is the thought that actions come in kinds, and that these kinds are determined by ends conceptualized as objects. It is objects that, for Aquinas, fundamentally determine the goodness of the will, because, by framing actions as kinds of actions, they allow actions to be apprehended by reason; and the will can only desire good as it is "apprehended by reason (*a ratione apprehendatur*)."²⁹⁰ This is why prudence is fundamentally syllogistic in form. Prudence works from ends. But ends can only be intended as apprehended by reason,²⁹¹ which means as kinds. The work of prudence, therefore, is fundamentally susceptible to analysis in terms of the subsumption of particulars under kinds.

From this we can also better see why Thomas holds prudence to be necessary. Law and virtue can deal only with kinds of action. Laws concern kinds of action, which are determined by objects. Objects are also the ends aimed at by the will, and so are implied within virtuous desires, and specify the virtues.²⁹² But action is about the realization of kinds of action in particular situations of potentially endless complexity, involving, as Thomas stresses, "an infinity of singulars."²⁹³ Law

---

286. ii-II.49.2 ad3. In *SLE* 6.9.14 Aquinas says that singulars are principia ad modum causae finalis.

287. *SLE* 6.9.15: Et quod singularia habeant rationem principiorum, patet, quia ex singularibus accipitur universale. Ex hoc enim, quod haec herba fecit huic sanitatem, acceptum est, quod haec species herbae valet ad sanandum.

288. See Aquinas's comments in *SLE* 6.1.11-15 about the role of the sensitive powers in practical thinking in his discussion of Aristotle's distinction in *EN* 6.1, discussed briefly in Section 1, above.

289. I-II.57.5, and above; emphasis added.

290. I-II.19.3.

291. See also I-II.12.1.

292. See again I-II.54.2, and our comments above in Section 2, n. 80 and Section 3a. Further discussion is needed regarding the place of law in practical reasoning, for Aquinas. See below, Chapter 3, Section 3b.

293. ii-II.47.15 ad3; cf. ii-II.47.3: Operationes autem sunt in singularibus.

and virtue can thus provide the starting points for action, the general premises of practical reasoning, because "the purpose [*finis*] plays the same role in practical reasoning as the first premise does in demonstrative reasoning."[294] But they cannot prosecute the movement to action. Law can declare the kinds of action that accord with reason, and virtue can shape the will to desire them, but to realize them in action requires a movement of thought, of practical reason, from the universal to the particular, a discernment of how a particular action instantiates an action of a moral kind. To make this movement well is the work of prudence. Prudence rightly prosecutes the movement of practical reason from desired kinds of action to particular acts.

5 Deliberation and the Practical Syllogism

Let us clarify. What we have argued above is that the central feature of Aquinas's account of prudence is the way it unites the idea of thinking from ends to means with a syllogististic conception of reasoning, and that it is the theory of kinds of action that allows this union. Our final task is to discern what this means for the idea of deliberation. Aquinas follows Aristotle in distinguishing a number of aspects of the movement to action, including the key concepts we noted above: choice, or decision (*electio*), and counsel, or deliberation (*consilium*). In Chapter 1, we noted difficulties with the attempt to make a clear-cut distinction between deliberation and choice as two stages of practical reasoning. We suggested that the reason for this is that the determination of the right means to an end, particularly in moral reasoning, is frequently a matter of subsumption, of a discernment about how to construe a particular action, and that this kind of process is analyzable as a syllogism. Daniel Westberg has argued that Aquinas makes a similar distinction between deliberation and choice, or decision, as part of his theory of action.[295] He writes:

> Deliberation and decision differ with respect to their ordering in the process of practical reasoning, their function, and their style of reasoning. While deliberation starts with an end and proceeds to identify a means or series of means to achieve the desired end, decision is a process of reasoning about a particular means or action in relation to actually achieving that end.[296]

Deliberation works discursively from a fixed end to the best means. Decision realizes the relation between the end and a means in action. One is about "specification" of

---

294. I-II.54.2 ad3. See also I-II.90.1.

295. Westberg, *Right Practical Reason*, 119–35. Westberg's arguments on this point reappear in his more recent *Renewing Moral Theology: Christian Ethics as Action, Character, and Grace* (Downer's Grove, IL: IVP, 2015), 45–57.

296. Westberg, *Right Practical Reason*, 149.

means, the other is about "choice" of an action.[297] The practical syllogism, Westberg says, properly belongs only to the latter. "The practical syllogism is a psychological account of human decision," an explanation of voluntary action.[298]

Westberg argues that this distinction has significant consequences for the place of law in Aquinas's system. Aquinas, he suggests, sees law as having a direct role in practical reasoning only "when the agent does not know the right relation of means to end."[299] Only with deliberation, that is, is law considered explicitly, although it is always implicitly relevant.[300] The significance of this is that it means Thomas does not see law, "as a source of moral action,"[301] in the sense of a motivating force.[302] Law is "a standard by which to judge the rightness and wrongness of actions,"[303] but it is not the thing that generates action. That is the perception of the relationship between action and the good, which is what is established in the syllogistic process of decision.[304] This, Westberg argues, allows Aquinas to avoid the problems associated with legalism.[305]

Westberg's overall reconstruction of Aquinas's theory of action is persuasive. He is surely right to highlight the ways in which Aquinas sees a complex interrelationship between reason and will at work in action. He is also right that Thomas distinguishes between deliberation-consent and judgment-choice. This is clear, for example, in Aquinas's discussion of whether consent is about the end or the means. One objection to the idea that consent is about the means is that this would make consent identical to choice.[306] Not so, insists Aquinas, because consent and choice are different kinds of acts of will. Consent is about the approval of a means, or indeed more than one means, as good; choice is about a preference for one means in particular.[307] *Electio*, moreover, clearly *is* specially related to the practical syllogism: "The conclusion of a practical syllogism is the work of reason; it is ... called the sentence [*sententia*] or judgment [*judicium*], from which choice [*electio*] follows."[308] Westberg also highlights Aquinas's assertion that "when the judgment about an action is clear, then deliberation is not required."[309] We can

---

297. Westberg, *Right Practical Reason*, 127, 130.
298. Westberg, *Right Practical Reason*, 154.
299. Westberg, *Right Practical Reason*, 174.
300. Westberg, *Right Practical Reason*, 239. Cf. 1-II.90.1.
301. Westberg, *Right Practical Reason*, 240.
302. Westberg, *Right Practical Reason*, 153–4.
303. Westberg, *Right Practical Reason*, 240.
304. Westberg, *Right Practical Reason*, 234–8.
305. Westberg, *Right Practical Reason*, 23–39, 240–4.
306. 1-II.15.3 arg3.
307. 1-II.15.3 ad3.
308. 1-II.13.1 ad2.
309. Westberg, *Right Practical Reason*, 147; cf. 1-II.14.4 ad.1. It is noteworthy, though, that in the body of the article, Thomas makes it clear that the things he has in mind are of two kinds: things that have a fixed way of being done, like how to write letters, and

agree with Westberg, then, that, formally speaking, deliberation and decision are for Aquinas two different kinds of movement: one concerns approval of a course of action, the other is already setting out upon it.

This distinction may not, however, be quite as neat in practice as Westberg argues it is. In particular, it is difficult to sustain the view that this distinction correlates to the presence or absence of syllogistic reasoning. The problem is that deliberation and decision overlap at least in that both begin, in a sense, from the end. In relation to choice, which is exercised through the practical syllogism, Aquinas says that "the end stands like a principle, not a conclusion."[310] But the same point is relevant to deliberation. Deliberation has to take an end for granted.[311] Yet deliberation, like decision, may be indirectly about ends, for it may be, "that an end in one situation is subordinate to the end in another, as, to draw the parallel, a premise in one demonstration may be the conclusion in another."[312] Aquinas draws similar analogies elsewhere. For example, in discussing *euboulia*, the virtue that corresponds to deliberation, Aquinas draws an analogy between end–means reasoning and syllogistic inference: "There is no good counsel either in deliberating for an evil end, or in discovering evil means for attaining a good end, even as in speculative matters, there is no good reasoning either in coming to a false conclusion, or in coming to a true conclusion from false premises through employing an unsuitable middle term."[313] These parallels between ends and premises remind us that deliberation navigates territory that can be charted by the practical syllogism.

Westberg's argument about the motive force of decision hinges on the idea that in decision, a connection is established between action and the first, fundamental principle of practical reason, namely "do good and avoid evil."[314] This first principle "remains the basic ground of all voluntary action."[315] There is, however, a problem with this argument, which is that a movement of thought to an action that begins from the first principle—the good is to be pursued and done, the evil avoided—is not susceptible to analysis as a simple syllogism, but is necessarily more complex. The processes of thought that Westberg discusses under the heading of choice, which move from an end to an action through a means, reflect this. He discusses two examples from Aquinas that have to do with sexual temptation.[316] In the first,

---

things that are of minute importance. Some of Westberg's examples do not fall into these categories. Anticipating our argument in what follows, it is possible that what Aquinas means here is simply that in some cases, subsumption is not complicated and so does not acquire the character of an act of deliberation.

310. I-II.13.3.
311. I-II.14.2.
312. I-II.14.2; cf. 13.3.
313. II-II.51.1 ad1, Benziger Brothers edition. See also Aquinas's comments on craftiness as a sin in II-II.55.3.
314. Westberg, *Right Practical Reason*, 162–3; cf. I-II.94.2.
315. Westberg, *Right Practical Reason*, 163, 236.
316. Westberg, *Right Practical Reason*, 150–2.

Thomas moves from "evil is to be avoided," through "adultery is evil," to "this adultery is to be avoided." Westberg correctly observes that this syllogism is missing a step: the perception that "This is adultery." He suggests that Thomas's syllogism would be better constructed as: "Evil is to be avoided; this act is evil because it is adultery; this act of adultery is to be avoided." This solution is problematic, however. For now the second item has become a complex premise, involving its own kind of "perception": that adultery is evil. In fact, this example cannot be reduced to a simple syllogism, but requires a two-part chain of reasoning: A. Evil is to be avoided; adultery is evil; adultery is to be avoided. B. Adultery is to be avoided; this is an act of adultery; this act is to be avoided. The same is true of the other example Westberg refers to here, in which Thomas moves from "nothing prohibited by the law of God is to be done," through "lying with this woman is prohibited by the law of God," to "this sexual union must be avoided." Again, Westberg points out that there has also been a conflation, because the law speaks only of kinds, and so in order for sexual intercourse with a particular person to be in view there must be a further term, for instance, lying with another man's wife is prohibited by the law of God. But then we have again a more complex chain of reasoning. The logic would have to run: A. Nothing prohibited by the law must be done; x kind of act is prohibited; x kind of act must not be done. B. x kind of act must not be done; this is an instance of x kind of act; this must not be done.

This hidden complexity is not limited to these examples. Westberg's first example in his discussion of the syllogistic structure of decision highlights this. He imagines a woman who through deliberation has determined that getting up early and walking to work are the best way to get fit. He goes on like this. "Now the decision to act: 'I want to become fit; getting up early to walk is the best way to start; I'd better set the alarm clock for 6:00. There!'"[317] This description, however, conceals the fact that there are actually two syllogisms contained within this one. First, I want to get fit; getting up early and walking are the best way to get fit; I will get up early and walk to work. Second, I want to get up early and walk to work; to do that, I need to set the alarm. There, I've set it.

This complexity is irreducible, if the starting point is a generalized first principle like "do good" or "act well." Westberg's condensed form of the syllogism—Do good and avoid evil; this is good; do this[318]—obscures this fact. The problem is that in any actual case, the process would be more complex and extended. We cannot move to a particular action—pour a drink of water, give my wife a kiss, limit the amount of time my daughter spends watching television—simply by derivation from the universal premise, do good. Other, more proximate determinations are necessary—it is good to have enough to drink, it is good to show my wife I love her, it is good to make sure my children do not watch too much television. But each of these is complex, to a greater or lesser extent. Moreover, each of these requires further difficult discernments: how much water is enough? Is the water

---

317. Westberg, *Right Practical Reason*, 149–50.
318. Westberg, *Right Practical Reason*, 163.

clean? Am I kissing my wife to show her I love her, or out of my own anxiety? How much television is too much? Do I need to be flexible today because she is tired? The result is that the ideal pattern Westberg describes relates to no actual process of practical reasoning. In fact, practical reasoning, if it begins from first principles, always requires a longer, and more complex, chain of reasoning. Westberg's account of decision as giving to action the motive force of the first principle of practical reason only works by subtly incorporating into the process of decision thinking that is strictly deliberative.

The above analysis might appear to take us back to the kind of two-stage picture of practical reasoning described by Cooper in relation to Aristotle. In the first stage, practical reason moves *to* the choice of a kind of action. In the second stage, practical reason moves from this choice to a particular action. The reality remains more complex, however. In fact, the one process of reasoning is often simultaneously deliberative and decisive. This is because, as we argued in Chapter 1, especially in relation to moral questions, the determination of the right means to an end is often a matter of how to construe an action. That is, it is a kind of perception. It is a great virtue of Westberg's work to have highlighted the role of perception of particulars in Aquinas's thought. The difference between good and bad action, he sees Aquinas as saying, arises particularly as a result of how a situation is interpreted.[319] Prudence is "mainly a matter of seeing things in the right way so that proper judgments about good and bad can be made."[320] Prudence is finally about judgment, right apprehension of situations under the guidance of law and the Holy Spirit.[321] The key to prudent action using the syllogistic pattern, writes Westberg, "is in the accurate perception of the quality of actions."[322] With all this we can gladly agree. The word "quality," though, gives away the fact that this perception can have deliberative, as well as decisive, significance. Determining the right means to an end is frequently a matter of perception of the quality of an action: that this or that particular action would instantiate this or that kind of action.

This is why in practice the complex, two-stage, process of practical reasoning is frequently truncated, and the two minor premises are collapsed into each other, as happens in each of Aquinas's sexual examples: "*x* kind of lying with someone is prohibited," and "lying with this woman would be *x* kind of lying with someone," becomes "lying with this woman is prohibited." "Adultery is evil," and "this is adultery," becomes "this act is evil because it is adultery." Rather than preceding decision as a prior stage, deliberation is implied within the process of decision.

---

319. Westberg, *Right Practical Reason*, 213.
320. Westberg, *Right Practical Reason*, 240.
321. Westberg, *Right Practical Reason*, 244.
322. Westberg, *Right Practical Reason*, 149; cf. 204–13. Jean Porter makes the same point by talking about how the role of prudence is to determine what, in concrete circumstances, "will best instantiate the mean of a given virtue" (*The Recovery of Virtue*, 159).

We can further illustrate this point by considering another passage in the treatise on prudence, which also allows us to recall Aquinas's understanding of kinds of action as we conclude:

> We have seen that the main function of prudence is to order things well for an end or purpose. This cannot be done aright unless the end be good, and also the means be good and adapted to the end [*conveniens fini*]. Yet because prudence is about individual actions [*singularia operabilia*], as we have explained [II-II.47.3], and these involve many factors, it may happen that a means good and suitable in the abstract becomes bad and inopportune owing to a combination of circumstances. For instance, to display affection for someone seems in itself to be well-calculated to touch his heart [*secundum se consideratum videtur esse conveniens ad alliciendum eius animum ad amorem*], yet if in fact his mood be haughty or suspicious of flattery, then it will not be well-designed for its purpose [*conveniens ad finem*]. Accordingly prudence calls for circumspection in order that what is done for an end may match the circumstances of the situation.[323]

We may begin by noting the ways in which this example illustrates aspects of Aquinas's theory of kinds of action. First, when we ask what kind of action this is, we see that it may be viewed from two perspectives: as an external act and as an internal act. The external act is specified by the object "to display signs of affection." This is what the pat on Fred's back or friendly hug *is*, considered in the abstract. Morally speaking, however, the more important question is what kind of act this is as an act of the will. Here, the object that specifies the action is "to arouse love in his heart" (or perhaps "to encourage"). That is *what* I am trying to do; it is the end I intend that constitutes the object of the internal act. Second, the example illustrates a point Thomas makes in question eighteen about circumstances. Particular circumstances may make an act good or bad, because they may materially alter the nature of the object of the act.[324] In this case, Fred's suspiciousness may turn what was intended to be an act of love into an act of flattery. This would be an error of reason on my part. Failing to grasp the reality of the situation, I willed something (a pat on the back) as good (encouraging to Fred) which was in fact evil (flattery).[325] Third, whether this failure of reason is

---

323. II-II.49.7.
324. I-II.18.10.
325. For many, this may be the hardest part of Aquinas's thinking to understand. It neatly highlights the difference between Aquinas's perspective and some modern perspectives, such as Kant's. For Aquinas, in the end, the goodness of actions is never purely a function of the quality of the will, but always involves *what is in fact willed*. If in fact what was willed was an act that effected flattery, then the action lacks in goodness, even if it is not wholly bad. Compare, by contrast, Kant's statement that "A good will is not good because of what it

culpable or not depends on whether I ought to have known how Fred would take the pat on the back. If Fred is generally a trusting and modest fellow, then perhaps my ignorance was not culpable. This would mean that what had in fact happened was that I had acted involuntarily—I did something I did not will at all. If, on the other hand, this was something I should have known—perhaps I know that Fred has just been betrayed by a friend—then I might be culpable for this failure of reason.[326] Prudence calls for circumspection, Thomas maintains.[327] Fourth, if we extend the example we can be reminded of the possibility that the act of the will may not quite match the intention. To display signs of affection seems in itself to be well-calculated to touch Fred's heart, but it might not be in fact. It might have hardly any effect on Fred. My intention may simply have been better than what I willed,[328] because I calculated wrongly.

This leads us back to the question of deliberation. The example also shows us that in the process of thinking to action, the external and internal actions are related as means and end. Encouraging Fred is the end, displaying signs of affection is the means. But this means may not actually be a good means, given the circumstances. The awareness that Fred is suspicious of flattery may cause us to rethink our choice to show him signs of love. Why is that? Because these signs might no longer touch his heart, but instead only arouse suspicion. As we have just noted, what this amounts to is the recognition that the action in question, which considered from without remains the same pat on the back, may turn out to be different in kind to what we intended: it is an act of flattery rather than of encouragement.

The interesting thing is that this is not really a process of discursive deliberation, in which an end is fixed and the agent is trying to find the best means. The question is not about a choice *between* various means to an end, but about one particular kind of action, and what it would amount to in a given situation. The end—touching Fred's heart—is not fixed, but in a way in question. The whole process only makes sense if this aim is referred to a more fundamental one, of acting well or doing good. If showing signs of love turns out not to be a fitting way to touch Fred's heart, then it may be that touching Fred's heart should not after all be aimed at. The end and the means arise together as a possible way of acting well. Yet neither is this simply a process of decision, in Westberg's sense, where all that is required is the recognition that "*this* is the best way to touch Fred's heart." A real, deliberative

---

effects or accomplishes, because of its fitness to attain some proposed end, but only because of its volition" (*Groundwork of the Metaphysics of Morals*, trans. Mary Gregor [Cambridge: Cambridge University Press, 1998], 8 [4:394]). In contrast to the famous beginning of the *Groundwork*, for Aquinas the will can only be good *because* it is possible to think of something "in the world, or indeed even beyond it, that could be considered good without limitation" (7 [4:393]).

326. See I-II.6.8; 19.6.
327. II-II.49.7, and above.
328. I-II.19.8.

question is raised here by the perception that at the moment Fred is in a haughty mood, or susceptible to flattery. But the form of this deliberative enquiry is not a choice between different means to an end, but about the meaning of one particular means in a certain situation. It is a question of whether this kind of action would turn out to constitute a way of encouraging Fred, or to be something different. The whole difficulty, as we said earlier, lies in determining what the truly important "end" *is* in this situation. This determination is primarily a matter of perception, of how to construe one particular, proposed kind of action; it is about how it "seems." This is why it is a work of prudence, a work of perception of particulars. The reference back to question forty-seven emphasizes this point. There Thomas develops the fundamental point we highlighted above, that prudence involves the subsumption of particulars under universals: "actions are in singular matters: and so it is necessary for the prudent man to know both the universal principles of reason, and the singulars about which actions are concerned."[329] What we have here, that is to say, is a process of deliberation in which the determination of the means is essentially a matter of perception of particulars.

In practice, the clear, two-stage process of a (discursive) deliberative journey from an end to a choice of means followed by a (syllogistic) decision which moves from the choice of means to the doing of the action is complicated by the fact that deliberation is frequently a matter of perception, the discernment of the meaning and significance of proposed actions and their consequent relation to proposed ends, and that the perception of particulars very often has consequences that are strictly deliberative. We have here a good example of the point we raised against Cooper's contention that the subsumption of the particular under a kind is a simple process, and not really part of practical reason. On the contrary, as David Wiggins reminded us earlier, the reality of putting into action a choice of a kind of act may cause us to rethink that choice in the light of the end. The circumstances may make what appeared to be a good choice problematic. The subsumption of particulars under universals may be precisely what deliberation involves, and where, in a particular situation, the challenge lies for practical reasoning.

Arguably, this fact—that deliberation is often a matter of discerning how in particular circumstances actions ought to be construed, and so can take the form of the subsumption of particulars under universals—explains why many have failed to appreciate the distinction between deliberation and decision that Westberg argues Thomas makes.[330] This does not mean that Aquinas never makes such a distinction. It may be, however, that this distinction does not hold the weight for Aquinas that Westberg claims it does. This would have implications for Westberg's wider argument. In particular, it calls into question Westberg's claim about the place of law in Thomas's thinking. If the practical syllogism frequently has deliberative, as well as decisive significance, then law should not be excluded

---

329. II-II.47.3, Benziger Brothers edition.
330. See Westberg, *Right Practical Reason*, 119–35; cf. McInerny, "Ethics," 205–8; and MacIntyre, *Whose Justice?*, 190–1.

as a "source" of action. As we noted above, law, like virtue, can provide the major premises of practical syllogisms, because it declares the kinds of action that accord with reason. And kinds of action are determined by their objects, which are the ends of internal acts. For Aquinas, thinking about ends means thinking about kinds of action, and this exposes practical reason to the judgments of eternal reason, and of wisdom. For wisdom, we recall, "judges things according to divine truth."[331]

Conclusion

Jean-Pierre Torrell writes of Aquinas that "everything he owes to Aristotle or other thinkers, Stoics and the like, is radically transformed, not to say subverted from within, by the simple fact of identifying the God of Jesus Christ with the Good that all men pursue, even without knowing it."[332] When it comes to Aquinas's account of practical reason, there is undoubtedly truth in this statement. By anchoring practical reason in eternal, divine reason, Aquinas puts Aristotle's conception of practical reason in a quite different setting. The instabilities in Aristotle's account produced by its dependence on the *polis* are steadied. Kinds of action, the lynch-pin for relating a teleological account of the moral life to a syllogistic conception of moral reasoning, are anchored in the eternal law; and the ambiguities in the relation of theory and practice are, at least to some extent, explained. Moreover, recognition of the significance of the coming of Christ opens practical reason to a further horizon that demands we look beyond natural powers for insight. Aquinas's distinction between the natural and supernatural ends of human life is a way of allowing the gospel to introduce something genuinely new into practical thinking. Nevertheless, there are questions to be asked about whether Aquinas's appropriation of Aristotle is quite what is required by Christian theology. Certain aspects of Aristotle's thought appear to go unchallenged, such as the idea of making as executing a preconceived form, the idea of reasoning from an end to the means, and the assumption that wisdom is a perfection of speculative knowledge. Susan Parsons has written that "It is at least arguable that the reconciliation performed by St Thomas Aquinas between Aristotle's philosophical analyses and Christian faith brought *techne* into a then unforeseen prominence," and suggested that this introduced various distortions into theological thinking.[333] Should, therefore, Aquinas be praised for overcoming the weaknesses implicit in Aristotle's

---

331. II-II.45.1 ad2, and above Section 1.

332. Torrell, *Saint Thomas Aquinas, Volume 2*, 270.

333. Susan F. Parsons, "The Practice of Christian Ethics: Mindfulness and Faith," *Studies in Christian Ethics* 25, no. 4 (2012): 448.

account, and giving it a solid foundation? Or should, perhaps, the identification of the good that all seek with the God of Jesus Christ have led him in some different directions? These are the questions we hope to address by looking at the book of Proverbs, and what it says about the wisdom that the Lord "got" at the beginning of his way, by which he "established the earth," who "dwells with prudence" (Prov. 3:19; 8:12, 22), but who also, ultimately, must be seen in the light of Jesus Christ.

Chapter 3

PRACTICAL REASON AND THE WAYS OF WISDOM

By wisdom a house is built.

—Prov. 24:3

Introduction

The theological foundation of Aquinas's understanding of eternal law, and so his overall understanding of good and evil action, lies in the idea that God created the world "through his wisdom."[1] As we have seen, the most important biblical exposition of this idea, for Aquinas, is Proverbs ch. 8. This text provides him with a crucial biblical ground for the eternity of eternal law, the derivation of all laws from eternal law, and the idea that eternal law encompasses "every motion and every act in the whole universe."[2] This chapter attempts to allow the book of Proverbs to speak in its own, distinctive voice about the questions we have identified in terms of the nature and foundation of practical reasoning, and to see how this compares to the perspectives of Aquinas and, to a lesser extent, Aristotle. It begins from this most important point of contact in Proverbs ch. 8, exploring the challenges this text presents and the different ways it has been understood (Section 1). It is then suggested that the key to reading this text lies in the wider account of wisdom in the book of Proverbs (Section 2). Wisdom in Proverbs is inextricably linked to action. It can be understood as a kind of practical knowledge that arises out of the character of the world. Wisdom is about the way creation extends hospitality to good action. This account of wisdom in Proverbs has significant implications for aspects of Aquinas's system. The final section of this chapter (Section 3) explores these. It suggests that the idea of eternal law is problematic, because of its dependence on a speculative conception of divine wisdom. It also suggests that several features of Aquinas's account of prudence and deliberation make more sense when we think along lines made available by Proverbs. This discussion opens a number of constructive possibilities for thinking about the nature of created order and the shape of moral deliberation. The following chapters seek to develop

---

1. *ST* I-II.93.1, and above, Chapter 2, Section 3b.
2. *ST* I-II.93.5.

these further, first by engaging with the work of Oliver O'Donovan (Chapter 4), and then by elaborating them more directly, by way of conclusion (Chapter 5).

1 The Puzzle of Proverbs Chapter Eight

In seeing the voice of wisdom in Proverbs 8 as the voice of Christ, Aquinas follows a well-worn path of patristic exegesis. We may fruitfully begin from this point.

At the beginning of the fourth of his Five Theological Orations, Oration 30, Gregory of Nazianzus makes the following argument about Proverbs 8:

> This is one passage they have very ready at hand: "The Lord created me as the beginning of his ways for his works." How are we to treat it? Are we not to denounce Solomon? Shall we not cancel his earlier words because of his later lapse? Must we not take the statement as that of Wisdom herself in the poetical sense of the skill, the systematic principle on which the universe is composed [*ton logon, tēs hoion epistēmēs kai tou technitou logou, kath hon ta panta sunestē*]. Scripture consciously personifies many inanimate objects; for example "The Sea said such and such," "The Deep said, 'It is not in me,'" and "The Heavens declare the glory of God." A sword, to continue the examples, is given an order; mountains and hills are asked why they skip. We adopt neither of these approaches, though they have been taken as forceful by some of our predecessors. No, let the statement stand as that of the Savior himself, the true Wisdom. Let us look at it together for a moment. What reality has no cause? Godhead—no one can talk of the "cause of God," otherwise it would be prior to God. But what is cause of the manhood, which God submitted to for us? Our salvation, of course, what else could it be? The passage is now free of complication, seeing that we find there clearly both expressions "created" and "begets me." Whatever we come across with a causal implication we will attribute to the humanity; what is absolute and free of cause we will reckon to the Godhead. "Created" has a causal implication, has it not? The text in fact runs: "He created me as the beginning of his ways *for his works*." "The works of his hands are truth and judgment," and for the sake of these works he was anointed with deity—deity being the humanity's anointing. But the expression, "begets me," has no causal implication—indicate, if you can, some qualifying term (*proskeimenon*) for it. What objection will there be, then, to Wisdom's being called "creature" in respect to earthly generation, but "offspring" with regard to the primal and less comprehensible one?[3]

---

3. Gregory of Nazianzus, *On God and Christ: The Five Theological Orations and Two Letters to Cledonius*, trans. L. Wickham (Crestwood: St. Vladimir's Seminary Press, 2002). Greek text from A. J. Mason, ed., *The Five Theological Orations of Gregory of Nazianzus* (Cambridge: Cambridge University Press, 1899).

In seeing Wisdom in Proverbs 8 as referring to the Son, and understanding the different statements as corresponding to the two natures of Christ, Gregory was following an established strategy of interpretative opposition to Arian theology. Athanasius, in particular, had forcefully championed this interpretation of the passage.[4] It is interesting, however, that Gregory makes some space to note the possibility of interpreting the passage along a different line, and seeing Wisdom as a kind of cosmological ordering logic, a *logos* of knowledge and skill according to which "all things were constituted." We will see that this summary of the interpretative options still basically covers the field.

Gregory maintains that with the orthodox interpretation the passage is freed of complication. Two features of the Septuagint translation of Proverbs 8 make this judgment seem optimistic. First, in the Hebrew text, the verb in v. 22 (*qnh*) usually means "got" or "acquired," rather than "created," as it is translated in the LXX (*ektisen*). In the context of the book of Proverbs as a whole the argument for that translation is strong. Other than the present case, the verb is used ten times, and in each instance there is no difficulty understanding it to mean "get" or "acquire."[5] Sometimes the verb is connected to terminology to do with money and transactions, making this meaning all the more secure.[6] Furthermore, in every case, the thing that is "gotten" is wisdom, or some related idea. The exhortation in 4:5 and 7, *qĕnēh ḥokmâ*, "Get wisdom," could be said to represent the flagship use of the verb in Proverbs. These considerations strongly suggest that in 8:22 we ought to seek to understand what it might mean for Wisdom to say that the Lord "got me" or "acquired me."[7]

---

4. See, for example, *De Decretis* 3.13-14; *Ad Episcopos Aegypti Et Libyae Epistola* 2.17; and, especially, "Four Discourses Against the Arians" [*Orationes Contra Arianos*] 2.19.44-82; 2.20.53. (*NPNF*, Series II, Vol. 4.)

5. Prov. 1:5; 4:5, 7; 15:32; 16:16; 17:16; 18:15; 19:8; 20:14; 23:23.

6. See Prov. 16:16; 17:16; 20:14; 23:23.

7. The verb *qnh* can mean, as the LXX renders it in Proverbs 8 (*ektisen*), "create." See especially Gen. 14:19, 22; Deut. 32:6; and Ps. 139:13; and Michael Fox, *Proverbs 1-9* (Anchor Bible; New York: Doubleday, 2000), 280. Against Fox, however, the difference between these translations is not moot. Certainly, "one way something can be acquired is by creation" (p. 279). However, it matters whether that specific implication is present here. As a variant of *both* "create" and "get," the meaning "beget" or "bring forth" has also been urged. See, for example, Bruce Waltke, *Proverbs 1-15* (New International Commentary on the Old Testament; Grand Rapids: Eerdmans, 2004), 408-10; Roland E. Murphy, *Proverbs* (Word Biblical Commentary 22; Nashville: Thomas Nelson, 1998), 48, 52; and Daniel J. Treier, *Proverbs & Ecclesiastes* (Brazos Theological Commentary on the Bible; Grand Rapids: Brazos, 2011), 48. The argument for such a translation, however, rests largely on the parallel with *ḥôlāltî* in 8:24 and 25, as well as what is seen to be a gain in sense. Against this has to be weighed the fact that "acquire" or "get" is far more common in the Old Testament, and is the way the word is consistently used in Proverbs. If sense can be made of "get," it should be preferred. See also Bruce Vawter, "Prov 8:22: Wisdom and Creation," *Journal of Biblical*

The second point to note concerns the phrase "for his works" (*eis erga autou*) in the second half of v. 22. This phrase allows Gregory, and Athanasius before him,[8] to distinguish the relation in v. 22 from that in vv. 23 and 24. The former implies causation—"cause" meaning, in this case, "final cause"—but "the expression, 'begets me,' has no causal implication." Combined with the verb "create," this allows Gregory to interpret v. 22 as referring to the incarnation. The "works" of God in question are his works of redemption: "What is cause of the manhood, which God submitted to for us? Our salvation, of course, what else could it be?" The problem with this is that the Hebrew text does not say "for his works" at this point, but rather, "the beginning of his deeds of old" (*qedem mipʿālāyw mēʾāz*). In the Hebrew text, it is much more difficult to see a distinction between the relation described in v. 22 and that described in vv. 23 and 24.

It is better to see the whole poem in vv. 22-31 as describing a single story of Wisdom's primordial relation to the LORD.[9]

The LORD got me at the beginning of his way, the first of his ancient deeds.
Out of time before, I was formed—before the origins of the earth.
When the deeps yet were not, I was brought forth; when there were no springs flush with water.
Before the mountains were settled, before the hills, I was brought forth.
When he had not yet made earth and its spaces, or the first dust of the ground;
When he fixed the heavens, there I was; when he inscribed a circle on the face of the deep;
When he made the skies above firm; when he strengthened the fountains of the deep.
When he set a limit for the sea, so the waters should not transgress his command;
When he inscribed the foundations of the earth:
I was beside him reliably [ʾāmôn]; and I was his delight, day by day, always playing before him, playing in the world his earth, and delighting in humankind.[10]

Literature 99, no. 2 (1980): 205-16; and Stuart Weeks, *Instruction and Imagery in Proverbs 1-9* (Oxford: Oxford University Press, 2007), 180. A final alternative, "possess," was the option known to Aquinas (*Dominus possedit me*), but it is not preferable, as the verb far more commonly refers to the process of coming into possession than to an ongoing state of possessing. See again Fox, *Proverbs 1-9*, 279.

8. See Athansius, *Orationes Contra Arianos* 2.20.56; cf. 2.19.50 (*NPNF*, Series II, Vol. 4.).

9. See also Treier, *Proverbs & Ecclesiastes*, 52-3.

10. The meaning of ʾāmôn in v. 30 is uncertain. It may mean either "little child," "Schoßkind"—see Gerlinde Baumann, *Die Weisheitsgestalt in Proverbien 1-9* (Forschungen zum Alten Testament 16; Tübingen: Mohr, 1996), 131-8; and Katharine Dell, *The Book of Proverbs in Social and Theological Context* (Cambridge: Cambridge University Press, 2006), 143; or "faithfully"—see Stuart Weeks, "The Context and Meaning of Proverbs

It is not that there is no way to find a reference to eternity in these phrases. Verse 23, in particular, can be taken to imply that Wisdom's formation goes back forever (*mē ʿôlām*). However, such a thought must be balanced against what appears to be the main emphasis of the poem: that Wisdom was "formed,"[11] "brought forth,"[12] or "gotten" by God prior to and for the sake of his creative work, so that she was present throughout this work, making some sort of impact upon it.[13] Wisdom was "gotten" as a *beginning* of God's creative activity, the start of his *way* (*rē ʾšît darkô*).[14]

There are also features of the passage that make Wisdom appear as a reality that is immanent within the creaturely realm. The same vocabulary is used of "Lady Wisdom" and human wisdom.[15] "By me (*bî*) kings reign," says Wisdom

---

30a," *Journal of Biblical Literature* 125, no. 3 (2006): 433-42; and Waltke, *Proverbs 1-15*, 391, 420. However, there are also good arguments for taking it to mean "craftsman," including the association between wisdom and house-building in chapter 9, and elsewhere in Proverbs. See Raymond C. Van Leeuwen, *Proverbs* (New Interpreter's Bible, Vol. 5; Nashville: Abingdon, 1997), 94-5. Although this connection will be important in what follows, I have here opted for a less adventurous translation that still makes room for the conceptuality of craftsmanship ("reliably"), on the basis of Weeks's argument that *ʾāmôn* is a noun/adjective being used adverbially to mean "faithfully." However, I am not persuaded by his argument that this is a reference to Wisdom's ongoing presence with God throughout history. In contrast to Weeks (and, following him, Treier—*Proverbs & Ecclesiastes*, 47-8), I do not think the second aspect of his argument is required for the first. I think, rather, that the idea is that Wisdom was present, faithfully, throughout the process of creation. This understanding rests partly on the argument in Section 2, below.

11. It is probably right to read *nissaktî* as the niphal of *skk*, or its by-form *nsk*, rather than as from the main form of *nsk*, meaning "pour out," which would imply an idea of appointing. See Waltke, *Proverbs 1-15*, 411; and Fox, *Proverbs 1-9*, 281. The verb may suggest a metaphor of weaving. The arguments for this rest largely on the parallel in Ps. 139:13, which also uses *qnh*.

12. The verb *ḥyl* in vv. 24 and 25 is used more widely than of natural begetting, as, for instance, in the closely parallel Psalm 90:2: "Before the mountains were birthed, or you brought forth (*watĕḥôlēl*) the earth and the world."

13. These words are chosen carefully, partly given the contested meaning of v. 30a. Fox argues that, in fact, the figure of Wisdom "was not an active agent in creation" (*Proverbs 1-9*, 354). However, Wisdom's presence at this early moment, and apparent connection to God's ordering of creation, which closely parallels Job 28:25-27, suggests that her presence makes some impact. Below, we will argue for a way of understanding wisdom as having an impact of creation that does not depend on v. 30a.

14. The precise significance of v. 22 is crucial, and we will return to it below. For now, however, I note that in my view, Treier's argument that these phrases are generally "trying to convey Wisdom's distinctiveness, not her fit within creaturely patterns" (*Proverbs & Ecclesiastes*, 48-9), while fair so far as it goes does not adequately take in the way in which these phrases are also trying to describe a particular, distinctive relation to creation.

15. Fox, *Proverbs 1-9*, 354.

(vv. 15-16). "In the path of justice I walk, on the tracks of judgment" (v. 20). These statements imply a link between the figure of Wisdom and wisdom in human action. Other passages in Proverbs make this point more strikingly. "She is a tree of life for those who grasp onto her," declares 3:18. If Wisdom is something that can be "taken hold of," "grasped," it surely cannot be simply a divine attribute. Perhaps most importantly, Wisdom consistently "calls" from locations within creation—from crossroads, heights, in public spaces.[16] These factors lead Katharine Dell to the conclusion that "Wisdom as presented in Proverbs is a two-sided coin; there is the human side and there is the divine, and, in my view, the figure of Wisdom provides a bridge that links the two."[17] Similarly, Gerlinde Baumann concludes, "Die Weisheitsgestalt vereinigt in sich göttliche und menschliche Weisheit."[18]

These observations create difficulties for the assumption that the voice of Wisdom in these verses must be the voice of, as Gregory puts it, "the Savior himself, the true Wisdom." If the eternal, divine Son is in view, then his eternity and consubstantiality with God seem to be in jeopardy. The alternative thought, that it might somehow be the human nature of Christ that is speaking, not just in v. 22 but throughout the passage, should not be hastily rejected. Clearly, however, it has challenges to overcome: it has, as Robert Jenson points out, an unsettlingly "Antiochene ring" to it.[19] It also requires us to explain what it means for Christ's human nature to pre-exist creation, as well as why it would be personified as female.[20]

It should be stressed, however, that the passage is theologically challenging even without the assumption that the voice of Wisdom is somehow the voice of Christ.[21] For the central, difficult thought is the way in which Wisdom is differentiated from the Lord himself. The Lord "gets" wisdom, brings it forth somehow before the

---

16. Prov. 8:1-3; cf. 1:20-21; 9:1-6.

17. Dell, *The Book of Proverbs*, 129.

18. Baumann, *Die Weisheitsgestalt*, 312. Translation: "The figure of Wisdom unites in herself divine and human wisdom." It seems to me that Treier underestimates these points in arguing that "the exhortation to choose Wisdom instead of, not just better than, such creaturely treasures, hints at a qualitative distinction according to which Wisdom is divinely valuable, associated first with the Creator rather than just the creature" (*Proverbs & Ecclesiastes*, 53). While Wisdom is indeed divinely valuable, She is also available within the world as a possibility of human action. While in the end I agree with Treier that Jesus Christ is "the resolution of a mystery latent in the text" (p. 51), Treier's discussion lacks a thick explanation of how human action can be "by wisdom," and how wisdom can be "taken hold of."

19. Robert Jenson, *Systematic Theology, Volume 2: The Works of God* (Oxford: Oxford University Press, 1999), 159.

20. These problems lead Jenson to suggest that the voice of Wisdom in these verses is the voice of the *totus Christus*, Israel, and the church. *Systematic Theology, Volume 2*, 159. We will return to this suggestion below.

21. Cf. Treier, *Proverbs and Ecclesiastes*, 46.

origin of his creative work. Wisdom is present at God's side and "before" him. Yet, is it not strange to think of God as going from not having wisdom to having it? Athanasius would ask, "Has not a man himself lost his mind who even entertains the thought that God was ever without Reason and without Wisdom?"[22]

This might appear to lead us back to the second interpretative option noted by Gregory: to say that the wisdom spoken of here is not after all *God's* wisdom in the sense of a divine attribute, but something else, perhaps some kind of attribute of creation. A "*logos* according to which all things are constituted," in Gregory's summary. This approach, whose resonance with Stoic thought was noted as early as Philo,[23] is a common one taken in modern biblical scholarship, especially since Gerhard von Rad's *Wisdom in Israel*.[24] In chapter 9 of that book, "The Self-Revelation of Creation," von Rad considers the major poems about wisdom in Job 28 and Proverbs 8, along with other passages from Proverbs, Sirach, and elsewhere. He argues that these passages clearly present the idea of a wisdom that belongs "to the sphere of that which is created," that is "immanent in the world."[25] The picture in Proverbs 8 is shaped by Israel's radical monotheism. Wisdom is not a goddess like Egypt's *Maat*, or a "hypostasized attribute of Yahweh," but rather "something created by Yahweh and assigned to its proper function."[26] "Although it is clearly differentiated from the whole creation, it is an entity which belongs in the world, even if it is the first of the works of creation, the creature above all creatures."[27] Wisdom is the "primeval order" or "world reason," "the mystery behind the creation of the world," whose presence had been "felt in Israel from the earliest times";[28] "not an attribute of God but an attribute of the world, namely that mysterious attribute, by virtue of which she turns towards men to give order to their lives."[29]

However, such an understanding of wisdom is difficult to maintain in view of the connections wisdom *does* have with God. Most readers, including, as we have seen, Thomas Aquinas, recognize that Prov. 8:22-31 should be interpreted in connection with 3:19-20, and so with the wider idea that God created the world "by wisdom" (*běḥokmâ*).[30] The only other text in Proverbs 1–9 that treats creation,

---

22. Athanasius, *Orationes Contra Arianos* II.18.32 (*NPNF* Series II, Vol. 4). Other early Christians also deployed such an argument. See, for example, Origen, *On First Principles* 4.4.1, quoted in ACCS, 61–2.

23. See Michael Baris, "Iniquities Ensnare the Wicked: The Ethical Theory of Proverbs 1–9," *Hebrew Studies* 56 (2015): 129–33.

24. Gerhard von Rad, *Wisdom in Israel* (London: SCM, 1972).

25. Rad, *Wisdom in Israel*, 145, 152.

26. Rad, *Wisdom in Israel*, 153.

27. Rad, *Wisdom in Israel*, 154.

28. Rad, *Wisdom in Israel*, 155, 157, 161.

29. Rad, *Wisdom in Israel*, 156.

30. Athanasius also insists on this connection. See *Orationes Contra Arianos* 2.18.32, 40 (*NPNF* Series II, Vol. 4). Von Rad accepts this point in *Wisdom in Israel*, 155. See also

in Katherine Dell's words, "in any cosmic sense," is 3:19-20.[31] This text also mirrors 8:22-31 in being set within a wider passage that pictures wisdom as a woman (3:13-20), and there are significant structural parallels between the two passages.[32] Prov. 3:19-20 reads as follows:

> The LORD by wisdom (*běḥokmâ*) established the earth, setting firm the heavens by understanding.
> By his knowledge (*bědaʿtô*) the deeps burst open, and the clouds drop the dew.

What is striking here is the pronominal suffix on the word "knowledge" in v. 20—it is *his* knowledge. This sentence parallels and expands v. 19, and thus implies that the wisdom, understanding, and knowledge by which the LORD acted were his own. This thought is found in a number of other places within the Old Testament.[33] Parallel statements in the book of Jeremiah also contain pronominal suffixes, including on the word "wisdom." Twice, God is said to have established the world "by his wisdom" (*běḥokmātô*).[34] This makes it difficult to claim that the wisdom in question is not God's own. Von Rad himself is only able to maintain his interpretation by unsatisfactorily minimizing this point.[35]

The function of Prov. 8:22-31 within the poem as a whole, and indeed within the wider literary context, also points toward seeing the figure of Wisdom as super-creaturely. The overall purpose of Proverbs 8 is to highlight the value of wisdom, and to exhort those addressed, "my sons" (v. 32), to listen to wisdom, to take it up (v. 10), and to "be wise" (v. 33). Verses 22-31 play an important role in relation to this purpose: they ground this appeal in the exalted status of Wisdom.[36] Wisdom is supremely valuable, worth choosing over gold, silver, jewels (vv. 10-11), because she was there in the beginning with God, his faithful companion and joy. Although its meaning is contested, v. 30, in particular, describes a relation between Wisdom

---

Raymond Van Leeuwen, "Cosmos, Temple, House: Building and Wisdom in Mesopotamia and Israel," in *Wisdom Literature in Mesopotamia and Israel*, ed. Richard J. Clifford (SBL Symposium Series 36; Atlanta: Society of Biblical Literature, 2007), 79.

31. Dell, *The Book of Proverbs*, 139.

32. See Leo Perdue, *Wisdom and Creation: The Theology of Wisdom Literature* (Nashville: Abingdon, 1994), 80–93; and Dell, *The Book of Proverbs*, 139.

33. The most significant parallels are Ps. 104:24; Jer. 10:12; 51:15. While not a direct parallel, Job 28:25-27 is also important.

34. Jer. 10:12; 51:15.

35. While acknowledging that the reader would most likely assume that the wisdom spoken of in v. 19 was God's wisdom, von Rad argues that it "could also be understood as an attribute of the earth," and then suggests that the question is in fact "superfluous," because "it is actually impossible to separate from the former statement the idea that creation has to be credited with the attribute of wise orderliness" (*Wisdom in Israel*, 155–6). This is true, but it does not make the question superfluous.

36. See Weeks, "The Context and Meaning of Proverbs 30a," 436.

and God that seems to be different to the normal Creator–creature relation.[37] Wisdom is, in Dell's words, "Yahweh's companion in the creation of the world, his intimate friend and part of the very construction of the world."[38]

These factors make it difficult to maintain the idea that Wisdom is thoroughly creaturely. At a minimum, Wisdom is "the creature above all creatures," as von Rad puts it.[39] Other commentators, however, are compelled to say something more than this, and to describe Wisdom as occupying some kind of intermediate position between God and creation. Raymond van Leeuwen, for instance, writes that in Woman Wisdom, "we have the 'self-revelation' of an archetypal normativity built into the cosmos, a *tertium quid* that mediates between God and the world, a something embedded in the fabric of creation, but which is not simply to be identified with created things."[40] Leo Perdue calls Wisdom "the Queen of Heaven and the firstborn of Yahweh."[41] Gerlinde Baumann describes Wisdom as "ein himmlisches, also transzendentes Wesen … JHWHs transzendentes Geschöpf."[42] We also noted Dell's argument that there is a human and divine side to wisdom in Proverbs, and that the figure of Wisdom is a kind of "bridge" between them.[43] Bruce Waltke attempts to carve out a different position. He argues that *qānānî* in v. 22 should be translated "brought forth," yet insists that Wisdom should not be identified with a hypostasis of God, but is the personification of Solomon's wisdom. He therefore concludes that "the metaphor 'brought me forth' signifies that Solomon's inspired wisdom comes from God's essential being; it is a revelation that has an organic connection with God's very nature and being, unlike the rest of creation that came into existence outside of him and independent from his being."[44] This suggestion raises a number of questions.[45] Here, however, we note only the way in which Waltke ends up describing Wisdom as an intermediate entity between creation and God. At one point he apparently endorses the language of "heavenly mediatrix."[46]

---

37. The precise meaning of *ʾāmôn*, on which see above, n. 10, is not especially important for the argument. Whether or not Wisdom had an active role in creation, her presence at creation is sufficient to establish her exalted status.

38. Dell, *The Book of Proverbs*, 143.

39. Rad, *Wisdom in Israel*, 154.

40. Raymond C. Van Leeuwen, "Liminality and Worldview in Proverbs 1–9," *Semeia* 50 (1990): 116.

41. Perdue, *Wisdom and Creation*, 94.

42. Baumann, *Die Weisheitsgestalt*, 312.

43. Dell, *The Book of Proverbs*, 129.

44. Waltke, *Proverbs 1–15*, 409.

45. Not least what it means to say that Solomon's wisdom pre-existed creation, and had some role in the work of creation. See the review by Thomas McCreesh, "The Book of Proverbs: Chapters 1–15," *Catholic Biblical Quarterly* 70/2 (2008): 352–3.

46. Waltke, *Proverbs 1–15*, 85–6.

These kinds of interpretations are theologically problematic. Athanasius's response would be to ask what a *tertium quid* means, theologically speaking. What does it mean to speak of a "bridge" between God and creation? Precisely this problem provided Athanasius with weighty arguments against the Arians. He pointed out, for example, that were the Arian understanding right, and Prov. 8:22 meant that Wisdom was in some sense *created*, then it would be impossible to distinguish Wisdom from creation. In that case, Wisdom's being a "beginning" would mean simply that Wisdom was the initial part of creation: "It would follow that He (the Son, divine Wisdom) and all other things together make up the unity of the creation."[47] Either wisdom is part of creation, or it is divine. There can be no creature *above* all other creatures in the fullest sense; there are simply creatures.

An apparent alternative is the proposal of Michael Fox that Wisdom be understood as a "universal" in a realist sense—the figure of Wisdom in Proverbs 8 symbolizes the *form* of wisdom.

> Lady Wisdom symbolizes the perfect and transcendent universal, of which the infinite instances of human wisdom are imperfect images or realizations. Like a Platonic *idea*, the wisdom-universal exists objectively and not only as an abstraction or mental construct. It dwells in special proximity to God—"before him," present to his mind—while maintaining a distinct and separate existence. As a universal, it exists simultaneously in the supernal realm (universal, extra-temporal, extra-mundane) and the human world (time-bound, worldly, belonging to particular peoples, realized in specific words). This transcendent wisdom now and ever presents itself to humanity, meaning that the wisdom that people can learn, such as the wise teachings of Proverbs, are manifestations or precipitates of a universal, unitary wisdom. God's wisdom and man's wisdom, though incomparable in magnitude, are in essence the same.[48]

This suggestion seems to solve a number of problems. It appears to explain how Wisdom can be both distinct from God and yet transcendent of creation; indeed, how Wisdom can be God's own in some significant sense—because God's wisdom, too, is a particular instantiation of this universal. Precisely here, however, lies the difficulty. The theological tradition has generally recognized that there are major problems with the idea of forms existing outside the mind of God. Thus, as we saw above in connection with his understanding of eternal law, Aquinas cites Aristotle's rejection of Plato's notion of ideas existing outside the intellect, and insists that the ideas by which God knows things are within the divine mind indeed are ultimately forms of divine self-knowledge.[49] The problem is that the notion of an atemporal

---

47. Athanasius, *Orationes Contra Arianos* II.19.48 (*NPNF* Series II, Vol. 4).

48. Fox, *Proverbs 1–9*, 356.

49. See above, Chapter 2, Section 3, and *ST* I.14.5; 15.1 ad1. From the reformed tradition, compare Polanus, "The divine ideas of the things created are forms existing in the divine

idea outside of God compromises his freedom, setting conditions upon the form of his creative work. Although Fox himself rejects the idea that Wisdom was "an active agent in creation,"[50] the concept of Wisdom as a universal requires that Wisdom play a kind of role in creation, insofar as it represents a limit placed upon God's activity. It will be apparent, then, that from a theological perspective Fox's suggestion offers no real advance on the ideas noted above. Wisdom is still a kind of intermediary between God and creation.

The theological challenges of Proverbs 8 cannot, then, be resolved just by refusing the identification of Wisdom with Christ. The Wisdom spoken of cannot be seen as something properly other than God, a part of creation. It is, somehow, God's wisdom that is personified. And yet, there is no doubt that Wisdom *is* other than God in some sense. Wisdom is pictured *before* and *beside* God, *gotten, set up*, and *brought forth* by him. Wisdom is directly involved in creaturely life. "By me kings reign," we are told. In this respect Dell is justified in seeing Wisdom as like a bridge between the divine and human. Wisdom does have such a role in Proverbs 8 and elsewhere. Here, then, lies the genuine theological challenge of this passage: to understand how *God's* wisdom can be a reality *within* creation, so as to constitute a possible form of human action.[51] In Stuart Weeks's account of the matter, the problem is to discern how wisdom can be "*in* humans but *of* God."[52]

It could be that the book of Proverbs itself resists resolution of this theological problem. Gerlinde Baumann suggests that the mystery is purposeful. Reflecting on the difficulty in determining the meaning of the terms in 8:22-31, she comments:

> Eine derartige Anhäufung uneindeutiger Termini wird kein Zufall sein. Eher wird ihr die Absicht zugrundeliegen, mit Hilfe der Wortwahl das Verhältnis JHWHs zur Weisheitsgestalt *gerade nicht* festzulegen. Gesagt wird, daß die Weisheit JHWHs transzendentes Geschöpf ist. Ob beide nach dieser Erschaffung nebeneinander oder in einem hierarchischen Verhältnis zueinander stehen, bleibt offen.[53]

---

mind from eternity, not really distinct from the divine essence, but which are actually the same as the divine essence"; and J. H. Heidegger, "Like the eternal decrees of God the temporal creation had itself no cause outside God whether principal or instrumental; could not have had one. In the beginning nothing existed outside God, and no ideas or exemplars of work outside God had been set up, such as Plato imagined that God had in view when creating; This on the evidence of Aristotle, though others contradict this." Cited in Heinrich Heppe, *Reformed Dogmatics*, ed. Ernst Bizer, trans. G. T. Thomson (Eugene, OR: Wipf and Stock, 2007), 191–2. These statements exactly match Aquinas's position. For a brief, but lucid, discussion of this issue, see Karl Barth, *CD* III/2, 153–4.

50. Fox, *Proverbs 1–9*, 354.

51. Cf. Treier, *Proverbs & Ecclesiastes*, 49–50.

52. Weeks, *Instruction and Imagery*, 124, emphasis original.

53. Baumann, *Die Weisheitsgestalt*, 312. Translation: "Such a conglomeration of ambiguous terminology is no accident. Rather, at its basis is the intention not precisely to specify, by means of word selection, the relationship of YHWH to the figure of Wisdom.

While this may be a suitable conclusion from a range of viewpoints, it is not an adequate reading of Proverbs as Christian Scripture. The possibility that a transcendent creaturely figure might exist in equal partnership with God is not one that Christian theology can entertain with equanimity. It is Jesus Christ who is the firstborn of all creation (Col. 1:15), and so if that is the position the figure of Wisdom occupies, there is no alternative but to understand them in connection.

If we are not to begin to reconsider the first option noted by Gregory (saying that "Solomon's" words here must be rejected), this might seem to lead us back full circle to the patristic interpretation, and to say that, after all, we must find a way to understand the voice of Wisdom as the voice of Christ. And if we cannot see the figure of Wisdom as divine, then to understand it in relation to Christ's human nature. The awkward aspects of such a reading remain, though. The orthodox patristic tradition did not countenance the idea that the whole passage might refer to the human nature of Christ, because it saw a significant difference in time reference between v. 22—"the beginning of his way," referring to God's work of redemption—and v. 24—"before the hills," referring to eternity. As we noted above, the problems with such a thought lead Robert Jenson to reject it, and to instead suggest that the figure of Wisdom be understood as a personification of the *totus Christus*, the bride of Christ in Israel and the Church. It may be, however, that we can find a better solution by attending to the wider ways in which the book of Proverbs imagines wisdom, getting wisdom, and acting in wisdom.

2 The Nature of Wisdom in the Book of Proverbs

We have noted that in explaining what it means for God to create all things "through wisdom," Aquinas more than once deploys a metaphor of house-building.[54] Athanasius had used the same analogy, stressing the difference between building and begetting.[55] This metaphor parallels a logic deep within the book of Proverbs. House-building is the archetypical wise act. "A wise woman builds her house" (14:1). "The wicked are overthrown and come to nothing, but the house of the righteous stands" (12:7). Most significantly: "By wisdom a house is built, and by understanding it is established; by knowledge its rooms are filled with all precious and lovely riches" (24:3-4). This final text, with its threefold sequence of "by wisdom (*bĕḥokmâ*) ... by understanding (*ûbitĕbûnâ*) ... by knowledge (*ûbĕda'at*) ... " along with its use of the verb "established" (*kwn*), represents the

---

It is said that Wisdom is YHWH's transcendent creature. But the question remains open whether both, following this creation, stand alongside one another or in a hierarchical relationship."

54. See *ST* I.14.8; 15.1–3; I-II.93.1; II-II.52.3; and above, Chapter 2, Section 3.

55. See, for example, *De Decretis*, 3.13; *Orationes* 2.22.73–77; 3.30.62 (*NPNF* Series II, Vol. 4).

closest parallel to Prov. 3:19-20 in the book.[56] Each of these units, Raymond Van Leeuwen argues, "presents *in nuce* an Israelite formulation of ancient Near Eastern ideas of building and filling with wisdom"[57]—house-building being a "fundamental metaphoric domain used by ancient Near Eastern societies" to talk about wisdom.[58] In its reference to house-building, 24:3-4 also makes contact with the figure of Woman Wisdom. In Prov. 8:34, Wisdom speaks of her "doors," "doorposts," and "openings," imagery that leads the way to ch. 9, where we hear that "Wisdom has built her house" (9:1). With this image, we confront again the enigma in Proverbs of Wisdom's "bridging" the divine and the human. Both God and human persons "build" things "by wisdom." Indeed, Van Leeuwen says that in the Hebrew Bible there is often an "almost casual ... assumption that God's wisdom in creation is best presented in architectural terms."[59]

Aquinas's use of the analogy of house-building to speak about God's creative work makes contact, then, with the logic of Proverbs' understanding of wisdom.[60] The significance Thomas finds in this metaphor is, however, somewhat different to the implications it has within the thought of Proverbs. Aristotle, as we noted above, saw "house-building" (*oikodomikē*) as the paradigm example of a *poiēsis* that could be done with *technē*.[61] This was a process in which an intellectual form was executed in matter. As we have also seen, this conception exercised an influence on Aquinas's account of practical knowledge, and his understanding of eternal law as the *ratio* of divine wisdom. God is like a governor in relation to the acts and movement of creation, and in a governor's mind, we recall, there pre-exists "the *ratio* of the order of those things that are to be done by those who are subject to his government," just like the pre-existing conception by which an artisan makes.[62]

---

56. Despite this fact it has regularly been ignored because of the tendency to read chapters 1-9 in isolation from chapters 10-31. On this point see especially Raymond Van Leeuwen, "Cosmos, Temple, House," 77-9.

57. Van Leeuwen, "Cosmos, Temple, House," 80.

58. Van Leeuwen, "Cosmos, Temple, House," 89.

59. Van Leeuwen, "Cosmos, Temple, House," 77.

60. In the discussion that follows, we will sometimes use the term "wisdom" to speak of what the book of Proverbs uses a wide range of terms to speak of, for example, *ḥokmâ, daʿat, těbûnâ, ʿormâ*. These terms do, of course, have distinct shades of meaning, and our generalizing discussion is not intended to avoid this point, on which the discussions in Fox (*Proverbs 1-9*, 29-43) and Waltke (*Proverbs 1-15*, 76-8, 93-100) are instructive. However, it is also the case that, as Gerhard von Rad observes, through parallelism and juxtaposition, these terms "become intertwined almost to the point of a synonymity which is often difficult for us to understand" (*Wisdom in Israel*, 53). For all the differences between the terms used, there is a unifying "wisdom" that Proverbs is about.

61. *EN* 6.4, 1140a7; and above, Chapter 1, Section 3.

62. *ST* I-II.93.1; and above, Chapter 2, Sections 1 and 3.

Something quite different is in view when the book of Proverbs speaks of a house being built by wisdom. Let us note three significant points. First, although we might initially think that we have here an instance of "making," in fact the emphasis is elsewhere. The significance of "building a house" does not lie only in its being a complex structure, which requires a craftsman's skill in order to make it; it lies also in its being a major life-achievement. Building a house is not viewed in the abstract, but as something one accomplishes within the living of one's life. The wisdom by which it is built is not merely the wisdom of the craftsman, but perhaps more the wisdom of the overseer, or organizer; it is a social act, with ramifications for others. The point of a house is a house*hold*. Otherwise, it is unlikely, within that social context, that it would have been said that the wise *woman* builds her house (14:1). It also explains the second part of the proverb, about the filling of rooms with precious goods. The point is not merely the construction of the house, but the building of a house as a key part of, and symbol of, a successful life lived among others. This is not to deny any connection with practices of "making." This link is important. The other categories deployed in 24:3-4: understanding, or better, skill (*tĕbûnâ*), and knowledge (*da'at*) are terms frequently associated with craftsmanship.[63] For Proverbs, however, what is not to be overlooked is that acts of making do not occur in a vacuum; they are moments within a life, and they are more or less fruitful.

Second, the house-building metaphor pushes us to think more carefully about the relationship of wisdom to action. What does it mean to say that a house is built *by* wisdom, or that God *by* wisdom founded the earth? The Hebrew preposition *bĕ* can have a number of meanings. Possible in this connection are "by," "with," "using," "through," and "in." In the Old Testament, the most common sense of *bĕḥokmâ* is instrumental,[64] especially when the phrase is used adverbially.[65] The question remains, however, what it means for wisdom to be *used* to do something. Doing something "with a hammer" is very different to doing something "with care" or "with instructions." What is actually being envisaged when Proverbs speaks of something being done by wisdom? Perhaps we could still maintain that this means that something is done according to a pre-existing intellectual conception. As we have seen, however, this interpretation is based on an appeal to a picture of making that may be unwarranted. Moreover, as we saw Joseph Dunne argue in relation to

---

63. See Van Leeuwen, "Cosmos, Temple, House," 83, and note the parallels in 1 Kings 7:13-14; 10:4-8, 23-24 and Exodus 31:3; 35:31; 36:1; 35:35. Van Leeuwen points out that English translations unfortunately tend to translate the key terms differently in Exodus and Proverbs, and suggests that the reason for this may lie in Whybray's characterization of Proverbs as part of "the intellectual tradition." Fox states that "*T^ebunah* is the pragmatic, applied aspect of thought, operating in the realm of *action*" (*Proverbs 1–9*, 37).

64. See, for example: Exod. 35:26; 2 Sam. 20:22; Isa. 10:13; Ezek. 28:4; Job 4:21; 38:37; Prov. 28:26; 31:26; Eccl. 1:13; 2:3; 2:21; 7:23; 9:15.

65. Although there are exceptions, for example, Jer. 9:22-23.

Aristotle, the picture itself may be problematic.⁶⁶ Can we, then, discern a different way of understanding wisdom and its relation to action in the book of Proverbs?

Finally, and related to both points, it is critical to see that the purpose of this proverb, "by wisdom a house is built," is not just to illustrate the exercise of wisdom, but to tell us something about what wisdom is. Building and filling a house, that is to say, is not merely an arbitrary example of an impressive achievement that requires intelligence and skill; rather it is something good and significant for the living of life, the achieving of which is the substance of wisdom. Wisdom is here being described not merely formally as in "that by which difficult and great things are done," but concretely as "that by which a house is built."

These observations point us toward a distinctive way of understanding wisdom implied within the book of Proverbs, which it is the purpose of this section of our discussion to draw out. We will begin from the second point, exploring the way in which Proverbs presents wisdom as a determinate reality that is in a sense *other* to us (part a). This will provide us with a new perspective from which to consider what it means to "get" and "have" wisdom (part b), and with new tools for understanding Proverbs 8 (part c). All of this will allow us, in the final section of this chapter, to return to Aquinas with new questions. To anticipate, however, let us simply note the striking fact that perhaps the most profound and formative description in the Bible of wisdom—the category that not only Aquinas but also the wider philosophical and theological tradition has used to speak about speculative knowledge—is of a fundamentally practical reality. Lady Wisdom of Proverbs 8 is thoroughly oriented toward action (8:32-35). Represented, as Van Leeuwen highlights, by *two* terms, ḥokmâ and tĕbûnâ (8:1; cf. 2:2; 3:13; 9:1),⁶⁷ she might just as easily be called Lady Competence. This must make us reconsider both what it means for God to have made the world "by wisdom" and the nature of human prudence.

a. The Alterity of Wisdom

Wisdom, Proverbs tells us, "calls." In every passage in which Wisdom speaks in the first person, she is depicted as calling, or crying out.⁶⁸ Von Rad recognized that this is a striking and distinctive feature of the book.⁶⁹ Wisdom calls in public—outside (baḥûṣ; 1:20), in the squares (bārĕḥōbôt; 1:20), at the top of "bustling streets"⁷⁰ (bĕrō'š hōmîyôt; 1:21), at entrances and gates (1:21; 8:3), at high points along the way (ʿălê-dārek; 8:2), and in the town (9:3), at crossroads (8:2). Her call is general—"to all humanity," in 8:4—but more specifically it is for "the simple" (1:22; 8:5; 9:4). Her offer, essentially, is to give the knowledge that leads to life. In this call

---

66. See above, Chapter 1, Section 3. We will return to this point below, in Section 3a.
67. Van Leeuwen, "Cosmos, Temple, House," 83.
68. Prov. 1:20-21; 8:1-4; 9:3-6.
69. Rad, *Wisdom in Israel*, 157–66.
70. This phrase is Murphy's, *Proverbs*, xxxii.

of Wisdom, von Rad thought, we see something like, "the religious provocation of man by the world."[71] This, he suggests, is the deep reason wisdom is personified, because "the primeval order" is "oriented towards man, offering him help; it is concerned about him, indeed addresses him directly."[72] Von Rad sees a link between Wisdom's speech, and the notion in the psalms of creation praising God, the heavens "telling the glory of God."[73] Yet although Wisdom speaks *of God*, and "bears all the marks of a divine address," calling man to itself and even promising salvation, the voice of Wisdom is emphatically *not* Yahweh's voice, but the voice of "the self-manifesting primeval order."[74] Von Rad further argues that these ideas must be linked to the imagery of love used of wisdom.[75] "Esteem her, and she will exalt you; she will honor you when you embrace her" (4:8). This imagery, von Rad argues, suggests that "the existence in the world of the man who seeks knowledge is in a relationship of love to the mysterious order. It is in a state of tension through being wooed, through seeking and being sought, through having to wait for and, at the same time, anticipating precious intellectual fulfilment."[76] The notion of wisdom in Proverbs, von Rad concludes, speaks to a fundamental experience of the world as benevolent toward man, as a source of blessing, which "awakens trust, bestows order and healing."[77]

Above (Section 1), we saw that there are problems with von Rad's identification of Personified Wisdom with world-order. It cannot adequately recognize the sense in which Wisdom must be, in some way, *God's* wisdom.[78] However, there is much to appreciate in von Rad's analysis of Wisdom's call. Most important, von Rad highlights something other commentators struggle to recognize: the way in which the call of wisdom implies that wisdom is somehow differentiated from the moral subject, encountering her as *other*. Stuart Weeks, for instance, suggests that the device of personification actually gets in the way of the core ideas being developed. He writes,

71. Rad, *Wisdom in Israel*, 156.
72. Rad, *Wisdom in Israel*, 162; cf. p. 174.
73. Rad, *Wisdom in Israel*, 162; cf. Ps. 19:1.
74. Rad, *Wisdom in Israel*, 163. On this point, von Rad changes his earlier view that only the Lord could speak as Wisdom does. See Gerhard von Rad, *Old Testament Theology, Volume 1: The Theology of Israel's Historical Traditions*, trans. D. M. G. Stalker (Edinburgh: Oliver and Boyd, 1962), 444.
75. Rad, *Wisdom in Israel*, 166–76.
76. Rad, *Wisdom in Israel*, 173.
77. Rad, *Wisdom in Israel*, 175–6.
78. In this respect, I agree with Paul Fiddes's criticism of von Rad in *Seeing the World and Knowing God: Hebrew Wisdom and Christian Doctrine in a Late-Modern Context* (Oxford: Oxford University Press, 2013), 186–7. See below, however, for further comments about Fiddes's argument.

The personification of wisdom is … creating an issue that does not exist in the underlying thought. As we characterized it earlier, wisdom is literally to be conceived of as something that is within humans, an attribute or condition that allows them to discern the good and understand what is required of them by God; it is also, however, as 2:6 says, something that he gives or proclaims. The concept, then, is of a means by which God offers humans access to his will, and wisdom is therefore *in* humans but *of* God. This is not something that can be sustained once the concept is personified, and although much emphasis is laid upon Wisdom's relationships with humans, on the one hand, and God on the other, her very presence separates the two.[79]

We must, says Weeks, entertain "a suspicion that the author has not picked an ideal vehicle for expressing what he is trying to say."[80] Wisdom's call, on this assumption, is an awkward feature of Proverbs. By contrast, for von Rad, personification is "the most precise expression available for the subject matter to be explained,"[81] because wisdom is not simply a human characteristic but a feature of the created world. Even if we cannot agree with every part of von Rad's interpretation, he acutely recognizes that the idea of wisdom's call only makes sense with an understanding of wisdom as somehow a predicate of the world, rather than just of the subject. Wisdom is in some sense an *other* to be loved.

Weeks's view follows from his conceptuality of wisdom as an attribute, something "in humans." Michael Fox, among others, develops a similar view in discussing of "the lectures" in Proverbs 1–9, that is, the passages in Proverbs 1–9 where a father addresses a son.[82] Fox observes that the actual teachings of the father "do not seem all that difficult." "The message of the lectures is plain and unambiguous, and the precepts tell nothing that anyone would admit to being ignorant of: Don't rob; don't kill; don't commit adultery; be honest; trust God. As great as these principles are, having wisdom must mean something more than simply *knowing* them."[83] Fox concludes that what the father is aiming at in these speeches is wisdom "as a power": "The knowledge of wisdom, once achieved, resides in the learner as a potential and must be activated by God in order to become the power of wisdom, an inner light that guides its possessor through life."[84] This wisdom, he goes on to suggest, has

---

79. Weeks, *Instruction and Imagery*, 124.
80. Weeks, *Instruction and Imagery*, 124.
81. Rad, *Wisdom in Israel*, 174.
82. Fox, *Proverbs 1–9*, 347–51. Fox argues that Proverbs 1–9 is a composite text, combining five lectures and five interludes ("Ideas of Wisdom in Proverbs 1–9," *Journal of Biblical Literature* 116, no. 4 [1997]: 613–33). Overall, I am more persuaded by the argument of Stuart Weeks that Proverbs 1–9 is a single, coherent composition (*Instruction and Imagery*, 1–66).
83. Fox, *Proverbs 1–9*, 347. Emphasis original.
84. Fox, *Proverbs 1–9*, 347.

a moral component, "because inert wisdom would not provide protection"; it is "a configuration of soul; it is *moral character*."[85] Later, Fox elaborates this idea in a discussion of the affinity of Proverbs with Socratic ethical ideas. Proverbs, he suggests, is fundamentally about "the exercise of the human mind";[86] wisdom is a capacity that can be likened to "the Socratic art of metrics," an ability to weigh goods judiciously.[87] Wisdom in Proverbs is an intellectual capacity of some kind, a power that resides *within* the subject, and more specifically within the mind, and that enables good action.

There is, however, another way to interpret the legitimate observation that much of the teaching of Proverbs is relatively rudimentary. This is to see Proverbs as less interested in wisdom as a subjective, intellectual capacity and more interested in wisdom as a concrete or objective reality, wisdom as having to do with determinate forms of action that lie before us and are, in a sense that is reflected in the device of personification, really other than us. As we observed in the introduction to this study, when the mother of 1:8-19 tells her son not to join a violent gang, what she is seeking is not primarily for her son to build a moral and intellectual capacity, but for him to act in a good way, for him to take one road rather than another. The wisdom she is seeking is not so much an ability as it is a concrete form of life. The aim in Proverbs is not primarily to *be* wise—although there is a place for this—but to *act by* wisdom, to *walk in* wisdom. Wisdom in Proverbs can actually be *contrasted* with capacity for self-direction. To have to rely on one's own devices is a calamity and an alienation from wisdom (1:31; 3:5-7). "One who trusts to his heart—he is a fool; one who walks in wisdom (*běḥokmâ*)—he will escape" (28:26). Wisdom in Proverbs is not so much an internal capacity for thinking as it is an objective reality, a concrete opening for action that somehow belongs originally to the world itself.

We may call this idea, somewhat inadequately, the "alterity" of wisdom, aiming to highlight the determinate otherness of wisdom in Proverbs' presentation. It is my contention that this idea is of fundamental importance for understanding the book of Proverbs, throwing light on its central ideas and images. In the remainder of this part of our discussion (part a), we will try to demonstrate this by reference to various aspects of the book. Let us first turn our attention to the remarkable second chapter of Proverbs,[88] which Stuart Weeks suggests "is intended to condense or foreshadow major interests or motifs," and "probably comes as close as anything to epitomizing Proverbs 1–9 as a whole."[89]

---

85. Fox, *Proverbs 1–9*, 348. Emphasis original.

86. Fox, *Proverbs 10–31*, 934.

87. Fox, *Proverbs 10–31*, 939, 936.

88. Proverbs 2 is a semi-acrostic (22 lines of poetry) that constitutes one enormous conditional sentence, fully justifying, it seems to me, Weeks's contention that Proverbs 1–9 should be read as "sophisticated poetry" (*Instruction and Imagery*, 60). In what follows, I am indebted to Weeks's discussion in the same book, pp. 60-4.

89. Weeks, *Instruction and Imagery*, 62.

At first sight, Proverbs 2 might appear to support the idea that wisdom should be thought of primarily as an intellectual capacity. It seems to describe a process whereby zealous attention to words of instruction (vv. 1-4) leads to a new understanding (vv. 5 and 9, "then you shall understand"), until a point is reached (v. 10) at which "wisdom will enter your heart, and knowledge shall be pleasant to your soul," after which one is protected, by this new capacity, from going astray (vv. 11-20). While this reading has an alluring simplicity, there are reasons to think that the logic of the text is more complex. For one thing, v. 10 is not structurally central in the way this reading makes it. The two sections in vv. 5-8 and 9-11, both beginning with *'āz tābîn ... kî ...*, stand in parallel, and they do not necessarily represent a temporal progression from one moment to the next. Rather, they can be taken as describing the one reality from two angles: from the perspective of divine agency (vv. 5-8), and from the perspective of wisdom's agency (vv. 9-11).

The parallel between these sections also highlights that the wisdom in question is inextricably linked to particular words. Verse 6: "The LORD gives wisdom; from his mouth are knowledge and understanding." The LORD's giving wisdom happens through his words. This is the logic behind the way the poem begins, where the father calls his son to pursue wisdom by cleaving to his words:

1   My son, if you take hold of my words, and store up my commands (*miṣwōtay*) with you,
2   so you make your ear attend to wisdom and extend your heart to understanding,
3   if you cry for insight and call out for understanding,
4   if you seek it like silver and search it out like hidden treasure ...[90]

Verses 2-4 are dependent on v. 1 both grammatically[91] and conceptually. They effect a very close connection between wisdom and the father's teaching. It is in the actual teaching of the father—the *words* and *commands* in their particularity, and not merely, for instance, in its principles, or in the intellectual abilities they inculcate—that wisdom, insight, and understanding are to be sought. Indeed, as Fox recognizes, there is a sense in which "the father's words are not only the way to wisdom, they are wisdom itself."[92] The reason for this lies in the fact that the wisdom and understanding in view here have a definite shape and content. What is "found" through this search for wisdom is something specific: "Then you will understand [*'āz tābîn*] the fear of the Lord, and the knowledge of God you will find" (v. 5). "Then you will understand [*'āz tābîn*] righteousness, and judgment, and rectitude—every good path" (v. 9). These verses, which structurally and

---

90. This translation is my own, but is indebted to Weeks, *Instruction and Imagery*, 61; and Fox, *Proverbs 1-9*, 106-7.

91. As Fox states, the infinitive beginning v. 2, *lĕhaqšîb*, "is a gerund, specifying the circumstances of the preceding verb," *Proverbs 1-9*, 109.

92. Fox, *Proverbs 1-9*, 108.

verbally parallel one another, make it inadequate to imagine "wisdom" as a kind of neutral, instrumental skill, like a capacity to deploy reasoning in a particular way, an "art of metrics." Wisdom relates to *these things*: the fear of the Lord, the knowledge of God, righteousness, justice, rectitude.[93] The father's words are the way to wisdom—even, in a way, *are* wisdom—because wisdom is a determinate, specified reality, with this particular shape and substance.

Similarly, the *knowledge* that "will be pleasant to your soul" (v. 10) is not a subjective capacity, like "intelligence," but something concrete that is known. It is knowledge *of God* that will be found (v. 5). Certainly, there is a subjective element; knowledge is not a reference to mere content, but something that a person may have and that enables action. The prudent, Prov. 13:16 tells us, "act by knowledge" (*bĕdā'at*). Yet, within Proverbs, this ought to be understood to mean not that they act by means of general intelligence, but that they act according to substantial and particular knowledge. This is why elsewhere knowledge is something that needs to be guarded (5:2), that is found (8:9, 12); it is something to be possessed, like gold and silver (8:10), "laid up" (10:14). It is also why knowledge is constantly tied to speech. It is about "words of knowledge" that can be abandoned or strayed from (19:27; 23:12; cf. 19:2), "lips of knowledge" (14:7; 20:15), "sayings of knowledge" (22:20). It is contrasted with "the words of the treacherous" (22:12). Knowledge, in Proverbs, refers less to an intellectual capability, and more to knowledge *of* something—a purchase on what is true.[94]

This way of perceiving things emerges throughout Proverbs. Above, we noted how the statement "by wisdom a house is built" is not an arbitrary illustration of how wisdom enables the doing of difficult things but is meant quite specifically: wisdom is that by which houses are built. The same emphasis can be seen in the descriptions in Proverbs of animals as wise. In Prov. 30:24-28, we hear that ants, rock-badgers (*šĕpannîm*), locusts, and lizards are "exceedingly wise" (*ḥăkāmîm mĕḥukkāmîm*). Why? Because the ant can prepare its food in summer despite its lack of strength. Rock-badgers, though not mighty, manage to make homes in rocks. Locusts, though having no king, go out in ranks. And little lizards live in king's palaces. A common way to interpret this is to say that these animals illustrate aspects of what it means to be wise: having foresight, being clever, being organized, being crafty. This interpretation emphasizes the contrast between the animals' size and strength and their achievements, and to this extent makes sense. What is missing from it, however, is recognition of the significance of the particular

---

93. In this respect, Proverbs 2 parallels the conclusion of Job 28, that wisdom and insight consist in the fear of the Lord and turning away from evil (v. 28).

94. See also the interesting contrast in Prov. 29:7 between the righteous, who know the cause of the poor, and the wicked, who do not appreciate knowledge. Similarly, Gerhard von Rad notices that the problem with "the fool" in Proverbs is "only to a very small extent" about "an intellectual defect." It is much more about "a lack of ability or readiness to accommodate himself to the orders, the knowledge of which the wise men taught." Fundamentally, says von Rad, the problem with the fool is his "lack of realism" (*Wisdom in Israel*, 64).

achievements listed. Within the thought of Proverbs, storing up food in summer, making one's home secure, marching in ranks, and being in the king's palace are achievements that are significant in and of themselves. They are concretely wise forms of action.[95] In this sense, the description of these animals as wise should be taken quite literally. These animals really are wise, because they take up objectively wise positions and courses of action. The ant is wise not simply because without an overseer it achieves a lot, but because without an overseer it *gathers food*. This is what makes it worthy of consideration for the sluggard, because the risk the sluggard faces is poverty and hunger (6:6-11). Proverbs does not think of wisdom in merely formal terms, as a capacity, but understands it with reference to material descriptions of what it involves. Animal similes are deployed in Proverbs partly because they illustrate forms of action that simply are wise or foolish, *without* reference to subjective ability: "Like a bird that flees from its nest, so is he who flees from his home" (27:8).[96]

The determinate alterity of wisdom in Proverbs also explains the prominence given to the metaphor of paths and ways. As is widely recognized, path imagery is central to the book of Proverbs, and especially to chs 1-9. Consider ch. 2 again, for example: the LORD is a shield "for those who walk (*hlk*) in integrity ... guarding *the way* (*derek*) of his saints" (vv. 7-8). It is "every good *path*" (*kāl-ma 'ĕgal-tôb*) that will be understood (v. 9); and wisdom will deliver from the "evil way" (*miderek rā '*), "ways of darkness" (*darkê-ḥōšek*), which consist in "doing evil"—from those "whose paths are crooked and who go wrong in their tracks" (vv. 12-15). Norman Habel called this metaphor of paths the "nuclear symbol" of Proverbs 1-9.[97] If this description risks overlooking the significance of other "root metaphors,"[98] it is nevertheless true that ways and paths are of fundamental importance. As Weeks comments, "It seems hard to escape the conclusion that this imagery is important to the writer, and that it goes far beyond the common figurative use of 'ways' that Hebrew shares with English and many other languages."[99] The imagery occurs throughout the book—not only in chs 1-9[100]—and appears at noteworthy points. Weeks instructively notes that "all the settings involve roads, implicitly or

---

95. This is particularly evident in relation to the ant. Prov. 10:5 uses the same terms to describe the same action: "Whoever gathers ('gr) in summer/harvest (*baqqayis*) is a prudent son." Similarly, as we have noted, building a house is used as a fundamental metaphor for wise action (see also 12:5; 14:1, 11). The other two actions—marching in ranks and being in kings' palaces—are not mentioned elsewhere directly. Both, however, are clearly understandable as objectively desirable. To have the favor of a king is a blessing (14:35).

96. See also Prov. 6:5; 7:22-23.

97. N. C. Habel, "The Symbolism of Wisdom in Proverbs 1-9," *Interpretation* 26, no. 2 (1972): 131-57.

98. See Van Leeuwen, "Liminality and Worldview," 111-44.

99. Weeks, *Instruction and Imagery*, 74.

100. See, among many examples, Prov. 10:9; 11:20; 12:28; 14:2; 15:10, 24; 16:29; 20:24.

explicitly, and in a work that displays a strong interest in the figurative use of ways and roads, it seems unlikely to be a coincidence that the speeches of significant characters are associated with them in this way."[101]

Proverbs constantly draws a contrast between two kinds of ways, of the wicked and the righteous, the wise and fools. This does not, however, imply a strong narrative logic, whereby a fundamental choice for or against wisdom determines one's life course definitively.[102] There are indeed, in the end, two ways, one that leads to life and one that leads to death. But Proverbs does not paint a simple picture of what it looks like to take them. Fox sums up the imagery in this way:

> In spite of the importance of the two paths dichotomy, the author does not picture life as a landscape with two highways running through it and instead has a much more complicated map in mind. There are a vast number of paths … crisscrossing the landscape. Even within the two paths metaphor, there are a plurality of "paths of life," actions and types of behavior that lead to life (2:19); these are the "ways of the righteous" (2:20). Likewise, a single sinner takes many roads on his way through life, but each one leads to death.[103]

There is a sense in Proverbs in which, as Anne Stewart observes, "one is always at a crossroads between competing paths."[104] Partly for this reason, Stewart argues that in Proverbs, "character is not linked to a larger narrative arc." Proverbs does not, she maintains, operate with a "narrative model of selfhood."[105] The focus of Proverbs is not on the development of character over time, but instead on moments, the particular courses of action that make up one's character. Proverbs, Stewart writes, "privileges discrete episodes, conjures up the emotions evoked by particular moments, and features a string of isolated situations that are not of necessity connected into a coherent whole."[106]

---

101. Weeks, *Instruction and Imagery*, 79.

102. For this point, see especially the arguments in Anne W. Stewart, *Poetic Ethics in Proverbs: Wisdom Literature and the Shaping of the Moral Self* (New York: Cambridge University Press, 2016), 20–8, and 203–19.

103. Fox, *Proverbs 1–9*, 130.

104. Stewart, *Poetic Ethics*, 208–9. Stewart points out that "only the path of the foreign woman is said to set a person on a path from which one cannot return (2:19)" (p. 208).

105. Stewart, *Poetic Ethics*, 207, 209.

106. Stewart, *Poetic Ethics*, 209. In his discussion of the implied reader of Proverbs, William P. Brown argues for a different position, in which the student of wisdom progresses throughout the book from child to king ("The Pedagogy of Proverbs 10:1–31:9," in *Character and Scripture: Moral Formation, Community, and Biblical Interpretation*, ed. William P. Brown [Grand Rapids: Eerdmans, 2002], 181). Stewart, however, argues that this is a stretch, that the poetic genre of Proverbs works against such a scheme, and that "it is vital to the book's pedagogy that the reader is positioned differently in different episodes," so that "the addressee is always renegotiating character" (*Poetic Ethics*, 210).

Stewart notes that this means Proverbs "bears some resemblance to a rule-based ethic that privileges acts, not character." However, she maintains that Proverbs is still primarily focused on character. "The emphasis remains on the quality of the agent rather than the act itself."[107] I think, however, that Stewart's arguments lend more support for the kind of perspective advocated here, in which what we have called the "alterity" of wisdom is foregrounded. Proverbs is focused on wisdom, which is first and foremost a quality of the world, rather than of the moral subject. This explains both the emphasis on the image of paths and how it is used. Proverbs is interested in the ways of wisdom, which first means the character of the world, rather than just the character development of wise individuals. The path metaphor is singularly appropriate, because it highlights the way in which wisdom is first and foremost about the way the world, in a sense, extends hospitality to good action.

Another significant feature of Stewart's treatment of the ethics of Proverbs also makes good sense in this light. In her study of the different models of *mûsār* (discipline) used in Proverbs, Stewart highlights the place of "imagination."[108] By this she means the ways in which moral reasoning in Proverbs does not primarily work in terms of "the application of absolute laws or rigid doctrine," but rather creates space for indeterminacy.[109] Stewart draws on the idea of "cognitive prototypes," developed by cognitive linguists such as Mark Johnson. Cognitive prototypes are central, exemplary instantiations of moral kinds or categories.[110] Stewart argues that this is a useful category for understanding Proverbs, and the way it foregrounds "the prototypical moral features of the cosmos," while still allowing the "non-prototypical" to appear.[111] She also highlights the way moral reasoning in Proverbs works through "primary generating metaphors," such as "moral accounting," "moral strength," and "moral authority."[112]

In all this there is much to be appreciated. However, a number of responses are also in order. First, the contrast Stewart draws from Johnson's work, between an imaginative mode of moral reasoning and an ethics of law, is misleading. "The Moral Law folk theory" she refers to does not represent the tradition in its best formulations.[113] As we have seen in our discussion of Aquinas, there is room within a law-based ethic for indeterminacy, because law is fundamentally about kinds of action, and recognizing a kind always involves indeterminacy. This leads to a second point, which is that to speak of kinds is arguably a better way of getting at the account of moral reasoning implied in the book of Proverbs.

---

107. Stewart, *Poetic Ethics*, 213.

108. Stewart, *Poetic Ethics*, 170–200. See also Stewart, "Wisdom's Imagination: Moral Reasoning and the Book of Proverbs," *Journal for the Study of the Old Testament* 40, no. 3 (2016): 351–72.

109. Stewart, *Poetic Ethics*, 175, 182.

110. Stewart, *Poetic Ethics*, 173–7.

111. Stewart, *Poetic Ethics*, 180–1.

112. Stewart, *Poetic Ethics*, 181–91.

113. Stewart, *Poetic Ethics*, 173–7.

Stewart concludes that "the cultivation of moral imagination is a central goal of the book's pedagogy."[114] I think it is more accurate to say that the book aims to enable the student to recognize actions and ways of acting according to their kind, and that imagination assists such recognition. When Proverbs says, for example, that "a calm tongue is a tree of life" (15:4), or describes an honest answer as "a kiss on the lips" (24:26), evocative metaphors are being deployed to reveal these kinds of action—speaking calmly, answering honestly—for what they really are. Yet the goal is not so much the cultivation of the imagination as a familiarity with kinds. Imagination is not the end, but a means to that end.[115] Third, this way of describing things allows us more clearly to affirm the *reality* of moral kinds in the book of Proverbs. Stewart frequently implies such an affirmation, such as in her references to the "moral features of the cosmos," and "the reliable and discernible nature of the moral order."[116] Her emphasis on the imagination and the place of mental interpretative structures, however, could be seen as open to a Kantian interpretation, in which moral categories are only structures of the human mind, categories of moral understanding imposed upon a morally neutral world. In the book of Proverbs, moral kinds are real, and this is the reason that wisdom is not simply a subjective quality, but a determinate other, to be encountered, respected, and loved. It is also the reason why, as Stewart emphasizes, wisdom can be taught. This leads us to another point of discussion.

Above, we noticed the way in which in Proverbs 2 wisdom is linked to particular words. Other passages display the same emphasis. Prov. 6:20-24 parallels ch. 2 in a range of ways:

> Guard, my son, your father's commandment (*miṣwat*), do not forsake your mother's instruction (*tôrat*).
> Bind them constantly on your heart, tie them round your neck.
> As you walk, it shall lead you; when you lie, it shall guard you; when you wake, it will advise you.
> For the commandment is a lamp and the instruction is a light, and the way of life (*derek ḥayyîm*) is discipline's corrective,
> To guard you from the evil woman, from the smooth tongue of the foreign woman.

The way of life, and the avoidance of the destructive paths symbolized by the foreign woman, is accessed through remembering and constant attention to a form of teaching that has been handed down. Similarly, 22:17-21 emphasizes how particular words, "words of wisdom," "thirty sayings of counsel and knowledge," will lead to one's confidence being "in the Lord," and to a life that is full of truth and truthful speech. The crucial thing is simply that "you incline your ear to words

---

114. Stewart, *Poetic Ethics*, 177.

115. This does not mean imagination is optional; it may be that imagination is a necessary means to our knowledge of kinds. See below, Chapter 5, Section 1.

116. Stewart, *Poetic Ethics*, 181, 199.

of wisdom and set your heart on knowledge. For it will be pleasant if you guard them in your belly and they are established on your lips."

These passages, to which we might add others,[117] also highlight a connection between Proverbs and the life of Israel. References to *miṣwōt* and *tôrâ*, the image of the lamp, and of instruction bound in the heart and round the neck, clearly make contact with wider Israelite theology.[118] Chapter 2 is rich with such allusions. The reference to "commandments" (*miṣwōt*) in v. 1 and the idea of knowledge and understanding coming "from God's mouth" (v. 6) evoke ideas about law. The notion of the fear of the LORD (v. 5) is similarly evocative.[119] The image of the strange or foreign woman in vv. 16-19 also, most likely, makes contact with biblical prohibitions on intermarriage, and the interpretation of this as having a fateful impact on Israel's history.[120] The language of vv. 21-22 is suggestive, with its reference to dwelling in the land (*yiškěnû 'āreṣ*), and the wicked being "cut off" (*yikārētû*).[121] Finally, the central metaphor of ways and paths has significant wider biblical resonance.[122] All these allusions suggest, in one way or another, a link between the wisdom in question and the concrete way of life set before Israel by God.[123]

What do these points of contact mean? Stuart Weeks argues that such allusions ought to lead to the conclusion that the instruction referred to in Proverbs simply *is* the Torah. "When … the work repeatedly advocates adherence to instruction," he writes, "and when it evokes the Deuteronomic idea of God as instructor, it is hard to believe that the writer would not expect his Jewish readership to see in this a reference to the Torah."[124] A reference, certainly. Yet this does not mean that the Torah is all that is in view when Proverbs 1–9 speaks of instruction. For to say that problematizes the relationship of these chapters to the rest of the book, making them a singularly bad introduction to the Proverbs of Solomon.[125] It is better to understand the link between Proverbs and the Law of Israel conceptually.

---

117. Most notably Prov. 30:1-6, and 29:18b: "Blessed is he who keeps *torah*!"

118. Compare, for example, Deut. 6:6-9; Ps. 119:105-7.

119. See Dell, *The Book of Proverbs*, 90–124, 146–50.

120. Including, of course, in relation to Solomon: 1 Kgs 11:1-6. Compare the references to "foreign" women in Ezra 10:2, 10, 11, 14, 17, 18, 44; and Neh. 13:27. See the discussion in Weeks, *Instruction and Imagery*, 128–47.

121. Compare Deut. 28:1-14, 63; Ps. 37:3, 9, 29. Cf. Weeks, *Instruction and Imagery*, 170. Although see the arguments against this view in Fox, *Proverbs 1–9*, 122–5.

122. Weeks argues that although there are important Ancient Near-Eastern parallels to this metaphor, the most important context is the extensive biblical use of the ways imagery (*Instruction and Imagery*, 148–152). See, for example, 2 Kgs 22:2; Deut. 5:32-33; 8:6; 11:22; 19:9; 26:17; 28:9; 30:16; 7:4; and throughout Ps. 119.

123. See also von Rad, *Wisdom in Israel*, 60–4.

124. Weeks, *Instruction and Imagery*, 104. Note his arguments against Fox on p. 104, n. 11.

125. See our discussion of this point above, in the Introduction, n. 12.

Proverbs understands wisdom as about particular, determinate forms of life, which are accessed and held onto by disciplined attention to particular words. Within Proverbs, it does not seem to be the case that these words are limited to the Torah. Rather, they encompass the wider teaching given throughout the book. However, the connection between wisdom and definite commands and instructions clearly opens the way to a focus on Torah as wisdom, which goes some way to explaining later developments in Israel's wisdom tradition.[126] The idea of wisdom in Proverbs is open to an emphasis on Law because the primary question, for Proverbs—and indeed for Israel's wisdom tradition more broadly, is not "how may I become wise?" but "where shall wisdom be found?"[127] This is a question that demands an answer with material content. Job's answer to it is the same in kind as Proverbs: "The fear of the LORD, *that* is wisdom, and to turn from evil is understanding" (Job 28:28).

"The fear of the LORD" indicates the point of connection between wisdom and Law. The beginning of wisdom is the fear of the Lord, in Proverbs,[128] because wisdom has determinate content: it is about the *good* paths one may take through life, which the world God has made makes available. It is a "beginning," because it is a beginning *of a path*. It is not something merely formal, like a posture of submission or piety, but a "first step," in the sense that a guide might point to a stone in a river-crossing and say, "that's the first step."[129] Wisdom is about a purchase on the ways of life that are right and good. That is why its beginning is the fear of the Lord, and why it is open to being related to Law.

---

126. Consider the identification of wisdom and Torah in, for example, *Sirach* 24; cf. Rad, *Wisdom in Israel*, 165–6.

127. Job 28:12.

128. See Prov. 1:7; 4:7; and 9:10.

129. The idea of a beginning of wisdom is debated. Two words are used to express it: rēʾšît (in 1:7 and 4:7) and tĕḥillâ (in 9:10). The second of these tells in favor of the idea of a beginning in the sense of a "first part" or "starting point," rather than a translation like "essence," "principal part," or "basis" (See Weeks, *Instruction and Imagery*, 113–19; and Fox, *Proverbs 1–9*, 67–9). Weeks argues that what is meant is that the fear of the Lord is "the first product of knowledge," "something that one gains from wisdom and knowledge, not *vice versa*" (*Instruction and Imagery*, 118). This leads him to understand the acquisition of wisdom as a kind of once-and-for-all moment of transition. "A proper internalization of the Law brings one to a condition beyond the risk of corruption, expressed in terms of accepting wisdom" (p. 144). However, this does not seem to be how things are really imagined in Proverbs. As we noted above, there is a sense in Proverbs in which "one is always at a crossroads" (Stewart, *Poetic Ethics*, 209). I think things are simpler if we keep the emphasis on wisdom as an objective reality, rather than on subjective states of development. Weeks actually comes close to our position when he says that 9:10 "implies that wisdom is to be viewed as a continuing state or process, rather than as a simple skill or attribute, and the verse would seem to be suggesting that the fear of YHWH is the first point (in the process or continuing situation) of being wise" (p. 118).

With this, we may appreciate what is perhaps the deepest theological claim of Proverbs: its identification of wisdom with righteousness.[130] My biggest quarrel with Fox's account of the ethics of Proverbs lies at this point. Fox argues that the central principle of ethics according to the book of Proverbs is that wisdom is righteousness. But what he means by this is that "the exercise of the human mind is the necessary and sufficient condition of right and successful behaviour in all reaches of life: practical, ethical, and religious."[131] This, in effect, treats wisdom as the known term and righteousness as the unknown term. Wisdom is understood as an intellectual capacity that enables righteousness, allowing Fox to say, "the principle that human knowledge is a sufficient precondition for virtue allows Proverbs to provide a comprehensive guide to individual behaviour without recourse to divine Torah or other communication."[132] In my view, the identification of wisdom with righteousness that Fox rightly observes points to the exactly reverse thought: *righteousness* (the known term) *is wisdom* (the unknown term). The claim is that true wisdom—which the whole ancient world sought—is found in righteousness. Proverbs does not so much teach that, as Fox puts it, "hearkening to wisdom guarantees that one will walk the path of righteousness,"[133] as that the path of righteousness *is* the path of wisdom, that it is wise to be righteous. "I have instructed you in the way of wisdom, I have led you in tracks of uprightness" (4:11). What Fox leaves out is the idea we have emphasized here, of the determinacy and alterity of wisdom.[134] The deepest claim of Proverbs is that

---

130. While rarely made in a simple way in Proverbs, this claim is constantly being pointed to by sayings that either parallel wisdom and righteousness or folly and wickedness (e.g., 3:33-35; 4:11; 9:9; 23:22-25), or contrast folly and righteousness (e.g., 10:19, 21; 13:15); and also by the constant emphasis on the inevitable consequences of wickedness and righteousness (among many examples, see 10:2-3, 27-30; 11:4-8, 23, 30-31; 13:6, 9, 15; 14:11, 14, 19, 32; 21:7, 12, 21). I think that the editorial arrangement of sayings often aims chiefly to highlight this identification (e.g., 14:1-3, 32-35; 15:5-9).

131. Fox, *Proverbs 1–9*, 934.

132. Fox, *Proverbs 1–9*, 944.

133. Fox, *Proverbs 1–9*, 937.

134. Notably, the fear of the LORD is emptied of particularity in Fox's account, coming to mean essentially humility before the divine, rather than being a category that makes deep contact with the theology and faith of Israel (*Proverbs 1–9*, 69–71). Contrast Gerhard von Rad: "The statement that the fear of the Lord was the beginning of wisdom was Israel's most special possession" (*Wisdom in Israel*, 68). See also R. W. L. Moberly, *The Bible, Theology, and Faith: A Study of Abraham and Jesus* (Cambridge: Cambridge University Press, 2000), 80–97; Dell, *The Book of Proverbs*, 90–124, 146–50; and Weeks, *Instruction and Imagery*, 114. Ansberry makes a similar criticism of Fox to the one made here, and links this to his argument that Aristotle's thought makes for a better parallel ("What Does Jerusalem Have to Do with Athens?: The Moral Vision of the Book of Proverbs and Aristotle's *Nicomachean Ethics*," Hebrew Studies 51 [2010]: 159–66).

wisdom consists in righteousness: the way of righteousness, which is marked out by words of instruction, *is* the way of wisdom.

b. "Getting" Wisdom: Wisdom and Practical Knowledge

A clarification is needed. The point is not that wisdom is simply a determinate other in the sense of something wholly external to and standing over against the subject. There is a subjective side to wisdom, knowledge, and life-competence. These are things someone can *have* in some sense. A person may "get wisdom" (4:5, 7; 16:16). "Wisdom rests in the understanding heart" (14:33).[135] The question, though, is how this subjective possession of wisdom should be conceptualized. What does it mean for someone to "get wisdom" (4:5), to "guard discretion" (5:2), "to say to wisdom, 'you are my sister'" (7:4)?

We noticed at the beginning of this discussion that wisdom in Proverbs has to do with *action*. By wisdom a house is built. Throughout Chapter 2, this orientation to action is constant, and is expressed especially through the metaphor of ways and paths that we have already highlighted. Paths are for *walking* and keeping to (2:7-8). The "ways of darkness," on the other hand, consist in "doing evil" (2:13-14). The aim of wisdom is "that you may walk in the good way and guard paths of righteousness." The path metaphor serves, in part, to secure the link between wisdom and certain kinds of action.

Wisdom enables good action. The path metaphor disciplines the way in which we understand this relation. Wisdom enables good action in that it opens up good paths—not, that is to say, that it equips one to make good paths, or to carve them out, but wisdom allows one to appreciate good paths for what they are, and to take them. The paths metaphor reminds us that wisdom is something that involves the world as well as the subject. It rests upon the hospitality of the world to good action. Wisdom involves a relation, a kind of correspondence between action and the moral reality of the world.

The acquisition of wisdom cannot, then, be understood purely in the sense of the development of an intellectual capacity, for this does not reflect the way in which Proverbs sees wisdom in terms of a relation to the reality of the world. Here we must again disagree with Fox, who describes wisdom as a "faculty," "a higher state of conscience," which "allows one to classify each path and deduce its end point from its quality at point of entry."[136] Such a view is too remote from activity, from the sense in which wisdom is something acquired on the way, in the course of walking and in the face of danger. The "understanding" developed in 2:9 is not the understanding of the impartial observer, surveying from a privileged standpoint; it is the understanding of the skilled walker, who has become adroit at picking out the way, or better, for whom the path is becoming familiar. The striking thing in

---

135. Similarly, in 1 Kgs 10:24, the whole world comes to Solomon "to hear his wisdom, which God had set in his heart."

136. Fox, *Proverbs 1–9*, 116, 131.

2:10 is that it is *wisdom*, not the heart and the soul, that is the active agent: wisdom "enters" the heart; knowledge "befriends" the soul.[137] The development we see in Chapter 2 is not the development of "a reasoned, cognitive conscience,"[138] but the development of a relation between the subject and the reality of the world. The subject "gets wisdom" in the sense that they become rightly comported toward, or perhaps "attuned to," good paths.[139]

How can we characterize the subjective aspect of this relation more precisely? We may begin by recalling von Rad's attention to the affective dimension of our engagement with wisdom. Wisdom and folly are both attractive. They are likened to two women, inviting young men to their table (9:1-18). As Raymond Van Leeuwen puts it, there is a "bi-polar human *eros* for the beauty of Wisdom, who prescribes life within limits, or for the seeming beauty of Folly, who offers bogus delights in defiance of created limits."[140] *Eros* may not be the best term here, because it may not adequately catch the way Wisdom and Folly appeal in different kinds of ways—a point Van Leeuwen does recognize. Wisdom's attractions are profoundly different in character to those of Folly. Folly's attractions are finally illusory, leading to death (9:18). Wisdom's attractions, on the other hand, are real and deep: She holds out the chance to walk in the way of insight (9:6) that leads to life (9:11). Wisdom deserves to be *loved*.[141]

This affective dimension is a central feature of Proverbs' understanding of wisdom. It points toward the way of thinking about wisdom we have been arguing for, in particular the idea that the subjective acquisition of wisdom is not so much

---

137. The verb form *yin'ām* in v. 10 is normally translated, as we have above, "will be pleasant to." However, with the preposition *lĕ* it often means "be friendly with." The central point, though, is that it is *knowledge* that is the subject of the action.

138. Fox, *Proverbs 1–9*, 111.

139. Fox expresses something close to this when, commenting on 2:15, he says, "Just as he who goes in the straight path is himself straight [cf. 3:32], so he who walks the crooked track becomes deformed." *Proverbs 1–9*, 117.

140. Van Leeuwen, "Liminality and Worldview," 116.

141. Within Proverbs, the metaphorical contrast is accompanied by a more concrete contrast, between the "strange woman" (*zārāh, nokrîâ*; e.g., 2:17) and "the wife of your youth" (5:18). This is because in its own way the young man's choice between faithfulness to his wife and adultery with a stranger (or foreigner; see the detailed discussion in Weeks, *Instruction and Imagery*, 128–41) embodies the choice between wisdom and folly. The strange woman, too, holds out an illusory appeal. Her lips are sweet (5:3), her speech seductive (2:16), yet "her paths go to the dead" (2:18), "her steps hold to Sheol" (5:5). With the wife, on the other hand, lies blessing and true satisfaction (5:18-19). If we extend our view to the rest of Proverbs, this point is all the clearer. The "strong and noble wife" of 31:10-31 represents the real-life correlate of Woman Wisdom, in the same way that the strange woman is the correlate of Dame Folly. The young man's temptation illustrates, and in turn is illumined by, the metaphorical contrast between Wisdom and Folly.

a matter of "attaining an attribute"[142] as about a relation to something. Wisdom is about the love of something genuinely *other*. "Love her," says the father, "and she will watch over you" (4:6).[143]

At this point, we should note an aspect of the picture in Proverbs that will assist us to characterize this relation further. The element of affectivity is connected with speech. The strange woman attracts especially through her speech: "she smoothes her words" (2:16), "her mouth is smoother than oil" (5:3). Indeed, she is depicted as persuading through "her instruction" (*liqḥāh*, 7:21). Likewise, the sinners of the first chapter "entice" with their speech (1:10-11). Correspondingly, Wisdom draws attention to the genuine beauty of her speech. "Listen, for I speak admirable things … truth is what my mouth mutters" (8:6-7). In ch. 9, both wisdom and folly call out to attract.[144] Wisdom's affective appeal is extended and given form through words. Here may lie part of the significance of the structure of Proverbs 1–9, with its alternating of parental speeches and wisdom poems.[145] This may be a way of showing how the call of wisdom is mediated by the instruction of tradition, the teaching the parents pass on to their children.

We need to be careful how we construe this relationship, however. Commenting on the two halves of ch. 1 (1:10-19, 20-33), Van Leeuwen concludes, "The juxtaposition of these two warning speeches effects an identification of the parent's teaching and the voice of Woman Wisdom."[146] Identification is too strong. As we have seen, there is certainly a real and important connection between wisdom and the teaching that opens it to us. Yet equating the two risks obscuring the crucial point that wisdom involves a relation to a real feature of creation. The father's words "are wisdom" not of themselves, but by virtue of the reality they disclose, the ways of life they make available to the son. This is why the parental instruction can also speak *of* wisdom, commending her as a distinct entity (e.g., 3:13-18; 4:3-9). The interspersing of Wisdom's speeches and parental speeches reflects a profound theological claim: that on the one hand the created order is, of itself, hospitable to good action, while on the other hand our appreciation of and access to this truth depend upon our attention to particular words of instruction.

In the book of Proverbs, these words are words of poetry. More specifically, they are didactic poetry, that is, poetry that aims to teach, and that, in Stewart's words, "thus figures, either implicitly or explicitly, the relationship between author

---

142. Weeks, *Instruction and Imagery*, 154.

143. Stewart is conscious of this emphasis. "Within Proverbs," she writes, "wisdom is not simply a set of precepts that the student must memorize, but rather it is figured as an appealing and desirable object that the student must imbibe, delight in, and even love (2:10; 4:6; 8:17)" (*Poetic Ethics*, 60).

144. See Weeks, *Instruction and Imagery*, 143–5.

145. On the structure of Proverbs 1–9 see Fox, "Ideas of Wisdom in Proverbs 1–9," 613–33; and Weeks, *Instruction and Imagery*, 1–66.

146. Van Leeuwen, "Liminality and Worldview," 115.

and reader as one between teacher and pupil."[147] Moreover, the poetic form is not incidental to the teaching, a mere vehicle for content that could be expressed in prose propositions. Rather, the form of the poetry is itself critical. Why is this? Stewart argues that it is because what the poems of Proverbs aim to teach is not simply what wisdom is, but how to act wisely. Proverbial sayings aim not just at "clarity," but at the cultivation of skills.[148] She quotes Willard Spiegelman's comment that the didactic poem aims at not only "a sharing of enthusiasms and an imparting of knowledge, but also an understanding of a process ... Teaching, in the final analysis, does not take a direct object: the poets teach us *how*."[149] I think this is right. Proverbial sayings are designed not simply to disclose truth but to make the hearer notice it. The tight formulation of their insights forces the hearer to slow down. They aim to draw out not only insights into life in the world, but also their value to the living, so that the student does not just learn something in abstract but begins to learn how to do it. The poetry of Proverbs aims, that is, not at a *theoretical* knowledge of wisdom, but at a *practical* knowledge of it.

The idea of practical knowledge is one that we have already had occasion to note. Examining it more fully now will clarify our discussion. In Chapter 2, we introduced the idea of practical knowledge in the course of discussing Aquinas's account of divine knowledge; and we wondered whether there is a kind of knowledge that uniquely attends action.[150] Such a thought has been explored in different ways by Elizabeth Anscombe and Gilbert Ryle. In *Intention*, Anscombe builds on Aquinas's claim that practical knowledge is "the cause of what it understands,"[151] to describe practical knowledge as knowledge of "how to do things."[152] But that, she says, does not mean merely theoretical knowledge of how to do things, such as the knowledge of someone giving a lecture about how to do something; rather it means knowledge that can be enacted. "In the case of practical knowledge the exercise of the capacity is nothing but the doing or supervising of the operations of which a man has practical knowledge."[153] Practical knowledge, she clarifies, means not merely the knowledge *of* what I am doing when I do something—as I might observe the movements I am making as I act—but the knowledge *by which* I act.[154] It is the kind of knowledge, she illustrates, by which, during the course of building

---

147. Stewart, *Poetic Ethics*, 42. I am indebted to Stewart's wider discussion of the poetic form of Proverbs (pp. 29–69) at this point.

148. Stewart, *Poetic Ethics*, 50.

149. Quoted in Stewart, *Poetic Ethics*, 42.

150. See above, Chapter 2, Section 1.

151. Elizabeth Anscombe, *Intention* (Oxford: Basil Blackwell, 1976), 87, where Anscombe cites only *ST* I-II.3.5 arg1 for this idea. It is, however, found more clearly elsewhere, for example, *ST* I.14.16.

152. Anscombe, *Intention*, 88.

153. Anscombe, *Intention*, 88.

154. Anscombe, *Intention*, 88–9.

a house, a multitude of detailed decisions, which are not on the plans but which nevertheless require skillful judgments, get made.[155] In Kieran Setiya's more recent articulation of Anscombe's view, "knowledge how to φ is a capacity to execute one's intention, not to form an intention in the first place … knowledge how mediates between intention and action."[156]

A similar thought was developed a few years before Anscombe's argument by Gilbert Ryle. In *The Concept of Mind*, Ryle argued that there is a fundamental difference between "knowing how" and "knowing that."[157] There is a kind of knowledge, "knowing how," that is not reducible to knowledge of propositions, but rather subsists in action. Acting intelligently involves a kind of intelligence that is essentially practical, rather than simply the application of theoretical knowledge. In making this argument, Ryle was resisting what he saw as an overly intellectualized account, in which all the most important aspects of human existence were hidden in the inaccessibility of "other minds." Instead, Ryle insisted that in our actions, our minds are really on display: "In making sense of what you say, in appreciating your jokes, in unmasking your chess-stratagems, in following your arguments, I am not inferring the workings of your mind, I am following them."[158]

David Wiggins has recently defended Ryle's core insights against his critics.[159] He suggests that Ryle's account is strengthened if we include alongside the idea of "knowing how" the notions of "knowing when to," "where to," and "knowing to do p at V."[160] He also highlights the different ways in which practical and theoretical knowledge are interconnected. Wiggins illustrates how propositional knowledge can derive from practical knowledge (using an example of one of the kinds of *technē* that Joseph Dunne argues have a significant affinity with *phronēsis*[161]):

> A ship's pilot who is retained by the maritime authorities to bring large ships safely to anchor in an awkward or difficult harbour can tell us, on the basis of his competence and experience, that when the wind is from the north and the tide is running out, the best thing to do is steer straight for such-and-such a church tower until one is well past a certain bend in the channel. Almost anyone can come to possess that propositional knowledge but the information they get in this way will probably rest indispensably upon the experience and practical knowledge of a handful of people with a different

---

155. Anscombe, *Intention*, 81.
156. Kieren Setiya, "Practical Knowledge Revisited," *Ethics* 120, no. 1 (2009): 136.
157. Gilbert Ryle, *The Concept of Mind* (New York: Barnes and Noble, 1950), 26–60.
158. Ryle, *The Concept of Mind*, 59.
159. David Wiggins, "Practical Knowledge: Knowing How To and Knowing That," *Mind* 121 (2012): 97–130.
160. Wiggins, "Practical Knowledge," 113.
161. See above, Chapter 1, Section 3.

kind of knowledge, namely practical ... The propositional knowledge is *the stepchild* of the pilot's practical or agential knowledge.[162]

Wiggins further argues that theoretical knowledge can subsequently enrich practical knowledge. Practical discoveries in land measurement contributed to early geometry, but geometry then vastly enriched the practice of land measurement. Practices can be improved by subsequent, exploratory theoretical reflection upon them.

All this is not far from the way Proverbs imagines wisdom. Wisdom, like practical knowledge or "knowing how," is a form of knowledge that fully exists only in and with action. It is not, fundamentally, a theoretical knowledge that is subsequently applied to action, but a knowledge that attends upon action—although perhaps it may be open to theoretical enrichment. And wisdom is "other" in a parallel way to the way Ryle sees the workings of a mind as accessible in concrete operations like chess stratagems and determinate trains of thought.

A final observation about this philosophical discussion will take us a step further. Richard Moran contests the interpretation of Anscombe's concept of practical knowledge given here.[163] Moran argues that what Anscombe means by understanding practical knowledge as the cause of what it understands is the formal rather than the efficient cause. Practical knowledge is the non-observational knowledge that makes an action an intentional action. Using Anscombe's words, it is "the knowledge that one denies having if when asked e.g., 'Why are you ringing that bell?' one replies 'Good heavens! I didn't know *I* was ringing it!'"[164] While this kind of knowledge clearly is of interest to Anscombe, it does not, I think, do justice to Anscombe's idea of practical knowledge, which is knowledge *how* and so causal in a different sense than merely formal.[165] Moran's argument highlights an important point, however, which is that there is a connection between knowing how to do something and being able to say *what* one is doing. We see this connection in the way the question "what are you doing?" often seeks not merely a factual description of a person's actions but a description in terms of an intelligible purpose. If, in surprise, I ask a driver, "what are you doing?" as she makes a turn I was not expecting, I am asking her to show that she knows *how* to get where I have asked her to drive me. Similarly, the child surrounded by a floury mess who says "I'm making a cake" gives a mistaken description of their action because they lack the knowledge of how to make a cake. Finally, improvising on one of Moran's examples: imagine a painter observes his apprentice putting yellow paint on a wall,

---

162. Wiggins, "Practical Knowledge," 109, emphasis original.

163. Richard Moran, "Anscombe on 'Practical Knowledge,'" *Royal Institute of Philosophy Supplement* 55 (2004): 43–68.

164. Anscombe, *Intention*, 51, quoted by Moran in "Anscombe," 49.

165. Anscombe speaks of practical knowledge as "presupposed" by intentional action on p. 89 of *Intention*.

but doing a singularly bad job of it, and he shouts, "what are you doing?" What is actually in question here is not whether or not the apprentice *thinks* they are "painting the wall yellow"—no doubt they do. The question, rather, is a challenge to their knowledge of how to paint the wall yellow. Their lack of knowledge of *how* to paint properly means that *what* they are doing, in the sense that matters most, is not "painting the wall yellow."

The significance of this is to show us that practical knowledge is derivative upon the reality of the world. Knowing how to do things depends upon there being things available to do, actions that are intelligible and so open to question. "Knowing how" is the knowledge of how an intelligible kind of action, a "what" that can be done, falls within my power to effect; it is the knowledge of how that "what" can be done *by an agent*. Here, I believe, we make solid contact with the conceptuality of Proverbs. The wisdom by which a house is built is correlated to what houses actually are, the limited range of ways in which they can be well-built, and to the significance the building and filling of houses tends to have within the living of a life. Wisdom, like practical knowledge, is about *intelligible* action. It exists only insofar as it enables the doing of particular kinds of things. Anscombe does deploy the language of capacity to describe practical knowledge. Yet she also stresses that this capacity is only exercised in action. Practical knowledge, like wisdom in Proverbs, is a "capacity" that depends upon the availability of certain kinds of action, and that derives its meaning from them.

This underscores the appropriateness of the relational conception suggested above: wisdom is about a relation between the subject and the reality of the world, or as we put it, the world's hospitality to certain kinds of action. In closing this part of the discussion, we note that another way we might get at this understanding of wisdom is through Aquinas's notion of *connaturalitas*. As we saw, Thomas deploys this concept in his discussion of the gift of wisdom (as opposed to simply the intellectual virtue), as well as in his discussion of the way in which the virtues are related to prudence.[166] He explains it as an "instinctive affinity" or *compassio* for the objects of wisdom.[167] One advantage of this concept is that it is affective, and so reflects the way in which Proverbs frequently, as in 2:10, links wisdom with the heart—the heart being both like the mind, but also not merely "rational."[168] Wisdom's "entering the heart" (2:10) suggests an affective attunement to good forms of action, a "connaturality" with the ways of wisdom.[169]

---

166. See above, Chapter 2, Sections 1 and 4.

167. *ST* ii-II.45.2.

168. See Fox's instructive discussion of the heart in *Proverbs 1–9*, 109. Correspondingly, Proverbs deploys a distinctive expression for imprudence: "lacking heart" (*ḥăsar lēb*). See, for example, 6:32; 9:16; 10:13, 21; 24:30. I think Fox is mistaken in ruling out an affective element in this expression (*Proverbs 1–9*, 39–40), for the reasons he himself sets out in the discussion of the heart mentioned here.

169. In *Seeing the World* (pp. 374–82), Paul Fiddes also uses the musical metaphor of attunement. For Fiddes, however, attunement to wisdom means, fundamentally, attunement to God. I think it is primarily about attunement to creation.

c. Proverbs 8 Reconsidered

Finally, bringing our discussion around full-circle, the account of wisdom given here may provide a different way to understand the problem of Proverbs ch. 8. For it allows us to think of the Wisdom described in 8:22-31 in terms not simply of a divine *attribute*, but in connection with divine *action*. Weeks's discussion is, again, instructive:

> We are on our own, then, if we wish to understand just how wisdom in Proverbs 1–9 can at once be a divine attribute or possession, and at the same time have a personality distinct from God. It seems likely, though, that we are dealing with the same sort of idea that allows humans each to have wisdom, while wisdom itself remains a concept that transcends the individual: when the divine attribute of wisdom comes into being, so, simultaneously, does the whole concept of wisdom, the general arising from the first instance of the particular.[170]

Weeks rightly identifies the problem we outlined above: of understanding how wisdom can be somehow *God's* and yet also a human possibility, and hence, "of creation" in some sense. As we have seen, Weeks recognizes that his solution, that we think in terms of a concept that transcends the individual and is, in some way or other, instantiated both in God and human beings (which is not dissimilar to Fox's idea of Wisdom as a universal), renders the device of personification problematic. "The author's decision not only to use a character to represent wisdom, but also to use a personification of the concept, rather than a type like the woman or the sinners, has left him with problems both in correlating their roles, and in dealing with the implications of Wisdom (the person) for wisdom (the concept)."[171]

The same concerns lead to different results in Paul Fiddes's important recent theological engagement with Proverbs 8.[172] Fiddes, too, sharply recognizes the challenge posed by the way Wisdom seems to be "continually transgressing the boundary between self and world," and by "the ambiguity and overlap between divine and human exercise of wisdom which the figure of Lady Wisdom expresses."[173] However, because Fiddes is committed to understanding wisdom as an attribute of God's being, a "subjective faculty," he cannot, ultimately, take the creatureliness of wisdom seriously—or rather, taking it seriously leads to significant theological problems. "It does not matter," he says, "that … Lady Wisdom is said to be 'created' by God." This is merely a poetic device that is "balanced" by the images of being set-up and born.[174] In fact, Wisdom just is God, which is why "seeing the world is knowing God,"[175] a sentence that traverses into theologically perilous territory.

---

170. Weeks, *Instruction and Imagery*, 123.
171. Weeks, *Instruction and Imagery*, 125.
172. Fiddes, *Seeing the World*, especially pp. 175–88.
173. Fiddes, *Seeing the World*, 187.
174. Fiddes, *Seeing the World*, 188.
175. Fiddes, *Seeing the World*, 188.

The difficulty arises from thinking about wisdom primarily in terms of an attribute independently of determinate forms of action, something that is "possessed" by a subject in the sense of being a characteristic of that subject. It is assumed that to "have" wisdom is to *be* a certain way; and insofar as wisdom is related to action it is about thought that precedes and enables action. If, then, both God and humans "have" wisdom, then we either imagine wisdom as transcending those instantiations in the way a general concept does—an idea that we have already found theologically problematic, and that makes the personification of wisdom awkward—or we embrace the implication of personification and end up blurring the distinction between God and creation. If, alternatively, we focus on wisdom's connection with action, a different possibility may emerge. God's wisdom is a quality by which he *worked*, and Woman Wisdom is the personification of this quality. She is the wisdom "by" which he created—not simply in the sense of being a capacity first possessed (perfectly in the mind) and then put to work, but in the sense of an excellence only truly manifest *in the work*, a predicate not simply of his eternal knowledge, but of his action. She is the wisdom the LORD "got," "at the beginning *of his way*, at the outset *of his works* of old" (8:22); that is to say, Wisdom is intrinsically connected to God's action. Against Fiddes, we must insist that it *does* matter that Wisdom is said to be, in some sense, created, and that the other images, while complementing the metaphorical picture, do not change this reality. There is a real sense in which God's wisdom is *of creation*. God's wisdom is divine, in that it is *God's* work that is done by wisdom; but it is also creaturely, in that it is a quality of his *work*.

Above (Section 1), we noted the way in which vv. 22-31 play an important role in their context of grounding the appeal to listen to wisdom. They clearly ground this appeal in the status and antiquity of Wisdom. Now we may also see a way in which these verses ground the appeal in the example of God. In this respect, the translation of *qānānî* in v. 22 as "get" is important. As we noted, this word is frequently used in Proverbs to speak of "getting" wisdom, or a related good, as in the prologue's promise of "getting counsel" (1:5), or the call to "Get wisdom!" in 4:5 and 7. The statement in 8:22 should be understood in connection with these texts. It grounds the appeal to listen to wisdom and to be wise, and the wider call in Proverbs to get wisdom, in the example of God. God himself "got wisdom" in the beginning, in that he set to acting in a particular kind of way.

The point of analogy between divine and human wisdom lies in determinate action.[176] By wisdom God founded the earth: by wisdom a house is built. Yet Proverbs 8 also highlights a clear dis-analogy, signaled especially in the additional metaphor of God's giving birth to Wisdom used in 8:24-25. Although both God and humans may be said to "get wisdom," in the sense that they take up action in a particular way, only God "gave birth" to Wisdom. Wisdom never "called" to God; but She calls to humankind. God "has" wisdom, therefore, in a quite different way

---

176. Against, for example, Fiddes, who says that "The wisdom of God and humanity is the same kind of faculty, differing only in degree" (*Seeing the World*, 186).

to human beings. In this respect, Weeks is quite right to speak of wisdom arising from the first instance of it (God's): God's wise action is foundational, opening up a derivative possibility for creaturely action by participation.

Which returns us, at the close of this discussion, to theological reflection. Although we cannot yet develop the point in full, we should notice that this position might clarify the form Christological interpretation of Proverbs 8 should take. As we noted above, the New Testament explicitly links Christ to the wisdom of God, and alludes to Proverbs 8. Yet when it does so, it is never in isolation from the person, and the work, of Jesus of Nazareth. "He is the image of the unseen God, the firstborn of the whole creation. For in him everything was created … For in him all the fullness was pleased to dwell, and through him to reconcile everything to himself, by making peace through the blood of his cross" (Col. 1:15-20). Similarly, when the apostle Paul speaks of Christ as "God's power and God's wisdom" (1 Cor. 1:24), it is explicitly "Christ crucified" who is in view (1 Cor. 1:23). And in Rev. 3:14, "the Amen" (*ho amēn*, which appears to echo the contested term *'āmôn* in Prov. 8:30[177]), "the beginning (*archē*) of God's creation," is also "the faithful and true witness." This is simply to notice that in the New Testament, Christ's identification with God's wisdom is never removed from the historical action of Jesus.[178] The way Proverbs conceives of wisdom, we can now see, might allow us to understand why this is the case. It is because God's wisdom has to do with his action. Wisdom is essentially about action; to speak of God's wisdom is, therefore, to speak of the form his action takes. Jesus Christ crucified is the wisdom of God, because he is the determinate form of God's good action.

This, in turn, clarifies the way in which Proverbs 8 should be read as Christian Scripture. The Wisdom who speaks in Proverbs 8 cannot be separated from Jesus Christ. For if indeed he is "the firstborn of creation," and all things were made "through him and for him,"[179] then Jesus Christ, in his person and work, must somehow be the Wisdom the Lord "got" at the beginning of his works. He, Christ crucified, is the way of God's action, the Wisdom "by which" God founded the earth. In a way, this is a vindication of the patristic intuition that what was being spoken of in Prov. 8:22 was the human nature of Christ, that, in Augustine's words, "according to the form of a slave it was said, 'The Lord created me in the beginning of his ways.'"[180] What this recognizes, somewhat obliquely, is that God's wisdom cannot be disconnected from his action in the human being, Jesus Christ.

---

177. See Weeks, "Context and Meaning," 439, n. 24.

178. These observations are not dissimilar to those of Karl Barth in *CD* III/2, 55-60. I do not, however, wish to draw the same conclusions as Barth—that the distinction between the person and work of Christ should be collapsed (see pp. 61-2), and that human being consists in union with God—but only to say that Christ's being the wisdom of God cannot be separated from his work.

179. Col. 1:16; 1 Cor. 8:6.

180. *DT* 1.12.24; quoted in *ACCS*, 66.

And yet, the wisdom that speaks in Proverbs 8 is also not straightforwardly Jesus Christ. To note the most obvious point, already observed by Robert Jenson: the Wisdom of Proverbs 8 is personified as female. Less strikingly, but still significantly, when we first meet this figure in Proverbs, She appears to have a character that jars with the New Testament's presentation of Jesus. "I will laugh at your calamity and mock when your terror arrives" (1:26). Christ does not laugh looking over Jerusalem, but weeps.[181] These differences need at least to be explained if we are to connect Proverbs 8 with Jesus. I think the key, again, lies in the connection of wisdom with action. Although the New Testament identifies Jesus as the wisdom of God, and involves him in God's work of creation, it does not collapse the distinction between God's acts of creation and reconciliation. Although they are both acts of the same wisdom, the name of which is ultimately Jesus Christ, they are distinct acts. The female personification of wisdom is a pointer to an irreducible distinction between God's works of creation and reconciliation. This is a point we will need to take up again. For now, it is time to pause and clarify where the discussion so far has brought us.

3 Reflections on Aquinas's Understanding of Practical Reason

The remainder of this study will chiefly be an effort to explore the meaning and implications of the reading of Proverbs set out above. We begin by observing and clarifying a number of questions that now seem important about Thomas Aquinas's thought. The preceding remarks about the Christological significance of Proverbs 8 direct us to a first point of discussion: Aquinas's ideas of wisdom and eternal law.

a. Wisdom, Creation, and Eternal Law

Above, we suggested that there were important similarities between the idea of wisdom and the concept of practical knowledge. Both attempt to describe a relation to intelligible action that is in some way derivative upon the possibilities afforded by reality. What does this understanding of wisdom mean for Aquinas's account of eternal law and divine wisdom?

As we noted, Anscombe's reflections on practical knowledge are inspired, at least partly, by Aquinas. But does Thomas really have room for the kind of practical

---

181. In my view, this point should moderate the argument of Susanne Guenther Loewen, that the connection between Woman Wisdom and Christ complicates the gender of Christ ("Jesus Christ as Woman Wisdom? Complicating the Gender of Christ," *Religious Studies and Theology* 30 [2011]: 71–82). In contrast to Loewen, I do not think it is quite right that Woman Wisdom's actions and identity correspond to Jesus', such that "Woman Wisdom is another name for the same Christ" (p. 74). There are similarities, certainly; but there are important differences too.

knowledge we have described? In Chapter 2, we saw that Aquinas certainly does think that God has practical knowledge of creation.[182] In the prologue to his commentary on Lombard's Sentences, he makes this clear with reference to the category of wisdom, and to our central text:

> The second thing that pertains to the wisdom of God is *the production of creatures*. He not only has speculative but also operative wisdom—like that of the artisan to his works—concerning created things. Thus Psalm 103.24: 'Thou hast made all things with wisdom.' And Wisdom itself says in Proverbs 8:30: 'I was with him, forming all things.' This attribute is especially found in the Son insofar as he is the image of the invisible God, in whose likeness all things are formed: 'He is the image of the invisible God, the first-born of every creature, for in him were created all things' (Colossians 1:15); 'All things were made through him' (John 1:3). Rightly then does the person of the Son say, 'I, like a brook out of a river of mighty water,' in which is noted both the order and mode of creation.[183]

We also saw, however, that Aquinas understands this to be true because God's simple act of self-knowledge encompasses all forms of knowledge. God's practical knowledge is enclosed within the "one single insight," by which "God enjoys eternal and unwavering knowledge of everything."[184] This act of self-knowledge is fundamentally speculative in character. In being practical, Aquinas explains, God's knowledge "loses nothing of the excellence of speculative knowledge, because he sees all things other than himself in himself, and himself he knows with speculative knowledge. Thus in his speculative knowledge of himself he has knowledge both speculative and practical of all other things."[185]

The principle of the superiority of speculative knowledge, supported here by the authority of Aristotle,[186] dominates the picture. The question that presses is whether it prevents Aquinas from taking fully seriously his own recognition that God must have knowledge of things that is practical in its *mode*, and that God's wisdom is also "operative wisdom."

Such a thought would have been difficult in light of the tradition. "Wisdom," said Augustine, summarizing his account in book fourteen of *De Trinitate*, "consists in the contemplation of eternal things."[187] This principle represented a powerful point of connection between Aristotle and Augustine that helped Thomas to place

---

182. See above, Chapter 2, Section 1.

183. "Commentary on *Sentences* I, Prologue," in *Thomas Aquinas: Selected Writings*, trans. Ralph McInerny (London: Penguin, 1998), 52.

184. *De Substantiis Separatis*, 14.70–72, and above, Chapter 2, Section 1.

185. *ST* I.14.16 ad2.

186. *ST* I.14.16 s.c.

187. *DT* 15.3.5.

Aristotle's thinking in a theological setting. Moreover, the theological objections to any alternative seem formidable. Augustine had written, for instance:

> He [God] does not ... know all His creatures, both spiritual and corporeal, because they are, but they ... are because He knows them. For He was not ignorant of what He was going to create. He created, therefore, because He knew; He did not know because He created. He did not know them differently when they were created, than when they were to be created, for nothing has been added to His wisdom from them; it has remained the same as it was, while they came into existence as they should and when they should.[188]

God's knowledge is not derived from creation. That truth represented a not insignificant barrier to thinking about God's wisdom as truly practical.

Yet there were also barriers within Aquinas's thought to exploring the distinct character of practical knowledge. In particular, underpinning Thomas's position is a conception of practical knowledge oriented by the idea of production. Aquinas's fundamental metaphor for "operation" is the artist or the builder, as the passage above from the sentences commentary illustrates once again. He pictures someone with a form in mind who then may or may not instantiate this form in matter. The category of "virtually practical knowledge," as we have seen, depends upon this point that "there is a type of knowledge that is capable of being ordered to an act, but this ordering is not actual. For example, an artist thinks out a form for his work, knows how it can be made, yet does not intend to make it."[189] Aquinas draws on this model to connect speculative and practical knowledge,[190] and to maintain the superiority of speculative knowledge. As we have observed, this conception draws heavily upon Aristotle, and his account of *technē*, according to which, "things are produced from *technē* if the form of them is in the mind."[191]

Two questions arise about this conception, both of which have been pursued with great clarity by Joseph Dunne, in his study of *technē* and *phronēsis* in Aristotle.[192] First, is this an adequate picture of *productive* knowledge? The picture has an intuitive appeal. Hannah Arendt wrote of "the division between knowing and doing," which "is an everyday experience in fabrication, whose processes obviously fall into two parts: first, perceiving the image or shape of the product-to-be, and then organizing the means and starting the execution."[193] The craftsman,

---

188. *DT* 15.13.22.

189. *De Veritate*, 3.3; and see above, Chapter 2, Section 1.

190. See *ST* I.14.16.

191. *Metaphysics* 6.7, 1032a32; and above, Chapter 1, Section 3.

192. Joseph Dunne, *Back to the Rough Ground: "Phronesis" and "Techne" in Modern Philosophy and in Aristotle* (Notre Dame and London: University of Notre Dame Press, 1993), especially 237–356.

193. Hannah Arendt, *The Human Condition* (Chicago: University of Chicago Press, 1958), 225.

she thought, could be guided by an "absolute, 'objective' certainty."[194] No doubt it is possible for an artisan to conceive some works in great detail before beginning them. Yet does it do justice to the knowledge involved in making to envisage it this way? Arguably, the kind of knowledge an artist might have prior to the actual making is only a shadowy knowledge; true productive knowledge comes in the making of the thing. This is what Dunne concludes, arguing that Aristotle's formal conception of making does not do justice to the kind of knowledge displayed, for example, by "the gifted carpenter who, when confronted with crooked walls and warped timber, contrives nonetheless, to produce an excellent finished job."[195] There is a need, he argues, for an account that "does justice to feedback that one can receive from the materials in the actual process of making."[196] Although Aristotle's formal account of *technē* does not provide this, Dunne notices the way Aristotle often makes reference to experience, and highlights a passage from *Metaphysics*, where Aristotle speaks of how "the act of building resides in the object of building."[197] This hints at an idea of making "that is itself intelligent, endowed with a know-how which is learned and actualized in the very process of making,"[198] a

> concept of techne ... in which *noēsis* and *poiēsis* are not separable, linear sequences, such that one retraces in reverse order the steps marked out by the other, but are, rather, interwoven in one process which is at the same time intelligent *and* productive, and must be said to go on in the materials as much as in the mind of the *technitēs*.[199]

There is a kind of productive knowledge, that is to say, that can only be had *in action*. In this case there is a real difference, beyond the "addition of the will," between virtually practical and genuinely practical knowledge. Or, put differently, the addition of the will significantly alters the kind of knowledge present.

The second question is whether, however we may understand the knowledge involved in making, this formal account of making is an adequate basis for an account of practical knowledge more broadly. The argument above seems to be more forceful when we are thinking about *praxis* rather than *poiēsis*. Dunne thinks that this is certainly the case. Aristotle's distinction between *technē* and *phronēsis* reflects a basic insight that action has its own distinctive character and logic. *Phronēsis*, as we have already observed,[200] is a knowledge that arises only in and with action, and which, therefore, is bound up with experience. This, Dunne says, is what Aristotle is recognizing, sometimes despite himself, when he says things like,

---

194. Arendt, *The Human Condition*, 226.
195. Dunne, *Back to the Rough Ground*, 283.
196. Dunne, *Back to the Rough Ground*, 315.
197. Dunne, *Back to the Rough Ground*, 324, 345; cf. *Metaphysics* 9.8, 1050a28.
198. Dunne, *Back to the Rough Ground*, 285.
199. Dunne, *Back to the Rough Ground*, 338. Emphasis original.
200. Chapter 1, Section 2.

"A person is practically wise not only by knowing, but also by being disposed to act."[201] In many kinds of action, and especially actions that are all about a relation to other persons—managing, teaching, listening, bringing up children, giving advice, caring—is it not the case that there is a knowledge of how to act that is manifest only in the process of acting? In each of these cases, although a practitioner might be able to give an account of how and why they did what they were doing, this derivative, theoretical account would be a different kind of knowledge. Anscombe and Ryle, as we have seen, distinguish between the kind of knowledge that issues in action, and the theoretical account that might be given of that knowledge. Practical knowledge is not simply the execution of theoretical knowledge; it is knowledge that subsists in action. Hannah Arendt, for whom the distinctive characteristic of action is its relation to other persons and the unpredictability this entails,[202] is in agreement here. The division between knowing and doing, she maintains, is "alien to the realm of action, whose validity and meaningfulness are destroyed the moment thought and action part company."[203]

Now it is possible to see how Aquinas's core account of divine knowledge could accommodate these ideas. For there is indeed a profound difference between divine and human knowledge. Augustine was right that God "did not know because He created." Thomas neatly highlights the significance of this:

> As the natural objects of knowledge are prior to our knowledge, and are its measure, so, the knowledge of God is prior to natural things, and is the measure of them; as, for instance, a house is midway between the knowledge of the builder who made it, and the knowledge of the one who gathers his knowledge of the house from the house already built.[204]

While it may be true that human wisdom depends upon the reality of the world, the way creation is hospitable to good action, this is not true of God's wisdom. God's wisdom must be understood to be constitutive of this hospitality.[205]

Yet, while we certainly do not want to say that God's knowledge is derived from creation, should we assume that this means embracing an essentially speculative account of divine wisdom? If, following Proverbs, the point of analogy with divine wisdom is a form of practical knowledge, then ought we not, rather, attempt to conceive of a form of divine knowledge that is genuinely active? As far as wisdom is concerned, the "house" that God "built" (creation) mediates not primarily between divine speculative knowledge and derived human speculative understanding—knowledge *of* the house—but between divine practical knowledge and a derivative practical wisdom *by which* things, like building houses, are achieved.

---

201. *EN* 7.10, 1152a8–9; and above, Chapter 1, Section 2.
202. On this point, see also Dunne, *Back to the Rough Ground*, 359.
203. Arendt, *The Human Condition*, 225.
204. *ST* I.14.8 ad3, Benziger Brothers edition.
205. This point is also made with great clarity in *ST* I-II.93.1 ad3.

Again, it might be possible to see room in Aquinas's theology for such an emphasis. After all, Aquinas understands God's knowledge as an *act*, his act of pure existence that is also pure understanding. To dethrone speculative knowledge in this way would, however, be a significant shift in the light of the tradition. Fundamental theological questions are raised here about the eternity of God's acts and the nature of his triune existence. These are beyond both the scope of this study and the competence of its author. Even if these could be resolved without jettisoning Aquinas's basic account of divine simplicity, however, one idea of particular interest to us would seem to be in trouble. Aquinas's account of eternal law depends for its intelligibility upon the idea that divine wisdom is fundamentally speculative. As we saw in Chapter 2, the purpose of the description of eternal law as a *ratio* of divine wisdom is to anchor eternal law in God's speculative knowledge.[206] Eternal law is like the "conception of the things he makes by his art," that "pre-exists in an artist's mind."[207] If, however, such a framework mischaracterizes the nature of practical knowledge, and the wisdom by which God made the world, then the concept of eternal law becomes problematic. If the wisdom by which God created the world is to be understood primarily by analogy—though only by analogy—with practical human wisdom, then we are no longer justified in imagining a preconceived theoretical pattern on which everything is based.

What does this mean for the idea of eternal law? It does not mean that there is no place for speaking of a moral order that inheres in creation, an order that is "natural" in some sense. On the contrary, some such idea seems to be well-founded. That God made the world by wisdom must mean at least that the world is well-made, that it is not randomly thrown together or fundamentally misconceived. Anne Stewart's comment is right: "Proverbs implicitly insists that its vision of moral authority is enshrined in the natural order."[208] Moreover, that the wisdom by which God made the world calls to humankind, offering life, means that the world's order constitutes a foundation for good human action. God's creation by wisdom means that the world coheres in such a way as to make available to human beings ways of acting well. Wisdom calls, because creation is hospitable to the successful living of human life. Furthermore, Proverbs could be seen to suggest that thinking in terms of kinds of action may be a key way to articulate what this order of wisdom means. Proverbs, as we have observed, abounds with descriptions of kinds of action—restraint, slander, heeding instruction, giving surety—and of virtues and vices correlated to kinds of action—laziness, anger, hastiness of speech, quarrelsomeness—perhaps for just this reason. Wisdom has to do with certain intelligible kinds of action. We will return to this point below.

Yet such affirmations do not amount to the same thing as the idea of eternal law. To begin with, such a conception of created order is only ambiguously "eternal." God is eternally wise, and, recalling Athanasius, could therefore never be without

---

206. See above, Chapter 2, Section 3b; cf. *ST* I.15.3.
207. I-II.93.1.
208. Stewart, "Wisdom's Imagination," 369.

his wisdom. Yet if God's wisdom is also something related to his action, then there must be a sense in which God's wisdom is also temporal, appearing in and with his work of creation, related to the finitude of nature. This, arguably, is just what Proverbs 8 points to. That text does speak of the pre-existence of Wisdom. "Out of time before, I was formed … before the hills I was brought forth." Yet, the primary point is not, as Thomas interprets it, that God's mind "has an eternal concept,"[209] but that Wisdom accompanied God's action from the very first. "The LORD got me at the beginning of his way." The wisdom by which God created was realized in his creative action. Now Aquinas, as we have seen, also understands the eternal law to be somewhat ambiguously eternal, in that it cannot imply that creation is eternal.[210] Yet, as we have also seen, Aquinas resolves this in a way that allows him to strongly affirm the eternity of eternal law: "While not as yet existing in themselves things nevertheless exist in God insofar as they are foreseen and preordained by him."[211] Our argument suggests that the emphasis should be reversed. While the wisdom by which creation was made is indirectly "eternal," insofar as the one who made it is eternal, it is itself temporal and contingent. There is no timeless order that transcends creation and precedes it as a pattern. There is only the wisdom by which creation was made, that now belongs to it and subsists with it. To return to our metaphor, the wisdom in which we may participate is not the wisdom of the plans according to which the house was built, but the practical wisdom by which it was actually constructed, and by which it continues to hold together.

This leads to a second point, which concerns Aquinas's founding the idea of eternal law on divine *providence*. For Aquinas, the *ratio* of divine wisdom that is eternal law is a conception of the whole movement of all things to their end—a *ratio* of divine *government*. As such, it encompasses all eventualities and even the decree of predestination. As we have noted, this point is crucial for the status of eternal law as *law*, which involves direction to the common good. Yet precisely here the picture seems different from the way Proverbs speaks of wisdom. Wisdom's call can be refused (1:24). Her advice can be disregarded (1:25). The wisdom by which God made the world is not his government of all things, but an order that belongs to creation and defines the character of the world vis-à-vis human action. It is an order that is genuinely *of creation*, rather than of providence. This also explains why the order of wisdom is not readily comprehended as *law*. Law commands; it "prescribes and prohibits."[212] It has to do, as Thomas says, with a rule or measure that "binds" or "obliges."[213] Wisdom does not primarily command. Wisdom *calls*; it beckons, seeks to persuade, and invites. Wisdom entreats: "How long, simple ones, will you love simplicity?" (1:22) "Happy are they who guard my ways!" (8:32). This is the voice with which the created order speaks, and it is not the voice of

---

209. *ST* I-II.91.1.
210. See above, Chapter 2, Section 3b.
211. *ST* I-II.91.1 ad1.
212. *ST* I-II.90.1 s.c.
213. *ST* I-II.90.1.

law. It is formally eudaemonistic, holding out the prospect of a successful life (e.g., 1:33). This is not to say there is no place for law. Proverbs, as we have seen, holds instruction, including *tôrâ* and *miṣwâ*, to be crucial. It is simply to say that the order of wisdom should not be understood *as* law. There is a place for speaking of a natural order, but not necessarily of a natural *law*. Law is related to the order of wisdom; but it is not itself that wisdom. To speak of the order of wisdom as law involves a significant change of grammar.

Eternal law represents an attempt to encompass the whole course of salvation history within a single, overarching idea, a "*ratio* of divine wisdom, as moving all things to their due end,"[214] which takes in both creation and reconciliation. This is possible only on the assumption that God's wisdom is fundamentally speculative, and that his action proceeds according to a pre-existing conception that is complete prior to actual action. It is important to remember, of course, that Aquinas is cautious in his articulation of this concept, and appreciates the difficulties in thinking in these terms.[215] Still, Proverbs suggests that this is not the right way to think about God's wisdom. God's wisdom is a perfection, not of speculative, but of practical knowledge. As such, it is inextricable from action, which is why it is ultimately connected to the figure of Jesus Christ in and with his work.

We will have to think further about what this implies about the idea of created order, and of its relation to God's action in Christ. In the end, we will suggest that thinking along these lines ought to lead us to maintain a clear sense that God's action in creation and reconciliation is irreducibly twofold. Creation must be allowed to retain its integrity as a distinct act. It is this that justifies the language of "nature." In fact, Aquinas's distinction between humanity's natural and supernatural ends aims at something very similar. For, as we have seen, it aims to recognize the way in which the gospel introduces something genuinely new into practical thinking.[216] In seeing the Old Law as pointing toward the coming of Christ, but still fundamentally about the natural order, Aquinas articulates a position that, we will argue, is in important ways correct.

Finally, all of this has consequences for the kind of knowledge available to us. The idea of eternal law invites the thought of a global understanding, a wisdom that consists in a total picture of how things fit together. The idea of wisdom as we have understood it in Proverbs, however, resists such a perspective. For any such global understanding can only be an abstraction. Wisdom resides in the distinct, concrete realities of God's work of creation and reconciliation, and not in an overarching account of how they fit together. That does not mean there is no place for such an account. Yet it does relativize its importance. Where this may start to pinch for Aquinas is with the idea of first principles of practical reason.

---

214. *ST* I-II.93.1; and above, Chapter 2, Section 3b.
215. See, for example, *ST* I-II.93.5.
216. Recall the discussion of David Decosimo's book, *Ethics as a Work of Charity*, in Chapter 2, Section 3a.

The idea of knowledge from first principles suggests knowledge from outside, from an observer's perspective. Aristotle thought, "This person who understands everything for himself is best of all, and noble is that one who heeds good advice."[217] Aquinas will not quite agree with this. Partly on the basis of Prov. 3:5-6, he insists that docility, or teachableness, is a part of prudence.[218] Yet his ideal of a wisdom that "rightly judges all things and sets them in order, because there can be no perfect and universal judgment that is not based on the first causes,"[219] hints at an aspiration to move beyond dependence on instruction to a self-sufficient speculative understanding.

b. Deliberation, Prudence, and Words of Instruction

This leads us back to Aquinas's understanding of practical reasoning. Deciding upon action, for Aristotle and Aquinas, involves thinking about means to ends. In emphasizing the metaphor of paths and ways, Proverbs can be seen to support this claim. Paths, after all, have destinations. However, the kind of means-end thinking involved is different, because the implied perspective is different. The agent, in Proverbs, is not surveying the landscape from on high, deciding which path to take. Rather, she is already on the way, in the thick of things; the decisions are made up close, and under pressure. "Clear the path for your feet, and make all your ways firm; do not turn right or left—do not step into evil!" (4:26-27).

To the extent that Aquinas's account envisages deliberation in ways that imply a sovereign perspective, in which the agent knows the end from the outset, and calculates the best means to achieve it—recall Aquinas's claim that "the order of reasoning about actions is contrary to the order of actions"[220]—it will be addressed with skeptical questions from the book of Proverbs. For Proverbs implies that often we cannot see the end clearly enough to be in a position to calculate the way to get there. All we can see is the path or the paths that lie before us. As we saw in Aquinas's example about showing affection in order to encourage someone, the end of action and the means to it arise together as a course of action that is in question. We cannot "take the end as fixed." The idea of deliberating from a fixed end therefore requires us to begin from a more remote, general end—acting well, doing good. We may happily accept that we do indeed "know" such an end—at least, as Aquinas helpfully explains, formally.[221] That *is* where we want to end up. We have seen, however, that moving from such a general premise to a particular action necessarily requires a long chain of reasoning: evil is to be avoided; adultery is evil; I should avoid adultery; this is an act of adultery; I should avoid this act. Proverbs, however, raises serious objections to such a conception of deliberation.

---

217. *EN* 1.4, 1095b10.
218. *ST* II-II.49.3.
219. *ST* I-II.57.2, Benziger Brothers edition.
220. *ST* I-II.14.5.
221. See *ST* I-II.1.8; 2.7; 3.1; 5.8.

Rather than such long chains of reasoning, in the book of Proverbs what we find is a proliferation of pieces of what we could call more proximate instruction. "One who restrains his words has real knowledge" (17:27). "Food gained by fraud tastes sweet, but you end up with a mouthful of gravel" (20:17). "Fools show their irritation at once" (12:16). The focus on such proximate instructions suggests that the battle is already lost if we are asking ourselves how to do good or avoid evil. Such abstract surveying of the terrain might assist the task of walking the path at certain rare moments, but mostly we need nearer, more intimate guidance.

Now Aquinas, we must remember, actually shares much of this caution. As we saw, he notes that "it happens sometimes that general principles known by understanding or science are swept away in the particular case by a passion." This, he says, is why prudence needs the moral virtues, to supply the "particular principles of action" that are needed in the situation.[222] The question, however, is whether this reliance on the virtues achieves the embeddedness in reality that Proverbs suggests is needed.

At stake here is Aquinas's characterization of prudence. In defending the claim that the chief act of prudence is to command, Aquinas faces a curious objection: Augustine says that it is an act of prudence to "avoid ambushes."[223] Although Aquinas is justified in replying that Augustine was here particularly concerned with the discontinuity of the virtues in heaven,[224] there is in fact an important difference at stake. Command as the chief act defines prudence formally, without necessary reference to what is commanded. The idea of "avoiding ambushes," on the other hand, implicitly sees prudence with reference to the world and the possibilities and dangers it presents. In this, it is closer to the thinking of Proverbs. "The prudent sees evil and hides, the simple carry on and suffer" (22:3; 27:12). Prudence, that is to say, cannot in Proverbs be defined without concrete reference to the world and its possibilities.

Aquinas begins the treatise on prudence with the question, "Whether prudence is in the cognitive or in the appetitive faculty."[225] He holds that it is the former, because it is about knowledge of the future, of what is "far off"; and through the sensitive faculty we know only "what is within reach and offers itself to the senses." Accepting these terms of discussion, the book of Proverbs might be felt to call this response into question. The domain of wisdom in Proverbs seems very much "what is within reach." It is about a comportment toward the task of living that is at least as much affective as it is cognitive. Being wise, in Proverbs, is about love and discipline as much as reason: it is about the heart, and the ways to which it turns (7:25). To these objections a defender of Aquinas might respond that these things are taken into account with the principle that prudence cannot exist without the moral virtues.

---

222. i-II.58.5. See above, Chapter 2, n. 277.
223. *ST* ii-II.47.8 arg1; cf. Augustine, *DT*, 14.9.12.
224. *ST* ii-II.47 ad1.
225. *ST* ii-II.47.1.

In fact, however, the challenge raised by Proverbs is more fundamental. It is to question whether prudence should be understood as *in* the subject at all. Prudence, rather, should be understood in the sense described above, not as a subjective capacity but as a relation to an aspect of creation. To hold that prudence depends upon the moral virtues is to move in this direction. The moral virtues are, from one perspective, a way of talking about what we have called the determinacy of wisdom, its distinct form and content.[226] Yet they remain qualities within the subject, rather than a relation to a world that engages the subject from without.

An example may clarify the point we are reaching for along with its importance for our discussion. In explaining the point noted above, how "general principles known by understanding" are sometimes "swept away" by a passion, Aquinas gives the example of how "to one who is overcome by lust, the object of his desire seems good, although it is opposed to the universal judgment of reason."[227] This is a situation that the book of Proverbs dwells on at some length with the figure of the "strange woman."[228] In Prov. 7:6-23, for example, the father paints a picture of a young man "steered" (*hiṭṭattû*) by her speech, "overwhelmed" (*taddîḥennû*) by her "smooth talk," so that "all of a sudden" (*piṯ'ōm*) he goes with her (vv. 21-22). The verbs used suggest a powerful moving force that resonates with Aquinas's language of being "swept away" and "overcome." Yet this similarity highlights an accompanying dissimilarity between the two perspectives. Whereas for Aquinas this possibility is an argument for the necessity of the moral virtues, for Proverbs it is an argument for the critical importance of words of instruction. What the son needs, above all, is to keep the father's words, to hide them close, to "not turn aside from the words of his mouth" (7:1-3, 24; 5:7). What will save the son when his thinking is scrambled in the face of temptation is not virtue, but the recollection of words that have come from without, and that put him in contact with wisdom, with the reality of the world's hospitality to action. The virtues might point us to the path of wisdom, but will they do so with enough force and clarity to enable right action? For Proverbs, it is words that enable us to discern the right path.

Here is the point to recall the question of the place of law in Aquinas's moral thought. In Chapter 2, we emphasized the way in which Aquinas's generic understanding of action allows him to connect law and virtue, and we suggested that this point is sometimes overlooked by those who argue that his ethics is fundamentally an ethics of prudence and virtue.[229] We also noted, however, that this view is not without warrants. When it comes to how Aquinas pictures moral deliberation in practice, prudence and the moral virtues do dominate. Following Aristotle, it is the virtues, rather than laws, that tend to supply the ends of action

---

226. Decosimo's discussion of the relation of the virtues to "honest goods" displays this point (*Ethics as a Work of Charity*, 178–98), as does Bowlin's discussion of the connection of prudence and the virtues in *Contingency*, 83–5.

227. *ST* I-II.58.5. See above, Chapter 2, Section 4.

228. See Prov. 2:16-19; 5:1-23; 6:20-35; 7:1-27; 23:26-28.

229. See above, Chapter 2, Sections 2 and 3a.

in concrete situations.[230] Here Aquinas parts ways with Proverbs, in which it is very much *words* that supply the "particular principles of action" that are needed in concrete circumstances. Wisdom (or prudence) lies in words that allow the relevant kinds of action to appear at the point of action. By emphasizing kinds of action, Aquinas's moral thought makes room for this perspective just as it makes room for law. And yet, it does not become decisive for practical reason.

Arguably, though, several other aspects of Aquinas's thinking make more sense from this perspective. Most notably, Aquinas maintains that prudence cannot, strictly speaking, be in sinners, but is in all who have grace.[231] He maintains the first point because he holds that "genuine and complete prudence" involves "a view to the final good for the whole of human life."[232] The second point depends upon an idea set out already in the treatise on virtue, that one can have a virtue without yet fully exercising it.[233] In defending this position, Aquinas also argues that being guided by the counsel of others is not at odds with the possession of prudence.[234] Each of these points may make more sense if we think of prudence not as simply a subjective capacity, but as a kind of relation to the character of the world. We may speak, as Proverbs does, of the distinction between the righteous and sinners as a distinction between wisdom and folly, because this is the fundamental, concrete difference between the path of wisdom and the path of folly. The fear of the Lord is the beginning of wisdom. Righteousness *is* wisdom. Rather than trying to maintain, which Aquinas can do only with contortions,[235] that someone may have prudence without exercising it, we can instead reflect that someone—the young, for example, who constitute a special problem[236]— may be on the right path without full cognizance of it. Indeed, this step into self-conscious responsibility for the path one is already taking seems to be precisely the "liminal threshold" that is in view in the early chapters of Proverbs.[237] Finally, the need for counsel is no longer an embarrassment on such a view of prudence. Aquinas's recognition that "in matters of prudence no one is wholly

---

230. See the discussions in Daniel Mark Nelson, *The Priority of Prudence: Virtue and Natural Law in Thomas Aquinas and the Implications for Modern Ethics* (University Park: Pennsylvania State University Press, 1992), 69–104; and John Bowlin, *Contingency and Fortune in Aquinas's Ethics* (Cambridge: Cambridge University Press, 1999), 55–92.

231. *ST* II-II.47.13–14.

232. *ST* II-II.47.13.

233. See *ST* I-II.65.1 and 66.2.

234. *ST* II-II.47.14 ad2.

235. See *ST* I-II.65.1 and 66.2.

236. See *ST* II-II.47.14 arg3, ad3, where Aquinas disagrees with Aristotle's view that the young cannot be prudent.

237. See Leo G. Perdue, "Liminality as a Social Setting for Wisdom Instructions," *Zeitschrift für die alttestamentliche Wissenschaft* 93, no. 1 (1981): 114–26; and Van Leeuwen, "Liminality and Worldview," 111–44.

self-sufficient"[238] can be taken further. Docility, willingness to take counsel, is almost the center of prudence: "Trust the LORD with all your heart, and do not rely on your own capability, in all your ways, know him, and he will straighten your paths" (3:5-6).

The differences between Aquinas and Proverbs correspond to a basic difference in orientation. Proverbs, especially in chs 1–9, examines moral reasoning with the relatively immature person in mind, the youth on the verge of responsibility, set before adult life and its perilous choices. Aquinas's account of moral reasoning, on the other hand, sometimes seems to project a perspective of moral maturity: the agent envisaged is a person who possesses the virtues. The question is whether the perspective of Proverbs is relevant only to a particular, immature stage of spiritual development, or whether the distinctive character of this stage in fact illuminates what is true of the moral life as such. If we take the second view,[239] then we would have to see Aquinas's account of moral reasoning as unrealistically optimistic.

Despite these differences, however, Proverbs and Aquinas share a significant focus, namely, the importance of kinds of action. In outlining both Aristotle's and Aquinas's accounts of deliberation and choice, we highlighted the way in which, particularly in relation to moral decisions, deliberation can take the form of subsumption, because it is a matter of a discernment of the way this particular action constitutes an instantiation of a certain kind. This is a way of thinking that seems to find support from the book of Proverbs. As we suggested above, Proverbs abounds with evaluative descriptions of actions and courses of action. Although there is great variety in these descriptions, the variety is far from endless. A set of distinct themes emerges, which in chs 10–30 are gone over again and again, with variations: "a kaleidoscopic and paradigmatic portrait of the wise life," in Ansberry's description.[240] Some key examples include good speech, which includes consideration of lying, keeping silent, taking care in speech, and secrets and counsel;[241] listening as a fundamental aspect of wisdom;[242] right handling

---

238. *ST* II-II.49.3 ad3.

239. As is suggested by Stewart's reading of the pedagogy of Proverbs discussed above (Section 2a). Despite his argument for a narrative progression through Proverbs, William P. Brown concludes similarly that the reader addressed as king at the end of the book remains in need of correction (Brown, "The Pedagogy of Proverbs 10:1–31:9," 181). See n. 106 above and also Stewart's comments in "Wisdom's Imagination," 369.

240. Ansberry, "What Does Jerusalem," 172.

241. In chs 10–30, see following proverbs (with room for some debate): 10:6, 10-11, 13, 14, 18-21, 31-32; 11:9, 11, 12; 12:6, 8, 13, 14, 17, 18, 19, 20, 22, 23, 25; 13:2, 3, 5; 14:3, 5, 7, 15, 23, 25; 15:1, 2, 4, 7, 23, 26, 28, 30; 16:1, 10, 13, 20, 21, 23, 24, 27, 30; 17:4, 7, 9, 20, 27-28; 18:2, 4, 6, 7, 8, 13, 20, 21; 19:1, 5, 9, 22, 27, 28; 20:15, 19, 25; 21:6, 23, 28; 22:6, 11, 12, 14, 17-21; 23:6-8, 9, 12, 15-16; 24:1-2, 7, 26, 28-29; 25:11, 12, 15, 18, 23; 26:2, 4, 5, 7, 9, 20, 22, 23, 24, 25, 26, 28; 27:2, 11, 14; 28:23; 29:5, 19, 20; 30:1-6, 7-9, 32-33.

242. In chs 10–30, see the following proverbs (with room for some debate): 10:8, 17; 11:14; 12:1, 5, 15, 26; 13:1, 10, 13, 18; 15:5, 10, 12, 22, 31-32; 16:20, 29; 17:10; 19:16, 20, 25, 27; 20:18; 21:11; 24:6; 25:12; 29:1.

of money and wealth;[243] and self-control, including restraining anger, diligence, integrity, and moderation.[244] These themes, to which we could add others,[245] reflect something of the social circumstances in which the proverbs were originally fashioned. Yet we can learn much from the fact that such groupings are clearly possible. Although Proverbs is deeply engaged in discerning the significance of particulars, it does not present us with a mere "infinity of singulars," to use Aquinas's phrase. There are more or less distinct kinds of action, and walking in wisdom involves recognizing them.[246] The teaching of Proverbs inducts the reader or the hearer into a rich vocabulary of kinds of action. The student learns sets of names for actions and ways of acting over time,[247] and is invited to notice their connections. This can be seen as attesting the importance of the acts of recognition we have drawn attention to, in which actions are perceived as the kinds of acts they are.

243. In chs 10–30, see the following proverbs (with room for some debate): 10:4, 15, 22; 11:4, 16, 24, 25, 26, 28; 12:9, 11, 27; 13:7, 8, 11, 19, 22, 23, 25; 14:4, 20, 21, 23, 24, 31; 15:6, 15, 16, 17; 16:8, 19, 26; 17:1, 5, 16; 18:11, 16, 23; 19:1, 4, 6, 7, 10, 14, 15, 17, 22; 20:13, 21; 21:5, 13, 17, 20, 26; 22:1, 2, 7, 9, 16, 22-23, 26-27, 29; 23:4-5, 6-8, 19-21; 24:3-4, 30-34; 27:7, 23-27; 28:3, 6, 8, 11, 15, 19, 20, 21, 22, 24, 25, 27; 29:3, 7, 13, 14; 30:7-9, 11-14, 15-16.

244. In chs 10–30, see the following proverbs (with room for some debate). Anger: 12:16, 18; 14:17, 29; 15:1, 18; 16:32; 17:27; 19:11, 19; 20:2, 3; 21:14; 22:24-25; 24:19-20; 25:15, 23; 26:17; 27:3, 4; 29:8, 11, 22. Laziness and diligence: 10:4, 5, 26; 12:14, 24, 27; 13:4; 14:23; 15:19; 18:9; 19:15, 24; 20:4, 13; 21:5, 25; 22:13, 29; 23:4-5; 24:27, 30-34; 26:13, 14, 15, 16; 27:23-27; 28:19. Integrity: 10:9, 29; 11:3, 5, 20; 13:6; 14:32; 19:1; 20:7; 28:6, 10, 18; 29:10. Moderation: 20:1; 23:1-3, 19-21, 29-35; 25:16, 17, 27, 28; 27:7, 20; 30:15-16.

245. See the lists and categories in K. A. Farmer's thematic study of Proverbs: *Who Knows What Is Good? A Commentary on the Books of Proverbs and Ecclesiastes* (Grand Rapids, MI: Eerdmans, 1991), especially pp. 73–102. For Proverbs 15–22, see also B. W. Kovacs, *Sociological-Structural Constraints upon Wisdom: The Spatial and Temporal Matrix of Proverbs 15:28–22:16* (PhD diss., Vanderbilt University, 1978), 535–7, 540–2, 546–79.

246. Stewart's work on the significance of "cognitive prototypes" in Proverbs moves in the same direction. See Stewart, *Poetic Ethics*, 177–91; and "Wisdom's Imagination," 359–63.

247. It is important to note that the kinds of which Proverbs speaks apply not only to individual actions, but also to more extended policies of action or ways of acting. In relation to speech and anger, for example, Proverbs can give particular advice—"put your hand over your mouth!" (30:32)—but also speak of wider policies of action—"one who restrains his words has real knowledge" (17:27). Such policies of action lead naturally to virtue language: "slowness of anger quietens a quarrel" (15:18); "a cool spirit makes a man of understanding" (17:27). The virtues certainly have a place in Proverbs, but they are not primary; they depend upon the coherence of kinds of action. The virtues in Proverbs are names for extended courses of action.

Conclusion

The arguments of this chapter require further exploration. Most broadly, we need to better understand what it means to think about wisdom as a kind of practical knowledge that depends upon the hospitality of creation to good action. More particularly, the comments made about the idea of created order and its relation to salvation history need to be taken further. What precisely is being claimed, and what difference does that make to our understanding of moral reasoning? The significance of kinds for moral reasoning also invites closer attention. We have suggested that Proverbs can be understood as providing some support to the idea that kinds of action are crucial in practical reasoning. As we have seen, however, kinds of action are no simple thing to understand. What, then, does it mean to maintain such an emphasis on kinds? What account of moral deliberation and discernment follows from it?

Another significant question has also been hinted at in the discussion, but has not so far received proper attention, namely, what all this means for the distinction between theoretical and practical reasoning. Proverbs, as we have seen, does not straightforwardly support the idea of a wisdom that "consists in the contemplation of eternal things." In itself, this might be taken to call into question the idea of an independent, theoretical reason. Nevertheless, the very existence of Proverbs ch. 8 must qualify this conclusion. For although the overall purpose of that poem is to make an argument for the pursuit of practical wisdom, it is a theoretically rich argument that is made. Within the process of defending the value of (practical) wisdom, space opens for truthful speech about the *nature* of wisdom—speech that appears to have its own internal logic that needs to be carried through in thought. Can we, then, clarify the relation of such thought to practical reason?

These questions are serious concerns of the work of Oliver O'Donovan, in which we find an attempt to articulate a concept of created order that is different to Aquinas's, and to struggle with how history impacts such a conception. O'Donovan's understanding of moral reasoning is oriented by an emphasis on the significance of kinds; and it pays careful attention to the place of Scripture in Christian ethics. It also involves a significant account of the nature of practical and theoretical reasoning, developed with reference to the concept of wisdom, and to Proverbs 8. In the next stage of the discussion, therefore, we shall hear from O'Donovan.

Chapter 4

WORLD ORDER AND DELIBERATION IN THE WORK OF OLIVER O'DONOVAN

Does not Wisdom call?

—Prov. 8:1

Introduction

At an important moment in his influential outline of Christian ethics, *Resurrection and Moral Order*, Oliver O'Donovan draws attention to a problem that he sees as unresolved within the thought of Paul Ramsey: "how can we defend the generic character of moral wisdom, while still allowing that a particular judgment can be an exercise of rational thought?"[1] One way to understand not just *Resurrection and Moral Order*, but also O'Donovan's more recent trilogy *Ethics as Theology*,[2] is as a sustained attempt to answer this question by integrating Ramsey's basic insights about moral deliberation into a robust doctrine of creation. This project leads O'Donovan to a powerful account of Christian ethics that our discussion so far puts us in a position to appreciate. O'Donovan comes to sophisticated judgments about the central questions of this study: the place of created order in Christian moral reasoning, the nature of practical reason, and the structure of deliberative thinking. Furthermore, near the center of his account is a conception of wisdom, which in the more recent works is developed with significant attention to Proverbs. "The call of wisdom," O'Donovan writes in the central chapter of *Finding and Seeking*, "is the call of the world's temporal openness to knowledge."[3]

O'Donovan's work provides the vantage point we need in order to take our enquiries further. Attaining this vantage point, however, is no simple task. This chapter, therefore, takes shape largely as a long, reflective overview of O'Donovan's account of the structure of Christian moral thinking. Many aspects of O'Donovan's work are still passed over quickly. Our interest is focused on

---

1. *RMO*, 197.

2. *Ethics as Theology* is composed of three works: Volume 1, *Self, World, and Time* (*SWT*); Volume 2, *Finding and Seeking* (*F&S*); and Volume 3, *Entering into Rest* (*EIR*).

3. *F&S*, 100.

O'Donovan's understanding of the way in which we think to action, and why that is. The two major works that contain this account[4]—*Resurrection and Moral Order* and *Ethics as Theology*—are separated by a period of roughly thirty years. Despite this, they form an impressively unified picture.[5] However, the works are also different in important ways. We will therefore attend to them in order, seeking to observe the continuities and developments in O'Donovan's thinking (Sections 1 and 2). The movement through these works is punctuated by a series of pauses to make observations in the light of our previous discussions. These provisional discussions lead to a final, critical reflection on O'Donovan's work (Section 3), in which we will argue that, the many strengths of O'Donovan's work notwithstanding, his account of wisdom and of created order in terms of a timeless "whole" compromises the structure of salvation history in certain ways. This conclusion highlights the significance of what we have seen in the previous chapter about the presentation of wisdom in Proverbs. The practical character of wisdom directs us to a different understanding of created order and its relation to God's work in Christ. The final chapter of the study will attempt to draw this out in more detail, and explore its implications for moral discernment, and the place of Christian ethics as a discipline.

1 The Generic Character of Moral Reasoning in Resurrection and Moral Order

In chapter 9 of *Resurrection and Moral Order*, O'Donovan refers back to the discussion of created order in chapter 2 and calls it "a modest footnote" to Paul Ramsey's essay, "The Case of the Curious Exception."[6] This essay is formative not only for the argument of *Resurrection*, but also for the discussions of deliberation and discernment in *Ethics as Theology*. It remains, as O'Donovan says in *Finding and Seeking*, "decisive."[7] Beginning our discussion by taking stock of this important influence will help us orient our overview of O'Donovan's work.[8]

---

4. We will draw on a number of other works at various points; however, those mentioned above will orient and dominate the discussion.

5. It is striking, for example, that O'Donovan can still refer the reader of *Entering into Rest* to a discussion in *Resurrection and Moral Order* (*EIR*, 43, n. 9).

6. *RMO*, 197. Ramsey's essay is: Paul Ramsey, "The Case of the Curious Exception," in *Norm and Context in Christian Ethics*, edited by Gene H. Outka and Paul Ramsey (London: SCM, 1968), 67–135.

7. *F&S*, 226, n. 13; cf. 207, n. 29.

8. O'Donovan's own discussion in *RMO*, 196–7 is also a good guide to Ramsey's article. For our purposes, however, it will be useful to view it independently, before looking at O'Donovan's reading of it.

a. Paul Ramsey's "The Case of the Curious Exception"

The purpose of Ramsey's essay was to examine the idea of "justifiable violations of moral principles."[9] Against those, particularly those situationist ethicists, who thought such exceptions important, Ramsey argued that there were, in fact, no such things. For, "an exception would be a *sort* of thing."[10] For something to qualify as a *justifiable* exception to a principle, that is, it would have to have certain "morally relevant features" that justified it.[11] But in that case, it would not be an exception at all, but rather an intelligible kind of thing that, Ramsey further argues, clarifies the principle itself. For instance, the recognition that it would not be wrong to take some apples that did not belong to you if it was the only way to feed your starving family does not amount to an exception to the prohibition on theft, but to a clarification of what theft is.[12] When we make such discernments that a moral rule or principle does not apply, Ramsey suggests, what happens is that our knowledge of the principle itself is "deepened and clarified."[13] Thinking, to take another example, about the famous question of whether it is justified to lie in order to save life: rather than say either that this was an exception to the rule that one should not lie, or that saving life is a condition under which not speaking truth is not wrong—thus saying there is such a thing as a "justified lie"—it is better, Ramsey argues, to say that here we discover something new about "the meaning of … the forbidden lie."[14] Apparently exceptional cases are in fact moments at which we learn some important further thing about the meaning of the principle to which they appear to take exception.

Underpinning this argument is an understanding of moral reasoning as generic in character. "We can and may and must always think about the meaning of right and wrong in terms of the *sorts* of things that are right-making and wrong-making."[15] Genus-species language, though problematic in some respects, has validity as a "heuristic device for keeping it quite clear that in ethics we are talking about *definable sorts* of actions, which may have great 'specificity.'"[16] Moral reasoning, Ramsey argues, involves moving from broader to more specific principles.[17] At one end of the "spectrum" are "ultimate norms." Further down are "general principles" and "definite-action rules." The process ends in the "subsumption of cases."[18]

---

9. Ramsey, "The Case," 67.
10. Ramsey, "The Case," 93, emphasis original.
11. Ramsey, "The Case," 79.
12. For this example, see Ramsey, "The Case," 78, 89.
13. Ramsey, "The Case," 87.
14. Ramsey, "The Case," 90.
15. Ramsey, "The Case," 119, emphasis original.
16. Ramsey, "The Case," 75, emphasis original. For Ramsey's comments on genus-species language, see 74–5, 91.
17. Ramsey, "The Case," 82.
18. Ramsey, "The Case," 75.

The production of a particular deed is always a matter of the subsumption of a case; because of its features or because of the claims discerned in some situation, under the last *specific* to which moral reasoning has led us, for which there is some statable moral warrant. The latter must always be in terms of repeatable *kinds* of cases. One can say, of course, that one is moving along a spectrum of increasing "particularity"; but that is only a manner of speaking. Moral reasoning is always a matter of surrounding the particulars of actions by increasingly specific general terms—i.e., increasing illumination—for the direction of concrete actions.[19]

Ramsey acknowledges that actual thinking to action rarely corresponds to this process. The person who does a "fitting thing," he suggests, mostly just "senses the wise or good thing to do without much elaboration of why."[20] Yet that, for Ramsey, is not an adequate account of ethics. Ethics involves tracing the moral reasoning implied within good action, displaying the reasons that *could* be adduced by the one who does a fitting thing.[21]

Later in the essay, Ramsey also makes clear that the prudent subsumption of cases always represents a distinct step in the process of acting, a step that, in a sense, lies "outside ethical reasoning," in being "the actual practice of morality."[22] There is always a distinct moment of movement to application that was classically understood to be the work of prudence, and that cannot be removed either by even more detailed rules, or by application-governing rules.[23]

b. Resurrection and Moral Order

There are many other interesting aspects of Ramsey's essay. Now, however, we must consider how O'Donovan draws on Ramsey in *Resurrection and Moral Order*. As will hopefully become clear, this is also a good vantage point from which to appreciate much of the book.

O'Donovan's discussion of Ramsey appears in the third part of *Resurrection and Moral Order*, in which O'Donovan undertakes to describe "the form of the moral life," "the shape that love takes in the world."[24] In the first instance, this means attending to "the kinds of action which the gospel evokes,"[25] which means considering "the moral field."

"The moral field" is a way of speaking about how it is the world itself which affords certain possibilities for action. It is "the world as it presents itself to us

---

19. Ramsey, "The Case," 76, emphasis original.
20. Ramsey, "The Case," 76.
21. Ramsey, "The Case," 76.
22. Ramsey, "The Case," 105.
23. Ramsey, "The Case," 104–5.
24. *RMO*, 179, 182.
25. *RMO*, 183.

at any particular moment as the context and occasion of our next action."[26] It describes how various "possible ends-of-action" are presented to us by "the changing world."[27] With this arises what O'Donovan calls "the central problem of historical existence," namely, "the problem of novelty."[28] New historical contexts throw up new possibilities for action such that our ability to understand what we are doing is put in jeopardy. "The task of acting is rendered perilous by the historical dimension of our path through the world; we are threatened at each turn by a universe which we do not know and cannot recognize, in which memory will not serve us or may even mislead us."[29] Conservatism and consequentialism both represent responses to this problem that share an underlying historicist framework of thinking.[30] Neither gives any place to "transhistorical mediation," and so neither, ultimately, can truly secure against the radically new. Only the idea of "objective world-order" can truly enable us "to live with confidence rather than terror in the face of history."[31] At this point, in what is for our purposes an important paragraph, O'Donovan introduces the concept of wisdom:

> Only if we are endowed with a vision of what is in the world which measures changes and so stands beyond it, can we dare to encounter change. Such a vision is what the ancients meant by the term 'wisdom'. Wisdom is the perception that every novelty, in its own way, manifests the permanence and stability of the created order, so that, however astonishing and undreamt of it may be, it is not utterly incommensurable with what has gone before. This does not imply a pretence that the unlikeness of the new to the old is unreal. Even unlike things can be seen as part of the same universe if there is an order which embraces them in a relation to one another. The plurality of situations and events which characterizes the experience of history, the fact that every event is 'new' and different from every other, can be seen as a pluriformity in the world-order, which is a capacity for different things to transpire and succeed one another within a total framework of intelligibility which allows for their generic relationships to be understood. Without a generic order new things would indeed be incomprehensible, for they would be absolutely particular, which is beyond the power of human thought to grasp. The utterly 'unique situation', if we were ever to encounter it, would destroy us and the universe. Wisdom liberates us from the persistent fear of that unutterable and unknowable uniqueness by enabling us to interpret each particular thing, in all its newness to us, generically, and so measure its difference from other things and respond to it appropriately according to

---

26. *RMO*, 191.
27. *RMO*, 184.
28. *RMO*, 184.
29. *RMO*, 185.
30. *RMO*, 185–8.
31. *RMO*, 188.

its kind. Thus wisdom greets new things with recognition, and new moral decisions can be made.[32]

Wisdom means the knowledge of the generic, transhistorical created order that enables action in the midst of historical existence. It is a "vision" that "perceives" the underlying order that subsists in all new situations and events, making "particular things" recognizable as kinds and so enabling coherent moral action.

Here O'Donovan is approaching territory charted by Ramsey's article. Before this, however, O'Donovan introduces the category of law. He does this through a discussion of the way Israel interpreted wisdom as *torah*.[33] *Torah* "re-presented" the wisdom spoken of in "the tradition of proverb-making common to Israel and her neighbours," as law, and so made it available to all, in contrast to the "cool observational detachment" of wisdom, with "its inherent restriction to the educated."[34] From this point O'Donovan moves to say that "the moral agent approaches every new situation … equipped with the 'moral law,'" which means, "that wisdom which contains insight into the created order when it is formulated explicitly to direct decisions, i.e. deontically."[35]

Before we continue, we must express a reservation about this train of thought. "Cool observational detachment" is an unhappy summary of the wisdom of Proverbs, which pulses with the intensity of parental anxiety (e.g., 5:7-20; 31:2) and with a keen sense of danger (e.g., 4:20-27; 19:18). The importance of this observation lies in its potential to unsettle the characterization of wisdom as *knowledge* that can subsequently be "conceived and organized" in law.[36] If Proverbs reflects the fact that wisdom is fundamentally about *practical* knowledge, then the relationship of law—and in particular, Israel's law—to wisdom may need to be formulated somewhat differently.

The preceding discussion leads O'Donovan to the topic of "casuistry and moral learning."[37] When we think toward action, whether in deliberation, reflection upon action, or abstract exploration of possible action, the particular situation in view and the moral law with which we approach it are mutually illuminating: the law shows us the meaning of the situation, while the situation enables us to understand the law more deeply. Casuistry, O'Donovan infers, is properly "not just a matter of solving problems, but of growing in wisdom."[38] O'Donovan carefully rejects a conception of moral reasoning as classification, where there is on the one hand *synderesis*, knowledge of principles, and on the other *conscientia*, their application. Such an account fails to appreciate the processes involved in *recognizing* particulars

---

32. *RMO*, 188–9.
33. *RMO*, 189–90.
34. *RMO*, 190–1.
35. *RMO*, 190.
36. *RMO*, 191.
37. *RMO*, 190.
38. *RMO*, 191.

as kinds.³⁹ The formal rules employed by the scholastic tradition, such as the principle of double effect, in fact reflect certain ways in which particular cases may increase our understanding of the meaning of rules.⁴⁰ The introduction of formal principles to enable the application of principles to particulars frequently invites disastrous abuse. Far better just to say that,

> [W]e learn more about the moral law as we think about difficult cases. The particular discloses to us aspects of the generic to which we have not previously been sensitive … moral learning … is not a matter of accumulating new information about the moral order, but of discovering in closer detail that which we already know in broad outline. We penetrate behind the straightforwardness of the moral code through which we first learnt the moral law, to discover that that law is as complex and pluriform as the created order itself which it reflects.⁴¹

This understanding of moral learning picks up the account of knowledge set out earlier in the book.⁴² It is also deeply indebted to Ramsey, and at this point O'Donovan discusses Ramsey's essay directly. Failure to learn in this way, he says, manifests itself in systems required to posit exceptions.⁴³ Ramsey's argument failed only in not following where the truly theological meta-ethic he hinted at should have led: to a position where "we root the generic character of morality in the order of the *world,* rather than in the structures of the *mind,*" so that the subsumption of particulars under generic categories becomes "a matter of truthful recognition."⁴⁴ This would resolve Ramsey's unresolved difficulty of "how we can defend the generic character of moral wisdom, while still allowing that a particular judgment can be an exercise of rational thought."⁴⁵ O'Donovan draws attention to the way (noted above) that Ramsey separates the subsumption of particulars that is the work of prudence from moral reasoning properly speaking.⁴⁶ This is a mistake, O'Donovan argues, which derives from the absence of a conception of created order in Ramsey's account.

> It may be a rational judgment to subsume a particular under a generic principle. For it is not a *bare* particular which we encounter, until we randomly throw the cloak of generic order around it. It is already ordered

---

39. *RMO*, 191–2.
40. *RMO*, 192–4.
41. *RMO*, 195.
42. See especially *RMO*, 91–3.
43. *RMO*, 195.
44. *RMO*, 197.
45. *RMO*, 197.
46. See Ramsey, "The Case," 93–105.

generically and teleologically by virtue of its relations to other things, and it discloses to us its generic and teleological relations in disclosing itself.[47]

This claim, O'Donovan says, has been one of the "persistent contentions" of *Resurrection and Moral Order*.[48]

O'Donovan goes on to explain that moral learning takes place in situations in which there is a struggle to know how to interpret or properly "name" a situation.[49] Such situations, or dilemmas, arise, O'Donovan argues, because the moral field is "pluriform" and "specifically differentiated."[50] "The order of reality holds together a multitude of different kinds of moral relation, and orders them without abolishing their differences."[51] For this reason, moral codes can never be based on a single principle, but are always variegated. Yet this is an ordered complexity. Differentiated moral claims are ultimately related to one another in a unity, and so dilemmas are susceptible of "rational resolution."[52] "What happens when we think through a dilemma is that we gain some view of the universal order within which different species of moral claim are related."[53] The moral law can, therefore, be understood more deeply. Its internal logic can be grasped more fully (though never completely). Wisdom, O'Donovan suggests, is especially about understanding how individual elements of the moral law, such as items in a moral code, stand in relation to one another and to the whole. The Bible, therefore, must be read with a view to forming a "comprehensive moral viewpoint." "We must look within it not only for moral bricks, but for indications of the order in which the bricks belong together."[54] In this, O'Donovan is concerned to avoid a view where the task of moral thinking is merely to accumulate more information, compiling more comprehensive lists of rules. O'Donovan is aware that his way of describing things may raise "forebodings of a totalitarian theological construction which will legislate over questions where it would be better to respect the Bible's silence";[55] but he argues that there is no real alternative. If we refuse to seek to understand how the different elements of the Bible are ordered to one another, and thus to develop a sense of how a whole picture hangs together, then we will be unable to counter skeptical claims about the relevance of biblical teaching to situations. The Bible itself, he suggests, leads us to the task of attending to the principles by which the law is ordered, supremely in the pre-eminence given to the twofold command of love for God and neighbor.[56]

47. *RMO*, 197.
48. *RMO*, 197.
49. *RMO*, 198.
50. *RMO*, 199.
51. *RMO*, 199.
52. *RMO*, 199.
53. *RMO*, 199.
54. *RMO*, 200.
55. *RMO*, 200.
56. *RMO*, 200–3.

With this, we have broached an issue that will be at the heart of this chapter's engagement with O'Donovan: the idea that moral reasoning involves some kind of knowledge of "the whole." It reflects a conception of wisdom as fundamentally theoretical, making it a point at which our argument in the previous chapter suggests questions ought to be raised. It will be important to observe the way in which this thought is developed in O'Donovan's later work. However, we must also note the important discussion of this theme earlier in *Resurrection and Moral Order*.

Chapter 4 anchors the ideas explored in chapter 9 in a Christological account of moral knowledge. Moral knowledge, or "wisdom," O'Donovan there argues, must mean an "apprehensive" knowledge of "the 'shape' of the whole."[57] Yet it is also knowledge from within, which means it is never transcendent but always incomplete—knowledge of "a mystery which envelops us."[58] "Man's wisdom does not afford him a total purchase on the cosmos and its history; he can reach out towards apprehension only from within."[59] It is this that grounds the idea that moral knowledge must be open to improvement. We know "kinds," but only provisionally; our conceptions must always be "open to clarification in the light of new particulars."[60] Furthermore, this knowledge "from within" can only be from a particular position within, namely, humankind's position as that being called to worship God and have authority over the rest of creation. This means it must reckon with the reality of sin.[61] Finally, this knowledge must be secured against the threat presented by ignorance of the end of history. We need to know that the good we apprehend will not be "engulfed in novelty."[62] That knowledge can only come from "God's revelatory word."[63] This is what is given to humanity in Jesus Christ. This is the particular, exclusive point of access to the inclusive field of vision of created order that moral knowledge seeks.[64] Rebuking the idolatrous tendencies of our knowledge, the gospel gives us an authoritative center from which we may gain "a grasp of the total shape" of the moral order.[65]

---

57. *RMO*, 77–8.
58. *RMO*, 79.
59. *RMO*, 80.
60. *RMO*, 80.
61. *RMO*, 81–2.
62. *RMO*, 83. O'Donovan cites Revelation 4–5, and the image of the sealed scroll, in connection with this idea of history as threatening. The sealed scroll represents "the opacity of history." This reading of this text, which is developed in much more detail in O'Donovan's essay, "The Political Thought of the Book of Revelation" (*Tyndale Bulletin* 37 [1986]: 61–94; revised as "History and Politics in the Book of Revelation," in *Bonds of Imperfection: Christian Politics, Past and Present*, ed. Oliver O'Donovan and Joan Lockwood O'Donovan [Grand Rapids: Eerdmans, 2004], 25–47), is formative for O'Donovan's thinking. We will see it again in his later work.
63. *RMO*, 85.
64. *RMO*, 85.
65. *RMO*, 89.

The final step in this part of our outline of O'Donovan's thought must be to note how the opening chapters of *Resurrection and Moral Order* ground this conception of moral thought in a theology of created order and its relation to salvation-history. The second chapter defends the idea that "morality is generic,"[66] through an account of created order. Creation is "an ordered totality," with "a complex network of teleological and generic relations."[67] O'Donovan initially discusses how *things* are ordered—"rocks are ordered to vegetables."[68] Yet the focus quickly shifts to kinds of *actions*. Kinds, O'Donovan explains, is a category that applies to "operations," rather than just "material entities."[69] Actions come in kinds and have their corresponding ends: "speech is ordered to truth, and marriage to fidelity."[70] The notion of generic kinds of action is the most important goal of O'Donovan's account of created order. It is what, for O'Donovan, is at stake in the fundamental "decision" moral thinking must take "early in its course," between the thought of "a universal world-order" on the one hand and the world as "raw material" upon which the will imposes its own order on the other.[71] Voluntarism receives such strong opposition because, by refusing the notion of kinds of action given in the nature of reality, it creates a situation in which "moral disagreements … reveal ultimate clashes of commitment which are incapable of resolution."[72]

O'Donovan sees that the central theological problem for such a conception is the idea of salvation-history.[73] "'Salvation-history' means change and innovation; it means that God can do a 'new thing.'"[74] But if that is so, and if morality must respond to that agency, then the idea that morality is generic appears to be at risk. "For any command or principle that changes in history thereby becomes a particular, a mere item in the history of ideas."[75] O'Donovan's response to this is not to deny that God is free to act within history, or to call individuals particularly and even, following Kierkegaard, in apparent contradiction to the demands of morality. His response is to insist that these acts of providence and vocation only make sense if there is also an "order which is not subject to historical change,"[76] a "transhistorical order of things," as he puts it later, which "measures change and so stands beyond it."[77]

---

66. *RMO*, 41, 45.
67. *RMO*, 31–2.
68. *RMO*, 33.
69. *RMO*, 34.
70. *RMO*, 34.
71. *RMO*, 35.
72. *RMO*, 16.
73. *RMO*, 38–45.
74. *RMO*, 42.
75. *RMO*, 41.
76. *RMO*, 45.
77. *RMO*, 188.

The fundamental issue raised by this section is whether this account of God's action in history does justice to his act of redemption in Christ.[78] The main category under which God's actions are discussed in this section is *providence*. What seems to be missing in these pages, though, is a sense of God's redemptive action as transformative. Created order endures history, and history is measured against created order. It is the natural order that "makes that change good."[79] We will complete our discussion of *Resurrection and Moral Order* by observing a number of features of the book that highlight why we should keep this issue in mind as we go on.

Throughout the book the categories for describing the significance of the resurrection that do the heavy lifting, so to speak, are *reaffirmation* and *vindication*.[80] This is a judgment that we venture cautiously. O'Donovan does speak explicitly about transformation. The early chapters contain significant statements about the "newness" of redemption.[81] The resurrection is "an affirmation that goes beyond and transforms the initial gift of life."[82] In Chapter 3 this point comes into explicit focus. While the language of redemption implies "the recovery of something given and lost,"[83] redemption must not be thought of as "*mere* restoration": it is also a matter of "fulfilment" and "transformation."[84] This also means that there *is* "an important place in Christian thought for the idea of 'history;" used in the sense of "an intelligible story."[85] The resurrection has a double aspect: it means both restoration and transformation.[86] Christian ethics, therefore, "looks both backwards and forwards ... It respects the natural structures of life in the world, while looking forward to their transformation."[87] Moreover, this chapter explicitly rejects thinking of this eschatological transformation in terms of immanent teleology.[88] O'Donovan argues, in fact, that this is the central mistake of historicism: it sees "the destiny of the world" as "immanently present within its natural orderings," rather than a work of God that comes "from outside."[89]

---

78. In what follows, accepting the risk created by Barth's usage of the word redemption to refer to eschatology, I will frequently use "redemption" as a shorthand for God's saving action in Jesus Christ.

79. *RMO*, 45.

80. See *RMO*, 15, 19, 31, 45.

81. e.g., *RMO*, 13–14, 15, 42.

82. *RMO*, 14.

83. *RMO*, 54.

84. *RMO*, 55.

85. *RMO*, 55.

86. *RMO*, 56–7. See also O'Donovan, *The Desire of the Nations: Rediscovering the Roots of Political Theology* (Cambridge: Cambridge University Press, 1996), 141–4, 181–3; and *On the Thirty Nine Articles* (Exeter: Paternoster, 1986), 34–7. The discussion in *The Desire of the Nations* is especially significant.

87. *RMO*, 58.

88. *RMO*, 64–7.

89. *RMO*, 64–5.

Yet, overall, the transformative side of the resurrection does less work than these statements lead us to expect, particularly in relation to the book's treatment of moral reasoning.[90] The order to which morality conforms is fundamentally *static*. It is "transhistorical."[91] A recurring motif in the book is of order as always already present, but temporarily obscured. The author of Hebrews, O'Donovan suggests, "sees in Christ, and in the order of the world to come, the vindication and perfect manifestation of the created order which was already there but never fully expressed," and which "existed from the beginning in God's creative conception."[92] Creation is *complete*, O'Donovan insists against historicism.[93] "Historical fulfilment means our entry into a completeness which is already present in the universe."[94] But this transhistorical order is still the order of creation, a *natural* order. The significance of the Christian's sharing, by the Spirit, in the authority of Christ is primarily that it puts us in a position to rightly understand and respect this order,[95] suggesting that what is required for obedience is pre-eminently clarification rather than a genuinely new orientation. Nature still provides the primary reference point for ethics. We may "follow the Stoic recipe for 'life in accord with nature'," O'Donovan says, provided we maintain "a measure of epistemological guardedness."[96] The gospel allows us to "overcome the epistemological barriers to an ethic that conforms to nature."[97] This is why when it comes to the actual work of ethics, history, as we have observed, features primarily as a threat. History threatens moral thinking, because novelty is a source of confusion and anxiety.[98] The "question of history" *is* "the problem of evil."[99] We will see O'Donovan return to this problem significantly in *Ethics as Theology*.

To these observations we add a related one, namely, that the primary challenge to ethics posed by sin is *epistemological*. Sin, in *Resurrection and Moral Order,* is chiefly a matter of confusion and intransigence. "In speaking of man's fallenness we point not only to his persistent rejection of the created order, but also to an inescapable confusion in his perceptions of it."[100] There is little talk of sin as involving a corruption of the conditions in which obedience takes place. The order itself is undamaged.

---

90. Again, significant exceptions notwithstanding, most notably: the discussion of marriage and singleness (pp. 69–71); the discussion of political justice, which anticipates some of the central insights of O'Donovan's political theology (pp. 71–5); and the discussion of how the twofold love command is fulfilled in the love of Jesus (pp. 240–4).

91. *RMO*, 67.
92. *RMO*, 53, referring to Heb. 2:5-9.
93. *RMO*, 60–1.
94. *RMO*, 62.
95. *RMO*, 24–5; cf. 191.
96. *RMO*, 19.
97. *RMO*, 20; cf. 68.
98. *RMO*, 82–3.
99. *RMO*, 83.
100. *RMO*, 19.

Certainly, "Human nature … is flawed not only in its instances but in its mould, so that to be human itself means that we find this order of things a problem and are rebelliously disposed towards it."[101] Yet this is still to see the effects of sin primarily in terms of human agency. Little attention is given, for example, to what it might mean for creation itself to be "made subject to futility" (Rom. 8:20). The order remains intact; the problem is that humanity "misconstrues" it.[102] As we will see, in the *Ethics as Theology* series this issue becomes a point of explicit focus. We will conclude that a weakness in O'Donovan's position does disclose itself at this point.

To conclude: our discussion has suggested that one way of understanding *Resurrection and Moral Order* is that it is shaped by a particular conception of what the work of ethics involves. The practical work by which ethics is oriented is the act of deliberating about a problem and seeking resolution through recognition, that is, through rightly perceiving the kind to which something corresponds. Although not limited to such thought, ethics must be able to encompass and must be amenable to the kind of "moralist's dilemma" discussed in chapter 9.[103] This kind of deliberation and moral learning is possible, however, only if we may think about actions generically, as kinds. The basis for doing so lies in the good news that in the resurrection of Jesus, God has restored creation, with its order, and given it back to human agency as the ground of action.

This way of seeing O'Donovan's position has highlighted a number of questions, particularly about the relation of created order to salvation history, and about his conception of wisdom. These questions also present constructive challenges to our argument. On the one hand, O'Donovan's argument forces us to consider whether it is possible to sustain a generic understanding of moral reasoning, that is, one that gives a central place to kinds of action, apart from the idea of a transhistorical order. On the other hand, O'Donovan's idea that wisdom is "the knowledge of the created order" invites us to clarify how understanding wisdom as *practical* knowledge affects our account of moral reasoning. First, however, it is significant that in his more recent works O'Donovan has returned especially to the themes developed in chapter 9 of *Resurrection and Moral Order*. We must now go on to examine how his positions are clarified and developed in these works, and how this affects the wider issues we have raised.

2 The Elevation of Moral Reason in Ethics as Theology

Resurrection and Moral Order begins from created order and moves to moral agency. *Ethics as Theology*, which this section seeks to consider as a whole, begins

---

101. *RMO*, 17.
102. *RMO*, 82.
103. *RMO*, 198–9. Hence, also, the modest defense of "quandary ethics" (185, 198). See also O'Donovan's argument that ethics is fundamentally "problematical," in "How Can Theology Be Moral?" *Journal of Religious Ethics* 17, no. 2 (1989): 82–3.

from moral agency and shows how it depends upon created order. Both conclude with a consideration of love and the end of the moral life.[104] *Ethics as Theology* is, O'Donovan says, a "necessary complement" to *Resurrection and Moral Order*.[105] The aim of the earlier work was "to validate the interest of Theological Ethics in elucidating worldly order."[106] Yet, there is more to say about the newness of restored human agency than was said there, O'Donovan believes. *Ethics as Theology*, therefore, turns to focus more on "the subjective renewal of agency and its opening to the forward calling of God"[107]—"Ethics after Pentecost," as it is called at the end of the series.[108] For O'Donovan, however, showing what this renewal involves means beginning from un-renewed, natural human agency and its practical reasoning.

This is where *Self, World, and Time* sets out from, beginning, self-consciously, from "commonsense morality"[109] and "general, not … specifically religious experience."[110] Practical reasoning, O'Donovan insists, is "our native element."[111] The experience of "waking," of "coming-to to what is happening and to how we are already placed," is something common to human life,[112] and practical thought is "the rational expression of our existence-towards-action."[113] Self, world, and time name the three key elements of natural moral reasoning.

Yet practical reason, when pressed, points beyond itself to a "wider wisdom," to the God who "besets it behind and before"; and so ethics, in due course, "opens up to theology."[114] "There is no moral thought," O'Donovan writes, "that is not, quite simply, human thought, no human being that was not born to think responsibly

---

104. Among the many important parallels between the final chapters of *Resurrection and Moral Order* and *Entering into Rest* are discussions of justification and sanctification, the kingdom of God, the nature of conversion, and perfection.

105. *SWT*, 94.

106. *SWT*, 93.

107. *SWT*, 94.

108. *EIR*, 228.

109. *SWT*, 21.

110. *SWT*, 6.

111. *SWT*, 1.

112. *SWT*, 2, 6. Although O'Donovan does not refer to him here, the metaphor of waking almost certainly owes much to Robert Spaemann, for whom "erwachen zur Wirklichkeit" is an important concept, especially in *Glück und Wohlwollen: Versuch über Ethik* (Stuttgart: Klett-Cotta, 1989), but also in *Personen*, which was translated by O'Donovan as *Persons: The Difference between Someone and Something*. The purpose of this idea in Spaemann's thought is, in Holger Zaborowski's words, to conceptualize "how a transcendent, absolute, and unconditional horizon is always already present in human life" (*Robert Spaemann's Philosophy of the Human Person: Nature, Freedom, and the Critique of Modernity* [Oxford Theological Monographs; Oxford: Oxford University Press, 2010], 236).

113. *SWT*, 19.

114. *SWT*, 19.

about being, living, and doing; yet there is no moral thought that does not depend for whatever effect it may have upon a gift for which no human source can be credited."[115] The human vocation to think morally is "conceivable," "only in the light of the second Adam, who is Christ."[116] This is why moral thought can only be properly understood by attending to the *renewal* of moral agency as faith, love, and hope.

A key discussion of this point in chapter 5 of *Self, World, and Time* will help us get our bearings on the series as a whole.[117] Moral theology, O'Donovan says, must attend to the Spirit's "eschatological elevation" of moral agency.[118] But what the Spirit does is to renew "old," natural forms of moral thinking, giving them "back to us incomparably more disciplined, more informed, more comprehensive, more inviting, than they could have been before."[119] Yet this is not, O'Donovan claims, a retreat from a Christocentric approach. Dietrich Bonhoeffer's stringent opposition to all ethics and emphasis on "the concrete" should not be seen as requiring the abandonment of all natural moral thought.[120] Bonhoeffer's central demand, O'Donovan argues, was that "saving history, with Christ at the centre and the Spirit at its circumference, should be the matrix of all moral reason."[121] This ought properly to embrace a retrieval of the moral thinking of "God's creaturely man."[122]

This leads us to the central, substantive claim made in this first volume, which comes into clear view in a significant passage:

> Natural moral experience takes shape as a threefold awareness, we have said, and moral reasoning as a movement among the three poles of attention—self, world, and time. This pattern is taken up and enhanced in the redemption of the moral life ... Faith anchors the moral life in an awareness of self and responsibility, for agency is disoriented and uncertain until we grasp hold of God's work in shaping us to be effective agents. Love structures our awareness of the world and our appreciation of its ordered values, rejoicing in the world as God's creation and its history as the stage of God's self-disclosure. Hope focuses our awareness of time upon the "works

---

115. *SWT*, 38.

116. *SWT*, 75. In my judgment, the reason that *Self, World, and Time* can be felt a difficult book lies at this point. For here we see that O'Donovan has a dual interest: on the one hand, to show how moral thought naturally points to theology, including how philosophical ethics as a discipline opens up to theology (see p. 76); on the other hand, to show how moral thought is renewed by the Holy Spirit.

117. *SWT*, 91–7.
118. *SWT*, 95.
119. *SWT*, 96.
120. *SWT*, 96–7.
121. *SWT*, 97.
122. *SWT*, 97.

prepared before us to walk in" (Eph. 2:10). Within these three perfections we find all else—and there is much else—that is important to moral awakening and moral thinking.[123]

Natural moral experience is formed by a threefold awareness—of self, world, and time—and the form this awareness takes as it is renewed by the Holy Spirit is faith, love, and hope. Faith, love, and hope are crucial "bridge-concepts between Doctrine and Ethics," allowing us to rightly relate "the final perfection of mankind" to "natural human activity."[124]

At stake in this thought, moreover, is a claim about the relation of creation and redemption, made clear by the way O'Donovan distinguishes his position from Aquinas's. Aquinas's identification of faith, hope, and love as theological virtues, he argues, separated them too much from natural human experience. There are, O'Donovan argues, natural virtues that belong with the theological ones and relate to them: "courage with faith, judgment with love, prudence and temperance with hope."[125] O'Donovan suggests that this issue is at stake in the way the virtues are ordered. He notes that the usual order in the New Testament is faith, love, and hope, and sees in this a pointer to the way these virtues represent the restoration of natural moral awareness.[126] Yet they can also be reordered with love at the end—most notably in 1 Corinthians 13—and here lies the truth in Thomas's position: these virtues also point to the way the moral life looks toward perfection in love.[127]

The logic of the whole *Ethics as Theology* series becomes visible from this vantage point. The second volume, *Finding and Seeking*, traces the sequence of virtues in their primary order, which corresponds to the restoration and renewal of natural moral experience: faith, love, and hope. The final volume, *Entering into Rest*, begins from Paul's "inverted triad,"[128] and seeks to unpack its significance for our understanding of the end of the moral life. Before turning to these, however, we should note that O'Donovan's challenge to Aquinas may also be a challenge to the line of thought we began to develop in the previous chapter, when we suggested that Aquinas's distinction between the natural and the supernatural was a way of affirming the distinction between God's works of creation and reconciliation.[129] O'Donovan warns us against overstating this distinction. The question in response will be whether his own account can adequately appreciate it. This is an issue we will need to develop further. First, however, we need to observe a little more closely the first volume's arguments about the shape of practical reason.

---

123. *SWT*, 102–3.
124. *SWT*, 102.
125. *SWT*, 102.
126. *SWT*, 98–9.
127. *SWT*, 103.
128. *EIR*, 1–9.
129. See above, Chapter 3, Section 3a.

a. The Shape of Practical Reason

The core of *Self, World, and Time* consists of discussions of different modulations of natural moral experience: moral thinking (chapter 2), moral communication (chapter 3), and moral theory (chapter 4). Each of these chapters also, to a greater or lesser extent, develops one of the three key concepts of self, world, and time. Understanding this train of thought will highlight points of connection and also dissonance with what we have said about the character of wisdom. The sequence begins with a focused discussion of practical reason.

"Commonsense morality," O'Donovan writes, hinges on "the conviction that we must act reasonably."[130] This implies, he argues, both that our action must be "in tune with reality,"[131] and that our action must be thoughtful. "Simple awareness is not enough to ensure a reasonable judgment. When someone says, 'Think what you are doing!' we are expected to give our minds to it, to harness our intuitions to a disciplined exercise of reason that will lead to a rightly formed resolution."[132] The emphasis on thinking here, and its accompanied rejection of "simple awareness," will have to occupy us later. For now, we note that the thinking in question is a discursive movement of thought between value and obligation, from the good to the right.

This conclusion is reached by way of a dense passage of argument, in which O'Donovan connects together a number of distinctions: theoretical and practical reason, knowledge and will, fact and value. The discussion is framed in terms of the question of culpable ignorance.[133] The goal of the argument is to show that morality cannot, in the end, be divorced from reality. The fact-value divide and the divorce of knowledge and will are dead ends. Errors of understanding can indeed be culpable. "It belongs to the whole logic of practical reason that we need to know what we need to know."[134]

Without gainsaying the overall value of this argument or the many interesting points raised in it,[135] there is a question as to whether something is lost in the speed with which the ground is covered—particularly in regard to the brief discussion of Aristotle. O'Donovan refers to the distinction between practical and theoretical reason in book six of the *Nicomachean Ethics*.[136] He suggests that the crucial interpretative question has to do with how Aristotle envisaged practical reason as invested in *truth*. Are practical judgments true only in the formal sense that they flow out of a logical chain of reasoning, or are practical judgments true in a deeper

---

130. *SWT*, 21.
131. *SWT*, 25.
132. *SWT*, 21.
133. *SWT*, 21–5.
134. *SWT*, 25.
135. Most notably the suggestion that the basic problem at issue in the debate between Philippa Foot and R. M. Hare, and Foot's solution, was prefigured in debates between Peter Abelard and his scholastic contemporaries.
136. Cf. above, Chapter 1, Sections 1 and 2.

sense that they accord with reality? The first, he says, was the route eventually taken by modern voluntarism; the second, by classical moral realism, which O'Donovan suggests is more likely to have been Aristotle's meaning. In Chapter 1, we agreed that Aristotle's purpose was not to support a Humean account, in which practical reason merely serves desire. Aristotle thought that there had to be an agreement between desire and truth: the *right* things needed to be desired and pursued. This, though, is not quite the same thing as saying, as O'Donovan does, that "the right and wrong of practical judgment … correspond in some sense to the true and false of theoretical judgment."[137] The problem with this formulation is that it suggests a relationship between practical and theoretical reason that is less clear in Aristotle's thought. The right goals that practical reason pursues are not, for Aristotle, supplied by theoretical reasoning, but by the virtues. They are the gifts of the *polis* to practical life and, as we have seen, there remains a deep tension between the pursuit of them and the call of theoretical reason.

The importance of this appears in O'Donovan's ongoing argument, in which he suggests that Aristotle's understanding implicitly supports Augustine's idea that knowledge and will are united, with different consequences, in "contemplation" and "cogitation."[138] Although it seems to me that O'Donovan is right to say that Aristotle's idea of wisdom as concerned with "the most honorable things"[139] must imply some kind of affective commitment,[140] there remains an important difference between Aristotle's conception and Augustine's. Aristotle's conception of practical reason does not support a smooth movement from theoretical conclusions to practical implications. Although *sophia* is superior to *phronēsis, phronēsis* has its own domain. It was only with Thomas Aquinas that the right of "wisdom" to judge practical matters was unequivocally asserted, and as we have seen, Proverbs gives us reasons to question this way of putting things together.

The main burden of O'Donovan's argument at this point, however, is simply to show that the involvement of practical reason in affective commitment does not undermine the commonsense conviction that we must act reasonably in the sense of acting in accordance with how things are. For things really *are* value-laden. And so the movement that practical thought must unavoidably negotiate is not so much from is to ought, but from a value-laden-is to ought, from value to obligation, or as ancient thought had it, from the good to the right.[141] The tension between the good and the right, between the value we perceive to lie in reality and the obligation laid upon us as agents, is a basic feature of moral experience. The challenge lies in working out how goods constitute reasons for particular acts at certain times.[142] And this, says O'Donovan, is what practical reason is about: the journey from the

---

137. *SWT*, 22.
138. *SWT*, 23.
139. See *EN* 1141a18, b3; and above, Chapter 1, Section 1.
140. *SWT*, 22.
141. *SWT*, 25–32.
142. *SWT*, 29.

"is" of value to the "ought" of obligation. "Practical reason correlates the actions we immediately project with the way things are."[143]

The ideas of self, world, and time relate to this movement. The journey from value to obligation is a journey from *world* to *time*. Such movements are sometimes trivial, but other times they are weighty; that is, they are movements in which our selves are invested; they go to the question of how we may live our lives successfully.[144] "Responsibility" names the moment where we experience this weightiness. "Responsibility is an awareness of ourselves as subjects of action, as those who conduct the passages of thought between world and time, who come to resolutions of which they know themselves to be the author and understand the weight and significance of what they do."[145] Moral reason is the way in which we find our*selves* accountable as we think from *world* to *time*. It is a *finding* of self and world that issues in a *seeking* of what is to be done at this moment of time: "Practical reasoning ... begins with *finding*: we awake to our responsible agency; we appreciate the vast array of goods that the created world presents to our admiration. But then it must narrow its scope, focus on what is to be done, and engage with its time."[146]

What is the nature of this focusing in upon action? It is not, O'Donovan says, "intuitive."[147] Practical reason is discursive. "It has to negotiate its way between the two poles of description and resolution, the one determinate and the other indeterminate, one in the sphere of the actual, the other in the sphere of the possible."[148] As evidence O'Donovan cites the New Testament pattern of exhortation following on from announcement: this is what God has done in Christ—therefore—do this.[149] The announced truths ground the practical demands.

Yet, nor is it simply the case that practical implications are *deduced* from theoretical announcements. The analogy with theoretical reason can mislead: "Practical reason," O'Donovan stresses, "is not deductive, but inductive." It is not "an inference from premises to conclusions." Indeed, it has "no premises, no points from which an uncontroversial start may be made, and it has no conclusions, on which its trains of reason come to rest. No premises, because the knowledge of the world on which practical reason turns is always contested knowledge, not agreed. No conclusions, because practical reason terminates in action, not in belief."[150]

---

143. *SWT*, 29.

144. *SWT*, 32-3.

145. *SWT*, 36.

146. *F&S*, 179. The motif of finding and seeking may be drawn partly from the beginning of *De Trinitate*, book 9: "Let us, therefore, so seek as if we were about to find, and so find as if we were about to seek. For 'when a man has done, then he begins'" (9.1).

147. *SWT*, 29.

148. *SWT*, 29.

149. *SWT*, 29.

150. *SWT*, 30.

The descriptive accounts of reality that afford an entrée for action are not agreed starting-points. They are complex readings of the world, and as such arguable from the beginning. Moral reason has, of course, its commonplaces and formal rules—"the good is to be pursued, the evil avoided," etc.—which work just like the formal rules of logic in theoretical reason. But these are not the substantive readings of the world and its order on which our judgments of the good are based.[151]

Practical reason begins from contested interpretations of the meaning of the world, and ends, not in logical conclusions, but in "moments of action which punctuate thought without bringing it to a final cadence."[152]

O'Donovan sees this understanding of practical reason as an important point of differentiation from Aquinas, whose employment of the idea of first principles of practical reason, he says, reflects the mistake of thinking of practical reason as deductive.[153] The practical syllogism (a concept O'Donovan expresses reservations about) differs from the theoretical dramatically in that in it, "the minor premise *never* follows easily, but is always the focus of whatever moral disagreement there may be."[154] Above, we too criticized the idea of practical reasoning from first principles. We also pointed out elements in Aquinas's thought that suggest an ambivalence about this procedure.[155] So with O'Donovan's argument about the non-deductive character of practical reasoning we can agree. The questions that remain have to do with the way he positively characterizes practical reason. What kind of "knowledge of the world" does practical reason begin with? Where do its "substantive readings" come from? And how does it make the movement to action?

The importance of these questions emerges as the concept of "world" develops in chapters 3 and 4 of *Self, World and Time*. Chapter 3 explores it with reference to wisdom. Our awareness of ourselves as agents, O'Donovan begins, is always a socially mediated awareness. "My practical thinking continually alludes to ends pursued in common by the society I belong to."[156] The goods that we admire and pursue have to be "shown" to us by others.[157] This allows O'Donovan to talk about advice, authority, and moral teaching, and also wisdom.[158] An advisor's task is to bring the one being advised into contact with "a moral wisdom that belongs to us as a human community."[159] This moral wisdom consists in knowledge of kinds, of how certain questions are understood universally. The "authority of wisdom" belongs

---

151. *SWT*, 30.
152. *SWT*, 30.
153. *SWT*, 30; cf. *F&S*, 185–6.
154. *F&S*, 228.
155. See above, Chapter 3, Section 3b.
156. *SWT*, 49.
157. *SWT*, 44.
158. *SWT*, 49–65.
159. *SWT*, 51.

to exercises of authority that effect a wide disclosure of reality, marking "one end of the spectrum of cognitive plenitude."[160] In passing, O'Donovan mentions "the breadth and scope of wisdom as it is spoken of in the Old Testament," in support of this view.[161] Furthermore, he goes on to explain that what necessitates this wisdom is "the dialectic of nature and history."[162] It is our need for "some word" that can bring this dialectic "to a resolution" that makes us look for wisdom, for "a doctrine that can put us in a position to live our lives in harmony with nature and events."[163] This is quite similar to the conception of wisdom we saw in *Resurrection and Moral Order*, where wisdom involves a grasp of things as a whole in the midst of historical novelty.

O'Donovan clarifies this point here by distinguishing, with reference to Ecclesiastes 12:9-11, between comprehensive and "eclectic" teaching:

> Eclectic human wisdom may be a stimulus, but it is inconclusive; it leaves the student as bewildered as it found him. What is needed is the doctrine of a single teacher, comprehensive, coherent instruction that does not stop at isolated observations but pulls everything together, liberating us to learn from them all and live in harmony with nature and events. Such a doctrine can dispose of the fragments of wisdom because it is authorised by the coherence of the world and its history.[164]

In *Entering into Rest*, this distinction is seen to correspond to the books of Ecclesiastes and Proverbs; it is the basis on which O'Donovan says that the compilers of Proverbs cannot be understood as philosophers.[165] One overall purpose of this study is to suggest that there is more consistency in the outlook of Proverbs than is often imagined. Yet we need not fiercely dispute the word "eclectic." The question to be asked at this point is simply whether such comprehensive teaching really liberates us to *live*, or only to *understand*. Is it possible, perhaps, that the value of such comprehensive teaching has more to do with theoretical reason than with practical? Arguably, when it comes to *living* in harmony with nature and events, what matters is not that we have a grasp of the whole, but that we appreciate the thing in front of us; and for this purpose, "eclectic" wisdom may sometimes be better suited. This has a bearing on the discussion that follows, in which O'Donovan discusses what it means for Jesus to be the wisdom of God.[166] The incarnation, he

---

160. *SWT*, 56. I have discussed these ideas, and O'Donovan's treatment of authority more broadly, in Andrew Errington, "Authority and Reality in the Work of Oliver O'Donovan," *Studies in Christian Ethics* 29, no. 4 (2016): 371–85.
161. *SWT*, 58.
162. *SWT*, 59.
163. *SWT*, 59–60.
164. *SWT*, 60.
165. *EIR*, 34; and in the Introduction, above.
166. *SWT*, 62–5.

says, means "the evangelical mediation of reality, breaking into and re-constituting all our pre-existing traditions of wisdom about the world."[167] While appreciating the power of this formulation, we should register a query about the idea that the Gospel means the *mediation of reality*. Does it suggest a conception of wisdom that is too theoretical, grounded in a conception of reality (of "world") that is too ahistorical?

This question arises again in the discussion of moral theory, in chapter 4. What Ethics as a discipline is about, O'Donovan argues, is the trains of thought that lead to action and how they ought to run. Within the orbit of Christian theology—that is, where Ethics is practiced as Moral Theology—this question takes the form of "how a decision can derive its authority from a teaching."[168] Christian Ethics seeks "to clarify the conditions of a faithful correspondence of action to text."[169] Behind this conception lies a point that should be brought into the open, which is that Scripture's primary function is to give us knowledge of "world." Scripture is the critical instantiation of the point made in the previous chapter, that our knowledge of the world is socially mediated. This is why Scripture cannot, of itself, effect for us the movement to action in time. "There is a necessary indeterminacy in the obedient action required by the faithful reading of the text."[170] Scripture can tell us about *kinds*, but it cannot determine the particular act we must perform here and now. Scripture is "the divine resource with which we confront the practical indeterminacy of decision."[171] Moral thinking can respond to the authority of Scripture only with "a deliberated and free action."[172] Obedience to Scripture is a matter of achieving a "correspondence" between trains of thought in the Bible and our own train of thought in the present.[173]

This discussion is similar to O'Donovan's description of wisdom, in *Resurrection and Moral Order*, as knowledge of the generic world order in the midst of historical novelty, and of the need to read the Bible with a view to understanding "how the bricks fit together." Wisdom is about a grasp of the whole that can overcome the dialectic of nature and history; Scripture gives us knowledge of the world, and the "kinds and types" of action it contains.[174] Again, the question is whether it

---

167. *SWT*, 62.
168. *SWT*, 74.
169. *SWT*, 78.
170. *SWT*, 77.
171. *SWT*, 78.
172. *SWT*, 79.

173. *SWT*, 79. Regrettably, space prohibits a thorough engagement with this account of obedient reading, which O'Donovan has developed in a number of places, including *Church in Crisis: The Gay Controversy and the Anglican Communion* (Eugene, OR: Cascade, 2008), ch. 4; "The Moral Authority of Scripture," in *Scripture's Doctrine and Theology's Bible: How the New Testament Shapes Christian Dogmatics*, edited by Markus Bockmuel and Alan J. Torrance (Grand Rapids: Baker, 2008), 165–75; and "Scripture and Christian Ethics," *ANVIL* 24, no. 1 (2007): 21–9.

174. *SWT*, 77.

is right to think of what Scripture gives practical thinking primarily in terms of theoretical knowledge of a transhistorical order.

There are two related concerns here. The first has to do with the *kind* of knowledge Scripture gives us. Is it sufficient to think of Scripture's place in practical reasoning in terms of giving us *theoretical* knowledge of the world? Or do we also need to think of Scripture's role in terms of *practical* knowledge? This is a question we will return to below when we discuss O'Donovan's account of discernment in *Finding and Seeking*.

The second issue has to do with salvation-history, and whether O'Donovan's conception of "world" really has room for it. This question is highlighted by O'Donovan's ensuing description of the relationship between the disciplines of doctrine and ethics. There is, he says, a "proper *vis à vis* between Doctrine and Ethics."[175] On the one hand, Ethics must not be collapsed into Dogmatics; on the other, it must not become too distinct.[176] O'Donovan illustrates the first danger with a discussion of sin. Dogmatics and Ethics, he suggests, treat the reality of sin in different ways. Dogmatics emphasizes the "impossible universality" of sin, "its significance as the defining qualification in the mis-relation between mankind and a holy God," whereas Ethics emphasizes the "possible contingency" of sin, its presence "as a horizon continually to be recognized and refused in each action."[177] This differentiation, which O'Donovan recalls in *Finding and Seeking*,[178] has an intriguing parallel in something Kant says in *Groundwork to the Metaphysics of Morals*—a passage to which O'Donovan elsewhere refers—about the different ways in which practical and theoretical reason consider freedom.

> [T]here arises a dialectic of reason since, with respect to the will, the freedom ascribed to it seems to be in contradiction with natural necessity; and at this parting of the ways reason *for speculative purposes* finds the road of natural necessity much more travelled and more usable than that of freedom; yet *for practical purposes* the footpath of freedom is the only one on which it is possible to make use of our reason in our conduct.[179]

The parallel is instructive because it is inexact. The question in relation to sin is not quite the same as the question of freedom and necessity. In the latter case, the explanation must be found (or not found) in a metaphysics, in which freedom is grounded in a world standing behind time and space.[180] In the case

---

175. *SWT*, 81.
176. *SWT*, 81–9.
177. *SWT*, 83.
178. *F&S*, 17–18.
179. Immanuel Kant, *Groundwork of the Metaphysics of Morals*, trans. Mary Gregor (Cambridge: Cambridge University Press, 1998), 60 [4:455-456]. O'Donovan refers to this passage in *F&S*, 68. Note also his comments about Kant in *SWT*, 83.
180. For an overview of Kant's thinking on this point, see Christopher J. Insole, *The Intolerable God: Kant's Theological Journey* (Grand Rapids, MI: Eerdmans, 2016), 56–92.

of sin, however, the explanation is historical: it is in the story of the fall, rather than the structure of reality, that theology finds its explanation for the unfreedom of the will, however that is understood. The distinction between the necessity and contingency of sin does not, therefore, map as directly onto the distinction between theoretical and practical reason, as Kant's distinction between necessity and freedom might do.

What is at stake here is whether O'Donovan's account of the "world," in which and from which practical reason acts in time, can really accommodate salvation-history. By imagining obedience in essentially the same framework that Kant understands freedom, O'Donovan implies a notion of "world" that is fundamentally ahistorical. The world that wisdom is given to know, and that obedience relates to, is not the world as it actually is—the creation itself, under the conditions of sin—but an order standing behind the world we experience, disclosed by theory. This is the central concern I will raise about O'Donovan's account. We cannot raise it properly, however, without first considering O'Donovan's understanding of the renewal of moral reason as faith, love, and hope, and particularly his discussion of love's relation to the world.

b. Faith, Love, and Wisdom

"Natural moral experience ... is taken up and enhanced in the redemption of the moral life."[181] The threefold awareness of self, world, and time that shapes the practical reasoning basic to human existence is renewed by the Holy Spirit in faith, love, and hope. This is the thought that O'Donovan outlines at the end of *Self, World, and Time*, and that structures *Finding and Seeking*. We will now survey the way this unfolds, with special attention to the points that relate to our theme. Here we will see O'Donovan develop the image of the call of wisdom in connection with the idea of "the whole." This is a point of some importance for our discussion.

Awareness of self is redeemed as faith. A central insight of the Reformation was, according to O'Donovan, that faith is already active. Faith is "the root of action."[182] In contrast to Aquinas, faith is not a cognitive disposition that becomes active only in love, but is already intentional,[183] "the subjective root from which the life of active love proceeds ... the awareness of the self made competent by an act of God."[184] It is "the consciousness of being called to life by God," which "reaches to embrace" the world and time in action.[185] Later, in *Entering into Rest*, O'Donovan expands and emphasizes this point. Love, he argues, must not be

---

181. *SWT*, 102, and above.
182. *SWT*, 105–12; *F&S*, 24–7; cf. *EIR*, 22.
183. *F&S*, 25.
184. *SWT*, 109.
185. *SWT*, 111–12.

made the foundation of action, for love cannot truly ground agency.[186] Love is not the starting point of practical reason, but something found, and reached again at the end.

Faith is awakened by the call of God. Yet, it "has no discursive content of its own,"[187] but has its essence in the immediate encounter of the self with God. Faith's sense of responsibility, therefore, requires the world to give it form and focus. We are "not called to life in a vacuum, but to life in the world."[188]

How can we understand this sense in which, following from faith, the world itself provides for our action? O'Donovan finds a key in the call of wisdom:[189] "'Does not wisdom call?' That is to ask," he writes, "does not the order and loveliness of the created world call us to know it and to love it?"[190] The call of wisdom is certainly the call of God, O'Donovan holds; and yet, "God's call reaches us only *through* the created world and as we are participators in it ... Whatever Christological extrapolation we may legitimately make from that, we must not miss the most obvious truth, that created order itself is not without voice, but has the resources to call us."[191] The call of wisdom is the purchase of the good order of the world upon us, an "existential condition," rather than an "episode."[192] The "mutual satisfaction of the wisdom of God in mankind, and of mankind in the wisdom of God," which Proverbs 8:30-31 describes, "is the ground of our moral perception," because "the wisdom in creation is itself of creation." Moral existence is made possible only by the moral field, "the world [God] has made so sure that it cannot be moved, the unnegotiable form of our unformed agency, the school of our first and last purposes, the gazette that announces our enlistment in God's service."[193] Wisdom calls because creation is good, evoking our love and knowledge—our *admiration*. As Augustine recognized, we may know things only as we know them as good, which means we may know them only as we love.[194] Such loving knowledge also discerns the interrelations of things, the way in which "the world of goods is joined up" in a complex network of relations of kinds and ends.[195] This is how faith works itself out in love toward action. "Loving attention to the world ... clothes the self in worldly concreteness, situating it within the world it enters."[196]

---

186. *EIR*, 9–14.
187. *F&S*, 47.
188. *SWT*, 112.
189. See *SWT*, 112–13; *F&S*, 48, 100.
190. *SWT*, 112; cf. *F&S*, 48.
191. *F&S*, 100–1.
192. *F&S*, 101; cf. O'Donovan's discussion of Augustine in *SWT*, 114–15.
193. *SWT*, 113.
194. See *F&S*, 77–81, and *SWT*, 114–19.
195. *F&S*, 76–7.
196. *F&S*, 83.

To what does wisdom call us? To know and to love the created order, O'Donovan has said, and to know it and love it in its interconnection. This means, as it did in *Resurrection and Moral Order*, an admiring grasp of the world as a whole.[197]

> In finding the world given as a total field of knowledge, we find it to be an object of affective appreciation as a whole, not merely a container for specialized objects of appreciation. When the world's reality speaks to us, it speaks to us with a claim: knowable and loveable in itself, it is the context for knowledge and love of ourselves, of all other reality and of God. This is the claim made upon us by "Wisdom," the paradigm of realities that cannot be loved without being known or known without being loved. It tells us, "Take my instruction instead of silver, and knowledge rather than choice gold, for wisdom is better than jewels and all that you may desire cannot compare with her." (Prov. 8:10-11)[198]

Wisdom's "project," O'Donovan argues, "is essentially holistic"; it involves "an effort to comprehend the pattern of the whole."[199]

This project is a *project*, rather than simply a fact, because it is a task that belongs to "creatures extended in time."[200] The call of wisdom, O'Donovan infers, means "the call of the world's temporal openness to knowledge, a call addressed to our powers of living through time."[201] Chapter 5 of *Finding and Seeking* begins from this point and explores what it means that wisdom *calls* to us, setting before us a task not simply of knowing and loving, but of *learning* and *seeking*.[202] We find wisdom, O'Donovan says, only to seek again. Wisdom is realized in intelligible "representations" of the order of things as a whole.[203] Yet time relentlessly challenges these representations by throwing up new perceptions and changing the shape of the world we have to reckon with.[204] "We achieve a grasp on the world as a whole, but the world as a whole does not remain quiescent in our grasp, but slips away and calls us to look further for it."[205] However much we come to know, "an erotic sense of the vast and unmapped universe of reality … continues to call us."[206]

The call of wisdom, then, means for O'Donovan the way reality as a whole endlessly holds itself before us as the object of our loving comprehension. Yet,

---

197. *F&S*, 81.
198. *F&S*, 81.
199. *F&S*, 80.
200. *F&S*, 100.
201. *F&S*, 100.
202. *F&S*, 100–3.
203. *F&S*, 108.
204. *F&S*, 104.
205. *F&S*, 102.
206. *F&S*, 108. O'Donovan's use of the term "erotic" follows a careful discussion of desire and eros (*F&S*, 103–8).

"we cannot settle down in our ideational constructions, just as we cannot make our home in a wayside inn."[207] The failure of "ideology" lies in refusing to accept the provisionality of the representations we attain.[208] Nevertheless, "the satisfying whole" remains a legitimate and necessary goal, for:

> God did not create a world of disjoined and unrelated moments, but one tied together as a whole in a multitude of ontological and temporal relationships. Symbolic representations of the whole may go astray, but we cannot do without them, for conceiving the whole is a power of mind with which human nature is endowed, and it needs to be taught and learned well. Christianity, it has often been said, has its own "worldview," its account of the whole ... The Gospel offers a central and normative focus of joy, the resurrection of Christ, which becomes a torch to illumine the goods of the world, a vantage point from which we can explore, discover, and appreciate all other objects of joy.[209]

O'Donovan stresses, though, that great care is needed with the idea of a worldview. He highlights the spareness of Augustine's "sketchmap of the objects of love," and suggests that "axiology" may be a more appropriate description of the kind of account that the science of Ethics may seek.[210] Yet an axiology is not all the moral *agent* needs. The moral agent needs not merely scientific knowledge, which "comes to rest in the knowledge of what has come to be known," but moral knowledge; and this "is, as such, its discovery." The knowledge of the whole that wisdom calls for comes in and as we "receive the good." As such, it will have a clear, simple center in "the disclosure of God's works in Christ," and otherwise not "too weighty a theoretical baggage."[211]

For it is only the gospel, O'Donovan goes on to stress, that tells us that "the possibility of wisdom" has been "decisively given."[212] In the final section of Chapter 5, O'Donovan takes up again the theme of the reconciliation of nature and history.[213] Awareness of time opens up a gap between the goods of "reality" and the possibilities of our time, a sense of loss that confronts us as threatening. History is beset with this threat of meaninglessness.[214] How can love of the world survive this threat? "The Gospel identifies a historical moment, at which time and the good are reconciled: the resurrection of Jesus Christ, an event at the centre

---

207. *F&S*, 102.
208. *F&S*, 108–11.
209. *F&S*, 111–12.
210. *F&S*, 112–13.
211. *F&S*, 113.
212. *F&S*, 118.
213. *F&S*, 114–19.
214. *F&S*, 115.

of history which vindicates the created order and heals the rift between history and the good."²¹⁵ Wisdom at its highest points to the need for this resolution, but cannot supply it.²¹⁶ For "the world does not contain within itself the resolution of the paradoxes of history."²¹⁷ It is only in Christ, along with his community, that the world's good can be saved for action from the threat of time's arbitrariness. For it is there that "the narrative of the Gospel has conferred moral sense upon the contingencies of time."²¹⁸

> Only by "following after" the one at the centre of history can we accomplish ourselves effectively. An opposition thus appears between the value-order of the world as perceived ahistorically and the word that holds the center of the world's history … Merely to affirm the created world's order of value is to ignore this opposition. To affirm Christ's death and resurrection is to acknowledge it, and to find it resolved in the rebirth of agency.²¹⁹

It is to this rebirth of agency that O'Donovan turns next.

Before we move on to this, however, we must pause once more to consider this significant exposition of the call of wisdom. There is much here that is recognizable from *Resurrection and Moral Order*. O'Donovan has found in the image of wisdom's call a biblical reflection of the way reality opens itself to our love and knowledge, which leads him to the now-familiar themes of knowledge of the whole and the dialectic of nature and history. Yet the discussion here also displays greater caution, particularly in relation to the idea of knowing the whole. This caution appears to be due, in part, to O'Donovan's awareness of the difference it makes to think of this knowledge as practical, rather than theoretical.²²⁰

The question, however, is whether the full force of this point has been felt. More precisely, is there a tension between the idea of wisdom as moral knowledge, and the idea of wisdom as an intellectual "representation of the whole"? Our discussion of the call of wisdom in the previous chapter suggests that this is indeed the case. At the beginning of Chapter 5, O'Donovan refers to the way "the world that offers us kinds and goods within a time over which they are distributed is hospitable to possibility."²²¹ This is strikingly similar to the language we have used to describe the call of wisdom. Yet for O'Donovan, the possibility in view is primarily the possibility of *knowledge*; on our account, it ought to be action. The call of wisdom,

---

215. *F&S*, 116.

216. *F&S*, 116. Here O'Donovan refers again to Revelation 4–5, the text that was crucial for this point in *RMO* (*F&S*, 117). See above, n. 62.

217. *F&S*, 118.

218. *F&S*, 118.

219. *F&S*, 118–19.

220. See *F&S*, 113, especially.

221. *F&S*, 100.

we said, is creation's hospitality *to good action*, the way the world is amenable to the successful living of life. The kind of knowledge wisdom calls for is more like practical knowledge, knowledge of how to act well in the world. What kind of grasp of the whole does such knowledge require, or make possible? There are moments in Proverbs that could be taken to suggest how a breadth of understanding will open up as one walks the path of wisdom. Consider the contrast between darkness and light made, for example, in 4:18-19, in which the fate of the wicked is to *not know* why they stumble; or the imagery of "straight paths." Yet, there are many other moments that suggest such a perspective will always elude, and is not what really matters. "From the Lord are one's steps—how can someone understand their way?" (Prov. 20:24). It is striking, too, that when the benefits of wisdom are listed (for instance in Prov. 3:13-18 or 8:12-21, 32-36), they are not primarily cognitive but practical. The understanding of wisdom as a representation of the whole, however "spare" and provisional, involves a conception of wisdom as fundamentally speculative in character. This is shown by O'Donovan's recognition that a theory of value has its proper place within a *science*.[222] Although O'Donovan rightly perceives that the practical orientation of Ethics will problematize such a theoretical conception, he still understands wisdom in terms of such an "imagined framework."[223] It seems to me that the practical character of wisdom calls for a more dramatic reordering. If we may speak of an intellectual representation of the whole, we will need to do so only by understanding it as a theoretical extrapolation made possible by a primary, practical purchase on reality. It is not itself the getting of wisdom. The importance of this criticism appears with O'Donovan's account of how renewed practical reason is completed in action, and especially in the way he understands prudence.

c. Hope and Prudent Deliberation

Faith sets the self in motion, love shows the world that gives direction, but it is hope that allows self to become effective. Here we reach what O'Donovan calls the "decisive" "third step in practical reason," the demand to attend to time, the "today" in which the future is open before us as an opportunity for action.[224] It is hope that secures the future for action. By contrast, anticipations, though inevitable and proper in their own way, cannot free us to act. For "action is adventure, the injection of new initiative into the stream of future events."[225] It therefore "requires thought about the character of the moment."[226] Anticipation, however, because it cannot truly *know* the future, but only the regularities of the past, tends to stifle

---

222. *F&S*, 113.
223. *F&S*, 113, 102.
224. *F&S*, 145; cf. *SWT*, 119.
225. *F&S*, 204.
226. *SWT*, 120.

such deliberative thought.[227] It is only the promise of God that gives the present moment to us as *open*, because "hope clears a space of freedom before our feet, even if that space is no larger than will allow for a disciplined and patient waiting."[228]

What precisely is involved in thinking to action? In the final chapters of *Finding and Seeking*, O'Donovan returns to questions with which we began our discussion of *Resurrection and Moral Order*. The discussion has two parts: deliberation and discernment. Overall, the conclusions reached in the earlier work are reinforced and given greater nuance. These chapters also traverse ground covered by Aquinas's theory of action.

Deliberation is a search for a purpose, that is, for "a mental representation of the action about to be executed."[229] It is a *search for* a given course of action, and not merely a *choice between* alternatives.[230] The central task of deliberation, O'Donovan argues, consists in a kind of narrowing of focus from the many goods of the world in upon the one thing to be done. As he writes in *Entering into Rest*, "We *narrow our view* of the field of possibility until we achieve whatever sharpness of focus we need in order to envisage a practicable action."[231] What deliberation seeks, therefore, is an "objective determination," a right answer to the question "what is to be done."[232]

O'Donovan's idea of a purpose, as it is articulated here, is close to Aquinas's concept of the interior object of an act. A purpose is an action intended to be performed. This is a central aspect of what Aquinas is interested in with the idea of an action's object.[233] This similarity is highlighted by the fact that O'Donovan links purposes to kinds, just as Aquinas links kinds to objects. "To purpose action," O'Donovan writes, "we must frame it in our minds … as a non-necessary event," and this means "we must conceive it as an act of a certain kind."[234] This is similar to the way Aquinas links objects, kinds, and reason. O'Donovan, like Aquinas, also sees the need to distinguish between actions and ends. He argues that we must distinguish purposes from "ends-of-action."[235] A purpose, he argues, is a conception *of* the action. An end-of-action is a state of affairs envisaged as a result of the action. It is an "anticipation" that necessarily accompanies a purpose, and

---

227. O'Donovan's critique of anticipation is found in *SWT*, 121–2, and *F&S*, 152–9. Regrettably, space prohibits a thorough discussion of this point. For the positive role of anticipation, see *F&S*, 159–66, 204; and *EIR*, 23–6.

228. *SWT*, 123.

229. *F&S*, 186.

230. *F&S*, 181, 183; cf. *SWT*, 77; *EIR*, 119.

231. *EIR*, 26, emphasis original. See also *SWT*, 123; and *F&S*, 182.

232. *F&S*, 184, 185.

233. See above, Chapter 2, Section 2. Recall that the notion of the object, although it is not merely a subjective aim, is very much linked to purpose: "fines objecta actuum interiorum" (*ST* I-II.54.2 ad3).

234. *F&S*, 231.

235. *F&S*, 186.

is, therefore, also in a sense intended; but it is not the same thing as a purpose.[236] This is not quite the same as the distinction Aquinas makes between what is willed and what is intended.[237] It would appear, for example, to weaken or at least qualify the principle that actions receive their species from their end.[238] It should be noted, though, that the term "purpose" itself reveals an impulse to understand actions from their ends. Moreover, we will see that the distinctions O'Donovan makes here unravel a little in *Entering into Rest*.

Now, just as for Aquinas, it is through the notion of kinds that O'Donovan introduces law. For "the moral law," as O'Donovan puts it later, "gives generic forms by which we can understand the moment in which we find ourselves placed."[239] O'Donovan introduces law, however, through a discussion of prudence, which requires consideration.

Prudence, O'Donovan says, is "the virtue of excellent deliberation."[240] For O'Donovan, its work lies in a sort of coordination of what has been learned about the world with the task at hand. Following Augustine, it is about "coordinating memory and intention."[241] This is an intellectual work. The goal of prudence is for our actions to "bear an intelligent relation to reality—'intelligent,' not merely 'intelligible,' since the intelligence of action is present in the agent's purpose, not only observable from outside."[242] Prudence involves a cognitive "bringing to bear" of the world's order upon action.[243]

Law is what this bringing to bear entails. Taking a cue from Aquinas's notion that the chief act of prudence is to command, O'Donovan argues that law is, in a sense, the product of prudence. Not that prudence generates law—it is reality's order of value that does that—but prudence discerns the normative significance of that value: "The specific role of prudence is to conceive [the] ordered good as *directive*, as a *normative* order that lays claim on our freedom to act ... prudence does not confer normativity on value, but recognizes the normative implications of value. We admire the goods of the created order affectively; in prudence we discern the system of moral law they imply."[244] Laws, O'Donovan clarifies, "are constructs, mediating the order of reality."[245] They are a normative representation of the created order.[246] For this reason, prudent deliberation involves grasping the

---

236. See *F&S*, 186.
237. Cf. *ST* i-II.19.7–8, and above, Chapter 2, Section 2.
238. Cf. *ST* i-II.1.3, and above, Chapter 2, Section 2.
239. *F&S*, 215; see also p. 199.
240. *F&S*, 193; cf. *SWT*, 16.
241. *F&S*, 194.
242. *F&S*, 194.
243. *F&S*, 195.
244. *F&S*, 195, emphasis original.
245. *F&S*, 207.
246. *F&S*, 195.

way moral laws form an "ordered system."[247] There are more and less fundamental laws, and it is discerning their order and relation that gives coherence to our agency.[248]

Prudence has the task, though, not merely of discerning the law, but of keeping it, which means "interpreting the present situation morally."[249] This involves a moment of "recognition" of the meaning of the particular situation: the recognition that *this* situation is of *that* kind. This element of deliberation cannot be conceived in terms of deduction; it is a "mysterious act, learned only by practice though usually performed without thinking."[250] In this movement, furthermore, both the particular situation and the generic law are illuminated.[251] The notion of subsumption misleads to the extent that it suggests we merely have to categorize the situation rightly. In fact, however, recognition involves a "re-learning of the law." Moral laws are not the moral order itself, but "formulae that represent the shape of moral reality."[252] They may therefore have exceptions, but these exceptions will be themselves rules, for there cannot be exceptions to the moral order itself.[253] There can finally be no purely particular obligation. What applies in one situation must apply in others, at least in principle.[254]

This discussion is another rendering of what O'Donovan sees as the central insights of Ramsey's paper on exceptions, to which he refers once more.[255] What is different from Ramsey is, again, the emphasis on moral kinds as present in reality. Here, however, O'Donovan also moves beyond *Resurrection and Moral Order* by following the point about recognition further. There is something "mysterious," he says, about the forming of a purpose that concludes, or better, cuts off the process of deliberation. Deliberation reaches resolution not by following a train of thought "to a logical resting place," but *by acting*.[256] Resolutions, O'Donovan explains earlier in *Self, World, and Time*, are "moments of action which punctuate thought without bringing it to a final cadence."[257] It is hope, O'Donovan thinks, that makes such discernments possible, for it is only hope that can "assure us that an exertion of our own could constitute a 'work' that might count good for eternity."[258]

The problem, O'Donovan explains in the final chapter of *Finding and Seeking*, is time. We encounter the moral order at a particular moment, looking into a future

---

247. *F&S*, 197.
248. *F&S*, 200–1; compare *RMO*, 200–3.
249. *F&S*, 207.
250. *F&S*, 206.
251. *F&S*, 207.
252. *F&S*, 207.
253. *F&S*, 207, 226.
254. *F&S*, 227–30.
255. *F&S*, 207, n. 29, 226, n. 13.
256. *F&S*, 206.
257. *SWT*, 30.
258. *SWT*, 124.

that we cannot know simply on the basis of the past. Hence, although the moral law can tell us what is to be done and not done in general, "it cannot tell us what is to be done *next*."[259] To know what *is* to be done, "deliberation must conclude in an act of *discerning the time*."[260]

Discernment involves a "coincidence" of "constraint and opportunity."[261] It is like finding a path, a course of action that appears to be going somewhere.[262] The metaphor of the path is "so potent in talk of practical attention to the future," because a path has a teleological form that is still unknown.[263] A path is finally what deliberation looks for:

> Deliberation is not an inferential train of reasoning, its conclusion contained in its premises and only waiting to be laid bare; it is a focusing of vision upon ourselves and our circumstances, so as to effect an act of discernment. It looks for the appearance of a path of life and action, a direction that will emerge within the complex of circumstances. When the search is successful, we light on something not already present in our thought, an immediate opening for action.[264]

We make such discernments not merely by feeling, nor deduction, but by "observing correlations." We seek a "congruence of normativities": the alignment of "the ordered demand of the creation," the "agential powers" we have, and "the moment of opportunity."[265] Discernment is an experience of "being led."[266] It thus opens up to the concept of vocation, which means "the way in which the self is offered to us" as a possibility opened up by God's promise.[267]

We have now begun to traverse the territory charted in the final volume of *Ethics as Theology*. Before we turn to that, however, let us pause again to reflect on this rich treatment of deliberation and discernment.

From the point of view of our reading of Proverbs, the most striking point in O'Donovan's account of deliberation has to do with the role of memory in relation to prudence and law. At first sight, this might appear to be a point in common with Proverbs, which also emphasizes the significance of memory for deliberation. "My son, do not forget my law (*tôrātî*)!" (3:1). Yet the ideas are not identical. For Proverbs, it is not memory itself that is critical for wise action, but the words that

---

259. *F&S*, 215.
260. *F&S*, 215, emphasis original.
261. *F&S*, 220.
262. *F&S*, 217.
263. *F&S*, 218. This is a point we highlighted above in connection with Proverbs. See Chapter 3, Section 3.
264. *F&S*, 220.
265. *F&S*, 220–1.
266. *F&S*, 221.
267. *F&S*, 222–4.

memory can recall: "The commandment is a lamp and the instruction is a light" (6:23). On O'Donovan's account things are slightly different. Commandments do not impact upon deliberation directly, but only as mediated by the mind. "Moral laws," O'Donovan writes, "are historical formulations, belonging to memory, as moral order belongs to understanding."[268] Prudence must weigh and reflect upon these laws, evaluating their place and significance, in order to bring the order of the world to bear on the moment of action. From the perspective of Proverbs, this appears to involve the danger of devaluing the significance of the particular forms of instruction that can disclose the path of wisdom. If a command is only "historical,"[269] then is it really a live element in the process of deliberation and discernment? Or is it now a piece of information that has to be filtered, by prudence, through the prism of a representation of the ordered system of law? It is tempting to hear in this conception an echo of Kant's idea that for obedience to law to be moral, we must, in a sense, give ourselves the law.[270]

What lies behind this difference is the primacy of the theoretical in O'Donovan's understanding of prudence. Prudence, as we saw, has to do with the *intelligence*, and not merely the intelligibility, of action. It "discerns the system of moral law" implied by created order and "brings it to bear" on action. "What theories are for reflection," O'Donovan suggests, "laws are for deliberation: capturing the changelessness of changeable realities, open to refutation and disproof, securing for thought the wisdom attained by reflection."[271] To this, Proverbs leads us to respond with some skepticism. Perhaps there can be great value in speculative conceptions of world order; however, prudence does not lie in the intellectual bringing-to-bear of such constructs on action, but in an affinity with wise action itself. Prudent action *does* mean action "in tune with reality," as O'Donovan says,[272] but it does not necessarily mean *intelligent* action in the sense of action in which one knows what one is doing comprehensively. If we may recall a point from our earlier discussion of *Self, World, and Time*, O'Donovan argues that acting reasonably means not only "that our actions must fit with how things are," but also "that we must think about what we propose to do in an ordered way." "When someone says, 'Think what you are doing!'," he writes, "we are expected to give our minds to it, to harness our intuitions to a disciplined exercise of reason that will lead to a rightly formed resolution."[273] By way of response, we might ask whether this is really what "commonsense morality" asks for. More often, the thing that would be said would be simply, "What are you doing?" And what such a question asks for is not necessarily an ordered process of thought—that may or may not be

---

268. *F&S*, 195.

269. *F&S*, 193.

270. See, for example, *Groundwork*, 42 [4:434]; *Critique of Practical Reason*, trans. Mary Gregor (Cambridge: Cambridge University Press, 2015), 30 [5:33].

271. *F&S*, 195.

272. *SWT*, 25.

273. *SWT*, 21.

required—but simply for action to "make sense" by conforming to the kinds of action to which the world is hospitable. (Even when what is said is, "what do you *think* you are doing?" the emphasis is not primarily on a failure of thought, but on a failure, to use O'Donovan's expression once more, "to keep our actions in tune with reality." Thinking is part of the equation not because it is what is lacking, but because it may provide the explanation for the otherwise inexplicable.) Prudence, to engage the point of reference in Augustine that is common to O'Donovan as well as Aquinas, is about "avoiding ambushes"; and that may indeed be a matter of "simple awareness," rather than a reflective grasp on the whole.[274]

d. The Perfecting of Agency

Our survey of the final stage in the journey of *Ethics as Theology* must be accomplished more briefly. We have already seen how O'Donovan's discussion of discernment opens up a further horizon of the fulfilment of action in eternity, and we have noted the claim in *Self, World, and Time* that this promise supplies the logic of the re-ordered sequence of virtues in 1 Cor. 13:13—faith, hope, and love. This is the point from which *Entering into Rest* begins, seeking the logic of this "inverted triad." By placing love "at the summit of the triad,"[275] O'Donovan argues, what Paul seeks to express is the way love appears in moral existence not only as that which gives form and focus to the self's activity, but also as the goal of that activity. Action also *seeks* love, which becomes a real anticipation of eternity in the life of the present community. Paul's characterizations of love in 1 Cor. 13:4-6 describe a love realized "as deference," love expressed in "'resting in' others' labours."[276] This "resting in" is "a foretaste of the Kingdom of God" in which the created order is restored.[277] It is a simultaneous "eschatological extension" and "ecclesiological orientation" of practical reason.[278] *Cooperation* is the form in which a provisional, anticipatory rest is offered to us.[279] But only anticipatory, for in the end eschatological disclosure must turn it to devotion.[280]

This claim, which is the heart of the third volume, rests on O'Donovan's particular understanding of, on the one hand, ends-of-action, and on the other, love. For our purposes, it will be sufficient briefly to draw out O'Donovan's arguments about these two concepts.

First: in the opening chapters of *Entering into Rest*, O'Donovan discusses the idea of ends-of-action in order to clarify why practical reason ultimately looks

---

274. Recall our discussion of this point in Chapter 3, Section 3b.
275. *EIR*, 3.
276. *EIR*, 2–3.
277. *EIR*, 4.
278. *EIR*, 8.
279. *EIR*, 19.
280. *EIR*, 14, 225–9.

toward fulfilment in community.[281] The heart of his answer is that ends-of-action represent a kind of coordination of our agency with the reality of the world. It is only reality itself that makes it possible to envisage an end-of-action.

> An end-of-action … is not a projection of the purposing mind; it is an anticipation made by the purposing mind of a future state, which the world we now encounter harbors, though concealed, among its possibilities. It is an anticipation that reflects the purpose back to itself, and discloses what it is about by representing what the world shall be in its wake.[282]

Because of this, ends-of-action are intrinsically exposed to judgment. Our intentions "lay claim" to an "objective intelligibility," and in so doing, implicitly appeal to a community of understanding.[283] "When we speak of a good that we may initiate, an end-of-action, we speak of a good that is not only *communicated*, but *communicable*."[284]

This emphasis on the intelligibility of intention ought to remind us of Aquinas's similar effort to hold together the objective and subjective elements of action. We will also need to consider whether O'Donovan's interpretation of this in terms of *communicability* might be an important development of the picture. In distinction from Aquinas, however, O'Donovan deliberately resists the conceptuality of means and ends. Practical thought, he maintains, certainly constructs a "succession of nearer ends leading to further ends."[285] Yet it is a mistake, he says, to conceive this in terms of means to ends, for to do so confuses two separate issues. On the one hand, ends are anticipations, and so further ends follow from nearer ones, without necessarily implying an order of value. For example, "if I anticipate writing a book that will make me a great deal of money, that does not mean that I think having money more important than writing a book."[286] On the other hand, "anticipations are taken into the formation of purposes," which may, indeed, be ordered to one another. I might plan a dinner in order to cultivate a friendship. Having a dinner is perfectly meaningful in itself, without the further aim. Although in this instance it is in fact "nested" within a further end, to call it a "means" obscures its status as an end-of-action in itself.[287] The term "means," O'Donovan suggests, should be reserved for what he calls "operations," in contrast to "acts" or "deeds." Operations are activities that are "intelligible only in relation to further ends." Deeds or acts, on the other hand, have "intrinsic ends."[288] Along with this, O'Donovan also

---

281. See *EIR*, 23, 45.
282. *EIR*, 39.
283. *EIR*, 46.
284. *EIR*, 51, emphasis original.
285. *EIR*, 31.
286. *EIR*, 32.
287. *EIR*, 31–3.
288. *EIR*, 31–2.

dismisses the "scholastic doctrine" of deliberation as a movement in which "an end is first settled on reflectively, and deliberation undertaken only to find the means to realize it."[289] In fact, he says, we discern ends-of-action only at the *end* of deliberation, as we come to discern the shape of a "practicable action."[290]

This final point is essentially the same as that which we made in connection with Aquinas, when we showed that often in deliberation, the end and the means arise together as a conceivable, which means intelligible, course of action.[291] However, O'Donovan's wider rejection of means-end conceptuality requires further clarification. The need for this emerges with O'Donovan's use of the language of "purposes." In clarifying, a little earlier, the nature of ends-of-action in relation to anticipations of the future, O'Donovan stresses, as he does in *Finding and Seeking*, that ends-of-action are not the same as consequences. We cannot be responsible for consequences in the same way we are for ends, for ends-of-action do not "lie beyond" actions themselves. They are "what we intend by our action."[292] This point is relatively clear. O'Donovan goes on, however, to say that the end "is the action itself from the point of view of what it purposes."[293] This is unexpected, given the careful distinguishing of purposes and ends-of-action in *Finding and Seeking*.[294] That distinction aimed to establish precisely that the end was *not* the action itself, which was what "purpose" referred to, but the state of affairs anticipated to result from the action. The ambiguity is reinforced when O'Donovan goes on to write, "Action is exertion to a purpose—exertion, on the one hand, because it is an event and not merely an idea, but purposed, on the other, because it is not a mere event, but an event shaped in conformity to an idea. The 'end' of action is not the exertion, but the idea, the 'object' as framed in the mind."[295] Here purpose (along with Aquinas's term, "object") is being used primarily in relation to the end-of-action, in contrast to the "exertion" that achieves it. A little later, however, O'Donovan seems to recover the earlier distinction to some extent, writing that "the end-of-action is ... a foresight ... of the world as it shall be when we have done what we purpose."[296]

O'Donovan is here navigating the same, complex territory that Aquinas charts by means of the concepts of internal and external objects, and ends. Aquinas, to recall, wanted to say both that the end *was* the internal object, and that there could be a distinction between the object of an act and the intention. The difficulties that O'Donovan has with the idea of "a purpose"—that it is the term he uses (in *Finding and Seeking*) to distinguish an action itself from its end, and yet it also draws him

---

289. *EIR*, 26.
290. *EIR*, 26.
291. See above, Chapter 2, Section 5; and Chapter 3, Section 3b.
292. *EIR*, 24.
293. *EIR*, 25.
294. *F&S*, 186, and above.
295. *EIR*, 25.
296. *EIR*, 25–6.

into understanding actions in terms of ends—precisely match the complexities Thomas faces with the term "object." The term that seems appropriate to designate the action—object or purpose—is naturally oriented toward the end of the action. In fact, O'Donovan is using the term "end" in two different ways. That this is the case is particularly clear from another contrast. In *Finding and Seeking*, he writes that whereas "a purpose needs to be clear, clear enough to channel the exertion of effort … an imagined end … need not be very clear."[297] In *Entering into Rest*, however, he writes that "ends are always precise," whereas "reasons may sometimes be diffuse and broadly conceived."[298] In both cases, O'Donovan's interest is in distinguishing between the action itself as an effecting of something in particular and the wider meanings that the action may have. What has happened, however, is that in the later work, the term "end" has come to refer to the action itself, that is, to do some of the work done by the term "purpose" in the earlier work. This is interesting. Earlier, we pointed out that the firm distinction between purpose and end made in *Finding and Seeking* appeared to call into question Aquinas's strong emphasis on ends as determinative. Now, however, it seems this distinction has come unstuck.

The uncertainty is itself evidence for a number of conclusions. The first is that Thomas is right to think that, in some sense, it is the end of an action that determines its kind. When O'Donovan writes that "An end of action is formed by a process of decision, and it forms the act decided upon,"[299] he is saying something very similar to Aquinas's claim that *actus humani habent speciem a fine*.[300]

Second, however, as we also noted in our discussion of Aquinas, this principle does not tell us very much, for when it comes to moral discernment, the whole difficulty lies in discerning *which* "end" is the determinative one. Actions can have many ends, in the sense that they can have many different anticipated meanings. To use O'Donovan's example: having a dinner can be a way of cultivating a friendship, which is in turn a way of relaunching life after a depressed period.[301] As Robert Spaemann points out, this sequence of integrated meanings is potentially endless, up to the end of *eudaimonia*.[302] O'Donovan's description of ends of action as nested within one another is a helpful one, and an improvement upon the framework of means and ends in that it resists instrumentalizing actions that have their own integrity. What it fails to capture, however, and what the framework of means and ends arguably has better success with, is the way in which there is often one end that is determinative of what the action is *morally*. If, for instance, my purpose

---

297. *F&S*, 186.
298. *EIR*, 25.
299. *EIR*, 28.
300. *ST* I-II.18.6.
301. *EIR*, 32.
302. Robert Spaemann, "Individual Actions," in *A Robert Spaemann Reader: Philosophical Essays on Nature, God, and the Human Person*, ed. D. C. Schindler and Jeanne Heffernan Schindler (Oxford: Oxford University Press, 2015), 147.

in having a dinner is to lure an enemy into a false sense of security, then it is *that* "end" that specifies the action morally: it is an act of deception. Fundamentally, Aquinas's distinctions between external and internal objects, and acts of will and intention, simply aim to get a purchase on this point.

Third, one of the keys to such discernment has to do with the clarity with which ends are envisaged. This is the insight in O'Donovan's desire to distinguish a clear end, or purpose, from vaguer ends (or reasons). What an action is has to do with how it is envisaged by the agent. That means that it matters how it is envisaged *at the outset*. An agent is not free, as Aquinas says, retrospectively to redefine her action through an added intention—"as when somebody wills to do something and then afterwards offers it to God."[303] In this sense O'Donovan rightly says that "ends are always precise."[304] Even when we do not know what we are doing, in the sense that we do not know *all* of what our action will add up to and mean, there is always a sense, however limited, in which we *do* know what we are doing, and that sense matters.

O'Donovan's discussion also helps us understand, finally, why intentions are open to interrogation. Actions are specified by their ends. That means that the way an agent sees an action matters, but it also means that a subjective construal of action is not unquestionable. For "seeing" an action, as Aquinas understood, involves the agent in the order of reason; it requires her to understand her action in a way that is intelligible, and hence, as O'Donovan recognizes, communicable. This means action is always exposed to judgment, divine, and human. For an action to be purposed, it must be able to be named. And this means that intentions can be questioned, not simply at the level of whether they are sincere, but at the level of whether they truly describe an action. The idea that actions have external objects, and that these make some actions intrinsically evil, is a way of maintaining that some actions are such that no subjective intention, or construal of the meaning of the action, can make it true that the act is good.[305]

These conclusions reflect valuable insights in the work of O'Donovan and Aquinas, which our final chapter will aim to consolidate and secure.[306] For now, however, we must complete our survey of O'Donovan's work in the same place he does, by considering love. At the beginning of *Entering into Rest*, O'Donovan writes,

> Love's *métier* is a world of meaning and goodness. Love is focused on an object, finding its rest in an objective world, not simply in its own exercise. God could have responded to the moral loss of mankind by making new

---

303. *ST* i-II.19.7.

304. *EIR*, 25.

305. This understanding of things is similar to that of Charles Pinches's reading of Aquinas, in *Theology and Action: After Theory in Christian Ethics* (Grand Rapids, MI: Eerdmans, 2002), 111–36.

306. See below, Chapter 5, Section 3b.

worlds of which mankind was not part; instead, he has restored the world of which we are part, making it hospitable to our purposive action.[307]

O'Donovan's understanding of love closely reflects one of the central themes of this study: the idea that right action depends upon the character of the world, the way it is "hospitable to purposive action." Love is evoked by the reality, the goodness, of the beloved. Love does not, as Anders Nygren thought, *create* value in its object; it finds it.[308] "Love cannot be without its world; it must have its object."[309] At the end of *Entering into Rest*, O'Donovan explores the impact of eschatology on this principle. The promise of God's kingdom draws love through the most dramatic of transformations. The world we love must pass away, and our love of it must be surrendered, for "friendship with the world is hostility to God."[310] And yet, because God will never be without his world, "with the disclosure of God and of love we are told of a 'new' world, a 'new heaven and a new earth.'"[311] Here and now, therefore, in and as we anticipate that new world in our "love of the brother,"[312] our loves may grasp hold of that new world as the rightful object of our loves. And here, at the end of *Ethics as Theology*, O'Donovan returns to a key theme: to know anything here and now, he says, presupposes "a love for the world as a whole." "When we order our loves … we affirm an order which we believe the world reveals … Our order of love embodies a love of order, an organization of things in terms of their real significance."[313] That is to say, our knowledge of the ordered whole, though always problematic and "subject to judgment,"[314] can be a provisional love of the world to come.

These thoughts rest on arguments made earlier in *Ethics as Theology*, especially in a chapter we passed over in our survey of *Finding and Seeking*. Closing our overview by attending to this chapter will lead us to the heart of our wrestle with O'Donovan's thought. In "Love and Testimony,"[315] O'Donovan argues that our talk of love must be able to encompass the normal patterns of affection and admiration that fill human life. "We must have in view," he writes, "the whole arc of love from the most commonly instinctual to the most godlike and self-outpouring."[316] He is critical of "katabatic" accounts of love that drive too great a wedge between God's

---

307. *EIR*, 4.

308. Compare also the discussion in O'Donovan's, *The Problem of Self-Love in Saint Augustine* (Eugene, OR: Wipf and Stock, 2006), 137–59.

309. *EIR*, 227.

310. *EIR*, 227; cf. Jas 4:4.

311. *EIR*, 227.

312. *EIR*, 225.

313. *EIR*, 227.

314. *EIR*, 227.

315. *F&S* chapter 6, 120–44.

316. *F&S*, 122.

redemptive love and creaturely loves.[317] Love is differentiated according to the goodness of its object, and by the different emotions that attend its object's presence or absence, but there is a univocal core to the idea of love: "the affective affinity that arises to bind us to states, objects, or persons."[318] This is why the community-love of which the New Testament speaks so often is still simply love. "'Charity,'" as he puts it in *Entering into Rest*, "is not something *other* than the focused love-of-the-world that allows faith and hope to bring human action to birth; it is the same love, but extended further, through another level of reflection."[319] Love, in all its forms, must be "the affective cognition of reality."[320]

O'Donovan goes on to say that this is also the key to understanding revelation. Revelation must be treated in connection with love because revelation means the disclosure of the good.[321] With this, O'Donovan returns to a theme we observed to be important in *Resurrection and Moral Order*. In Christ, he says, what we see is "the representative moment in history that gathers the intelligibility of world and time into itself."[322] The coming of God's kingdom means "the final reconciliation of the tension between history and the good." Yet, O'Donovan continues, "The opposition of 'earth' and 'heaven' makes it clear … that the sovereign rule of God supervenes not as an innovation on the world we know, but as a disclosure of what is and always and everywhere the truth."[323] The reconciliation of history and the good consists in the revelation of how they are not, and have never been, finally at odds. In O'Donovan's understanding of love, then, we see coming together the key concerns that we have raised throughout our discussion, and that will now be the focus of our concluding reflection: the place of salvation-history, and the idea of the whole.

3 The Reconciliation of Nature and History

Throughout our overview of O'Donovan's writing about the nature of Christian moral reasoning, we have drawn on the book of Proverbs to raise questions and concerns. In this concluding, critical reflection, we will continue to do so. Let us begin, therefore, by highlighting two other points in this connection. First, a point that contributes to the overall justification of this study: O'Donovan's own

---

317. *F&S*, 121. O'Donovan finds an example in the thought of Wolfhart Pannenberg. In the background lies the work of Anders Nygren.

318. *F&S*, 122.

319. *EIR*, 6, emphasis original.

320. *F&S*, 125. This emphasis on the univocity of love has some similarities with Ramsey. See especially O'Donovan's comment in *The Problem of Self-Love*, 167, n. 11.

321. *F&S*, 125.

322. *F&S*, 126.

323. *F&S*, 127; the repeated "and" here may be a typographical error, but I have retained it as it stands in the text.

work invites such comparison and reflection. He consistently draws on the idea of wisdom and relates it to moral reasoning, and his more recent work contains significant, deliberate reflection on the book of Proverbs, especially the texts at the center of this study.[324] Second, the concerns we have to raise should not obscure the many points at which O'Donovan's thinking coincides with the logic of Proverbs. Indeed, it is only the nearness of many of O'Donovan's ideas to Proverbs that allows us to raise the questions we have. The following, final chapter of this study will hopefully highlight how much there is to be appreciated in O'Donovan's work. Here, though, our aim is to draw together and connect the concerns we have raised on the way through our summary of O'Donovan's positions.

There is an ambiguity in O'Donovan's thought surrounding the question of how God's redemptive activity should be characterized. It is an ambiguity that emerges especially in his discussions of the reconciliation of history and the good. On the one hand, O'Donovan is conscious of the need to speak of God's work of redemption as transformative, a doing of a new thing that has a real impact on what has been before. This is especially clear in the third chapter of *Resurrection and Moral Order*. On the other hand, however, O'Donovan also persistently speaks of this reconciliation in terms of *disclosure*. The *word* of the gospel, he says, "heals the rift between history and the good," and so "confers moral sense" upon the contingencies of time.[325] "Historical fulfilment," that is, eschatological fulfilment, "means our entry into a completeness which is already present in the universe."[326] That God's will is done in heaven means that the coming of the kingdom can only be "a disclosure of what is ... always and everywhere the truth."[327] "The petition for history is a petition for the world, not simply as we see it, but as it is yet to take form in the conjunction of earth and heaven, of man's existence and God's rule. In making this petition we lend our active selves to the service of the world's good fixed in the purposes of God."[328]

This last quotation highlights that this point about disclosure has real practical importance in O'Donovan's thought. The notions of the whole and of wisdom as knowledge of the whole flow out of it. For it is "the world's good fixed in the purposes of God" that wisdom is given to know. *That* is what is truly real—that "transhistorical"[329] or "ahistorical"[330] order of things that has "existed from the beginning in God's creative conception."[331] And so wisdom is the "vision" of "what is in the world which measures change and so stands beyond it,"[332] the cognitive

---

324. As well as the examples above, see *F&S*, 86–7; *EIR*, 170, 217–18.
325. *F&S*, 116, 118.
326. *RMO*, 62.
327. *F&S*, 127.
328. *F&S*, 127.
329. *RMO*, 188.
330. *F&S*, 118.
331. *RMO*, 53.
332. *RMO*, 188.

"representation" of the world's good order.³³³ That is why "the invitation of wisdom" is "to turn from the visible to the invisible, from the beauties that confront us to the hidden ends in which our active lives may finally come to rest."³³⁴ The echoes here of Augustine's understanding of wisdom in *De Trinitate* are unmistakable: "to wisdom belongs the intellectual cognition of eternal things," that is, "those things which neither have been nor shall be, but which are."³³⁵

The central problem for such a conception of wisdom is ultimately historical and Christological. What can it really mean, on this account, to say that Jesus Christ crucified is the wisdom of God (cf. 1 Cor. 1:23-24)? For this is a claim that is inextricable from history. It is noteworthy that although O'Donovan acknowledges the legitimacy of "Christological extrapolation" from the figure of Wisdom in Proverbs ch. 8, his primary move is to forestall such reflection, warning that "too hasty a movement from the wisdom in creation to the divine Word can mislead us."³³⁶ With this we may readily agree. The burden of the previous chapter was precisely to avoid such over-hasty movement. We still aimed, though, eventually to achieve it, and found the key in the connection between wisdom and action. That connection allowed us to say why Jesus Christ is the wisdom of God, without overlooking the distinction between creation and redemption. The question is whether O'Donovan's account of wisdom can do the same, or whether this distinction tends to collapse.

Toward the end of *Entering into Rest*, there is a discussion that highlights this question. Under the heading of "The Communication of Meaning," O'Donovan discusses narrative and description as forms of discourse that correspond to the two fundamental realities of history and nature.³³⁷ Narrative and description have to exist in dialectical relation; neither "can convey reality on its own."³³⁸ Events have to be intelligible on the basis of "relations with an inherent logic." Formal relations are only meaningful because they are instantiated in events.³³⁹ There is a "complementarity" to narrative and description.³⁴⁰ Now, the obvious challenge to this picture comes from the event of the resurrection. Is that an event of which it can be said that "*this* thing has *happened, such* things happen?"³⁴¹ Implicitly, O'Donovan's answer is to say both no and yes. On the one hand, Christ's resurrection is obviously *not* the kind of thing that normally happens. Yet on the other hand, if it did happen, then "it was an event of such importance that other events and sequences of events must ultimately derive their meaning

---

333. *F&S*, 101, 108.
334. *F&S*, 121.
335. See *DT* 12.15.25, 14.23.
336. *F&S*, 101; *SWT*, 113.
337. *EIR*, 170-4.
338. *EIR*, 171.
339. *EIR*, 171.
340. *EIR*, 175.
341. *EIR*, 171.

from it."³⁴² God's redemptive action "does not disturb the claim we have made for a complementarity of narrative and descriptive functions. It simply narrates an event at the center of salvation history as the definitive moment for Christian proclamation."³⁴³ That is to say, what the resurrection disrupts is not created order itself, but the understanding we have had of it, hitherto. It discloses the inner truth of created order as an order of resurrection. The resurrection, to recall a comment from *Finding and Seeking*, is "a torch to illumine the goods of the world," showing us how things really are.³⁴⁴ The question is whether this picture does justice, on the one hand, to salvation history, to the newness of what God does in Christ, and on the other hand, to created order as an order that is genuinely of creation. It seems, rather, that history cannot be allowed to present a real disruption of order. There is room for a tension between creation and redemption in our understanding of them, but not in reality.

Does not salvation history demand more than this? "Behold, I do a *new* thing" (Isa 43:19). Consider the following attempt by Karl Barth to articulate the core notion of history by contrasting it with the concept of a "state" (*Zustand*):

> The concept of history in its true sense as distinct from that of a state is introduced and achieved when something happens to a being in a certain state, i.e., when something new and other than its own nature befalls it. History, therefore, does not occur when the being is involved in changes or different modes of behaviour intrinsic to itself, but when something takes place upon and to the being as it is. The history of a being begins, continues and is completed when something other than itself and transcending its own nature encounters it, approaches it and determines its being in the nature proper to it, so that it is compelled and enabled to transcend itself in response and in relation to this new factor. The history of a being occurs when it is caught up in this movement, change and relation, when its circular movement is broken from without by a movement towards it and the corresponding movement from it, when it is transcended from without so that it must and can transcend itself outwards.³⁴⁵

As we have seen, O'Donovan can speak in similar terms: the destiny of the world is a work of God that comes "from outside," he says.³⁴⁶ Yet in O'Donovan's account overall, it is not clear that history really rises to this kind of significance. History

---

342. *EIR*, 174.

343. *EIR*, 175.

344. *F&S*, 112; and above, Section 2b.

345. *CD* III/2, 158. It is striking that, somewhat despite himself, Barth requires the concept of nature in order to articulate what history means. This is instructive, and in the following chapter we will argue, against Barth, that this vis-à-vis between nature and history is critical for Christian ethics.

346. *RMO*, 64–5; and above, Section 1b.

means "an intelligible story,"³⁴⁷ but what kind of intelligibility is this? Is it one in which the circular movement of creation's state is transcended from without? Or is it simply one in which our understanding of creation is reconfigured? Is the "new thing" that God does genuinely new, *another* thing? Or is it only new from our perspective, new *for us*, but in reality, only what has always been the ultimate truth?

Throughout O'Donovan's work, one biblical text is consistently introduced in connection with these questions: Revelation 4–5.³⁴⁸ O'Donovan sees the drama of the four living creatures and the sealed scroll as an image of the "dialectic of nature and history."³⁴⁹ John weeps because of the "opacity of history" to created order.³⁵⁰ The appearance of the Slain Lamb causes joy because he is the one with "the right to make sense of history."³⁵¹ Accepting many aspects of this reading, we may still ask whether the drama has quite been presented rightly. What is it, exactly, that causes John to weep? For O'Donovan, it has to do with an epistemic tension necessarily present within the reality of free action.³⁵² "Narrative sequence," he writes in *Finding and Seeking*, "can never dispense with the actions of free subjects … which enter the course of events out of nothing, refusing to be subject to the generic order of cause and effect. Narrated events are part of reality, 'what there is,' yet they violate the framework of laws and regularities … History bursts out of the woven fabric of natural regularities, leaving loose threads of indeterminacy hanging."³⁵³ The fundamental problem posed by this tension is intellectual, which is why O'Donovan often emphasizes "intelligibility" in describing Christ's achievement. "The Lamb … affords to all creation the joy of having history, and with it the problem of evil, made intelligible."³⁵⁴

But is it a necessary, epistemic crisis that makes John weep, or is it a contingent, historical one? At one point in *Resurrection and Moral Order*, O'Donovan acknowledges a reason to think it is the latter.

> Perhaps thinkers need never have troubled themselves about the end of history had Adam not set in motion a train of happenings which threatened the good order of creation itself. As it is, Adam's children must find out, though they have no means of doing so, where the course of events is tending, for without that knowledge they cannot tell whether such knowledge of the

---

347. *RMO*, 55.
348. See *RMO*, 56, 85; *F&S*, 115, 117; also, O'Donovan, "The Political Thought of the Book of Revelation."
349. *SWT*, 59.
350. *RMO*, 85.
351. *F&S*, 117.
352. See *RMO*, 44–5, 184–5; *SWT*, 59; *F&S*, 114–19.
353. *F&S*, 115.
354. *RMO*, 85; cf. *F&S*, 126.

good as they possess is a real ground of hope or the last trace of a joy that is about to be engulfed in novelty.[355]

The threat posed by history to created order, that is to say, is not inevitable, but simply what has in fact happened—"as it is." Revelation 4–5 can be read felicitously from this perspective. That the scroll is sealed can be seen as unexpected, a shocking reflection of the fact that creation's history turns out to be threatened by the particular character of its history. The appearance of the Lamb *does* mean the reconciliation of nature and history, but it is not an intellectual reconciliation, necessitated by the formal dynamic of nature and history, necessity and freedom, but a real reconciliation, necessitated by the particular history that creation happens to have. The Lamb is able to open the seals because he "*has triumphed*" (5:5). This is not a disclosure of what has always been the case, but an achievement that overcomes evil's opposition and *effects* reconciliation. The good of creation may indeed be called "a ground of hope." Yet what is hoped for is more than merely the restoration of that good, because it is not "novelty" but sin that is the threat.

To see things in this way makes a difference. It undermines the idea that this tension is present in free action as such, an idea which O'Donovan emphasizes in the more recent works.[356] The point is the same as that which we made above, when we noted that O'Donovan's distinction between the way in which theology and ethics consider sin was not identical to Kant's distinction between the way in which theoretical and practical reason consider freedom. Sin, and our resultant un-freedom, is the result of a historical contingency, not a metaphysical necessity. The idea of a timeless "whole" standing beyond creation and *disclosed* by redemption is also brought in question. Without the assumption that the good is inherently threatened by novelty, there is no longer a need for the idea of reconciliation as disclosure, nor the idea of a timeless, transcendent whole. It becomes possible, rather, to understand created order as intrinsically open to historical transformation. Novelty is not intrinsically a threat to nature. Creation's order, though perhaps in a limited sense "transhistorical," in that it persists throughout creation's history, is *not* "ahistorical." It is an order *of action*, a quality of creation that, though problematized by the fall, is not inherently at odds with history.

This highlights the significance of our contention, in the previous chapter, that wisdom essentially has to do with action, that it is to be understood as a kind of practical knowledge. For O'Donovan, because created order is inherently at odds with history, wisdom must have to do with that which "measures change and so stands beyond it." Conversely, thinking about wisdom—even God's wisdom—in connection with action makes room to take salvation history with greater seriousness. Jesus Christ is the wisdom of God because God's wisdom is not a perfection of his speculative knowledge, but a perfection of his action. Human

---

355. *RMO*, 83.
356. *SWT*, 59; *F&S*, 115.

wisdom is not a participation in divine speculative knowledge, but a form of practical knowledge, derived from the reality of wise divine action. This means that, rather than human wisdom being about a grasp of a trans-temporal depth hidden behind the world as it actually is, we may understand wisdom as having a form which corresponds to the world as it is in this present moment: the world into which the kingdom of God has come, on the one hand, and the creation that awaits redemption, on the other.[357] Human wisdom in the present moment has an irreducibly twofold form, because it is a possibility afforded first by God's creation of the world by wisdom, and second by his work in Christ to reconcile all things to himself.

This is a way of picturing things that we will continue to develop in our final chapter. For now, however, we may clarify it somewhat by noting that O'Donovan's concern about thinking like this might run along the lines of his objections to historicism: does this not inevitably surrender the idea that morality is generic? For, "any command or principle that changes in history thereby becomes a particular, a mere item in the history of ideas."[358] To this worry we may respond that although commands and principles may not themselves change, their significance for us does. The coming of Christ means that the commandment not to commit murder must be extended to a prohibition of anger (Mt. 5:21-22), and the right to proportionate retaliation must be foregone (Mt. 5:38-39). In the same way, although created order does not change, it acquires a distinct significance by virtue of the salvation-historical moment.

We may avoid this only by positing a "real" creation subsisting behind the world we actually experience, a creation that is eternally complete and perfect, which the work of Christ discloses. But such a conception seems to reduce the fall to an epistemological crisis, and to curtail the transformative impact of Christ. Instead, we should maintain that created order is genuinely *creation's* order—a "natural" character of the world as it endures through time. This means, on the one hand, that it is an order that is not yet the kingdom of God, and on the other, that it is an order whose claim must now be heard in the light of the claim of the kingdom of God.

The coming of Christ makes possible a renewal of human wisdom. "Something greater than Solomon is here," Jesus proclaimed (Lk. 11:31), and was confident that he would be proved right. "Wisdom," he said, "is vindicated by all her children" (Lk. 7:35). In him, according to the apostle Paul, "all the treasures of wisdom

---

357. This contrast is similar to one made by David Kelsey, who criticizes conceptions in which, "God's actual creation" is a "'noumenal' reality, a depth far more meaningful than the quotidian itself, of which the quotidian is mere phenomena or appearance" (*Eccentric Existence: A Theological Anthropology*, 2 vols. [Louisville, Kentucky: Westminster John Knox, 2009], 191). Where this account differs is in its attempt to relate this to salvation history in a way Kelsey refuses. We will discuss this point at greater length below, Chapter 5, Section 2b.

358. *RMO*, 41.

and knowledge are hidden" (Col. 2:3). The Christian life can be characterized as "walking carefully in wisdom" (Eph. 5:15). A similar impulse can be seen in a surprising tradition of Christian interpretation, from Hippolytus to Johann Georg Hamann, which understood the house and the "seven pillars" in Prov. 9:1 to the church built by the Holy Spirit.[359]

This wisdom, however, is not simply the wisdom that corresponds to creation—the wisdom of which Proverbs speaks. For although, by the Spirit, we may be restored to the world, the world is not yet restored to us. The creation "waits," we are told, in anticipation, having been "made subject to futility" (Rom. 8:19-20). We might speculate that in the miracles of Jesus we catch glimpses of the restoration of creation's hospitality to renewed humanity. When Jesus walks on water and feeds the five thousand, may we not catch a glimpse of Wisdom's "delighting in humankind" (Prov. 8:31)? For the moment, however, creation remains in "slavery to decay" (Rom. 8:21)—a bondage that runs into every human life: we ourselves also groan, as we wait for "the redemption of our body" (Rom. 8:23). The wisdom in which Christ's followers are called to walk is a way opened up not only by creation's call, but by Christ's call within creation.

The only order that can help us to *act* is that which actually exists in creation at this time—for this is the only world that exists for us to act within. This, in fact, is the underlying reason for O'Donovan's hesitation, which we noted above, about the usefulness of an "axiology." Such a theory was, we saw him recognize, not itself the practical knowledge that we need, and it inevitably does not sufficiently grasp the "center" of such knowledge in "the disclosure of God's works in Christ."[360] Wisdom is about practical, rather than theoretical, knowledge of what to do. This means it is correlated to the distinctive character of the time. Our knowledge of "world order" must indeed, as O'Donovan says in *Resurrection and Moral Order*, be "existential" knowledge, "from within"; but in contrast to O'Donovan, this means it cannot be knowledge that "reaches out to understand the whole,"[361] but instead knowledge of how to act well in this moment of salvation-history.

This is why in the New Testament the theme of "waking" is persistently associated with being aware of the time, in the sense of the salvation-historical moment. "Keep awake, for you do not know when … " (Mk 13:33). "It is now the hour for you to wake from sleep, for salvation is nearer to us now than when we believed" (Rom. 13:11). In *Self, World, and Time*, O'Donovan recognizes this, but then explains it in more general terms. Being awake, he writes, means being "aware of the truth of a world," by which he means "an order of things that stands behind

---

359. See the references in *ACCS*, 72–4. Compare Hamann's comment on Proverbs 9:1: "Hier sind die sieben Pfeiler, die durch die ganze heilige Schrift erscheinen und in der Offenbarung Johannis am weitläufigsten offenbart sind." (*Londoner Schriften*, ed. Oswald Bayer and Bernd Weißenborn [München: C H Beck, 1993], 223.)

360. *F&S*, 113; cf. above, Section 2b.

361. *RMO*, 85.

and before" our existence, which "was and will be."³⁶² His primary aim in this is to defend the objectivity of the world: the world is not simply *my* world. Yet what is missing is a clear recognition that the world is something in motion, something to which certain critically important things have happened. This kind of recognition is in the foreground when the New Testament speaks of wisdom. "Be careful, then, how you walk—not as unwise but as wise, redeeming the time, because the days are evil" (Eph. 5:15-16). "The days are evil" is a claim about the character of the time, the way in which the powers, though overthrown, remain at work in this world (cf. Eph. 6:12). If wisdom means attunement to creation's hospitality to action, this now especially involves alertness to the fact that the world is not yet redeemed. The conditions of the time highlight the necessities of certain possibilities, modes of action, and have an impact upon the availability of others.

The same point can be made from another angle. O'Donovan connects the theme of waking to faith. Just as waking needs the presence of an objective world to give it form, so faith needs love of the world. Faith is inherently active, but this active impulse has no shape apart from the second call, of the good world. "Faith has no discursive content of its own."³⁶³ But is that quite right? The reason to hesitate comes from O'Donovan's own recognition that faith has to do with forgiveness. In *Finding and Seeking*, he connects faith to the fourth petition of the Lord's Prayer. The prayer for forgiveness, he says, "asks for the conditions of freedom."³⁶⁴ Yet in his exposition of the Lord's Prayer, which he calls "the beginning and end of moral thinking,"³⁶⁵ no attention is given to the second half of that petition, "as we also forgive our debtors" (Mt. 6:12). This *is* discussed in *Self, World, and Time*, and yet, even there, the emphasis is entirely on its being a prayer for a renewal of freedom to act.³⁶⁶ More ought to be said. What we see in this petition is that our waking comes at a certain salvation-historical moment, which gives a certain form to our action. Faith's active impulse is always already oriented in a certain direction, because it is only ever experienced as forgiveness. The faith that is formed by love is already oriented by the form in which it has arisen: through being forgiven.

Reflection on the practice of forgiveness is, overall, not prominent in the works we have surveyed.³⁶⁷ This is true even of *Entering into Rest*, in which O'Donovan especially attends to the fulfilment of practical reason in love. Part of the explanation may lie in the fact that the logic of forgiveness has everything to do with the peculiar realities of the time: the presence of sin and failure, and of the renewal of agency without the fulfilment of that renewal in perfection. O'Donovan's conception of world-order allows him to speak profoundly of admiration, which is the love that

---

362. *SWT*, 8–10.

363. *F&S*, 47.

364. *F&S*, 148.

365. *F&S*, 147.

366. *SWT*, 40–2. See also O'Donovan, "Prayer and Morality in the Sermon on the Mount," *Studies in Christian Ethics* 22, no. 1 (2000): 21–33.

367. It does appear, for example, *RMO*, 176; *SWT*, 41; *EIR*, 109.

corresponds to the continuing presence of creation's order in the present, and of devotion, which is the love that is perfected in creation's eschatological renewal, and that, like a miracle, we may glimpse anticipated in moments of cooperation here and now;[368] but it apparently does not spur him to speak of the distinctive way in which love in the present must be shaped by the logic of forgiveness.[369] "As I have loved you, so you must love one another" (John 13:34).

In making these criticisms we are, in a way, exploring comments O'Donovan himself makes at various points. In a sense, we are simply arguing for what O'Donovan calls a properly "eschatological" conception,[370] and attempting to explore further his idea that the gospel introduces "an opposition … between the value-order of the world as perceived ahistorically and the word that holds the centre of the world's history."[371] Similarly, O'Donovan's political theology is driven by salvation-history. O'Donovan's account of political authority reflects precisely the kind of dialectical tension between created order and the triumph of Christ that we are emphasizing.[372] Hence, his account of political ethics is deeply shaped by the practice of forgiveness and the imperative, "judge not!"[373]

Our final chapter will attempt to say how all this bears on O'Donovan's account of deliberation and discernment. Fundamentally, there is a great deal to appreciate in O'Donovan's description of this movement, especially as it is explored in *Finding and Seeking*. O'Donovan's description of deliberation as an inductive movement centering on a moment of recognition captures many of the conclusions we reached in our discussions of Aristotle and Aquinas. O'Donovan's notion of discernment as a "congruence of normativities"[374] can also assist us in understanding the function of created order in discernment. However, we will argue that these ideas fit better within a framework in which we follow the lead of O'Donovan's insight that there

---

368. See, for example *EIR*, 227.

369. Consider, for example, the exposition of 1 Cor. 13 in *EIR*, 2–4.

370. *RMO*, 70.

371. *F&S*, 118–19.

372. See *The Desire of the Nations*, especially 120–92; and *The Ways of Judgment* (Grand Rapids, MI: Eerdmans, 2005), especially 66, 127–48. See also Jonathan Chaplin, "Political Eschatology and Responsible Government: Oliver O'Donovan's 'Christian Liberalism,'" in *A Royal Priesthood: The Use of the Bible Ethically and Politically. A Dialogue with Oliver O'Donovan*, ed. C. Bartholomew et al. (Scripture and Hermeneutics, 3; Carlisle: Paternoster, 2002), 265–308; and Andrew Errington, "Between Justice and Tradition: Oliver O'Donovan's Political Theory and the Problem of Multiculturalism," *Studies in Christian Ethics* 27, no. 4 (2014): 417–30. In contrast to Jonathan Cole ("Towards a Christian Ontology of Political Authority: The Relationship between Created Order and Providence in Oliver O'Donovan's Theology of Political Authority," *Studies in Christian Ethics* [2018], https://doi.org/10.1177/0953946818775559), I think this aspect of O'Donovan's political thought is one of its virtues.

373. See, for example, *The Ways of Judgment*, 84–100, 231–41.

374. *F&S*, 220–1; and above, Section 2c.

is an element of mystery in such moments of congruence, and that in practice they are "usually performed without thinking"[375]—a point that, as we saw, Ramsey also acknowledged. This is a possibility opened up by the idea of wisdom as practical knowledge. It allows us, also, to give the central place to Scripture that O'Donovan himself calls for: to say why "practical reason looks for a word."[376] It is because what enables us to act wisely is not a theoretical grasp of the whole, but a practical grasp of where wisdom lies here and now, in the midst of danger.

---

375. *F&S*, 206.
376. *SWT*, 12.

Chapter 5

WISDOM, CREATION, AND CHRISTIAN ETHICS

In the path of righteousness, is life.

—Prov. 12:28

Introduction

At the end of the Sermon on the Mount, Jesus tells a parable to sum up the character of the moral task he has set before his hearers.

> Everyone, therefore, who hears these words of mine and does them will be like a wise man [*phronimō*], who built his house on the rock; and the rain fell down, the torrents came, and the winds blew and beat against that house—and it did not fall, for it was founded on the rock. And everyone who hears these words of mine and does them not is like a foolish man, who built his house on the sand; and the rain fell down, the torrents came, and the winds blew and struck that house—and it fell, and its downfall was great. (Mt. 7:24-27)

In deploying, alongside the language of wisdom and folly, images of house-building and of a storm that overthrows one and not another, Jesus is drawing deeply on central themes of the book of Proverbs. The metaphor of house-building, as we have seen, lies at the heart of Proverbs. "By wisdom a house is built" (24:3). "The wise woman builds her house" (14:1). Images of bad weather and of collapse are also important: "When the storm comes, the wicked are finished, but the foundation of the righteous endures" (10:25). "The wicked are overthrown and come to nothing, but the house of the righteous stands" (12:7).

This summoning-up of the core structures of Proverbs suggests that we are not mistaken to have looked to this text to clarify our thinking about the shape of practical reason in Christian existence. It also supports our decision to engage primarily with discussions that do not resist a formally eudaemonistic framework. In Jesus's parable, as in the book of Proverbs, the metaphor of house-building is central because of a sense that this action is emblematic of the successful living of a life. The collapse of the house is likewise an image of the failure of a life, and of judgment. The call to heed Jesus's teaching presupposes and draws on a fundamental desire for one's life to turn out well. "Happy," Proverbs insists, "the person who find wisdom" (3:13).

Jesus's parable also touches on the central themes of this study that are the focus of this final chapter. The use of the word *phronimos* for "wise man," and the emphasis on action—"putting into practice"—reminds us of the practical character of wisdom, and how the book of Proverbs complicates the distinction between wisdom and prudence. The first section of this chapter sums up what we have learned along these lines. The contrast between the wisdom of building on rock and the folly of building on sand reminds us of the theme of the objectivity of wisdom, which we have described with the language of creation's hospitality to good action. The focusing of this contrast upon the words of Jesus, however, especially in the context of earlier parts of the sermon (Mt. 5:17-48), raises the question of the impact of salvation-history upon this picture. The second section of the chapter examines these issues, attempting to clarify the notion of created order and its place within Christian ethics. The emphasis on heeding words of instruction also recalls a key emphasis of Proverbs. The third section of this chapter explores this point and clarifies what we are now in a position to say about moral discernment. Finally, the contrast and apparent gap between hearing and putting into practice remind us of the distinction between theoretical and practical reason. The final section of this study attempts to describe this dynamic afresh, and to say what it suggests about the work of Christian ethics. The aim of this concluding chapter is to appreciate the significance of the course our "discussion" has taken. This aim is pursued here partly through constructive proposals and engagements with new voices. The second section discusses the work of David VanDrunen and David Kelsey. The third section interacts with Karl Barth's critique of deliberation. These discussions should be understood as provisional attempts to suggest what the conclusions we have reached might amount to, and bring out their relevance. They invite further discussion and critical engagement.

1 Wisdom and Creation

The difference between the two basic conceptions of wisdom represented in this study, and discussed especially in Chapter 3, should not be underestimated. On the one hand, there is the view of Aristotle and much of the theological tradition, in which wisdom is fundamentally speculative. "Wisdom is knowledge having to do with certain principles and causes," as Aristotle puts it in the *Metaphysics*.[1] The result is a conception of wise action that emphasizes mental clarity: "It belongs to the wise man to order."[2] This leads to a conception of God's action in creation in terms of the implementation of a preconceived plan. God stands to creation,

---

1. *Metaphysics* 1.1, 982a1.

2. Aquinas, *Exposition of* Metaphysics I, preface (in *Thomas Aquinas: Selected Writings*, ed. R. McInerny [London: Penguin, 1998], 719).

in Aquinas's image, like a builder to a house, with "the form of the house" in his mind, as "something understood by him, to the likeness of which he forms the house in matter."[3] On the other hand, we have the way of thinking of wisdom that undergirds the book of Proverbs, in which wisdom is fundamentally practical, a quality that appears only in and with action. "By wisdom a house is built" (24:3). "Every prudent person *acts* by knowledge, whereas the fool (merely) disperses folly [*yiprōs' 'iwwelet*]" (13:16). Aristotle could actually describe *phronēsis* in a similar way: "A person is practically wise not only by knowing, but also by being disposed to act."[4] At its deepest, this is because wisdom has more to do with the nature of the world than with an excellence of the mind. Wisdom is about the hospitality of creation to action, which is why wisdom "calls." As we argued in Chapter 3, this understanding implies a conception of God's wisdom as an attribute of his action. The wisdom by which God made the world therefore comes to characterize the world. God's wisdom is genuinely of creation, which is ultimately why the man Jesus Christ in and with his work can be the wisdom of God.

A similar clash of conceptions of wisdom appears already to have been present within the world of the New Testament. "Who among you is wise [*sophos*] and understanding [*epistēmōn*]?" James asks; then responds, "Let him show by his good way of life [*anastrophēs*] the works that belong to the gentleness of wisdom" (3:13). This text, with its reference to "the wisdom from above" (3:15), is taken by Aquinas in his second inaugural lecture to reveal "the height of sacred doctrine."[5] However, the emphasis of the text is different. James is unimpressed by any so-called "wisdom" that fails to build up the life of the community (3:14-15). Wisdom, he says, is manifest in action: "The wisdom from above is first pure, then peaceable, yielding, persuadable, full of mercy and good fruit, straightforward, sincere" (3:17). For James, the most important thing to say about wisdom is that it means certain kinds of action.

When Proverbs tells us that the Lord "by wisdom" founded the earth (3:19), it suggests an analogy between God's work of creation and the human work of house-building (24:3-4). House-building, as we have observed, was also the archetypical example of "making" for Aristotle and Aquinas. In their thought, however, this connection introduced a distortion, for it allowed wisdom to be understood in terms of a formal model of making in which there was a two-stage process: in Hannah Arendt's description, "first, perceiving the image or shape of the product-to-be, and then organizing the means and starting the execution."[6] As Aristotle puts it in the *Metaphysics*: "things are produced from skill [*technē*] if the form

---

3. *ST* I.15.2, Benziger Brothers edition.

4. *EN* 7.10, 1152a8-9; and above, Chapter 1, Section 2.

5. Thomas Aquinas, "On the Commendation of Sacred Scripture [*Principium Rigans Montes*]," in *Thomas Aquinas: Selected Writings*, ed. R. McInerny (London: Penguin, 1998), 13.

6. Hannah Arendt, *The Human Condition* (Chicago: University of Chicago Press, 1958), 225.

of them is in the mind."⁷ This, however, is a reductive picture of "making," and becomes more problematic still when it is extended to other kinds of action. This Aquinas does when he explains how eternal law is the *ratio* of divine wisdom, a single, simple conception in the mind of the movement of all things to their end, which is like "a conception of the ordered actions to be done by those subject to his sway [that] pre-exists in a governor's mind."⁸ Our objection to this conception has been strikingly put by Hans Georg Gadamer, in terms that reflect this extension of the two-stage notion of making:

> The work of art is as little to be understood in terms of the planned execution of a sketch—even an infallibly unconscious one—as the course of history may be conceived for our finite consciousness as the execution of a plan. Rather, here as well as there, luck and success tempt us into *oracula ex eventu* that in fact hide the event—the word or deed—by which they are expressed … In truth, we may attribute a privilege to a poet in the explanation of his verse just as little as we may attribute it to the statesman in the historical explanation of events in which he had an active part.⁹

The wisdom by which a house is built, and the "knowledge" by which its rooms are filled (Prov. 24:3-4) are not a pre-conceived mental plan; they are the practical knowledge that attends those actions when they are well done.¹⁰

To speak of wisdom as "practical knowledge" in this way is not to speak merely of a theoretical knowledge that has practical implications, but to speak of a knowledge that is essentially connected to action. Arendt described something similar in saying that a division between knowing and doing was "alien to the realm of action, whose validity and meaningfulness are destroyed the moment thought and action part company."¹¹ More explicitly, Gilbert Ryle spoke of how in relation to acting, "'Intelligent,' cannot be defined in terms of 'intellectual' or 'knowing how' in terms of 'knowing that'; 'thinking what I am doing' does not connote 'both thinking what to do and doing it.' When I do something intelligently, i.e. thinking what I am doing, I am doing one thing and not two. My performance has a special procedure or manner, not special antecedents."¹² Aquinas gestures toward such

---

7. *Metaphysics* 6.7, 1032a32.

8. *ST* I-II.93.1; and above, Chapter 2, Section 3b.

9. Hans-Georg Gadamer, "The Nature of Things and the Language of Things," in *Philosophical Hermeneutics*, trans. David E. Linge (Berkeley and Los Angeles: University of California Press, 1977), 79–80.

10. To a certain extent, therefore, my argument supports that of Susan Parsons in "The Practice of Christian Mindfulness," especially pp. 448–9. In what follows, however, I make more space for theoretical thought than I think Parsons would advocate.

11. Arendt, *The Human Condition*, 225.

12. Gilbert Ryle, *The Concept of Mind* (New York: Barnes and Noble, 1950), 32.

an idea when he speaks of a knowledge that is genuinely practical "in its mode."[13] However, his account ends up unable fully to embrace such a thought. For the only thing that differentiates genuinely practical knowledge from knowledge that is still essentially theoretical is the addition of the will. In *Finding and Seeking*, O'Donovan recognizes this point, charging the distinction between reason and will with producing a conception in which, "we are reasonable beings who *also* act, not beings who *act reasonably*."[14] This is the right line of criticism. The question, though, is whether O'Donovan's own framework travels far enough along it. In contrast to Ryle's comment above, O'Donovan's account of the "intelligence" of action typically sees thought as preceding action: "we must think about what we propose to do in an ordered way."[15]

It is not that there is no place for thinking that precedes action. Such thought is frequently essential. The point, however, is that there is more to acting well—acting "reasonably"—than such thought. There is a further and yet more basic "knowledge" associated with acting well, which can be exercised only *in* action, not simply in the thought that precedes it. This is what wisdom is: the knowledge *by which* one acts well. To some extent, "knowledge" and "reasonableness" are no longer the right terms for such wisdom. For as we have stressed, wisdom is deeply *affective*; it involves a kind of attunement to good action that is not only cognitive.

To speak of wisdom in terms of attunement *to* good action highlights the other, critical point that we have emphasized, which is that this account of wisdom is also an account of creation.[16] It is creation and its finite patterns of action that underpins the idea of wisdom in Proverbs—a point often on view in the similes of Proverbs: "Pressing milk produces butter; pressing the nose gives blood; pressing anger gives strife" (30:33).[17] It is one of the great virtues of O'Donovan's work to have clearly recognized this point: that our capacity to act reasonably derives from the nature of the world. The fundamental question of Proverbs, and perhaps of the whole wisdom literature, is that put in Job: "Where may wisdom be found?" (Job 28:12).[18] The core question is not, that is, *how* does one *become* wise, but *where* one *finds* wisdom. To "get" wisdom means not merely to develop an intellectual capacity, but to get a purchase on something that remains, in a real way, other. Wisdom is something found, rather than developed. "Happy the person who *finds* wisdom" (3:13). The spatial metaphor reflects the way in which, in Proverbs, to speak of wisdom is to speak of creation, and the way it is hospitable to human action.

Three further, related comments about the form of this hospitality will lead us to our second section. First, it is fundamentally about the generic character of

---

13. *ST* I.14.16; *De Veritate* 3.3; and above, Chapter 2, Section 1.
14. *F&S*, 186.
15. *SWT*, 21; and above, Chapter 4, Section 2b.
16. See above, Chapter 3, Section 3a.
17. For other clear examples see Prov. 25:23, 26, 27.
18. The whole of Job 28 reflects this way of thinking about wisdom in spatial terms.

action. O'Donovan and Aquinas both see kinds of action as central to ethics, and the book of Proverbs supports them. Wisdom is about the way creation welcomes certain kinds of action. This is the sense of created order in which ethics must be most interested: an order of actions and ways of living. "The world," as O'Donovan puts it at one point, "contains patterns of fulfilling inter-human relations, which we could not invent from scratch but must simply accept as given."[19] Or in Aquinas's terms: "A human action is good or evil in its species."[20]

Second, and relatedly, at its heart, creation's hospitality involves a promise concerning language. Where may wisdom be found? "On the lips of the understanding will wisdom be found" (10:13). The proverbs themselves instantiate this promise. Standing over against the hearer, initially disconcerting but disclosing themselves with time, each tight formulation reflects the way wisdom comes to us from without, and yet is fundamentally welcoming. They represent a promise that the hospitality of creation can be extended through language. Naming actions is a possibility afforded by creation itself.[21] In the essay cited above, "The Nature of Things and the Language of Things," Gadamer suggests that language has a kind of primal relation to reality. "Is not," he asks, "language more the language of things than the language of man?"[22] Language, he argues, provides a basis for affirming a "correspondence of soul and world," without the need to have recourse to the infinite mind by which classical metaphysics "provided this correspondence with a theological foundation."[23] "The agreement about things that takes place in language means neither a priority of things nor a priority of the human mind that avails itself of the instrument of linguistic understanding. Rather, the correspondence that finds its concretion in the linguistic experience of the world is as such what is absolutely prior."[24] Without getting absorbed by this essay, we may simply point out that for the account of wisdom we have outlined here, there is no need to decide *between* a theological basis for our ability to engage the world meaningfully in action, and a linguistic basis. For there is a fundamental connection between wisdom and speech. The interweaving of passages of parental instruction and

---

19. O'Donovan, "John Finnis on Moral Absolutes," *Studies in Christian Ethics* 6, no. 2 (1993): 59.

20. *ST* I-II.18.5.

21. The basic difference between the perspective of this study and that of Charles Pinches lies in this claim that names for actions are grounded in creation itself. By contrast, Pinches, with Hauerwas and MacIntyre, sees narrative as the thing that supports action descriptions (*Theology and Action: After Theory in Christian Ethics* (Grand Rapids, MI: Eerdmans, 2002), 15-18, 50-8, 199-232). I agree with Pinches that actions "require a home" (p. 33). But their home is not just "human practices, purposes, and narratives" (p. 33), but the created world that lies behind them.

22. Gadamer, "The Nature of Things," 77.

23. Gadamer, "The Nature of Things," 78.

24. Gadamer, "The Nature of Things," 78.

passages about Wisdom in Proverbs 1–9 reflects this connection: the hospitality of creation to action essentially involves its openness to language. Wisdom *calls*.

Third, we can take one more step. In the book of Proverbs, wisdom extends her welcome not just through speech, but through *poetry*.[25] The call of wisdom comes through words, words of great value, formulations passed from generation to generation. They are words that carry authority, and this authority is expressed through their poetic form.[26] Proverbs' understanding of wisdom strikingly brings together a conviction about natural moral order, a confidence in moral teaching, and a poetic form. And it is poetry, albeit a distinct, didactic kind of poetry, that is most fitting, because what wisdom holds out is not primarily the possibility of scientific understanding, but of living well, of the practical wisdom that leads to life.

2 Nature, History, and Created Order

a. Moral Order and Resurrection

What does this understanding of wisdom mean for the notion of created order within Christian ethics? Stanley Hauerwas once made the following criticism of *Resurrection and Moral Order*: "O'Donovan seeks an account of natural law that is not governed by the eschatological witness of Christ's resurrection. We cannot write about *Resurrection and Moral Order* because any order we know as Christians is resurrection."[27] What Hauerwas asks for is that a Christian ethic be "governed" by resurrection in a deeper sense than merely an epistemological one. It is not enough, according to Hauerwas, to say that moral order may only be truly *known from* the perspective of its restoration in Christ. We must say something more: that the resurrection is somehow *determinative of* the moral order; that any order we know *is* resurrection. Hauerwas's criticism is driven by a sense that there is a tension between an ethic grounded in the gospel and ways of thinking that take their bearings from creation and its natural order.

A parallel impulse may perhaps be seen in the common patristic practice of interpreting the book of Proverbs with reference to the realities of Christian faith. To give a few among many examples: Wisdom's invitation to "eat my food" and drink wine can be interpreted as a reference to the eucharist,[28] as can the reference

---

25. Recall Anne Stewart's careful attention to the significance of poetry for the pedagogy of Proverbs in *Poetic Ethics*, discussed above, Chapter 3, Sections 2a and b.

26. Note Stewart's discussion of moral authority in *Poetic Ethics*, 187–9. The comments made about authority here could be taken to complement the understanding of authority developed in O'Donovan's work, on which see Andrew Errington, "Authority and Reality in the Work of Oliver O'Donovan," *Studies in Christian Ethics* 29, no. 4 (2016): 371–85.

27. Stanley Hauerwas, *Dispatches from the Front* (Durham, NC: Duke University Press, 1994), 175.

28. See the references in *ACCS*, 74–6.

to "dining with a ruler" (23:1-2).[29] Similarly, the "tree of life" of which Proverbs speaks (3:18; 11:30) is held to refer obviously to Christ.[30] "Solomon's hidden proverb had today its explanation," says Ephraim the Syrian.[31] Yet the same impulse also introduces tensions. The fathers struggle, for example, to understand some of the proverbs about money and wealth. Prov. 13:8, with its apparent reference to wealth as a ransom for one's "soul," is especially awkward.[32] To give another example, while Chrysostom, reflecting on Prov. 31:6, can endorse wine as a "remedy for depression," others are unnerved and feel the need to spiritualize it.[33] Some of the ideas in Proverbs are felt not quite to fit with a Christian ethic.

The central theological concern here is the relation between creation and redemption, nature and history. The impulse to avoid a natural ethic independent of Christ reflects an important truth, which the theme of wisdom brings into focus. In the end, there is a unity between God's works of creation and redemption, and that unity is focused upon Jesus Christ. He *is* the wisdom of God, through whom all things were made and in whom all things hold together. There can be no question of a natural order that is wholly independent of him.

Yet, this is a point that O'Donovan, in his own way, also accepts. From the perspective of this study, there is something ironic about Hauerwas's criticism. For we have argued that there is a way in which O'Donovan's work seeks to affirm precisely that the only order that we know is resurrection. At the heart of O'Donovan's work is the claim that the apparent tension between a creation-ethic and a gospel-ethic is ultimately *only* apparent. In reality, there is no tension, although there will be in our daily experience.[34] Yet ultimately, the order of creation and the order of resurrection are one, an abiding, eschatological reality, a whole that "measures change and so stands beyond it."[35]

The difference between Hauerwas and O'Donovan, then, does not actually lie in whether the order we know as Christians is resurrection. It lies, rather, in the way they each account for the tension between creation, with its natural order, and redemption. Where Hauerwas finds in this tension a reason to be wary of appeals to natural order, O'Donovan seeks to overcome this tension by making *world* an eschatological category. Created order is not the order of the world simply as it is, but the deep structure of the world as it subsists within the purposes of God, disclosed by the triumph of the Lamb.

---

29. See the references in *ACCS*, 145–6.
30. See the references in *ACCS*, 26–7, 87.
31. Quoted in *ACCS*, 27.
32. See *ACCS*, 93–5. The problem is heightened by the translation of *nephesh* as *psychē* in the LXX.
33. See the references in *ACCS*, 185.
34. O'Donovan is quite clear on this point. See especially *F&S*, 114–19; and *EIR*, 200–29.
35. See above, Chapter 4, Section 3.

In a way, therefore, this study raises a challenge for both O'Donovan and Hauerwas. For one of the burdens of the argument has been to show that the call of the wisdom by which the world was made is, on the one hand, genuinely *of creation* and so different to the demands made by God's work of reconciliation in Christ (*contra* O'Donovan), and on the other hand, the ongoing, unavoidable concern of Christian ethics (*contra* Hauerwas), because we live before the renewal of all things. The connection between creation and redemption cannot be described in terms of a single order. God's wisdom is indeed eternal, and the same; but—accepting, with Aquinas, that these categories must in some sense collapse when applied to God—God's wisdom is not primarily a perfection of speculative knowledge, but of practical. It is, that is to say, a perfection of action as much as knowledge. This makes room for a real and irreducible twofoldness in God's wisdom. Just as the wisdom by which God made the world both is and is not Jesus Christ, inasmuch as it can be personified as Woman Wisdom, different from the man Jesus, so creation is not redemption, although they are both works of the one wisdom. There is not one timeless intellectual order in which both moments participate; there is the twofold action of God's wisdom. So, while on the one hand there is a sense in which we might say that "any order we may know as Christians is resurrection"— for Christ is the wisdom by which creation was made—on the other hand, there is also a sense in which we really know an order that is not resurrection. For we are creatures, remaining part of a world that the resurrection is yet to transform. We are therefore, unavoidably, claimed by an order that belongs to God's action in creation, even if we now know it in the light of Christ. We cannot, in this age, set aside the tension between creation and redemption (or "nature and grace") implied in the apostle Paul's comment: "it is not the spiritual that is first, but the natural, and then the spiritual" (1 Cor. 15:46).[36]

Does this imply a conception in which an independent, closed, natural ethic of creation is juxtaposed to a different, Christian ethic of redemption, leaving their demands in conflict? It does not, for the same reason that in Aquinas's thought natural practical reason, though distinct, cannot be walled off from revelation: the former opens up to the latter, because it is the one wisdom that works both. Aquinas understands this continuity through the concept of eternal law, and we have argued that this is a mistake, because it fails to grasp the practical character of wisdom. Yet there *is* a real continuity between creation and redemption, despite their distinction.[37] This continuity can be glimpsed in the way Proverbs speaks about God. Thus, when the apostle Paul comments that "The spiritual person judges everything" (1 Cor. 2:15), he merely expresses, in a new way, what Proverbs

---

36. Professor O'Donovan himself first suggested to me this significance of this text, in a conversation for which I remain grateful.

37. I think we *may*, therefore, affirm Aquinas's attempt, highlighted by David Decosimo (David Decosimo, *Ethics as a Work of Charity: Thomas Aquinas and Pagan Virtue* [Stanford, CA: Stanford University Press, 2014]), to make space to welcome natural virtue by saying that, though not *strictly* true virtue, it is true virtue in an imperfect sense (see *ST* II-II.23.7).

had already said: "The evil man does not appreciate judgment; the one who seeks the Lord grasps all things" (Prov. 28:5). Although creation and redemption have their own distinct characters, which is why there may be moments at which the two orders do collide (contrast, for example, Lk. 12:51-53 and Prov. 19:26), they are not finally at odds. With Aquinas, we may see creation as having its own integrity and coherence; and hence, there is room for the language of "nature." Yet there can be no wholly self-referential *natura pura*.[38] Nature opens up to the action of God in Jesus Christ, which is its perfection just as nature is history's presupposition. However, the relation is not one of *immanent* teleology, in which the final perfection is contained, like a seed, in the first moment. Rather, something different takes place, a "new thing," which brings perfection precisely by being *un*anticipated. O'Donovan has in fact put the point perfectly: "the fulfilment of history is not generated immanently from within history."[39] Grace, we may say, presupposes nature—not as an oak tree presupposes a sapling, but more as an act of kindness presupposes those between whom it occurs. It is a *fitting* development, without being a *natural* development, generated from within.[40]

The book of Proverbs testifies to the openness of creation to redemptive history through its striking confidence that righteousness will ultimately be vindicated.[41] It is one thing to believe, in the words of the "friend" into whose mouth David Hume put this opinion, "that, in the present order of things, virtue is attended with more peace of mind than vice, and meets with a more favourable reception from the world."[42] It is quite another thing to affirm that "Whoever trusts in their wealth will fall; the righteous will flourish like new leaves" (11:28), or that "The light of the righteous shines gladly, the lamp of the wicked is put out" (13:9; cf. 21:21). The books of Job and Ecclesiastes, in which this point is a central concern, in the end also hope for the vindication of the moral order. But where these books affirm this only faintly, and at times with hesitation—"do not be *too* righteous" (Eccl 7:16)—Proverbs affirms it with boldness. Proverbs can therefore appear naïve. This need not be strictly dismissed; the point, however, is that this is a *naïveté* of faith, not of sheer optimism.[43] Proverbs affirms that wisdom lies in righteousness

---

38. On this point, see Robert Spaemann, "Nature," in *A Robert Spaemann Reader: Philosophical Essays on Nature, God, and the Human Person*, edited and translated by D. C. Schindler and Jeanne Heffernan Schindler, 139–53. (Oxford: Oxford University Press, 2015).

39. *RMO*, 64.

40. Here lies the difference between the view presented here and Barth's account, introduced in the last chapter (*CD* III/2, 158; see above, Chapter 4, Section 3). We may agree with Barth that history means being "transcended from without." Yet such transcendence from outside may still, in a sense, correspond to nature, still be *fitting*.

41. Recall above, Chapter 3, Section 2a.

42. David Hume, *An Enquiry Concerning Human Understanding* (Indianapolis: Hackett, 1993), 96 [section 11].

43. Consider, for example, Prov. 19:4-7.

not because of a refusal to acknowledge the way things are, but because of an underlying confidence in God. "Do not envy sinners in your heart, but live all your days in the fear of the Lord. For there *is* an end, and your hope will not be cut off" (23:17-18). This makes it possible to read Proverbs as, in its own way, a prophecy of the resurrection of Christ. It displays a bold confidence that the moral integrity of creation will be vindicated against evil, as if it has a promise that the one who made the world by wisdom will act again to bring it to perfection.

What, exactly, does all this entail for our understanding of "created order" as a normative source for Christian ethics? The outline of an answer will emerge if we triangulate our account with two recent attempts to say how the book of Proverbs bears on this question.

b. David VanDrunen and David Kelsey on Created Order in Proverbs

In the course of his recent efforts to recover the place of natural law within the Reformed tradition,[44] David VanDrunen has argued that Proverbs makes a significant contribution to "a biblical theology of natural law."[45] Proverbs, he argues, contains a robust affirmation that "God's wise formation of the world has instilled it with an orderly regularity that penetrates both the cosmic and the human social realms."[46] This natural order includes "a natural *moral* order, or natural law, that is accessible to human minds and apprehensible through their sensory and rational attributes."[47] Wisdom is the virtue that allows human beings "to perceive the natural order and to conduct themselves in a way that befits it."[48] The association made in Proverbs between wisdom and kingship leads VanDrunen to connect wisdom to the theme of the image of God, and to suggest that human wisdom facilitates a kind of royal rule that mirrors God's own sovereignty.[49]

Without doing justice to VanDrunen's account or drawing out the many points with which we can gladly agree,[50] we may say that from the perspective of this study there is a basic problem with this setup. What is missing is the

---

44. See David VanDrunen, *Natural Law and the Two Kingdoms: A Study in the Development of Reformed Social Thought* (Grand Rapids, MI: Eerdmans, 2010); *Divine Covenants and Moral Order: A Biblical Theology of Natural Law* (Grand Rapids, MI: Eerdmans, 2014); and "Wisdom and the Natural Moral Order: The Contribution of Proverbs to a Christian Theology of Natural Law," *Journal of the Society of Christian Ethics* 33, no. 1 (2013): 153–68. A similar effort has been made in Stephen J. Grabill, *Rediscovering the Natural Law in Reformed Theological Ethics* (Grand Rapids, MI: Eerdmans, 2006).

45. VanDrunen, *Divine Covenants*, 369.

46. VanDrunen, *Divine Covenants*, 380.

47. VanDrunen, *Divine Covenants*, 411, emphasis original.

48. VanDrunen, *Divine Covenants*, 380.

49. VanDrunen, *Divine Covenants*, 380–5.

50. Though we note with gratitude VanDrunen's discussion of the accessibility of wisdom (*Divine Covenants*, 393–8).

idea we have detected at the heart of Proverbs: the alterity of wisdom. For VanDrunen, wisdom is fundamentally a subjective capacity, whereas law is objective.[51] This permits him to draw a straightforward analogy between divine and human wisdom: both are about the sovereign knowledge that allows for kingly rule. But this leaves out the central, distinctive aspects of Proverbs' presentation of wisdom: the personification of divine wisdom, and the call of wisdom. It is striking, for instance, that in VanDrunen's discussion of the epistemology of Proverbs, the theme of the call of wisdom is absent.[52] For wisdom to call, wisdom must be objective, an attribute of creation itself. Human wisdom does not mirror divine wisdom, but really participates in it, by embracing it through the good action that it has made available, the paths it has beaten out. Yet to think in this way has two consequences for VanDrunen's overall framework. First, to think about created order in terms of *wisdom* unsettles the category of natural law, as we have already argued.[53] For law, as VanDrunen recognizes, *obliges*.[54] Wisdom, however, *invites*; wisdom *calls*, holding out an offer of success and life.[55] The idea of natural law implies that created order is implicitly deontological. Proverbs suggests it is basically eudaemonistic. It is creation's hospitality to *life*.

Second, to think along these lines unsettles the independence of natural law. For if created order is really the order of *God's* wisdom, then it must, as we have consistently stressed, be understood as essentially related to Jesus Christ. Although there *is* a distinction to be made between what follows from creation and from redemption, there is no natural order that is wholly unrelated to resurrection. The claim that lies upon us is in a sense twofold, in that creation and redemption are distinct works of the one wisdom. Yet it is still the one wisdom of God that makes this claim. The twofoldness of this claim persists only because the world is not yet perfected. It is a distinction whose destiny is to be swept away. This means that the temptation should be resisted to assign creation and redemption different spheres of influence, and to speak, for example, of our responsibilities as Christians on the one hand and as human beings or citizens on the other, as in the two kingdoms theology VanDrunen shows has gone hand in hand with Reformed accounts of natural law. There is no part of creation that has not been claimed by Christ through his death and resurrection, and no sphere of life in which that fact ought to be bracketed out. We may want to say that creation, with its hospitality to action, forms a basis for common moral discourse with all people; and saying that will have significance for social and political life. But we may not say that in

---

51. See VanDrunen, *Divine Covenants*, 371–2.

52. See VanDrunen, *Divine Covenants*, 386–98.

53. See above, Chapter 3, Section 3a.

54. VanDrunen, *Divine Covenants*, 371.

55. VanDrunen is, of course, aware of this aspect of Proverbs (e.g., *Divine Covenants*, 391–2). For him, however, the fundamental character of created order is deontological.

certain spheres of life it is legitimate to act as if Christ has not come,[56] and the term "nature" should not be used to legitimate such a view. For from the beginning, wisdom calls us to the fear of the Lord; and in this age, that means to the reverence of Christ.

A strikingly different reading of Proverbs appears in David Kelsey's theological anthropology, *Eccentric Existence*.[57] In this work, Kelsey argues that there are "three conceptually different ways in which the triune God actively relates to all that is not God"[58]: Creation, Consummation, and Reconciliation. At the foundation of his treatment of the first of these—and to some extent at the foundation of the whole work—is an interpretation of the ideas of creation found in the biblical wisdom literature, and particularly the book of Proverbs.

In many respects, Kelsey's reading of Proverbs is close to the one we have been developing in this study, and it is for this reason that we have left it until this point to consider. Kelsey highlights numerous themes we have argued are important. He recognizes the practical character of wisdom, arguing that its closest philosophical parallel is the classical notion of *phronēsis*.[59] Embodied in the figure of the capable wife of Proverbs 31,[60] wisdom, for Kelsey, is emphatically not a matter of knowing "the structure of reality," but rather a practice-oriented "capacity to discern order ad hoc in ordinary experience."[61] Kelsey highlights the way in which wisdom is centrally a matter of the right use of language, a fact which shows it to be an irreducibly social reality.[62] The book of Proverbs, he argues, is designed to produce such wisdom: "Wisdom's sentences do not offer a grasp of a set of universally applicable rules, much less a body of theory. Rather, they elicit insight in a student by depicting concrete situations in the most condensed way possible, often by rendering the same situation in more than one way."[63]

Kelsey also highlights the theme of the call of wisdom, and recognizes the way it comes from the created world itself: "the very context into which we are born has the force of a vocation."[64] His account of created order also supports the argument we have made above: "In Proverbs," he writes, "the sense of order that is of interest is not a metaphysical order that ontologically grounds a type of natural law, but

---

56. The problems surveyed by VanDrunen in *Natural Law*, 427–34, reflect the real difficulties this doctrine confronts. Overall, I think the argument here supports the careful alternative conception set out by O'Donovan in *The Desire of the Nations*. Cf. VanDrunen, *Natural Law*, 431 n. 16.

57. David Kelsey, *Eccentric Existence: A Theological Anthropology*, 2 vols (Louisville, Kentucky: Westminster John Knox, 2009).

58. Kelsey, *Eccentric Existence*, 893.

59. Kelsey, *Eccentric Existence*, 194–7.

60. Kelsey, *Eccentric Existence*, 222–3, 226.

61. Kelsey, *Eccentric Existence*, 173.

62. Kelsey, *Eccentric Existence*, 198–9.

63. Kelsey, *Eccentric Existence*, 218; cf. 223.

64. Kelsey, *Eccentric Existence*, 194.

rather a more pragmatic, context realistic, goal-oriented-action sense of 'order.'"[65] "God's actual creation" is not "'noumenal' reality, a depth far more meaningful than the quotidian itself, of which the quotidian is mere phenomena or appearance."[66] Rather, "what God creates is humankind's lived world in its concrete everydayness," what is on the surface.[67] This is what God delights in and is present to in hospitable generosity, extended through the practices that are constitutive of human life.[68] To a significant extent, this study should be seen as supporting, and in turn finds support from, Kelsey's reading of Proverbs.

Yet although there is much in Kelsey's work to appreciate, there are some important problems with it. Once again, the issues surface with the figure of Woman Wisdom. Kelsey argues that Wisdom is not merely an element of creation, but "the emblem of how God relates to human persons in and through their creaturely context."[69] She is a "pedagogical trope" for, "how God relates in creating."[70] With this point, Kelsey is wrestling with what we have argued is the central theological challenge of Proverbs: understanding how Wisdom can be in some sense both creaturely and divine. Kelsey, however, does not so much solve this problem as evade it. He is forced to do so because he is committed to understanding creation, not as a finished work of God, but as a present mode of God's "active relating."[71] This means, however, that despite Kelsey's recognition that Woman Wisdom is not God,[72] the two are in fact conflated,[73] as when Kelsey seeks to understand the order of wisdom in terms of "what God is up to."[74]

This loses sight of the distinctive creatureliness of Wisdom.[75] Woman Wisdom, in Proverbs, is not merely a teaching aid to show us how God relates in the present; she is a personification of the divine wisdom by which God acted in making the world, which is also in a real sense creaturely, because it is creation that is God's wise act. This conception, however, depends on creation's being an accomplished work. Kelsey insists that this is not how Proverbs sees things. "Wisdom's creation theology," he argues, "generally lacks any account of cosmic origins."[76] That God

65. Kelsey, *Eccentric Existence*, 237.
66. Kelsey, *Eccentric Existence*, 191.
67. Kelsey, *Eccentric Existence*, 191.
68. Kelsey, *Eccentric Existence*, 165, 191, 193–4.
69. Kelsey, *Eccentric Existence*, 170.
70. Kelsey, *Eccentric Existence*, 226.
71. This is a central concept in *Eccentric Existence*, developed throughout the work and structurally fundamental. See, e.g., pp. 8, 46, 115, 130–1, and 893–7.
72. See Kelsey, *Eccentric Existence*, 223, 239.
73. See Kelsey, *Eccentric Existence*, 227, 235.
74. Kelsey, *Eccentric Existence*, 241.
75. This criticism applies also to Fiddes, who accepts Kelsey's notion of "ordering" (See Paul Fiddes, *Seeing the World and Knowing God: Hebrew Wisdom and Christian Doctrine in a Late-Modern Context* (Oxford: Oxford University Press, 2013), 117, 188).
76. Kelsey, *Eccentric Existence*, 190.

created "by wisdom" does not mean, according to Kelsey, that "The LORD founded the earth by relying on divine wisdom." Rather, it means that God "evokes creation into being" here and now, by "using Wisdom's evocative discourse."[77] God *creates* the quotidian, "humankind's lived world in its concrete everydayness"—what is on the surface.[78]

This is not persuasive. Prov. 3:19-20 and 8:22-31 are indeed accounts of "cosmic origins," and they are of foundational importance.[79] The book of Proverbs does have plenty to say about God's ongoing, active relation to his creation, but what it says (e.g., Prov. 22:12) is far more readily comprehended under the idea of *providence*, a topic to which Kelsey gives little attention.[80]

What is at stake here for Kelsey is his conviction that it is a mistake to try to relate creation, consummation, and reconciliation in terms of a history of salvation:

> The logic of the relations among these three plots, each with a distinctive narrative logic that cannot be absorbed into or conflated with that of either of the other two, makes it impossible to relate them to one another in a simple linear fashion, as a sequence of different stories of three different ways in which God successively relates to all that is not God.[81]

This is because creation, reconciliation, and consummation refer, for him, not to a history of salvation but to simultaneous modes of divine action. Thus, although they are related—wound around each other, in Kelsey's image, "helixlike"[82]— there is no true order among them. In my view, this way of thinking is mistaken. Certainly, God's work of creation and his work of reconciliation are distinct works, each with their own integrity. This has been a crucial point in the argument thus far. Yet they are connected in ways that go far beyond Kelsey's account of their relation, which is why Proverbs is more connected to the story of Israel than Kelsey is willing to recognize.[83] As we argued above, particularly in its confidence

---

77. Kelsey, *Eccentric Existence*, 172.

78. Kelsey, *Eccentric Existence*, 190-1.

79. Kelsey is of course aware of these texts and acknowledges that they do "tell of something that has happened"; but he insists that "they tell no extended story about it" (*Eccentric Existence*, 163), such that, overall, the wisdom literature lacks "any genetic explanation of the origin of the world" (164). This is not an adequate account of these passages, in my view.

80. Kelsey acknowledges the distinction between creation and providence, but insists he is talking about creation (*Eccentric Existence*, 161). His brief discussion of providence does not clarify how this concept relates to God's "actively relating to create" (211-12).

81. Kelsey, *Eccentric Existence*, 476.

82. Kelsey, *Eccentric Existence*, 476; cf. 897-900.

83. See *Eccentric Existence*, 188. As well as the arguments made in Chapter 3, we should note the importance of the association—however credible—of Proverbs with Solomon (cf. 1 Kings 4:29-34 and Psalm 72). See also R. W. L. Moberly, "Solomon and Job: Divine Wisdom in Human Life," in *Where Shall Wisdom Be Found?*, ed. Stephen Barton (Edinburgh: T&T Clark, 1999), 1-17.

in the vindication of righteousness, Proverbs is already thoroughly "bent," to use Kelsey's imagery, toward the hope of reconciliation.[84] Creation and reconciliation are works of the one wisdom of God, which means they are both fundamentally related to Jesus Christ, in whom all things were created and in whom they hold together (Col. 1:15, 17). Kelsey deliberately resists such a framework.[85] Although he affirms that God creates through the Son, he is reluctant to connect this affirmation to "Christ in his humanity."[86] Yet such a connection must be made, precisely because of the idea of wisdom. Jesus Christ—and him crucified—*is* the wisdom of God (1 Cor. 1:24). In him we see, in a new and fuller way, the wisdom that was at God's side, rejoicing in creation at the foundation of the world (Prov. 8:30-31).

This difference has two consequences for the idea of created order. First, it allows us to recognize created order as genuinely *created* order, that is, as an order belonging to the world by virtue of its having been created a certain way. Certainly, we may affirm Kelsey's insistence that order is something that belongs to the world as it actually is, and not to some hidden, noumenal depth or beyond. Yet on Kelsey's account there is, I think, no way to avoid the historicist fluidity that O'Donovan so clearly warns against. For if the world's order is an active ordering, then we will not find any stability in the world itself, but only in God. This is not the view of Proverbs. While God is, of course, finally the only truly trustworthy one, he has by wisdom made a world that is a ground on which to stand, and that discloses paths in which to walk: "the world he has made so sure that it cannot be moved, the unnegotiable form of our unformed agency," in O'Donovan's words.[87] The order of creation is not infinitely flexible, changing with every movement of history quivering with significance. Although different times and contexts will reveal it differently, it is an order of *creation*, a hospitality to certain kinds of action "woven" into the world from its first moments (Prov. 8:23).[88]

In the second place, we are able now to see more clearly the place which created order must have within the Christian moral life. The ordered creation, the world in which we find ourselves, and that extends hospitality to us, is indeed the presupposition of all our action—"the unnegotiable form of our unformed agency." Yet O'Donovan goes on to call it "the school of our first and last purposes, the gazette that announces our enlistment in God's service."[89] Our first purposes, yes; but our last? Is it *the world* that announces our enlistment in God's service? In a sense, yes, in that the call of wisdom is a call to righteousness, and to the

---

84. For this image, and Kelsey's argument that Proverbs escapes such bending, see *Eccentric Existence*, 162, 176–86, 226.

85. See *Eccentric Existence*, 64–6, 78, 909–13.

86. Kelsey, *Eccentric Existence*, 912–13. For a similar criticism of Kelsey on this point, see Catherine Pickstock, "The One Story: A Critique of David Kelsey's Theological Robotics," *Modern Theology* 27, no. 1 (2011): 38.

87. O'Donovan, *SWT*, 113.

88. See above, Chapter 3, Section 1, n. 11.

89. *SWT*, 113.

fear of the Lord. But this call is refused (Prov. 1:24-26), so that another call is needed, from one who calls us to follow *him*, and perhaps even to "let the dead bury the dead" (Lk. 9:60). The school of our *last* purposes is not creation, but the fellowship of Jesus; the gazette that announces our enlistment in God's service is the cross. The call of creation's wisdom must give place to the call of Jesus, which, although it does not stand opposed to that wisdom, is still something different. "Something greater than Solomon is here!" (Lk. 11:31). Just as Jesus's fulfilment of the law was a complex fulfilment ("You have heard it said … but I say to you … "), so his impact upon created moral order is complex. In the teaching of Jesus, many aspects of wisdom are simply affirmed.[90] Other times, there is an intensification of wisdom, such as when the golden rule (Mt. 7:12) replaces "Do not say, 'As he did to me, I'll do to him; I will return to a man according to his deed.'" (Prov. 24:29). And at certain moments, wisdom's teaching is relativized, or effectively nullified. Such is the case with Jesus's teaching about generosity (Mt. 5:38-48), which stands out against the general tenor of Proverbs, with its assumptions about reciprocity and hesitation about lending (see, for example, Prov. 11:15; 17:18; 20:16; 22:7). A parallel example is found in the instinct shared by several of the fathers that the teaching of Proverbs about restraint in speech needed to be relativized by the imperative to preach the gospel.[91] Another parallel appears in Aquinas's discussion of temperance, referred to earlier, in which there is a jarring difference between natural temperance, in which "food should not harm the health of the body, nor hinder the use of reason," and infused temperance, where "it behooves man to 'chastise his body, and bring it into subjection' (1 Cor. 9:27), by abstinence."[92] Fundamentally, it is the same logic that leads the apostle Paul to say that "God chose the foolish things of the world to disgrace the wise" (1 Cor. 1:27). The coming of Christ means the wisdom that corresponds to the order of creation has been relativized.[93] Put starkly: the most honorable things (*ta timiōmata*) have been overshadowed by "things that are nothing" (*ta mē onta*; 1 Cor. 1:28). One of the central tasks of Christian ethics is to navigate these complex effects of the coming of Jesus on the normative significance of created order.

---

90. Compare, for example, Prov. 25:6-7 with Lk. 14:7-11; Mt. 23:6; Mk 12:39; Lk. 20:46; Prov. 25:8-10 with Mt. 5:25; Prov. 28:24 with Mk 7:10-11. Outside Jesus's teaching, note especially the use of Prov. 25:21-22 in Rom. 12:20.

91. Augustine, for example, commenting on Prov. 10:19, says, "Would that all my speaking were only the preaching of your word and the praise of you! Then I would not only escape sin, no matter how many words I spoke, but also obtain a good reward." See the references on Prov. 10:19 in *ACCS*, 82.

92. *ST* I-II.63.4, Benziger Brothers edition. See above, Chapter 2, Section 3a.

93. Despite the current unpopularity of this approach, in my opinion this is also the right line along which to interpret certain other teachings in the wisdom literature, such as Ecclesiastes' exhortation not to be "too righteous" (Eccl. 7:16). On this point, see O'Donovan's lucid discussion in *EIR*, 33-7.

To close this part of our discussion, let us illustrate by once more drawing on the metaphor of hospitality. Imagine a small farm that was home to a large family, who had worked the farm for many generations growing to understand it well, knowing the land and its rhythms intimately, so that they were able to cultivate it effectively and sustainably, and build flourishing lives upon it. That, in a way, is an image of the order that the world has by virtue of its creation by God's wisdom, and the practical wisdom that it affords. It is about the hospitality of creation to the activities of human life. Now imagine, however, that a political crisis creates a need to welcome large numbers of displaced people, and the family decide that they ought to use their farm to do so, taking in large numbers of refugees. In such a situation, the family's practical knowledge of the farm will be indispensable. It will not primarily be an obstacle to extending this welcome, but a help, enabling the family to use the farm to benefit others. Ignorance of the land and its rhythms would in fact be very damaging in such circumstances. Yet, the practical knowledge the family possess could not itself lead to the decision to welcome the refugees. It may point to it: a sense of the fruitfulness of the land may have been part of what opened the family up to extending this welcome. Yet by the same token, such knowledge could also be used to urge caution. The decision to welcome the refugees makes sense as a way of using the farm—it is fitting—but it is not inevitable; it requires also the event of the political crisis, and a recognition that it has placed a new obligation upon the family. It is a decision that will cause new tensions, placing various things under pressure and creating unanticipated challenges.

This, I believe, is a useful, though certainly limited, image of the place of the natural order within Christian ethics. Creation's order is the context and presupposition of Christian ethics. The practical knowledge of that order is very useful—indeed, essential—for effectively doing what is needed. Some breaches of this order will always constitute grave evils. Yet, such wisdom is not all there is to Christian ethics. There is a further wisdom, because there was a further event. Something has taken place that means that the ends to which our actions must be directed have changed. Something new has been asked of us, the pursuit of which is possible only through and with the wisdom that belongs to creation's order, but which is not contained within it. Indeed, from certain points of view the new task may represent a rebellion against the older wisdom. From another perspective, however, it is exactly what that wisdom was preparing for all along. The proof of such a perspective, though, is still to come. It is a perspective that reaches out in hope for a future that will vindicate it.

3 Moral Discernment and the Naming of Actions

What follows from all this for our understanding of the dynamics of moral discernment, which have been a central concern throughout this study? The apostle Paul wrote: "This is my prayer: that your love may grow more and more in knowledge and all insight [*aisthēsei*], so that you may discern the important distinctions [*dokimazein ... ta diapheronta*], and thus be pure and blameless on the day of Christ" (Phil. 1:9-10). The second word the apostle uses here to describe the knowledge that enables discernment, *aisthēsis*, is the word used by Aristotle for the perception on which practical reasoning depends.[94] It could be translated "attunement." It has to do with an appreciation of, or perhaps "feel for," the significance of the things that bear upon one. But what things are these? And what kind of "discernment of important distinctions" does this insight enable?

a. Hercules at the Crossroads

Let us begin by recalling a potent objection to one way of understanding such discernment. "The image of Hercules at the crossroads," inveighed Karl Barth, "is a pagan image for a pagan thing."[95] What Barth objected to was an image of moral discernment in which we are placed as judges, possessing some standard of goodness by which to assess the choices we confront. On the contrary, thought Barth, we are not judges, but judged; the will of God comes to us as a command, not inviting assessment, but demanding obedience. "Man will be and actually is told what is good and what the Lord requires of him—and with absolute definiteness, so that only obedience or disobedience remains, and there is no scope for his free appraisal and will in regard to the shape of his obedience."[96] Barth was conscious that passages such as the one above, which speak of the discerning or "testing" of

---

94. See above, Chapter 1, Section 4.
95. Karl Barth, *Ethics*, ed. D. Braun, trans. G. W. Bromiley (Edinburgh: T&T Clark, 1981), 74. What follows should by no means be taken as an adequate treatment of Barth's ethics. It seeks only to highlight an important critical element of Barth's thought, particularly as it is put forward in *CD* II/2 and the 1929 *Ethics*. O'Donovan's discussion of Barth in *F&S*, 188-93 takes a similar approach. For arguments that Barth's wider ethical thought opens up other possibilities less hostile to forms of deliberation, see Nigel Biggar, *The Hastening that Waits: Karl Barth's Ethics* (Oxford: Clarendon, 1993); Gerald McKenny, *The Analogy of Grace: Karl Barth's Moral Theology* (Oxford: Oxford University Press, 2010); and especially Derek Alan Woodard-Lehman's recent article, "Reason after Revelation: Karl Barth on Divine Word and Human Words," *Modern Theology* 33, no. 1 (2017): 92-115. In my view, however, these other possibilities are not entirely reconcilable with the critique of deliberation set out in *CD* II/2. Some of the reasons for this view are noted below; but I accept that this construal of Barth's thought is open to debate. Even if it is contestable, however, I hope it will serve its purpose of drawing out the significance of the arguments made throughout this book. I am grateful to Derek Woodard-Lehman for his engagement with me in relation to these questions.
96. Barth, *CD* II/2, 704. The language here is drawn from Mic. 6:8, where "told" translates *higgîd*. The common English rendering of this verb as "shown," however, is not unreasonable, and reflects the fact that the emphasis may not be on the verbal nature of the revelation, but on the making known itself. The differences between O'Donovan's way of thinking and Barth's are neatly encapsulated in their divergent readings of this text. See *F&S*, 70-2, 125.

God's will, apparently placed pressure on this framework.[97] He insisted, however, that these passages could only be understood if "test and approve" was taken in a responsive sense: we are not in a position to weigh and evaluate the command that comes to us; we are only in a position to receive it and submit to it.

Barth's account of this matter is shaped by the dominance of the concept of *command* in his thought. This emphasis is related theologically to his decision to ground ethics in the doctrine of divine election, and to understand this in terms of Gospel and Law.[98] This leads Barth to often use the categories of God's *will* and God's *command* interchangeably,[99] so that God's particular will is understood in terms of a particular command—"Man will be and actually is told what is good." This, in turn, shapes his interpretation of the passages noted above and of the idea of "testing." The point at issue in Philippians's reference to *dokimazein ... ta diapheronta*, he argues, is "the mutual relationship between this, that or the other possible line of action in this situation and the divine command."[100]

But must things take this shape? If God's will were not articulated wholly in terms of his command, then the definiteness that Barth legitimately holds to be entailed by divine election would not have to rule out any room for subjective deliberation and discernment of the kind Barth opposes. There is indeed a sense in which there can be no scope for our "free appraisal and will in regard to the shape of ... obedience." Yet that only rules out a subjective movement of deliberation and discernment if Barth is right that we are in fact *told*, in every moment, what the will of God is; if, that is, the will of God always encounters us as a "definite"[101] command, which "even to the smallest details ... is self-interpreting."[102] If, on the other hand, we say that God's will for us may be definite, but our purchase on it is a complex matter, not readily comprehended under the idea of "hearing a command,"[103] then space opens up to speak about deliberation in more fulsome

---

97. The other key passages are Rom. 12:2, and Eph. 5:10, 17. Barth discusses these passages briefly in *Ethics*, 75, and at length in *CD* II/2, 636–41.

98. See *CD* II/2, 509–13, 677, 701, 703, 708.

99. See, for example, *CD* II/2 566–7, 610–11.

100. *CD* II/2, 639. Compare *Ethics*, 75, where Barth's problem is with the idea of "testing the command." Gerald McKenny's account of Barth's ethics recognizes the importance of this motif of testing (*Analogy of Grace*, 230–5.) However, as Paul Nimmo observes, McKenny's account also underplays the significance of the idea of the definiteness of God's command in Barth's ethics ("Reflections on *The Analogy of Grace* by Gerald McKenny," *Scottish Journal of Theology* 68, no. 1 (2015): 91–2.

101. *CD* II/2, 661–708. On the theme of the definiteness of the divine command, see especially *CD* II/2, pp. 661–708; and Barth, *The Christian Life: Church Dogmatics IV, 4 Lecture Fragments* (Grand Rapids, MI: Eerdmans, 1981), 33–4.

102. *CD* II/2, 665. Note Nimmo's succinct highlighting of this theme in Barth's thought, in response to Gerald McKenny's account ("Reflections on *The Analogy of Grace*," 91–2).

103. Both McKenny and Woodard-Lehman maintain that Barth's understanding of hearing the command of God is in fact more complex than it can appear. McKenny insists

terms, which, as O'Donovan suggests, may better reflect the way the Bible talks about it,[104] and about the role of the Holy Spirit.[105]

In many ways, this study involves a decision not to travel the road laid by Barth's ethics. The reasons are marked out by different readings of Proverbs 8. Barth's reading of this text—which, on the whole, is notably absent from the *Church Dogmatics*—is driven by a desire to avoid the idea of God as "the immanent meaning of the world."[106] This leads him to argue that in Proverbs 8, "wisdom is equated with God himself,"[107] and to conclude that the idea "of an immanent divine wisdom accessible to and recognizable by man of himself," "is unambiguously eliminated."[108] The aim of our own reading has been to suggest that, while Barth is right that Proverbs does not support the idea of *God* as the immanent meaning of the world,[109] this does not mean that God's *wisdom* is not in

---

that for Barth the command of God is always "intersubjective" (*Analogy of Grace*, 239, 274). Similarly, Woodard-Lehman argues, on the basis of Barth's discussion of confession in *CD* I/2, that Barth assumes a social account of hearing the word of God, which, when it is taken seriously, makes space for practical rationality, understood in terms indebted to both Kant and Hegel ("Reason after Revelation," 92–115). He holds that for Barth "the ethical event in which divine command is given ... cannot be an immediate encounter with the Word of God as such," and therefore that "the encounter with the divine command is communal" (p. 99). Yet Woodard-Lehman also accepts that the criticisms cannot wholly be dismissed, and that his argument is really an argument for a particular way of receiving Barth's moral theology. I continue to think Barth's account of this matter is far too ambiguous. Some passages seem to me to clearly imply an existential and non-verbal experience of the command. For example, the command "secretly fills every moment of our life" and "is always being put to us afresh" (*CD* II/2, 613). Also, "it is indeed the case that—without prejudice to its particular form—the claim of God's command always wears the garment of another claim of this kind. An object with its question, the compulsion of a necessity of thought, one of those hypotheses or conventions, a higher necessity of life and particularly a more primitive, a necessity which in itself seems to be that of a very human wish or very human cleverness, a summons coming from this or that quarter, a call which a man directs to himself—all these can actually be the command of God veiled in this form" (*CD* II/2, 584–5).

104. Compare McKenny's comments about the weakness of the exegetical basis for Barth's account of ethical reflection (*Analogy of Grace*, 233).

105. Barth's account of ethics has consistently come in for criticism on this front, from the early, pietist response to his *Ethik* by Karl Heim (see Barth, *Ethics*, 114–15; and Barth, "Brief an Karl Heim," *Zwischen den Zeiten* 9 [1931]: 451–3), to O'Donovan's critique in *Finding and Seeking*, 188–93.

106. *CD* II/1, 427.

107. *CD* II/1, 429.

108. *CD* II/1, 430.

109. In which respect we have also parted company with Paul Fiddes's proposal that "seeing the world is knowing God" (*Seeing the World*, 188). See above, Chapter 3, Section 2c.

some way the immanent meaning of the world. For God's wisdom is an attribute of his action; God's wisdom is in what he *does*. This creates the space to speak of creation as somehow having a voice that is not simply God's own, and that calls to us to be wise.

It is instructive to compare Barth's disdain for the image of Hercules at the crossroads with the original account recorded by Xenophon.[110] As Xenophon records it, the event takes place as Heracles "was passing from boyhood to young manhood, when the young, now becoming their own masters, show whether they will approach life by the path of virtue or the path of vice." Heracles sits in a "quiet place ... pondering which road to take," when there "appeared two women of great stature coming towards him." One appears fair and noble, modest and sober, in a white robe. This, it turns out, is Virtue. The other is sensual, made-up, and provocative. "She kept eyeing herself and looking to see whether anyone noticed her." This one is "Vice," although her friends call her *Eudaimonia*. They approach Heracles, but Vice arrives first. She tells him to follow her on "the pleasantest and easiest road," which will lead to all life's pleasures, licit and illicit, and above all very little effort, "for to my companions I give authority to pluck advantage wherever they want." Virtue then speaks: "Heracles: I know your parents and have taken note of your character during the time of your education." She refuses to deceive Heracles, but instead sets before him the sober offer of hard work leading to success: "if you want land to yield you fruits in abundance, you must cultivate that land." Vice responds by pointing out how difficult this will be, but Virtue answers back, observing how sad and depraved Vice's outlook on life is.

The striking thing about this story is its resemblance to the imagery of Proverbs. We have the young man, at the threshold of adult life, confronted by distinctly different invitations, one to a life of sobriety, hard work, and honor, the other to easy pleasure. Promises and warnings accompany them. There is also the association of Wisdom or virtue with the man's parents. In contrast to Barth's sweeping denunciation of any kind of "Hercules at the crossroads" thinking, these similarities suggest that this kind of image reflects a way in which we are unavoidably situated in the world, because of the world's having been created by wisdom.

Nevertheless, there are also important differences between this image in Proverbs and in the story of Heracles, which point us to something in Barth's concerns about discernment that should not be jettisoned. The figure of Heracles is strikingly different to the young man envisaged in Proverbs 1–9. We find Heracles "pondering" in a quiet place. In Proverbs, there is no time for such pondering. The situation is too dangerous for that: "My son, pay attention!" (5:1), "Get wisdom, though it cost you all you have!" (4:7), "Guard it, for it is your life" (4:13). This urgency is not present in the story of Heracles, but much more closely

---

110. The account is found in Xenophon's *Memorabilia* II, 1.21–34. The translation used here, which uses the name "Heracles," is by E. C. Marchant (LOEB Classical Library; Cambridge, MA: Harvard University Press, 2013), 103–13.

matches Barth's account of the matter: "the next moment," he writes, "will bring to us the claim that judges us and should find us, not dreaming as Hercules at the crossroads dreams, but watchful."[111] We might therefore say that, according to Proverbs, although the Heracles story reflects something important about the nature of the world we live in, it is badly misjudged. There *is* a choice to be made between ways of life that lead to success, and ways that lead to failure; but it is far more urgent and perilous than it often appears, and we are not nearly so capable of making it well as we assume we are. Indeed, Proverbs points clearly toward the inevitability of our failure at such moments. Wisdom's very first speech is one of frustration and condemnation: "I called and you refused; I offered my hand, and no one paid attention." Well then, "I will laugh at your calamity" (1:23-26). The parental speeches are full of exasperation and fear for the same reason—that people "hate knowledge" and "do not choose the fear of the Lord" (1:29). The book's underlying confidence that righteousness will be vindicated is thus also an underlying consciousness that many face judgment.

In this respect, too, a Christian theological reading of Proverbs must see it opening up to the Gospel, to the place where the possibility of walking in wisdom is restored to us. Here is where Barth's ethics preserves something essential. For Barth reminds us that we confront such moments not as those capable of success, judges of good and evil, but as those who have already failed and so stand in need, not only of advice, but of salvation. Barth preserves the soteriological bearing of Christian moral discernment. "Ethics as the doctrine of God's command, and therefore as the doctrine of the sanctification given to man by God, is grounded in the knowledge of Jesus Christ. It can be attained and developed only as the knowledge of Jesus Christ."[112]

The virtue of Barth's discussion of discernment lies in the way it pursues this point. Discerning God's will, Barth argues, cannot be about "a kind of necessity immanent in the situation."[113] Why not? Because of "the demonism of the existing situation."[114] "Quite apart from the inclinations of our own fleshly nature, the existing situation as such is always ruled by all sorts of demons, and sensitiveness to it can have very little to do with sensitiveness to the will of God."[115] Discerning the will of God is, rather, about discerning which of "the various possibilities of action open to us" is "positively related" to the divine command:

> In face of our situation, we have to ask what is appropriate to us because it is pleasing to the Lord who is the Judge of goodness, righteousness and truth, and their opposite. This enquiry cannot be replaced by even the most penetrating systematic or intuitive analysis of the situation as such and the

111. *Ethics*, 75.
112. *CD* II/2, 777.
113. *CD* II/2, 639.
114. *CD* II/2, 640.
115. *CD* II/2, 639.

objective and subjective factors which condition it … this enquiry only begins where an analysis of that kind leaves off.[116]

For God's judgment "is not discoverable in the various possibilities open to us, but stands in sovereign transcendence over them."[117] This, Barth maintains, is "the difference between ethical reflection and every mere analysis of this situation."[118] It is the same difference, he suggests, that Jesus points to in Lk. 12:56, when he distinguishes between "discerning" (*dokimazein*) the earth and sky and discerning the *kairos*. The "time" that they cannot perceive is the Messianic advent.[119] "The accusation they [the Pharisees] incur is that while they are adept at analysing all kinds of different situations … they do not devote to the question of the will of God, as it is now manifest in the Messianic age, the attention which it deserves, and they therefore neglect the possible and demanded *dokimazein*."[120]

At this point, Barth's argument makes contact with our discussion in Chapter 4, where we suggested that despite O'Donovan's focus on the theme of time in *Ethics as Theology*, he does not give sufficient weight to time as salvation-history. We also suggested that this point surfaces with the theme of "wakefulness,"[121] a suggestion that we have seen Barth might support, with his contrast between Hercules's dreaming and the need to be watchful. Yet this does not mean we should wholly accept Barth's characterization of our ethical situation. The claim of Christ and his kingdom is the critical factor by which all moral discernment must be oriented. Yet it is not a claim floating in a vacuum, but one which bears on us as people always already called by wisdom in creation. This is the insight in O'Donovan's statement that "faith has no discursive content of its own."[122] In the previous chapter, we argued that this statement overlooks the way in which faith does come with its own, distinct form, focused in the call to forgive. What it rightly recognizes, however, is that the call of Christ only makes sense on the presupposition of an ordered call of creation. It is a call to something which is already itself morally oriented—a *re*-directing. We may therefore say, recalling O'Donovan's formulation, that what we seek in discernment is a "congruence of normativities." For O'Donovan, this means that "the ordered demand of creation, the agential powers which we are conscious of possessing, and the moment of opportunity into which we are thrust all flow together."[123] Our argument has tried to show that this list does not sufficiently accommodate the claim of Christ, which is neither simply part of the ordered demand of creation, nor encompassed by the

---

116. *CD* II/2, 639–40.
117. *CD* II/2, 640.
118. *CD* II/2, 640.
119. *CD* II/2, 640. On this theme, see also *CD* III/4, 565–94.
120. *CD* II/2, 640.
121. See above, Chapter 4, Section 3.
122. *F&S*, 47.
123. *F&S*, 220–1; and above, Chapter 4, Section 2c.

moment of opportunity. Christ's claim comes as another factor, which reorders, or in Barth's phrase, "stands over," all the others. We engage the world, with its natural order, conscious that something has happened within it that means its hospitality must now be accepted in a new way, turned toward the destiny to which it always reached out, but without hope of reaching it through its own resources. Yet we may still say that it is a "congruence of normativities" that we seek. The ordered demand of creation, like our own capacities and the uniqueness of the present moment, cannot simply be ignored, but forms the context and presupposition of all our discernments. In this sense, there is an important truth in O'Donovan's claim that "natural moral experience … is taken up and enhanced in the redemption of the moral life."[124]

b. Scripture and the Construal of Actions

How does such a congruence of normativities take place, so as to effect a moment in which we discern a path in which to walk, a course of action to be taken? In Chapter 3, we criticized a picture of deliberation that assumes a kind of sovereign perspective, with the moral agent surveying the terrain and picking out the best path. Such a picture, we said, is sometimes suggested by the framework of means and ends, especially when we imagine an agent being able to "take an end as fixed." That is not how things are in practice. In practice, we must make our choices in the thick of things, already walking the path, often reacting by instinct. Ramsey noted that the person who does a "fitting thing" mostly just "senses the wise or good thing to do without much elaboration of why."[125] Similarly, Anscombe comments, "It has an absurd appearance when practical reasonings, and particularly when the particular units called practical syllogisms by modern commentators, are set out in full."[126] Overall, she writes, "If Aristotle's account were supposed to describe actual mental processes, it would in general be quite absurd. The interest of the account is that it describes an order which is there whenever actions are done with intentions."[127]

In what sense, however, is an "order" described by a chain of practical syllogisms "there" if it is not present in actual mental processes? The answer returns us to the notion of ends of action. Every intentional action implicitly makes a twofold claim. First, it makes a claim to be an action of a certain kind. To act intentionally is to act for an end, which means an anticipation of how things will be through having acted. Someone who, in Ramsey's image, just "senses the wise or good thing to do" still imagines an end of action. That is, they have a sense that they are trying to do *something*. But to imagine an end of action is, implicitly, to construe an action as a certain kind. For actions really do receive their species from their end, in the

---

124. *SWT*, 102; and above, Chapter 4, Section 2.
125. Ramsey, "The Case," 22; and above, Chapter 4, Section 1a.
126. Elizabeth Anscombe, *Intention* (Oxford: Basil Blackwell, 1976), 79.
127. Anscombe, *Intention*, 80.

sense that any intention entails a claim about the kind of action an action is.[128] Second, intentional actions implicitly make a further claim, which is that acting in such a way *is a way of acting well*. This is another way of expressing the structural assumption that all human beings desire to live their lives successfully. It means taking every intentional action as implying a claim to be a way of acting well. This claim is not a starting point, from which a determination of the means to achieve it is reached. That is the mistake of thinking of deliberation as a deductive process. Practical reason, as O'Donovan acutely recognizes, is not deductive, but inductive. Moral discernment centers on a moment of recognition, in which the "means" and the "end" arise together, as we have said. Yet this is not to say that no further end—acting well—is envisaged; it is. Although it is a mistake to picture deliberation in terms of chains of deductive reasoning from first principles, it is not a mistake to think that moral choices reflect some such order. When we act, we really do, though mostly implicitly, make a claim that we are doing a particular kind of thing, and that this is a way of acting well. What happens in discernment is that *a kind of action appears as a way of acting well*. This is the "act of discerning the time" that concludes deliberation, in O'Donovan's formulation.[129]

For this reason, action is fundamentally exposed to interrogation and judgment, as both Aquinas and O'Donovan see. These two implied claims open action up to a common world of intelligible kinds of action and credible or incredible accounts of the successful living of life. Actions are intrinsically exposed to judgment in two ways. First, they are exposed to the criticism that what they really amount to—which construal is morally decisive—is different to what has been claimed for them. Second, they are exposed to the criticism that such a kind of action is not really a way of acting well.

Both these lines of criticism center on the notion of kinds of action. What this shows us is that acting well depends upon seeing actions for what they really are, recognizing which construal of an action is truest. If discernment is about the way a kind of action *appears as* a way of acting well, then genuine success in action depends upon the true recognition of the moral kinds to which actions belong. How is such recognition attained? How do we "see" what a course of action really amounts to? Two comments are necessary. First, the only way to clarify such seeing is through language, by *naming*. If we want to clarify what a course of action means morally, that is, if we want to make sure we have recognized it for what it really is, then what we need to be able to do is to *call* it what it is. Second, recognizing actions for what they truly are is not primarily theoretically challenging; it is primarily practically challenging. Being able to see and to name a course of action rightly is practically difficult, because it happens under the pressures of time, temptation, and misdirection. It requires *wisdom*: a practical, affective grasp on the reality of the action and what it means.

---

128. This was the conclusion we reached above, in Chapter 4, Section 2c.
129. *F&S*, 215; and above, Chapter 4, Section 2b.

All of this explains why the book of Proverbs is concerned not only to set out the relevant moral kinds that correspond with wisdom, but to equip its readers to recognize them. For the successful living of life depends not only upon knowing which kinds of action are morally important, but also upon the ability to recognize them in practice. Creation is hospitable to certain kinds of action, and wisdom consists in the capacity, not just to know what they are in theory, but to *take up* those actions—to recognize them and do them. This requires not so much a theoretical knowledge of the moral order as an intimate, practical knowledge of it. For it is entirely possible for someone to know in theory what is the right kind of thing to do, but to lack the ability to see it. It is also inevitable that kinds of action that are in fact good will, in the moment, appear to us not to be so.[130] We are surrounded by dangers and temptations, deceitful invitations, and smooth speech, which tempt us to mischaracterize our situation and mistake the path of wisdom. It is for this reason that Proverbs lays great stress on the importance of remembering words of instruction. "Guard my words, my son; hide my commands within you" (7:1). The crucial thing, when it comes to actual living, is to be able to recognize what a course of action "adds up to"; and for this, we may need a word, not just in the background of our thinking, but "bound around the fingers" and "written in the heart" (7:3), a word we can trust even against our own intuitions. "Whoever trusts in his heart is a fool, whoever walks in wisdom will escape" (28:26). The ability to act well is, for Proverbs, closely tied to which words one attends to: "The simple trust every word, but the prudent appreciate their steps" (14:15). Where shall wisdom be found? "On the lips of the understanding will wisdom be found" (10:13).

What about, however, when the challenge *is* essentially theoretical, when what is in doubt seems to be precisely and simply the correct naming of an action? These are the cases that are the concern in Ramsey's article,[131] and in some of O'Donovan's thinking: situations in which a course of action appears to constitute an exception to a moral rule. Ramsey's argument, which O'Donovan largely follows, is that in such cases what is needed is moral learning. For there cannot be exceptions to the moral order itself.[132] Dilemmas must be susceptible of "rational resolution."[133] As we think about such situations, we clarify the shape of the moral order, understanding, for example, that to give a false statement to the interrogators in order to save the innocents we are hiding is more truly a rescue than a lie.[134]

In response, we may ask whether we may be quite so confident about what we learn from such moments. A person, under pressure, discerns that to give a false statement to the interrogators is the way to act well in that situation. That

---

130. This is a point we noted in our discussion of the right and the good in Aristotle, in Chapter 1, Section 4.

131. See above, Chapter 4, Section 1a.

132. *F&S*, 207, 226.

133. *RMO*, 199.

134. O'Donovan mentions this example in *F&S*, 227.

discernment is exposed to judgment. Was it *really* the way to act well? O'Donovan's and Ramsey's account of the matter rightly perceives that the answer to this question hinges on the question of what kind of action it most fundamentally was. Was it a lie? Was it a rescue? Perhaps, with O'Donovan, we may indeed conclude that such an act is more truly a rescue than a lie. We should be very cautious, however, about the suggestion that such a conclusion constitutes a piece of moral learning that can inform further deliberations. The dangers of such an approach are apparent in Ramsey's discussion of "the case of Mrs Bergmeier,"[135] in which he argues that a certain woman imprisoned in a concentration camp was justified in sleeping with a friendly camp guard so as to fall pregnant and be released, based on a regulation about pregnant women, in order to return to her family, who desperately needed her. Ramsey suggests that such a case shows us something deeper about the meaning of marital fidelity, and so of adultery: it could be, he suggests, that "this was not the meaning of the forbidden adultery."[136] Although Ramsey expresses some caution about this line of thought, it is consistent with his overall approach. What it illustrates is the way in which an account driven by a theoretical moral order may begin to float free of Scripture, finding ways to go behind the words that have been given, and so around them. The book of Proverbs should lead us to be skeptical about the practical value of such operations. This is not the approach to words of instruction that assists us to live well. The relevant warning is put starkly in Prov. 30:5-6.

The difference in approach at this point is rooted in different conceptions of moral order. For Ramsey, and for O'Donovan, the moral order is a coherent, intellectual whole.[137] The assumption is that there is a depth behind moral rules that remains susceptible to articulation in terms of rules. For the book of Proverbs, on the other hand, the moral order is simply the way the actual creation hangs together to support action. Moral rules do reflect this order, but the order itself is not a legal order. Laws may describe the more stable aspects of creation's order. But they do not gain their authority from that order, but from God's having given them. Other sayings point to real but far less stable aspects, and hence are certainly capable of "exceptions": "Do not answer a fool according to his folly ... Answer a fool according to his folly ... " (Prov. 26:4-5).

This makes it possible to imagine how there could be situations which, because "the days are evil" (Eph. 5:16), are *not* susceptible of rational resolution. When Aquinas thinks about the example of the Hebrew midwives who lie to save the Hebrew babies from being murdered, he concludes that such an action was, in a

---

135. Ramsey, "The Case," 83–90.

136. Ramsey, "The Case," 87–8.

137. Ramsey and O'Donovan do differ on how they understand this point. For O'Donovan, the moral order belongs to reality in a way that it does not, for Ramsey. Nevertheless, as we have argued, from a certain perspective the "reality" to which it belongs is, for O'Donovan, fundamentally intellectual. See above, Chapter 4, Section 3.

sense, sin, yet not a mortal one—indeed, in some respects, it was admirable.[138] This is unsatisfying if we are sure that dilemmas are susceptible of rational resolution. But perhaps they are not always. Perhaps sometimes we face situations in which the evil of the time means that a commandment that really does apply should not be obeyed. This would not strictly be an exception, because the rule really does apply. And yet, it would be an exception in the sense that the rule should not be obeyed in such a case. The advantage of such a perspective is that it does not sacrifice the integrity of the commandment for the sake of rational resolution. Moreover, it reflects the fact that what is required in such terrible moments is pre-eminently *practical* wisdom. Faced with such decisions, it is not theory that we need. In such a situation, theory would more probably allow us to deceive ourselves or justify to ourselves a bad course of action.

It should be stressed that such situations would not be *good*. They are not the result of the tensions placed upon wisdom by salvation history, for example. They are not, that is, equivalent to the challenge that the gospel may pose to the command to honor one's parents. That *is* a dilemma that is susceptible of rational resolution, because we have the promise that creation and redemption are works of the one wisdom of God. But perhaps this cannot always be said. Perhaps sometimes the evil deeds of others force upon us a situation in which no action is available to us that is wholly right from our perspective, and so what is to be done must be done with remorse. This may be why Aquinas thought that the action of the midwives had to be called sin in some sense.

On the view we have been developing here, therefore, Christian ethics, which attends to the way the call of Christ determines our life within this world, need not be so concerned to resolve such moral dilemmas. The moral order is not a timeless, unchangeable whole; it is creation's hospitality to good action, and the obligations laid upon us by the gospel. When it comes to discernment, the purchase upon creation's order we need is not theoretical, but practical. That is why, to use O'Donovan's expression, "practical reason looks for a word."[139] But the words we need are not only the words that disclose the wisdom of creation to us—though those remain of great value—but the words that disclose to us the further wisdom of what God has done in Christ. Whoever "hears these words of mine and does them will be like a wise man, who built his house on the rock." This leads us to the final part of our discussion.

4 Theory, Practice, and Christian Ethics

At a turning point in the epistle to the Hebrews, the author makes a comment that deserves attention for what it says about the relation of theoretical and practical knowledge within the Christian life: "Solid food belongs to the mature, those whose senses [*ta aisthētēria*] have been trained [*gegumnasmena*] by habituation

---

138. See above, Chapter 2, Section 2.
139. *SWT*, 12.

[*hexin*] to distinguish [*diakrisin*] good from evil" (5:14). The sentence in its context suggests at least two things.

First, it suggests that the distinction between theoretical and practical knowledge is important and meaningful within the Christian life. On the one hand, there is such a thing as "solid food," teaching that goes beyond the "milk" that is the elementary truths of God's word (5:12). There are things to be taught and understood. On the other hand, maturity does not consist merely in theoretical knowledge, but in a habituated, practical knowledge that enables a person to distinguish good and evil. Maturity is about no longer being "unskilled [or, 'inexperienced,' *apeiros*] in the word of righteousness" (5:13). Theoretical and practical knowledge thus appear to each have their own distinct integrity and internal momentum.

Second, the sentence suggests that there is a complex relationship between theoretical and practical knowledge in Christian existence. On the one hand, theoretical knowledge has a kind of priority. It seems to be both the basis and the goal of practical knowledge. The milk of "the fundamental elements of the oracles of God" (5:12) is the foundation on which someone may begin to grow to practical maturity. Theoretical knowledge also appears as a kind of goal of maturity: solid food is *for* the mature; it is something that is *reached*. On the other hand, within this movement there is a sense in which practical knowledge assumes a kind of priority. Solid food is for *the mature*; a practical maturity is required before certain teaching can be appropriate, or perhaps, meaningfully engaged.

In these respects, this passage reflects a pattern that can be observed in a number of places in the New Testament. At a turning point in some epistles, for instance, we find the word "therefore" (e.g., Rom. 12:1; Eph. 4:1). Before it lies material that, broadly speaking, can be characterized as declarative, an announcement of the truth and reality of the Gospel. After it we encounter material that is more obviously practical: instruction, exhortation, guidance. This progression from "theory" to "practice" is often observed.[140] What is less often noticed is the significance of the fact that the "practical" material is there at all. Practice, it turns out, does need to be unpacked and explored in its own right; it cannot simply be *deduced* from the theory. There are clear and constant connections, but there are also new themes that need to be developed, new ideas that need to be introduced.

One of the aims of this study has been to highlight the importance of this second point: to argue that there is such a thing as genuinely practical knowledge, and that this is important for understanding Christian ethics. What, finally, can we now conclude about this, and about the relation of practical knowledge to theoretical knowledge, conscious that these questions have recently resurfaced in some scholarship?[141]

---

140. As we noted above (Chapter 4, Section 2a), O'Donovan sees it as a fundamental structural point for Christian ethics. See, for example, *SWT*, 29; also "John Finnis on Moral Absolutes," 65.

141. For example, in his essay, "What Makes Theology Theological?" (*Journal of Analytic Theology* 3 [2015]: 17–28), John Webster defends a Thomistic position, in which "primarily

Let us first consider the issue of the preeminence of theoretical knowledge. In Chapter 1, we observed that Aristotle distinguished theoretical and practical reason on the basis that there were two fundamentally different types of objects: things that could not be otherwise, and things that could be. We have also seen, however, that this way of making the distinction can be found obscure. For, as Anscombe and Aquinas recognize, it is perfectly possible to reason about nonnecessary things without a view to action. So the important distinction does not seem to be between types of objects, but between thinking to a conclusion in knowledge, on the one hand, and thinking to action, on the other.

It was the difference in objects, though, that provided the basis for the superiority of theoretical reason. For Aristotle, wisdom's contemplation was supreme because its objects were the "most honourable" (*ta timiōmata*). If the distinction is instead merely between different aims and modes of reasoning, then the superiority of speculation evaporates. This might be seen as a desirable conclusion, freeing us from awkward aspects of Aristotle's practical philosophy. The Christian tradition, however, has often been reluctant to surrender the primacy of theoretical knowledge (although it has been a point of debate). The basic reason for this reluctance is essentially the one we see above: the conviction that there is "solid food" that, although it is for the mature, is not only for maturity. To take an example somewhat at random: commenting on the Aristotelian distinction in the introduction to his incomplete commentary on the *Nicomachean Ethics*, Peter Martyr Vermigli writes, "The things in which we believe and that are contained in the articles of faith pertain to contemplation since we perceive them but do not create them."[142]

There is an important difference, however, between Peter Martyr's reformed account of the matter and Aristotle's. What they have in common is the conviction that there are objects that *cannot* be the objects of our action, and so cannot be practically known, and that among these objects are "the most honourable" objects. There is a difference, though, regarding what these objects are. For Aristotle, as for Aquinas, they are the "divine realities" that "are necessary and eternal in themselves."[143] For Peter Martyr, on the other hand, although he is influenced by this way of thinking and may not have fully recognized this point, the category of objects that "we do not create" cannot be defined only by a metaphysical

---

and principally, theological intelligence intends eternal and necessary truths, by the gift of God penetrating to their depths. But by derivation these truths are regulative, and theological intelligence would have too narrow a view of the interests of faith if it did not also consider the realm of human conduct" (24–5). By contrast, Stanley Hauerwas's recent book, *The Work of Theology* (Grand Rapids, MI: Eerdmans, 2015), aims to show why and how theology "is an exercise in practical reason" (4, 109).

142. Peter Martyr Vermigli, *Commentary on Aristotle's Nicomachean Ethics*, ed. E. Campi and J. McLelland (The Peter Martyr Library, Vol. 9; Sixteenth-century essays and studies, Vol. 73; Kirksville, Missouri: Truman State University Press, 2006), 14.

143. *ST* II-II.45.3 ad2.

distinction. For to it belong "the articles of faith," and these include not only God himself, but also *his works*. That is why for Peter Martyr the priority of theoretical knowledge is a reflex not simply of metaphysics but of the doctrine of justification by faith. "In scripture," he writes, "speculation occurs first, inasmuch as we must first believe and be justified through faith."[144] The fundamental issue is not these objects' *eternity* but their *gratuity*.

It is true, as Anscombe points out, that we can think about anything "theoretically," that is, without a view to acting. It is *not* true, however, that we can think about anything *with* a view to accomplishing it or making it. Some things can be thought about only with a view to knowing them, or contemplating them. Among these things are the most excellent things. This is an insight in Aristotle's account of the matter that Christian theology can affirm. However, Christian theology must go on to say something Aristotle could not say, which is that these most excellent things include the historical events that are the actions of God in which faith places its confidence. These are things that do not, from outside, appear to be *ta timiōmata* at all, but rather *ta mē onta* (1 Cor. 1:28)—supremely, the cross of Christ. Yet these are the things that lie beyond the scope of our practical knowledge—for they are things that took place apart from us and now lie completed, behind us—on which the true preeminence of theoretical knowledge is founded.

The preeminence of speculative knowledge, then, is not founded on the metaphysical priority of thought—on the fact, as Aquinas puts it in his exposition of Aristotle's *Metaphysics*, that "only through intellect is man united with separated substances."[145] It arises, rather, from the doctrine of grace. Faith comes through what is heard, and what is heard comes through the word of the gospel (Rom. 10:17). Because of this, theology rightly has a kind of preeminence. It is a discipline of reflection upon the word that is foundational, and that comes as God acts *apart from us*. But as such, it also simultaneously deflates its own importance. The word comes apart from us; hence, our theoretical elaboration of it is not in itself what matters, and in itself has no priority. The preeminence of theology has nothing to do with the intrinsic superiority of thought as opposed to action, but only with the fact that the objects that matter most are not given to us to accomplish, but to believe in. When it comes to our own activity, thought has no priority over other forms of action. Faith, to recall O'Donovan's reformation emphasis, is the root of action. As human action, theology is merely another human work, and as such no more important than anything else—indeed, it lies under judgment.

Which returns us, in closing, to practical knowledge. In an essay from 1793 entitled, "On the Common Saying: That May Be Correct in Theory, but It Is of No Use in Practice," Kant pilloried the idea of "a wisdom that can see farther and more clearly with its dim moles' eyes fixed on experience than with the eyes belonging to

---

144. Vermigli, *Commentary*, 14.
145. Aquinas, *Exposition of* Metaphysics I.1.4.

a being that was made to stand erect and look at the heavens."[146] By way of response we may point out that this only counts as a criticism if the aim of wisdom is to *see far*. If, on the other hand, the aim of wisdom is to take the right steps here and now, then "moles' eyes" may be more valuable. At the end of the first section of that essay, Kant concludes that "someone instructed by experience" cannot proudly "send the adherent of theory back to school. For all this experience does not help him at all to escape the precept of theory, but at most only helps him to learn how theory could be better and more generally put to work, after one has adopted it into one's principles; but we are not speaking here of such pragmatic skill but only of principles."[147] The whole problem, however, lies in this speaking "only of principles" and not of "pragmatic skill." This is why the common saying concerns not the truth of theory but its usefulness. The person of experience does not desire to send the adherent of theory back *to school*, but into the world, to discover that there is "more to it" than can be seen from the perspective of theory. The "putting to work" of theory is its own business; it involves "pragmatic skill," a "knowledge" that is truly practical, a know-how that consists in an engagement with the reality of the world. It was an instinct for this truth which led Aristotle to hold that "We should attend to the undemonstrated words and beliefs of experienced and older people or of practically wise people, no less than to demonstrations, because their experienced eye enables them to see correctly."[148] The same impulse lies at the heart of the book of Proverbs: "The wisdom of the prudent is to discern their way" (14:8).

Christian ethics is the discipline of thought that accompanies and reflects upon this practical wisdom. As an essentially theoretical enterprise, it is somewhat awkward, for the primary kind of "knowledge" required for action is not theoretical but practical. Christian ethics can only ever be a "step-child," to use Ryle's analogy, of the practical wisdom of the Christian life. Its legitimacy, however, derives from the same logic that makes the "practical parts" of the New Testament necessary. This logic is twofold. First, practical knowledge is genuinely distinct from theoretical knowledge. It is true that, as Aquinas held, "divine realities" are the "measure" of human actions. But there is more to action according to this measure than the theoretical knowledge of it. There is the practical maturity of wisdom. And for this, second, we need instruction. We come to the task of living well as novices,

---

146. Immanuel Kant, "On the Common Saying: That May Be Correct in Theory, But It Is of No Use in Practice," in *Practical Philosophy*, trans. Mary J. Gregor (Cambridge: Cambridge University Press, 1996), 280 [8:277]. The following comments do not, of course, do justice to this interesting essay. Nor is the aim to vindicate the arguments of Kant's critic, Christian Garve.

147. Kant, "On the Common Saying," 290 [8:288-289].

148. *EN* 6.11, 1143b11–13. Note that Aquinas agrees with this maxim of Aristotle (*ST* II-II.49.2); cf. Daniel Mark Nelson, *The Priority of Prudence: Virtue and Natural Law in Thomas Aquinas and the Implications for Modern Ethics* (University Park: Pennsylvania State University Press, 1992), 79.

with a long history of blunders and the habits that come with them. If we are to learn to walk on the right path, to "walk carefully," as wise (Eph. 5:15), we will need constant correction, instruction that can lead us "along straight paths" (Prov. 4:11), the voice of our teacher, telling us "This is the way, walk in it!" (Isa. 30:21). The task of Christian ethics is to attend to and reflect upon this instruction. In a sense, this puts Christian ethics "between" doctrine and practice, as O'Donovan situates it.[149] Yet in another sense it is perhaps better to say that ethics is located *alongside* practice. For the knowledge it serves has its own integrity and momentum, which, although it depends upon and arises from "the articles of faith," is not exhausted by the theoretical apprehension of them. Christian ethics serves that maturity to which "solid food" rightly belongs, which consists in a practiced ability to discern good from evil—to discern the ways of wisdom; which comes through "paying attention" and "guarding" words of instruction; and which rests upon the hospitality to good action of the world God has made, and redeemed.

---

149. *SWT*, 67.

BIBLIOGRAPHY

Allan, D. J. "The Practical Syllogism." In *Autour d'Aristote: Recueil d'études de philosophie ancienne et médiévale offert à Msgr A. Mansion*, 325–40. Louvain: Publications Universitaires de Louvain, 1955.
Ansberry, Christopher B. *Be Wise, My Son, and Make My Heart Glad: An Exploration of the Courtly Nature of the Book of Proverbs*. Beihefte zur Zeitschrift für die alttestamentliche Wissenschaft 422. Berlin: de Gruyter, 2011.
Ansberry, Christopher B. "What Does Jerusalem Have to Do with Athens?: The Moral Vision of the Book of Proverbs and Aristotle's *Nicomachean Ethics*." *Hebrew Studies* 51 (2010): 147–73.
Anscombe, G. E. M. *Intention*. Oxford: Basil Blackwell, 1976.
Arendt, Hannah. *The Human Condition*. Chicago: University of Chicago Press, 1958.
Aristotle. *Nicomachean Ethics*. Greek text and translation by H. Rackham. Loeb Classical Library 73. Cambridge, MA: Harvard University Press, 1926.
Aristotle. *Nicomachean Ethics*. Translated and edited by T. H. Irwin. 2nd ed. Indianapolis: Hackett, 1999.
Aristotle. *Nicomachean Ethics*. Translated and edited by Roger Crisp. Cambridge: Cambridge University Press, 2000.
Aristotle. *The Metaphysics*. Translated by Hugh Lawson-Tancred. London: Penguin, 1998.
Aristotle. "Movement of Animals" (*De Motu Animalium*). Translated by A. S. L. Farquharson. In *The Complete Works of Aristotle*, Vol. 1, edited by Jonathan Barnes, 1087–96. Princeton, NJ: Princeton University Press, 1984.
Aristotle. "On the Soul" (*De Anima*). Translated by J. A. Smith. In *The Complete Works of Aristotle*, Vol. 1, edited by Jonathan Barnes, 641–92. Princeton, NJ: Princeton University Press, 1984.
Augustine. *On the Trinity, Books 8–15*. Translated by Stephen McKenna. Edited by Gareth Matthews. Cambridge: Cambridge University Press, 2002.
Augustine. *The Trinity*. Translated by Edmund Hill. Brooklyn, NY: New City Press, 1991.
Baris, Michael. "Iniquities Ensnare the Wicked: The Ethical Theory of Proverbs 1–9." *Hebrew Studies* 56 (2015): 129–44.
Barnes, Jonathan. *Aristotle*. Oxford and New York: Oxford University Press, 1982.
Barth, Karl. "Brief an Karl Heim." *Zwischen den Zeiten* 9 (1931): 451–3.
Barth, Karl. *Church Dogmatics*. Translated by G. W. Bromiley and T. F. Torrance. Edinburgh: T&T Clark, 1956–1962.
Barth, Karl. *The Christian Life: Church Dogmatics IV, 4 Lecture Fragments*. Translated by G. W. Bromiley. Grand Rapids, MI: Eerdmans, 1981.
Barth, Karl. *Ethics*. Edited by Dietrich Braun. Translated by G. W. Bromiley. Edinburgh: T&T Clark, 1981.
Baumann, Gerlinde. *Die Weisheitsgestalt in Proverbien 1–9*. Forschungen zum Alten Testament 16. Tübingen: Mohr, 1996.
Biggar, Nigel. *The Hastening that Waits: Karl Barth's Ethics*. Oxford: Clarendon, 1993.
Bowlin, John. *Contingency and Fortune in Aquinas's Ethics*. Cambridge: Cambridge University Press, 1999.

Broadie, Sarah. *Ethics with Aristotle*. New York: Oxford University Press, 1991.
Brock, Brian. *Singing the Ethos of God: On the Place of Christian Ethics in Scripture*. Grand Rapids, MI: Eerdmans, 2007.
Brown, William P. "The Pedagogy of Proverbs 10:1–31:9." In *Character and Scripture: Moral Formation, Community, and Biblical Interpretation*, edited by William P. Brown, 150–82. Grand Rapids, MI: Eerdmans, 2002.
Chaplin, Jonathan. "Political Eschatology and Responsible Government: Oliver O'Donovan's 'Christian Liberalism'." In *A Royal Priesthood: The Use of the Bible Ethically and Politically. A Dialogue with Oliver O'Donovan*, edited by C. Bartholomew, J. Chaplin, R. Song, and A. Wolters, 265–308. Scripture and Hermeneutics 3. Carlisle: Paternoster, 2002.
Charles, David. *Aristotle's Philosophy of Action*. London: Duckworth, 1984.
Conley, Kieran. *A Theology of Wisdom: A Study in St. Thomas*. Dubuque, IO: Priory Press, 1963.
Cooper, John M. *Reason and Human Good in Aristotle*. Cambridge, MA: Harvard University Press, 1975.
Decosimo, David. *Ethics as a Work of Charity: Thomas Aquinas and Pagan Virtue*. Stanford: Stanford University Press, 2014.
Dell, Katharine. *"Get Wisdom, Get Insight": An Introduction to Israel's Wisdom Literature*. London: Darton, Longman and Todd, 2000.
Dell, Katharine. *The Book of Proverbs in Social and Theological Context*. Cambridge: Cambridge University Press, 2006.
Diem, W. M. "Review of Stephen J. Jensen, *Knowing the Natural Law*." *Studies in Christian Ethics* 29, no. 4 (2016): 356–9.
Dunne, Joseph. *Back to the Rough Ground: "Phronesis" and "Techne" in Modern Philosophy and in Aristotle*. Notre Dame and London: University of Notre Dame Press, 1993.
Elliger, K. and W. Rudolph. *Iob et Proverbia*. Biblica Hebraica Stuttgartensia, Vol. 12. Stuttgart: Deutsche Bibelstiftung, 1977.
Errington, Andrew. "Authority and Reality in the Work of Oliver O'Donovan." *Studies in Christian Ethics* 29, no. 4 (2016): 371–85.
Errington, Andrew. "Between Justice and Tradition: Oliver O'Donovan's Political Theory and the Problem of Multiculturalism." *Studies in Christian Ethics* 27, no. 4 (2014): 417–30.
Farmer, K. A. *Who Knows What Is Good? A Commentary on the Books of Proverbs and Ecclesiastes*. Grand Rapids, MI: Eerdmans, 1991.
Fiddes, Paul. *Seeing the World and Knowing God: Hebrew Wisdom and Christian Doctrine in a Late-Modern Context*. Oxford: Oxford University Press, 2013.
Finnis, John. *Aquinas: Moral, Political, and Legal Theory*. Oxford: Oxford University Press, 1998.
Finnis, John. *Fundamentals of Ethics*. Oxford: Clarendon, 1983.
Finnis, John. *Natural Law and Natural Rights*. Oxford: Clarendon, 1980.
Finnis, John. *Reason in Action: Collected Essays: Volume 1*. Oxford: Oxford University Press, 2011.
Ford, David. *Christian Wisdom: Desiring God and Learning in Love*. Cambridge Studies in Christian Doctrine. Cambridge: Cambridge University Press, 2007.
Fox, Michael V. "Ideas of Wisdom in Proverbs 1–9." *Journal of Biblical Literature* 116, no. 4 (1997): 613–33.
Fox, Michael V. *Proverbs 1–9*. The Anchor Bible. New York: Doubleday, 2000.
Fox, Michael V. *Proverbs 10–31*. The Anchor Bible. New York: Doubleday, 2009.

Gadamer, Hans-Georg. "The Nature of Things and the Language of Things." In *Philosophical Hermeneutics*, edited and translated by David E. Linge, 69–81. Berkeley and Los Angeles: University of California Press, 1977.
Gilby, Thomas. *St. Thomas Aquinas: Philosophical Texts*. London: Oxford University Press, 1951.
Grabill, Stephen J. *Rediscovering the Natural Law in Reformed Theological Ethics*. Grand Rapids, MI: Eerdmans, 2006.
Gregory of Nazianzus. *On God and Christ: The Five Theological Orations and Two Letters to Cledonius*. Translated by Lionel Wickham. Crestwood: St Vladimir's Seminary Press, 2002.
Gregory of Nazianzus. *The Five Theological Orations of Gregory of Nazianzus*. Edited by A. J. Mason. Cambridge: Cambridge University Press, 1899.
Habel, N. C. "The Symbolism of Wisdom in Proverbs 1–9." *Interpretation* 26, no. 2 (1972): 131–57.
Hamann, J. G. *Londoner Schriften*. Edited by Oswald Bayer and Bernd Weißenborn. München: C. H Beck, 1993.
Hardie, W. F. R. *Aristotle's Ethical Theory*. Oxford: Clarendon, 1980.
Hauerwas, Stanley. *Dispatches from the Front*. Durham: Duke University Press, 1994.
Hauerwas, Stanley. *The Work of Theology*. Grand Rapids, MI: Eerdmans, 2015.
Heppe, Heinrich. *Reformed Dogmatics*. Edited by Ernst Bizer. Translated by G. T. Thomson. Eugene, OR: Wipf and Stock, 2007.
Hintikka, Jaakko. *Knowledge and the Known: Historical Perspectives on Epistemology*. Dordrecht: D. Reidel, 1974.
Hoffmann, Tobias. "Prudence and Practical Principles." In *Aquinas and the Nicomachean Ethics*, edited by Tobias Hoffmann, Jörn Müller, and Matthias Perkams, 165–83. Cambridge: Cambridge University Press, 2013.
Hooker, Richard. *Of the Laws of Ecclesiastical Polity*. Edited by Arthur Stephen McGrade. Cambridge: Cambridge University Press, 1989.
Hume, David. *An Enquiry Concerning Human Understanding*. Indianapolis: Hackett, 1993.
Insole, Christopher J. *The Intolerable God: Kant's Theological Journey*. Grand Rapids, MI: Eerdmans, 2016.
Irwin, T. H. *Aristotle's First Principles*. Oxford: Clarendon, 1988.
Irwin, T. H. *The Development of Ethics: A Historical and Critical Study. Volume I: From Socrates to the Reformation*. Oxford: Oxford University Press, 2007.
Irwin, T. H. "The Metaphysical and Psychological Basis of Aristotle's Ethics." In *Essays on Aristotle's Ethics*, edited by A. O. Rorty, 35–53. Berkeley: University of California Press, 1980.
Jensen, Steven J. *Knowing the Natural Law: From Precepts and Inclinations to Deriving Oughts*. Washington, DC: Catholic University of America Press, 2015.
Jenson, Robert. *Systematic Theology, Volume 2: The Works of God*. Oxford: Oxford University Press, 1999.
Jordan, Mark D. *Ordering Wisdom: The Hierarchy of Philosophical Discourses in Aquinas*. Notre Dame: University of Notre Dame Press, 1986.
Kant, Immanuel. *Critique of Practical Reason*. Translated by Mary Gregor. Cambridge: Cambridge University Press, 2015.
Kant, Immanuel. *Groundwork of the Metaphysics of Morals*. Translated by Mary Gregor. Cambridge: Cambridge University Press, 1998.
Kant, Immanuel. "On the Common Saying: That May Be Correct in Theory, but It Is of No Use in Practice." In Immanuel Kant, *Practical Philosophy*, translated by Mary J. Gregor, 279–309. Cambridge: Cambridge University Press, 1996.

Kelsey, David. *Eccentric Existence: A Theological Anthropology*. 2 vols. Louisville, Kentucky: Westminster John Knox, 2009.
Kenny, Anthony. *The Aristotelian Ethics: A Study of the Relationship between the Eudemian and Nicomachean Ethics of Aristotle*. Oxford: Clarendon, 1978.
Kenny, Anthony. *Aristotle on the Perfect Life*. Oxford: Clarendon, 1992.
Kenny, Anthony. *Aquinas*. Oxford: Oxford University Press, 1980.
Kerr, Fergus. *After Aquinas: Versions of Thomism*. Malden, MA: Blackwell, 2002.
Kerr, Fergus. "Doctrine of God and Theological Ethics According to Thomas Aquinas." In *The Doctrine of God and Theological Ethics*, edited by A. J. Torrance and M. Banner, 71–84. London: T&T Clark, 2006.
Kovacs, Brian Watson. *Sociological-Structural Constraints upon Wisdom: The Spatial and Temporal Matrix of Proverbs 15:28–22:16*. PhD diss., Vanderbilt University, 1978.
Kraut, Richard. *Aristotle on the Human Good*. Princeton, NJ: Princeton University Press, 1989.
Kraut, Richard. "*Aristotle's First Principles*, by Terence Irwin. Book Review." *The Philosophical Review* 101, no. 2 (1992): 365–71.
Kraut, Richard. "Aristotle's Ethics." In *The Stanford Encyclopedia of Philosophy* (Summer 2014 Edition), edited by Edward N. Zalta. http://plato.stanford.edu/archives/sum2014/entries/aristotle-ethics/.
Kühn, Ulrich. *Via Caritatis: Theologie des Gesetzes bei Thomas von Aquin*. Berlin: Evangelische Verlagsanstalt, 1964.
Lisska, Anthony J. *Aquinas's Theory of Natural Law: An Analytical Reconstruction*. Oxford: Clarendon, 1996.
Loewen, Susanne Guenther. "Jesus Christ as Woman Wisdom? Complicating the Gender of Christ." *Religious Studies and Theology* 30 (2011): 71–82.
MacIntyre, Alasdair. *Whose Justice? Which Rationality?* London: Duckworth, 1988.
MacIntyre, Alasdair. *Three Rival Versions of Moral Enquiry: Encyclopaedia, Genealogy, and Tradition*. London: Duckworth, 1990.
McCarthy, David M. and Charles R. Pinches. "Craft as a Place of Knowing in Natural Law." *Studies in Christian Ethics* 29, no. 4 (2016): 386–408.
McCreesh, Thomas. "The Book of Proverbs: Chapters 1–15." *Catholic Biblical Quarterly* 70, no. 2 (2008): 352–3.
McInerny, Ralph. *Aquinas on Human Action: A Theory of Practice*. Washington, DC: Catholic University of America Press, 1992.
McInerny, Ralph. "Ethics." In *The Cambridge Companion to Aquinas*, edited by N. Kretzmann and E. Stump, 196–216. Cambridge: Cambridge University Press, 1993.
McInerny, Ralph, ed. *Thomas Aquinas: Selected Writings*. London: Penguin, 1998.
McKenny, Gerald. *The Analogy of Grace: Karl Barth's Moral Theology*. Oxford: Oxford University Press, 2010.
McWhorter, Matthew R. "Intrinsic Moral Evils in the Middle Ages: Augustine as a Source of the Theological Doctrine." *Studies in Christian Ethics* 29, no. 4 (2016): 409–23.
Moberly, R. W. L. "Solomon and Job: Divine Wisdom in Human Life." In *Where Shall Wisdom Be Found?* edited by Stephen Barton, 1–17. Edinburgh: T&T Clark, 1999.
Moberly, R. W. L. *The Bible, Theology, and Faith: A Study of Abraham and Jesus*. Cambridge: Cambridge University Press, 2000.
Moran, Richard. "Anscombe on 'Practical Knowledge.'" *Royal Institute of Philosophy Supplement* 55 (2004): 43–68.
Murphy, Roland E. *Proverbs*. Word Biblical Commentary 22. Nashville: Thomas Nelson, 1998.

Nagel, Thomas. "Aristotle on Eudaimonia." In *Essays on Aristotle's Ethics*, edited by A. O. Rorty, 7–14. Berkeley: University of Chicago Press, 1980.

Nelson, Daniel Mark. *The Priority of Prudence: Virtue and Natural Law in Thomas Aquinas and the Implications for Modern Ethics*. University Park: Pennsylvania State University Press, 1992.

O'Donovan, Oliver. *Church in Crisis: The Gay Controversy and the Anglican Communion*. Eugene, OR: Cascade, 2008.

O'Donovan, Oliver. *Common Objects of Love: Moral Reflection and the Shaping of Community*. Grand Rapids, MI: Eerdmans, 2002.

O'Donovan, Oliver. *The Desire of the Nations: Rediscovering the Roots of Political Theology*. Cambridge: Cambridge University Press, 1996.

O'Donovan, Oliver. *Entering into Rest. Ethics as Theology 3*. Grand Rapids, MI: Eerdmans, 2017.

O'Donovan, Joan. "From Justification to Justice: The Cranmerian Prayer Book Legacy." In *The Authority of the Gospel: Explorations in Moral and Pastoral Theology in Honor of Oliver O'Donovan*, edited by Robert Song and Brent Waters, 104–21. Grand Rapids, MI: Eerdmans, 2015.

O'Donovan, Oliver. *Finding and Seeking. Ethics as Theology 2*. Grand Rapids, MI: Eerdmans, 2014.

O'Donovan, Oliver. "How Can Theology Be Moral?" *Journal of Religious Ethics* 17, no. 2 (1989): 81–94.

O'Donovan, Oliver. "John Finnis on Moral Absolutes." *Studies in Christian Ethics* 6, no. 2 (1993): 50–66.

O'Donovan, Oliver. "The Moral Authority of Scripture." In *Scripture's Doctrine and Theology's Bible: How the New Testament Shapes Christian Dogmatics*, edited by Markus Bockmuel and Alan J. Torrance, 165–75. Grand Rapids, MI: Baker, 2008.

O'Donovan, Oliver. *On the Thirty Nine Articles: A Conversation with Tudor Christianity*. Exeter: Paternoster, 1986.

O'Donovan, Oliver. "The Political Thought of the Book of Revelation." *Tyndale Bulletin* 37 (1986): 61–94. Revised as "History and Politics in the Book of Revelation." In *Bonds of Imperfection: Christian Politics, Past and Present*, edited by Oliver O'Donovan and Joan Lockwood O'Donovan, 25–47. Grand Rapids, MI: Eerdmans, 2004.

O'Donovan, Oliver. "Prayer and Morality in the Sermon on the Mount." *Studies in Christian Ethics* 22, no. 1 (2000): 21–33.

O'Donovan, Oliver. *Resurrection and Moral Order: An Outline for Evangelical Ethics*. 2nd ed. Grand Rapids, MI: Eerdmans, 1994.

O'Donovan, Oliver. "Scripture and Christian Ethics." *ANVIL* 24, no. 1 (2007): 21–9.

O'Donovan, Oliver. *Self, World, and Time. Ethics as Theology 1: An Induction*. Grand Rapids, MI: Eerdmans, 2013.

O'Donovan, Oliver. *The Ways of Judgment*. Grand Rapids, MI: Eerdmans, 2005.

O'Donovan, Oliver. *The Problem of Self-Love in St. Augustine*. Eugene, OR: Wipf and Stock, 2006.

Owen, Joseph. "Aristotle and Aquinas." In *The Cambridge Companion to Aquinas*, edited by N. Kretzmann and E. Stump, 38–59. Cambridge: Cambridge University Press, 1993.

Parsons, Susan F. "The Practice of Christian Ethics: Mindfulness and Faith." *Studies in Christian Ethics* 25, no. 4 (2012): 442–53.

Perdue, Leo G. "Liminality as a Social Setting for Wisdom Instructions." *Zeitschrift für die alttestamentliche Wissenschaft* 93, no. 1 (1981): 114–26.

Pickstock, Catherine. "The One Story: A Critique of David Kelsey's Theological Robotics." *Modern Theology* 27, no. 1 (2011): 26–40.
Pinches, Charles R. *Theology and Action: After Theory in Christian Ethics*. Grand Rapids, MI: Eerdmans, 2002.
Porter, Jean. *The Recovery of Virtue: The Relevance of Aquinas for Christian Ethics*. Louisville, Kentucky: Westminster John Knox, 1990.
Rad, Gerhard von. *Old Testament Theology, Volume 1: The Theology of Israel's Historical Traditions*. Translated by D. M. G. Stalker. Edinburgh: Oliver and Boyd, 1962.
Rad, Gerhard von. *Wisdom in Israel*. London: SCM, 1972.
Ramsey, Paul. "The Case of the Curious Exception." In *Norm and Context in Christian Ethics*, edited by Gene H. Outka and Paul Ramsey, 67–135. London: SCM, 1968.
Rhonheimer, Martin. "The Perspective of the Acting Person and the Nature of Practical Reason: The 'Object of the Human Act' in Thomistic Anthropology of Action." In *The Perspective of the Acting Person: Essays in the Renewal of Thomistic Moral Philosophy*, edited by Martin Rhonheimer and William F. Murphy, 195–249. Washington, DC: Catholic University of America Press, 2011.
Rist, John M. *Augustine Deformed: Love, Sin, and Freedom in the Western Moral Tradition*. Cambridge: Cambridge University Press, 2014.
Roberts, A. and J. Donaldson, eds. *The Ante-Nicene Fathers*. Grand Rapids, MI: Eerdmans, 1989.
Ryle, Gilbert. *The Concept of Mind*. New York: Barnes and Noble, 1950.
Santas, Gerasimos. "Aristotle on Practical Inference, the Explanation of Action, and Akrasia." *Phronesis* 14, no. 2 (1969): 162–89.
Schaff, Philip, and Henry Wace, eds. *A Select Library of the Nicene and Post-Nicene Fathers of the Christian Church*. 2 series. Buffalo, NY: Christian Literature, 1887–1894; Reprint, Grand Rapids, MI: Eerdmans, 1952–1956.
Setiya, Kieren. "Practical Knowledge Revisited." *Ethics* 120, no. 1 (2009): 128–37.
Spaemann, Robert. *Glück und Wohlwollen: Versuch über Ethik*. Stuttgart: Klett-Cotta, 1989.
Spaemann, Robert. *Happiness and Benevolence*. Translated by Jeremiah Alberg. Notre Dame: University of Notre Dame, 2000.
Spaemann, Robert. "Individual Actions." In *A Robert Spaemann Reader: Philosophical Essays on Nature, God, and the Human Person*, edited and translated by D. C. Schindler and Jeanne Heffernan Schindler, 139–53. Oxford: Oxford University Press, 2015.
Spaemann, Robert. "Nature." in *A Robert Spaemann Reader: Philosophical Essays on Nature, God, and the Human Person*, edited and translated by D. C. Schindler and Jeanne Heffernan Schindler, 139–53. Oxford: Oxford University Press, 2015.
Spaemann, Robert. *Persons: The Difference between "Someone" and "Something"*. Translated by Oliver O'Donovan. Oxford: Oxford University Press, 2006. Translation of *Personen: Versuche über den Unterschied zwischen 'etwas' und 'jemand'*. Stuttgart: Klett-Cotta, 1996.
Spaemann, Robert. *Philosophische Essays*. Stuttgart: Reclam, 1994.
Stewart, Anne W. *Poetic Ethics in Proverbs: Wisdom Literature and the Shaping of the Moral Self*. New York: Cambridge University Press, 2016.
Stewart, Anne W. "Wisdom's Imagination: Moral Reasoning and the Book of Proverbs." *Journal for the Study of the Old Testament* 40, no. 3 (2016): 351–72.
Stewart, J. A. *Notes on the Nicomachean Ethics*. 2 vols. Clarendon: Oxford, 1892.
Thomas Aquinas. *Commentary on Aristotle's Nicomachean Ethics*. Translated by C. J. Litzinger, O. P. Notre Dame, IN: Dumb Ox Books, 1993.

Thomas Aquinas. "Commentary on Sentences I, Prologue." In *Thomas Aquinas: Selected Writings*, edited and translated by Ralph McInerny, 50–84. London: Penguin, 1998.
Thomas Aquinas. *The Disputed Questions on Truth [Questiones Disputatae De Veritate]*. 3 vols. Translated by R. W. Mulligan, S. J. Chicago: Henry Regnery Company, 1952–1954.
Thomas Aquinas. "Exposition of Metaphysics, Preface and I, 1–3." In *Thomas Aquinas: Selected Writings*, edited and translated by Ralph McInerny, 718–43. London: Penguin, 1998.
Thomas Aquinas. "Inaugural Sermons." In *Thomas Aquinas: Selected Writings*, edited and translated by Ralph McInerny, 5–17. London: Penguin, 1998.
Thomas Aquinas. *Opera Omnia. Iussu Leonis XIII*, Rome: Vatican Polyglot Press, 1882–.
Thomas Aquinas. *Scriptum Super Sententiis. Opera Omnia*, Parma: Fiaccadori, 1856. http://www.corpusthomisticum.org/snp2035.html#6903.
Thomas Aquinas. *Summa Contra Gentiles*. Translated by Anton C. Pegis. New York: Hanover House, 1955–1957.
Thomas Aquinas. *Summa Theologiae*. 61 vols. Cambridge: Blackfriars, 1964–1981.
Thomas Aquinas. *Summa Theologica*. New York: Benziger Brothers, 1911–1925.
Torrell, Jean-Pierre. *Saint Thomas Aquinas, Volume 1: The Person and His Work*. Translated by Robert Royal. Washington, DC: Catholic University of America Press, 1996.
Torrell, Jean-Pierre. *Saint Thomas Aquinas, Volume 2: Spiritual Master*. Translated by Robert Royal. Washington, DC: Catholic University of America Press, 2003.
Treier, Daniel J. *Proverbs & Ecclesiastes*. Brazos Theological Commentary on the Bible. Grand Rapids, MI: Brazos, 2011.
Treier, Daniel J. *Virtue and the Voice of God: Toward Theology as Wisdom*. Grand Rapids, MI: Eerdmans, 2006.
Van Leeuwen, Raymond C. *Context and Meaning in Proverbs 25–27*. SBL Dissertation Series 96. Atlanta, GA: Scholars, 1988.
Van Leeuwen, Raymond C. "Cosmos, Temple, House: Building and Wisdom in Mesopotamia and Israel." In *Wisdom Literature in Mesopotamia and Israel*, edited by Richard J. Clifford, 67–90. SBL Symposium Series 36. Atlanta: Society of Biblical Literature, 2007.
Van Leeuwen, Raymond C. "Liminality and Worldview in Proverbs 1–9." *Semeia* 50 (1990): 111–44.
Van Leeuwen, Raymond C. *Proverbs*. New Interpreter's Bible, Vol. 5. Nashville: Abingdon, 1997.
VanDrunen, David. *Divine Covenants and Moral Order: A Biblical Theology of Natural Law*. Grand Rapids, MI: Eerdmans, 2014.
VanDrunen, David. *Natural Law and the Two Kingdoms: A Study in the Development of Reformed Social Thought*. Grand Rapids, MI: Eerdmans, 2010.
VanDrunen, David. "Wisdom and the Natural Moral Order: The Contribution of Proverbs to a Christian Theology of Natural Law." *Journal of the Society of Christian Ethics* 33, no. 1 (2013): 153–68.
Vawter, Bruce. "Prov 8:22: Wisdom and Creation." *Journal of Biblical Literature* 99, no. 2 (1980): 205–16.
Vermigli, Peter Martyr. *Commentary on Aristotle's Nicomachean Ethics*. Edited by E. Campi and J. McLelland. The Peter Martyr Library, Vol. 9. Sixteenth century essays and studies 73. Kirksville, MO: Truman State University Press, 2006.
Vranas, Peter B. M. "Aristotle on the Best Good: Is 'Nicomachean Ethics' 1094a18–22 Fallacious?" *Phronesis* 50, no. 2 (2005): 116–28.

Waltke, Bruce. *The Book of Proverbs, Chapters 1–15*. New International Commentary on the Old Testament. Grand Rapids, MI: Eerdmans, 2004.

Webster, John. "What Makes Theology Theological?" *Journal of Analytic Theology* 3 (2015): 17–28.

Weeks, Stuart. "The Context and Meaning of Proverbs 30a." *Journal of Biblical Literature* 125, no. 3 (2006): 433–42.

Weeks, Stuart. *Instruction and Imagery in Proverbs 1–9*. Oxford: Oxford University Press, 2007.

Westberg, Daniel. *Renewing Moral Theology: Christian Ethics as Action, Character, and Grace*. Downer's Grove, IL: Imperial Valley Press, 2015.

Westberg, Daniel. *Right Practical Reason: Aristotle, Action, and Prudence in Aquinas*. Oxford: Clarendon, 1994.

Whybray, R. N. *The Composition of the Book of Proverbs*. JSOTS 168. Sheffield: Sheffield Academic Press, 1994.

Wiggins, David. "Deliberation and Practical Reason." *Proceedings of the Aristotelian Society* 76 (1975–1976): 29–51.

Wiggins, David. "Practical Knowledge: Knowing How to and Knowing That." *Mind* 121 (2012): 97–130.

Woodard-Lehman, Derek Alan. "Reason after Revelation: Karl Barth on Divine Word and Human Words." *Modern Theology* 33, no. 1 (2017): 92–115.

Wright, Robert, ed. *Ancient Christian Commentary on Scripture, Volume IX: Proverbs, Ecclesiastes, Song of Solomon*. Downer's Grove, IL: Imperial Valley Press, 2005.

Xenophon. *Memorabilia*. Translated by E. C. Marchant. LOEB Classical Library. Cambridge, MA: Harvard University Press, 2013.

Zaborowski, Holger. *Robert Spaemann's Philosophy of the Human Person: Nature, Freedom, and the Critique of Modernity*. Oxford Theological Monographs. Oxford: Oxford University Press, 2010.

GENERAL INDEX

Ackrill, J. L. 22 n.20, 25
action. *See also* practical knowledge
  and choice (*prohairesis*) 33–6, 73, 78
  and circumstances 83, 85
  construal of 31, 82, 85, 217–21 (*see also* perception)
  ends of (*see* ends *and* objects)
  generic character of (*see* kinds of action)
  goodness of 51, 53
  intelligibility of 176, 179
  and intention 54–7, 171, 176–9, 217–18
  internal and external 52–9, 83–4, 86, 170, 177
  intrinsically evil 50 n.89, 53–4, 210
  naming of 8, 121–2, 138–9, 198–9, 210–19
  policies of 139 n.247
  and principles 33–4, 75 n.277, 135, 137
  and purposes 53, 59, 170–1, 176–9
  and thinking 41–2, 160–2, 174–5, 197
admiration. *See under* love
analogy 67–8, 100–1, 124, 130–1, 195, 204
anger 131, 139, 197
Ansberry, Christopher 4, 12, 115 n.134, 138
Anscombe, Elizabeth 25, 30, 119–21, 126, 130, 217, 223–4
anticipation 169–70, 176, 217
Aquinas. *See* Thomas Aquinas
Arendt, Hannah 30–1, 45, 128–30, 195–6
Aristotle. *See also* practical syllogism; prudence; reason; wisdom
  distinction between practical and theoretical 7, 24–5, 42, 223
  happiness 18–25
  influence on Aquinas 39, 72, 74–5, 98, 101, 127
  Metaphysics 31, 129, 194–7
  Nicomachean Ethics 19–38
  and O'Donovan 157, 190
  poiēsis and *praxis* 30–1, 101, 128–9
  Polis 21, 23–5, 37–9, 158, 162

practical reason 11, 28–38, 48, 134, 211
prudence (*see under* prudence)
wisdom (*sophia*) 3, 26–8, 158, 194
  (*see also* eternal objects)
artisan 44, 67–8, 101, 127–9
Athanasius 91–2, 95, 97, 100, 131
Augustine
  higher and lower reason 42 n.16
  lying 9, 53–4
  and O'Donovan 158–9, 165, 167, 171
  and Proverbs 6, 125, 209 n.91
  prudence 135, 175
  wisdom 3, 15, 127–8, 183
authority 160–2, 190, 199, 220

Baris, Michael 12, 16
Barth, Karl 125 n.178, 184, 194, 202 n.40, 211–17
Baumann, Gerlinde 92 n.10, 94, 97, 99
Bonhoeffer, Dietrich 155
Bowlin, John 40–1, 58 n.140, 62, 137 n.230
Brown, William P. 4, 110 n.106, 138 n.239

call of wisdom
  and Christian ethics 195, 208, 214–16
  O'Donovan and 141, 164–6, 168
  in Proverbs 94, 103–6, 118, 131–3, 199, 204–5
casuistry. *See* moral learning
Chaplin, Jonathan 190 n.372
character 110–11
Charles, David 34–5
Christian ethics. *See* ethics
Cole, Jonathan 190 n.372
connaturality 46, 75, 122
contemplation 15, 22–6, 127, 140, 158, 223
contingency 40–2, 132, 163–4, 186. *See also* indeterminacy
Cooper, John 20, 31, 34–7, 82, 85
courage 37, 59

created order. *See also* creation; hospitality of creation; nature
   in Christian ethics 194, 210, 221
   and eternal law 131–3
   and kinds of action 138–9, 162, 172, 198
   and natural law 133, 203–4
   as natural moral order 3, 131, 199, 208–10, 216–17, 220–1
   in O'Donovan 140–1, 145–54, 162–5, 168, 174, 182–91, 220
   in Proverbs 112, 138–9
   and virtues 64
creation. *See also* created order; God; hospitality of creation; wisdom
   divine action 7, 66, 89, 207
   doctrine of 38, 66–9, 126–8, 132, 197, 205

Decosimo, David 64, 133, 136 n.226, 201 n.37
deliberation. *See also* action; ends
   in Aquinas 62, 78–86, 134–40
   in Aristotle 26, 29–32
   and construal of actions 177, 217–21
   in O'Donovan 170–2
   in Proverbs 134–40
Dell, Katharine 3, 11, 92 n.10, 94, 96–7, 99
deontology and teleology 36, 157–8, 204
desire 1–2, 26–7, 73, 117–18, 158, 171
discernment 78, 170–5, 210–21. *See also* deliberation; perception
discipline 111
discussion 7
Dunne, Joseph 22 n.20, 31–2, 102–3, 120, 128–9

ends. *See also* action; kinds of action; objects; virtues
   of action 62, 145, 175–81
   in creation 66
   and means 29–30, 78–80, 84, 134, 176–8, 217
   movement to action from 20, 26–7, 39
   in practical reasoning 29, 80
   specifying action 51, 55, 57, 170–1, 217–18
Errington, Andrew 161 n.160, 190 n.372, 199 n.26
eschatology 180, 199–200, 210. *See also* hope; salvation history

eternal law 18, 38–9, 44, 58–71, 89, 126–34
   as divine *ratio* 65–9, 101, 131–3, 196
eternal objects
   in Aristotle 15, 24–5
   in Christian thought 39, 47, 127, 183, 209, 223–4
ethics
   and created order 203, 210
   relation to theology 156, 162–3, 221–6
   task of 3, 10, 144, 151, 167
Eucharist 6, 199
Eudaimonism. *See* happiness
exceptions 143–4, 147, 172, 219–21
experience
   moral 154–9, 164, 217
   and practical wisdom 28, 120, 128–9, 195

faith
   and action 47, 63, 189
   and forgiveness 189, 216
   in O'Donovan 155–6, 164–5, 169
   and theology 224
Farmer, K. A. 139 n.245
fear of the Lord 2, 107, 113–15, 137, 205, 209
Fiddes, Paul 5, 13, 122 n.169, 123–4, 206 n.75, 213 n.109
Finnis, John 27, 47–8, 56 n.132, 60–1, 75 n.277
Foot, Philippa 157 n.135
Ford, David 14
forgiveness 189–90, 216
Fox, Michael 1, 11, 91 n.7, 98, 101 n.60, 105, 110, 113–17, 122 n.168
freedom 163–4, 171, 189

Gadamer, Hans Georg 196, 198
gender 126 n.181
God. *See also* Jesus Christ; wisdom of God
   ideas of 65, 98–9
   knowledge of 39, 43–6, 58, 66–71, 127, 130–1
   simplicity of 45, 131
   twofold action of 7, 14, 133, 156, 187, 200–1, 204–6, 224
   will of 66, 69, 105, 182, 211–12, 215
gospel
   in O'Donovan 152, 162, 167–8, 182, 190
   and salvation-history 133, 199–200, 212, 215, 221–2, 224

government. *See* providence
Grabill, Stephen J. 203 n.44
Gregory of Nazianzus 90–2, 94–5

Habel, Norman 109
Hamann, J. G. 188
happiness. *See also* Aristotle
   and created order 204
   and practical reasoning 2, 16–17, 37–8,
      178, 193–4, 218
Hare, R. M. 157 n.135
Hauerwas, Stanley 9, 198 n.21, 199–201,
   223 n.141
Hebrews, book of 152, 221–2
Heidegger, J. H. 99 n.49
Heim, Karl 213 n.105
Hercules at the crossroads 211, 214–15
Hintikka, Jaako 31
history. *See also* salvation history; sin
   and grace 202, 224
   historicism 151, 208
   as problem 145, 149, 152, 161–2,
      167–8, 184–6
Hoffmann, Tobias 46 n.57, 74 n.271
Holy Spirit 50, 82, 154–6, 164, 188, 213
Hooker, Richard 11
hope 155–6, 169–70, 175, 210
hospitality of creation. *See also* creation;
   created order
   and action 2, 118, 122, 175, 194, 208,
      210, 219, 221, 226
   and call of Christ 217
   and call of wisdom 131, 168–9, 195
   and language 198
   in O'Donovan 180
   and path metaphor 111
   and practical knowledge 140
   and wisdom 189, 197, 219
   and wisdom of God 130
   and words of instruction 136
house-building 31–2, 43, 65, 93 n.10,
   100–3, 108, 116, 130, 193, 195
   in Aquinas 43, 65, 195
   in Aristotle 31–2
   in Proverbs 93 n.10, 100–3, 108, 116,
      130, 193
Hume, David 16, 27, 158, 202

Indeterminacy 12, 62, 111, 129, 162, 185
Insole, Christopher J. 163 n.180

Intellect 26, 42, 65, 76 n.282, 168, 174, 201
Irwin, Terrence 21–2, 25
Israel 6, 95, 100, 113–14, 207

Jensen, Stephen J. 43–4, 48, 61
Jenson, Robert 94, 100, 126
Jesus Christ
   cross 3, 125, 208, 224
   miracles 188
   and moral knowledge 149, 215
   and Proverbs 90–1, 94, 100
   resurrection 151–2, 167–8, 183–4, 199,
      203–4
   teaching 187, 193–4, 209, 216
   and wisdom 14, 100, 133, 161, 186,
      195, 200–1
   and woman wisdom 99, 126, 201
Job (book of) 93 n.13, 95, 108, 114, 197, 202
Jordan, Mark 61
judgment
   divine 176, 179, 193, 215–16, 218, 224
   human 61, 63, 176, 179, 201
justification (doctrine of) 224

Kant, Immanuel
   and Aquinas 55 n.122, 62, 83 n.325
   division of disciplines 10
   and O'Donovan 163–4, 174, 186
   practical and theoretical reason 7,
      16–17, 224–5
Kelsey, David 6, 15, 187 n.357, 194, 205–8
Kenny, Anthony 22–3
Kerr, Fergus 40, 60–2
kinds of action. *See also* action; ends;
      moral learning; objects; practical
      syllogism
   in Aquinas 39, 41, 48–59, 71, 83–6, 170
   in Augustine 9, 53–4
   and creation 8, 122, 187, 197–8
   and law 51, 58–9, 111
   in O'Donovan 143–4, 146–7, 150, 153,
      170–9
   and practical reasoning 33–5, 77, 83–6,
      136–7, 217–21
   in Proverbs 122, 131, 138–9
   and Scripture 162, 195, 217–21
knowledge. *See also* God; practical
      knowledge; practical reason
   moral 149, 167
   in Proverbs 108, 133

scientific 26, 167
speculative 3, 66, 201, 223–4
of the whole 142, 166–9, 181–2, 186, 191
Kovacs, B. W. 139 n.245
Kraut, Richard 21–2
Kühn, Ulrich 49, 60, 63, 66–7

law. *See also* eternal law; natural law; Torah
  in Aquinas 49–51, 58–71, 85, 136
  and moral reasoning 12, 79, 111, 146–7, 171–4
  and Proverbs 112–14, 132
  relationship with virtue 49–51, 77
Lisska, Anthony J. 61, 63
Lombard. *See* Peter Lombard
love
  admiration 159–60, 165–6, 171, 180, 189
  in O'Donovan 155–6, 164, 175, 179–81, 189–90
  and wisdom 104–5, 117–18, 167–9
lust and adultery 74, 80–2, 134, 136, 219–20
lying 9, 53, 56–7, 138, 143, 219–20

MacIntyre, Alasdair 37, 38 n.140, 72, 198 n.21
making 28, 44, 65, 67, 101, 195
  and doing 30, 38, 45, 128–9
McInerny, Ralph 48–9, 51, 55 n.122, 85 n.330
McKenny, Gerald 211 n.95, 212 n.100, 213 n.104
McWhorter, Matthew R. 53 n.109
memory 171, 173–4
metaphor 12, 111
midwives (Ex. 1:19–21) 56–7, 220–1
Moberly, R. W. 6, 7, 10, 115 n.134, 207 n.83
moral dilemmas 148, 153, 219–21
moral learning 146–8, 153, 219–21
Moran, Richard 121
Murphy, Roland E. 1, 16, 91 n.7

Nagel, Thomas 23, 25
narrative
  and history 168, 183–5
  and practical reasoning 9, 198 n.21
  in Proverbs 4, 110, 138 n.239

natural law 15, 40–1, 50 n.89, 60–3, 133, 203–5
nature. *See also* created order; history
  and ethics 51, 152, 199–202, 205, 210
  and history 161, 167, 185, 202
  natural reasoning 22, 154–5
  and the supernatural 48, 50, 63–5, 86, 133, 156
Nelson, Daniel Mark 40 n.7, 62, 74 n.274, 137 n.230, 225 n.148
New Testament 159–60, 193, 195, 222
Nimmo, Paul 212 n.100
Nous. *See* intellect
Nygren, Anders 180–1

objects 50 n.89, 51–9, 77, 177–81
O'Donovan, Joan Lockwood 10
O'Donovan, Oliver
  and Aquinas 55 n.122
  and Barth 211 n.95, 213
  critique of 181–91, 197, 199–202
  on discussion 7
  Entering into Rest 175–81
  Finding and Seeking 164–75
  political theology 190, 205 n.56
  and practical reason 8, 153–64, 218–22
  and Proverbs 13, 141, 146, 161, 165–9, 173–4, 181–2
  Resurrection and Moral Order 144–53
  Self, World, and Time 153–64
  and wisdom 141, 145–6, 161, 166, 168, 182–3
order. *See* created order
Origen 5–6

Pannenberg, Wolfhart 181 n.317
parents 105, 107, 118, 214, 221
Parsons, Susan 86
path metaphor. *See* ways and paths
perception. *See also* practical syllogism
  in Aquinas 75–8, 82, 85
  in Aristotle 34–5, 38
  and deliberation 139, 218–19
  in O'Donovan 146, 153, 172
Perdue, Leo 97, 137 n.237
Peter Lombard 53–4, 127
Phronēsis. *See* prudence
Pinches, Charles R. 8–9, 51, 179 n.305, 198
poetry 118–19, 199

Poiēsis. See making
Polanus 98 n.49
Polis. See under Aristotle
Porter, Jean 65 n.204, 82
practical knowledge. *See also* wisdom
   in Aquinas 43–4, 101
   and Christian ethics 222, 224–5
   in modern philosophy 119–22
   and Scripture 163, 219
   and wisdom 3, 126–30, 153, 169, 186, 196–7, 201, 210
practical and theoretical reason (distinction). *See also* Kant, Immanuel; practical knowledge; practical reason; theoretical reason; reason
   in Aquinas 16, 41–2, 47, 71, 73
   in Aristotle 7, 19–20, 24–6
   interaction between 120–1, 221–6
   in O'Donovan 157–8, 163–4, 186
practical reason. *See also* ends; objects; practical and theoretical reason; prudence; reason
   in Aquinas 39–48, 60–3, 69, 75, 134–40, 201
   in Aristotle 20–7
   first principles of 42–3, 48, 76, 80–1, 133–4, 160, 218
   inductive nature of 28, 159, 218
   in O'Donovan 153–64
   Proverbs and 3, 11, 134–40
practical syllogism 28, 32–8, 75–86, 138, 143–4, 147–8, 160, 172, 217–18
   in Aquinas 75–86
   in Aristotle 28, 32–8
   and construal of actions 138, 217–18
   in O'Donovan 143–4, 147–8, 160, 172
practice 14, 31–32
Praxis. See under making
Prohairesis. See action
proverbial sayings 13, 118–19, 198
Proverbs (book of). *See also* practical knowledge; Thomas Aquinas; wisdom
   and Christology 89–100, 123–6, 208–9
   history of interpretation 10–17, 89–100, 188, 199–200, 205–7, 214–15
   in O'Donovan (*see under* O'Donovan)
   as prophecy 17, 202–3
   and Scripture 5–7, 220
   unity of 3–7
   and wisdom 89–126, 193–5, 214–15, 219–20, 225
providence
   in Aquinas 38, 66–71, 74, 101, 132, 196
   in O'Donovan 150–1
   Proverbs and 4–6, 207
prudence (*Phronēsis*). *See also* practical knowledge; wisdom
   in Aquinas 71–8, 82–4
   in Aristotle 23, 26–7, 30, 32, 128–9, 158, 195
   in O'Donovan 144, 147, 171–3
   in Proverbs 16, 132–5, 194, 205
   and virtue 27, 40, 62, 135
purposes. *See under* action

Rad, Gerhard von
   interpretation of Proverbs 3–4, 101 n.60, 108 n.94, 115 n.134
   and wisdom's call 95–7, 104–5, 117
Ramsey, Paul 141–4, 146–7, 217, 219–20
reality. *See also* O'Donovan; World
   and creation 3, 116–18, 122
   in O'Donovan 148, 157–8, 168, 171, 176, 220 n.137
   and reason 50 n.89, 55, 71–2
   and theology 46–7
reason. *See also* practical reason; theoretical reason
   and action 49–52, 58, 74
   and human nature 21, 23, 25
   moral 12, 61, 71, 111, 140, 152, 159
   natural and divine 58–60, 63, 72
recognition. *See* perception
responsibility 60, 72, 137–8, 154, 159–60, 165
revelation 58, 97, 201
Revelation, book of 125, 149 n.62, 168 n.216, 185–6
Rhonheimer, Martin 50 n.89, 55, 63 n.188
right and good. *See* deontology and teleology
Rist, John 19, 63 n.192
Ryle, Gilbert 119–21, 130, 196–7

salvation 6, 64, 92, 104, 215
salvation history
    in Aquinas 64–5, 86
    and Christian ethics 133, 194, 200–3, 207, 216, 221
    in O'Donovan 150–1, 156, 163–4, 167, 180–91
    and Proverbs 6, 126
Santas, Gerasimos 26–7
scripture 4, 7, 11, 140, 162–3, 191, 220
Septuagint 5, 70 n.245, 91, 200 n.32
Setiya, Kieran 120
simplicity. *See* God
sin 56–7, 149, 152–3, 164, 186, 189
skill 20, 30, 101, 128–9, 195
Solomon 97, 113, 116 n.135, 207 n.83, 209
soul 7, 24–6, 42, 74, 117, 198
Spaemann, Robert 17 n.77, 37–8, 57, 154 n.112, 178, 202 n.38
speech 118, 138–9, 198–9, 209, 219
Stewart, Anne W.
    ethics in Proverbs 12–13, 111–12, 131, 139 n.246
    poetry and narrative 4, 110, 118–19, 138 n.239, 199 n.25
Stoicism 12, 16, 86, 95, 152
subsumption. *See* practical syllogism
supernatural. *See* nature
syllogism. *See* practical syllogism
Synderesis 42, 76 n.282

Technē. *See* skill
theology 4–6, 12, 155 n.116, 156, 162–3, 224
theoretical reason. *See also* practical and theoretical reason (distinction); practical reason; reason
    in Aquinas 41–8, 127–8
    in O'Donovan 158, 161, 163, 174
    pre-eminence of 223
Thomas Aquinas. *See also* Aristotle; eternal law; law; natural law; objects; O'Donovan; practical knowledge; Proverbs; providence; salvation history; virtues
    deliberation 78–86
    eternal law 59–71
    kinds of action 48–59

    and Proverbs 11, 13, 69–71, 101, 126–40
    prudence 71–8
    wisdom 40–8
time (in O'Donovan) 157–9, 164, 167, 169, 172, 182. *See also* history; hope
Torah 4 n.12, 112–15, 146, 209. *See also* law
Torrell, Jean-Pierre 49 n.81, 72
tradition 13, 114, 118, 146, 162. *See also* parents
Treier, Daniel J. 7, 14, 91 n.7, 93 n.14, 94 n.18
truth 26, 42, 73, 157

understanding 48, 50, 63

VanDrunen, David 11, 194, 203–5
Van Leeuwen, Raymond C. 3, 93 n.10, 101–3, 118, 137 n.237
Vawter, Bruce 91 n.7
Vermigli, Peter Martyr 223–4
virtues
    dependence of prudence upon 27–8, 62, 74, 135
    and ends 27, 62, 74–5, 136
    intellectual 72–3, 203
    and law 49, 51, 58–9, 77
    natural 64, 201, 214
    in practical reason 22–3, 40, 136–7
    in Proverbs 131, 139 n.247
Vranas, Peter B. M. 20

Waltke, Bruce 16, 91 n.7, 97, 101 n.60
ways and paths
    and deliberation 134–6, 208, 217, 226
    in O'Donovan 169, 173–4
    in Proverbs 107, 109–11, 113, 115
Webster, John 222 n.141
Weeks, Stuart 1–5, 92–3, 99, 104–6, 109, 113–14, 118, 123, 125
Westberg, Daniel 9, 33, 58, 78–82, 85
the whole. *See under* knowledge
Wiggins, David 27, 30–1, 35–6, 85, 120–1
will 44, 51–9, 71, 78–9, 83–4, 179. *See also* action; God
wisdom. *See also* Aristotle; call of wisdom; O'Donovan; Proverbs; Thomas Aquinas; Wisdom of God

affective nature of 117–18, 122, 135, 166, 197, 218
alterity of 2–3, 103–16, 121, 136, 197, 204
of animals 108–9
as attribute 2, 105–9, 116, 123–4, 137, 204
and creation 95, 98–103, 111, 116, 183, 209
divine (*see* Wisdom of God)
and eternal things (*see* eternal objects)
human 93–4, 116, 122, 124, 187–8, 204
and Jesus Christ (*see* Jesus Christ)
literature 5, 95, 146, 161, 202, 205
personification 93–4, 103–6, 117, 123–6, 201, 206
practical nature of 15–16, 102–3, 116–23, 128–9, 194–5, 218, 221
and righteousness 2, 17, 115–16, 137, 202–3
as theoretical 32, 149, 166, 169, 182, 194–5
as universal 98–9, 123
wisdom of God. *See also* creation; eternal law; Jesus Christ; wisdom
and action 130–2, 213–14
and eternal law 65–71
in Proverbs 89–95, 123–6, 165
twofold form of 161, 186–7, 195, 201, 204
Woodard-Lehman, Derek Alan 211 n.95, 212 n.103
words of instruction 1, 173–4
and practical knowledge 219, 225–6
in Proverbs 1, 107–8, 112–14, 118, 173–4, 219
world. *See* creation; O'Donovan; reality

Xenophon 214

Zaborowski, Holger 154 n.112

INDEX OF SCRIPTURE REFERENCES

Old Testament

Exodus
  1:19–21   56

1 Kings
  4:29–34   207
  10:24   116 n.135

Job
  28   95, 114, 197 n.18
  28:12   197, 114, 197
  28:25–7   93 n.13, 96 n.33
  28:28   114

Psalms
  4:6   71
  72   207 n.83
  104:24   96 n.33, 127

Proverbs (In addition to the following references, see pp. 138–9, nn.241–4)
  1:2   16
  1:4   16
  1:5   124
  1:7   114
  1:8–19   1–2, 106
  1:10–19   118
  1:10–11   118
  1:20–33   5, 118
  1:20–1   94 n.16
  1:20   103
  1:21   103
  1:22   132
  1:23–6   215
  1:24–6   209
  1:24–5   132
  1:26   126
  1:29   215
  1:31   106
  1:33   133
  2   106–10, 113
  2:1–4   106
  2:2   103
  2:5   108, 113
  2:6–9   2
  2:6   105, 113
  2:7–8   109, 116
  2:9   1, 107, 109, 116
  2:10   2, 108, 116, 118 n.143, 122
  2:12–15   109
  2:13–14   116
  2:15   117
  2:16–19   113, 136 n.228
  2:16   117 n.141, 118
  2:17   117 n.141
  2:18   117 n.141
  2:19–20   110
  2:21–2   113
  3:1   173
  3:5–7   106
  3:5–6   138
  3:5   73 n.265
  3:13   19, 103, 194, 197
  3:13–20   96
  3:13–18   118, 169
  3:18   94, 200
  3:19   39, 87, 195
  3:19–20   95–6, 101, 207
  3:33–5   115 n.130
  4:3–9   118
  4:5   91, 116, 124
  4:6–9   2
  4:6   118
  4:7   91, 114, 116, 124, 214
  4:8   104
  4:11   115, 226
  4:13   214
  4:18–19   169
  4:20–7   146
  4:26–7   134
  5:1–23   136 n.228
  5:1   214
  5:2   108, 116
  5:3   117 n.141, 118
  5:5   117 n.141
  5:7–20   146
  5:7   136
  5:18–19   117 n.141
  6:6–11   109
  6:20–35   136 n.228
  6:20–4   112
  6:23   174
  6:32   122 n.168
  7:1–27   136 n.228
  7:1–3   136
  7:1   219
  7:3   219
  7:4   116
  7:6–23   136
  7:21   118
  7:24   136
  7:25   135
  8   11, 18, 69–71, 89–100, 123–6, 213
  8:1   11, 103, 141
  8:1–3   94 n.16
  8:2   103
  8:3   103
  8:4   103

8:5	103	10:25	193	24:26	112
8:6–7	118	11:28	202	24:29	209
8:9	108	11:30	200	24:30	122 n.168
8:10	96, 108	12:5	109 n.95	25:6–7	209 n.90
8:10–11	96, 166	12:7	100, 193	25:8–10	209 n.90
8:12–21	169	12:16	135	25:21–2	209 n.90
8:12	16, 87, 108	12:28	193	25:23	197 n.17
8:15	70	13:8	200	26:4–5	220
8:15–16	94	13:9	38, 202	26:26–7	197 n.17
8:17	70, 118 n.143	13:15	115 n.130	27:8	109
		13:16	195	27:12	135
8:20	94	14:1–3	115 n.130	28:5	202
8:22–31	5, 92–100, 123–6, 207	14:1	100, 102, 109 n.95, 193	28:24	209 n.90
				28:26	106, 219
8:22	70 n.244, 87, 91–2, 94, 97–8, 100, 124			29:7	108 n.94
		14:7	108	29:18	113 n.117
		14:11	109 n.95	30:1–6	113 n.117
		14:15	219	30:5–6	220
8:23	70, 92, 208	14:32–5	115 n.130	30:24–8	108
8:24–5	124	14:33	116	30:32	139 n.247
8:24	71, 92, 100	14:35	109 n.95	30:33	197
8:29	70	15:4	112	31:6	200
8:30–1	165, 208	15:5–9	115 n.130	31:10–31	117 n.141
8:30	92 n.10, 96, 125, 127	15:18	139 n.247	31:12	146
		16:16	116		
8:31	71, 188	17:27	135, 139 n.247	Ecclesiastes	
8:32–6	169			7:16	202, 209 n.93
8:32–5	103	18:13	9		
8:32	96, 132	19:2	108	12:9–11	161
8:33	96	19:18	146		
8:34	101	19:26	202	Isaiah	
9:1–18	117	19:27	108	30:21	226
9:1–6	94 n.16	20:15	108	43:19	184
9:1	101, 103, 188	20:17	135		
9:3	103	20:24	169	Jeremiah	
9:4	103	21:21	202	10:12	96
9:6	117	22:3	135	51:15	96
9:9	115 n.130	22:12	108, 207		
9:10	114	22:17–21	112	Micah	
9:11	117	22:20	108	6:8	211 n.96
9:16	122 n.168	22:28	6		
9:18	117	23:1–2	200	**New Testament**	
10:13	122 n.168, 198, 219	23:1	6		
		23:12	108	Matthew	
10:14	108	23:17–18	203	5:17–48	194
10:19	115 n.130, 209 n.91	23:22–5	115 n.130	5:21–2	187
		23:26–8	136 n.228	5:25	209 n.90
10:21	115 n.130, 122 n.168	24:3–4	100–2, 195–6	5:38–9	187
		24:3	15, 89, 193, 195	5:38–48	209
10:23	16			6:12	189

7:12	209	10:17	224	5:17	212 n.97
7:24–7	193	12:1	222	6:12	189
23:6	209 n.90	12:2	212 n.97		
		12:20	209 n.90	Philippians	
Mark		13:11	188	1:9–10	211
7:10–11	209 n.90				
12:39	209 n.90	1 Corinthians		Colossians	
13:33	188	1:22	3	1:15	100, 127, 208
		1:23	125		
Luke		1:23–24	183	1:15–20	125
7:35	187	1:24	125, 208	1:16	125 n.179
9:60	209	1:27	209	1:17	208
11:31	187, 209	1:28	209, 224	2:3	188
12:51–3	202	2:15	201	4:5	47 n.60
12:56	216	8:6	125 n.179		
14:7–11	209 n.90	9:27	65, 209	Hebrews	
20:46	209 n.90	13	156	5:12–14	222
		13:4–6	175		
John		13:13	175	James	
1:3	127	15:46	201	3:13–17	195
4:22	6				
13:34	190	Ephesians		Revelation	
		2:10	156	3:14	125
Romans		4:1	222	4–5	149 n.62, 168 n.216, 185–7
8:19–20	188	5:10	212 n.97		
8:20	153	5:15–16	189		
8:21	188	5:15	188, 226	5:5	186
8:23	188	5:16	220		

www.ingramcontent.com/pod-product-compliance
Lightning Source LLC
Chambersburg PA
CBHW050325020526
44117CB00031B/1778